ELECTRONIC COMPUTERS

FUNDAMENTALS, SYSTEMS, AND APPLICATIONS

EDITED BY

PAUL VON HANDEL
INSTITUTE FOR DEFENSE ANALYSES, WASHINGTON, D.C., USA

WITH THE COOPERATION OF

HANS W. GSCHWIND, MARTIN G. JAENKE
AND ROBERT G. TANTZEN
AIR FORCE MISSILE DEVELOPMENT CENTER,
HOLLOMAN AFB., NEW MEXICO, USA

WITH 160 FIGURES

Springer-Verlag Wien GmbH
1961

ISBN 978-3-662-23789-2 ISBN 978-3-662-25892-7 (eBook)
DOI 10.1007/978-3-662-25892-7

Ursprünglich erschienen bei Springer-Verlag in Vienna 1961.
Softcover reprint of the hardcover 1st edition 1961

Library of Congress Catalog Card Number 61-12942

Preface

The 19th century was distinguished by the construction of machines with enormous power. During the last decade rapid progress has been made in the development of a completely different type of machine. These new machines, the electronic computers, are not built to generate power or to do mechanical work, but to perform logical operations and calculations. This new concept will have a profound influence on engineering, science, and economy. In fact, the first effects of this development are already taking shape today.

It is the purpose of this book to give a survey of the basic principles and applications of computers for the benefit of those who hitherto did not work with them, but who might have use for them in the future. The rapid progress of the engineering science has, naturally, led to a situation in which the practicing scientist and engineer cannot keep abreast of the progress in neighboring fields. The chapters of this book were prepared by distinguished experts in the field of computers for the non-expert who does not intend to become an expert, but who wants to acquire a general understanding of the problems and solutions which he needs to effectively perform the work in his proper field.

We address this book to the engineers and scientists who want to know the performance of computers, as well as to the managers who are mainly concerned with their economic aspect.

The technical development of computing machines is going on at a rapid rate. Any detailed description of computer components would therefore become obsolete within a few years. The general principles underlying their operation will probably remain unchanged for a longer time. Accordingly, this book puts main emphasis on principles and methods rather than on engineering details.

Washington, March 1961.

Paul von Handel

Table of Contents

Chapter 1

Introduction

By

Dr. **Paul von Handel**

(Institute for Defense Analyses, Washington, D. C., USA)

Science, engineering, industry, and business today are confronted with problems continuously growing in size and complexity. Traditional methods and instruments are becoming less and less efficient for their solution. Many of these enormous computations simply would not be worth attacking, were it not for the modern electronic computers, which have improved the situation greatly by increasing computing speed and reliability by many orders of magnitude.

By far the greater portion of today's problems are solved by computing with discrete variables, i.e. numbers in digital format. The category of problems comprises all kinds of algebraic formulas in physics, engineering, statistics, accounting, census, etc., as well as problems in logic, theory of games, linear programming, circuit design, and others. Ever since the advent of science has man tried to make computations easier by inventing new machines and methods. Some milestones along this path are the abacus, Pascal's mechanical computer. mathematical tables, logarithms, the desk calculator, the punched card machine, The development to date has culminated in the large scale high speed digital computers.

Another sector of technical problems is presented in the form of differential equations. For these the computations can best be carried out using continuous variables. The traditional tools for this type of computations are graphical methods, and mathematical instruments like the slide rule and the planimeter. In many cases mechanical models have been built for certain types of problems. Here mechanical quantities are substituted for the actual physical quantities involved. The basic idea behind the modern computers is this: the physical quantities appearing in differential equations can always be interpreted as meaning some electrical quantity. Hence it is possible to build electric circuits to represent those equations. Computers which can do just this are called analog computers because they are able to simulate an electrical analog to a given problem.

There are other ways of solving differential equations. One of them is to apply a numerical method of integration and solve on a digital computer. Another way is to substitute the corresponding difference equations and solve those directly. Machines built especially for this purpose turn out to be much simpler and cheaper than general purpose digital computers. They are called digitoe differential analyzers and can be considered a hybrid between a digital and an analog computer.

Chapter 2

Digital Computers

By

Robert G. Tantzen (Dipl. Ing.)

(Chief, Digital Computer Branch, Analysis and Computation Division, Air Force Missile Development Center, Holloman Air Force Base, New Mexico, USA)

With 21 Figures

2. Digital Computers

2.1. Layout and Structure

In trying to understand the philosophy behind the layout of a modern electronic digital computer it may be helpful to see how the idea of automatic computers originated and how they were consequently developed in early designs. Unfortunately, the history of computers is rather complex, since many people have been working simultaneously on the same problems and contributing their often contradictory ideas. Moreover, the development frequently ended in a design which, at the time, was considered superior to anything else available only to be relinquished a short time thereafter in favor of a different principle.

Let us follow here only those developments which may be considered as direct steps toward the present day computer. Even though the following remarks may not be exactly historical in all respects, they are never far from reality and may help explain the reasons for the structures of a modern machine.

2.11. Early Automatic Computers

As so many other human achievements, automatic digital computers may have originally been inspired by the wish for more convenience. The earliest inventions, now about 200 years old, concerned themselves with the mechanization of the basic arithmetic operations. The crude manufacturing methods of those times prevented any really successful machines. Only the modern precision manufacturing techniques gave us the fast and reliable desk calculators of today. These machines, electrically driven, reduce the manual work to the mere pushing of buttons. The elimination of manual arithmetic from a computation is only the first step, but a very important one, toward an automatic computer. Anyone who ever performed a lengthy calculation on a desk calculator, going through the same motions again and again, knows how tiresome and boring it can get to push buttons. The process is, to a surprisingly large extent, purely mechanical and very seldom requires genuine thought of the operator, once the computation is started.

Since mechanical operations can be performed by mechanisms, there was no principal obstacle for constructing machines which would perform automatically all the arithmetic operations of a routine calculation in proper sequence. However, although a mechanical version of an automatic calculator had been attempted during the last century, a workable computer did not come into being until after World War II. Designers realized that an electrical machine is simpler to construct than a mechanical one. Such a machine could also use, to advantage, electrically operating punched card and punched paper mechanisms developed previously for different purposes. Associated devices like card sorters, collaters, printers, etc. became very convenient for the operation of the system.

Let us pause here for a moment to look at such a prototype of an automatic calculator. The familiar mechanical desk calculator is replaced by its electrical equivalent, an arithmetic unit. A punched card reading mechanism sends electrical signals to the calculator and performs essentially the same function as was previously accomplished by the human operator depressing buttons. Any desired signal or a combination thereof can be sent according to the code, i.e. the holes punched into the card. The operation of the computer proceeds in approximately the following manner: The first card of a previously prepared card deck is read. The codes on the card are sensed and corresponding signals are sent to the arithmetic unit. Let us assume a sample problem:

$$y = x_1 + x_2 + x_3 \ldots + x_n$$

and suppose the codes of the first card cause the arithmetic unit to be cleared from any previous contents. This is the equivalent of depressing the clear-button on a desk calculator. The next card contains the first number, x_1. When the card is read, x_1 is entered into the arithmetic unit, corresponding to a manual entry of a number on the keyboard of a desk calculator. The next card contains an add instruction which causes the entered number to be added into an accumulative register, or accumulator for short. The remaining cards alternately contain numbers and add instructions until finally with the last card, the computer is instructed to display the result (the sum of all numbers) and to stop.

It is not difficult to imagine that in this manner any calculation which can be performed on a desk calculator can also be performed by the computer. But now what have we gained? The answer is nothing, if we assume a calculation which has to be performed only once. In this case we have to push the same number of buttons to get the holes into the cards as if we had performed the computations directly. The advantage of this scheme becomes apparent for a calculation which has to be done repeatedly, each time with different numbers. Let us suppose we want to evaluate a polynomial for a large number of different sets of coefficients. For every new set of coefficients we have to perform the same operations like add, subtract, multiply, etc., in the same sequence, except that the numbers worked on are different every time. If we compare the cards necessary for two different runs on the computer we will find that all cards are the same which contain instructions like add, multiply, etc.; whereas the cards containing the operands are different for every run. We really have two decks of cards: one program deck which contains instructions, and one deck of operands which contains the numbers to be used. Only the operand deck has to be changed for every new run. The larger the number of runs that have to be performed and the higher the percentage of required instruction cards, the more pronounced is the advantage of the automatic calculator.

There is another convenience too. Suppose we have to perform another calculation, but part of this calculation is the evaluation of a polynomial. In preparing the program cards for this new problem we simply insert the existing program deck for evaluation of the polynomial as part of the new program deck. In this way we may use a library of existing basic programs to assemble program decks for more complicated problems.

The computer, as it stands now, is quite versatile, but not enough for all occasions. One difficulty is encountered when an intermediate result calculated by the computer has to be used later for another calculation. True enough, the computer can punch a card with the intermediate result and this card can later be inserted into the card reader. But this operation requires an interruption in the otherwise fully automatic operation. Therefore, the designers of even the earliest machines incorporated a memory. (So to speak, a piece of scratch paper on which the computer can write an intermediate result and refer to it later.) A memory able to store a few numbers for later reference is quite sufficient for most calculations for the type of computer which is considered here. The transfer of numbers between the computer proper and this memory, as all other operations, is under control of instruction cards.

Another inconvenience is encountered when a certain sequence of instructions appear within a lengthy computation again and again. Such a program may be called a sub-program. The program deck becomes very voluminous by the repetition of identical cards. This situation can be helped by punching the sub-program into a paper tape loop. Every time the main program has to perform the sub-program, it simply starts the tape reader for the sub-program. The paper tape now controls the computer, and, with the sub-program completed, transfers the control back to the main program.

Several of these sub-program tape readers can be used, when the main program contains several sub-programs or where different sub-programs have to be used depending upon previous results, e.g. do one thing if the present result is positive, and do another thing if the result is negative.

The concept of the computer is now already quite different from a desk calculator. Let us imagine its operation. The card reader and the readers for sub-programs control the operation for various lengths of time. Relays in the computer execute the program step by step and cards containing the results are automatically punched. No human interference whatsoever is required once the computation is started. It is understandable that such machines have inspired observers to call them robots. In reality, these machines (and also present day computers) have no capability, except for speed, beyond that of a simple desk calculator and a stupid but reliable operator who is told exactly what to do in every instance.

For the reasons of speed and perhaps for the fact that machines are less susceptible to errors than humans, these early automatic digital computers can be considered as an important historical mark. Several of them have been built in different versions. Since they used almost entirely relays for their internal operations, they became known as relay computers, and to distinguish them from their successors, they may be called externally programmed.

The next step toward the concept of a modern electronic machine was an enlargement of what may be called the control unit. This control unit is a sequencing mechanism which causes the computational or arithmetic unit to perform a certain cycle of operations. Even in a simple desk calculator there is such a sequencer which controls the order in which digits are taken in addition, and causes consecutive additions or subtractions in a multiplication. This sequencer was not very elaborate for the first relay computers. As a matter of fact, not all of them had a multiply command and practically none had a divide command. The main program or sub-programs had to take care of these operations by repeated add and shift instructions, or repeated add, subtract and test instructions.

The control unit in new computers was enlarged to a more or less universal sequencer which could be set up (programmed) by wiring connections on a plugboard to perform a number of different sequences. Once excited by an instruction from the main program it went automatically through its prescribed sequence, and caused the arithmetic unit to perform corresponding operations. This was an advantage insofar as the main program became simpler, and also because the control unit could replace the paper tape loop for certain sub-programs, e.g. the sine, cosine or square root.

Now, going a little further, sequencers have been built so that at the end of one cycle another one (which can be selected by another wire connection) is initiated automatically. In this way the sequencer can, by itself, take care of the control of the complete program for relatively simple calculations. For this type of operation only the operands have to be read while the program is controlled by wires on a plugboard. Plugboards can easily be interchanged for the computation of different problems. This type of computer is duly called: plugboard programmed.

2.12. Modern Electronic Digital Computers

The next step in the development of digital computers is characterized by two major improvements which are incorporated in practically all later machines. The concept of the stored program, and the replacement of electro-mechanical devices by electronic circuits created the modern computer. The salient features of automatic computers we have encountered so far are automatic arithmetic, input and output of data, external program control by cards or paper tape, limited internal program control by plugboard, and a small memory. Most of the individual operations of those machines make use of electro-mechanical devices and are therefore limited in speed. The development of new electronic devices opened the door to new possibilities in the design of computers. It is now practical to built a large memory. Proper design of the logical circuitry allows one to use this memory to store both the program and the data. On the one hand, this allows a completely internal program control. On the other hand, instructions and numbers are now of the same kind, instructions can be treated as numbers and the computer can compose its own instructions. Depending on conditions of intermediate results, instructions can be modified to do one thing or another, or the machine can select different parts of a program for execution. Modern computers exhibit a variety of different logical designs, but they do have a common general structure. The operations of the individual parts of a computer are very closely intermeshed, and it is difficult to draw a clear line between them. It may nevertheless be helpful to outline a functional block diagram of a modern computer. Such a diagram is shown in Fig. 1. It should be understood that the diagram does not indicate the layout of actual physical building blocks. Certain logical operations of a computer are closely related with a particular unit of the diagram. These auxiliary operations, or subsequences, will be considered as part of the particular unit. For instance, all the logic involved in performing a multiplication, i.e. the necessary number of repeated additions, and the breakdown of each addition into repeated additions of single digits, are considered to be a part of the

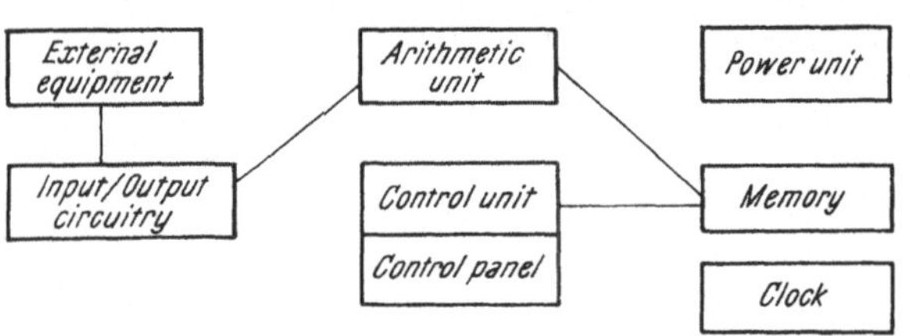

Fig. 1. Block Diagram of a modern Digital Computer. The connecting lines are the main paths of information flow.

arithmetic unit. The functions of the various units can then be stated as follows:

Arithmetic Unit: Execution of all machine instructions, except a few which are directly concerning external equipment. The unit has a few special small storage devices, called registers, for operands, intermediate and final results. Information transferred from one place to another usually passes through the arithmetic unit.

Control Unit: The control unit is the nerve center of the computer. It controls all events for proper sequence. There are special registers for the necessary logical information. Each instruction is analyzed in the control unit, and the necessary operations are initiated accordingly. A special function of the control unit is the automatic checking of computer malfunctions and of certain coding errors. Alarm signals are given and sometimes the machine is stopped if such conditions are found.

Control Panel: All switches and other manual control elements necessary to operate the computer are assembled on the control panel. The registers of the arithmetic unit and of the control unit are connected to indicators on the panel, so that their contents may be visually inspected. The state of the various external devices, like ready, not ready, busy, etc., may be displayed. Certain lights serve to show alarm conditions. Sometimes a cathode ray oscilloscope or a loudspeaker is connected to the control unit to help the operator in monitoring the operations. Fig. 2 shows the control console of the Univac Scientific

Fig. 2. Control Pane of the Univac Scientific, Model 1103 A (Remington Rand Univac)

as an example. The left panel indicates the input-output registers and information about the external equipment. It also has a clock for timing purposes. The upper half of the center panel shows the conditions of the arithmetic and control units. The lower part has the operating buttons and switches and also the fault indicator lights. The right panel pertains to the memory. The lower section has a series of switches which allow to vary the operating voltages for test and maintenance purposes. The top center panel holds an oscilloscope for observation of references to the core memory.

Clock: The clock is a device which generates a continuous sequence of pulses as soon as the start button is depressed. It governs the basic speed of all operations. Common clock rates lie between 100 kc and 5 mc. Some computers have options of reduced pulse rates or even the possibility to generate pulses manually, one at a time. These features are useful for the diagnosis of computer malfunctions.

Memory: The memory is a device which can store large quantities of information. It takes over the functions of two different devices of earlier computers. First, it stores intermediate results for short periods of time. In this respect it performs the same function as the small memory in early computers. Secondly, it stores the program and the data. This was done in the early computers by a deck of cards and by the sequencer. The memory is divided into a number of cells, or registers, each with an identifying number, called the address. Depending on the construction, the memory is called volatile or non-volatile. A volatile memory loses its information as soon as the computer is turned off, a non-volatile one retains it. Another distinction is sometimes made between internal and external memory. An external memory permits the physical removal of the storage medium from the computer, e.g. magnetic tapes.

Input-Output Circuitry: The timing of the external devices is determined by mechanical properties, such as the speed of a motor or the response time of a relay. Since these factors cannot be controlled to sufficiently close tolerances, the external devices cannot be synchronized with the clock pulse rate of the computer. The input-output circuitry serves as information buffer.

External Equipment: All devices which do not necessarily belong to the computer proper, although often directly connected to it, are considered external equipment. Examples are: typewriter, printer, card reader, card punch, magnetic tape units, plotter, and converter. In general, any device whose operation cannot be synchronized with the computer clock belongs in this category.

Power Unit: The power unit contains all the circuitry needed to generate and regulate all the voltages needed in the computer. There may also be an automatic cooling system to maintain suitable temperatures throughout the machine.

Small and medium sized computers are sometimes built as one physical unit. Large machines are always composed of several units, for engineering reasons. This permits easy modification or expansion of a computer system. As an

Fig. 3. Physical Layout of the Univac Scientific Digital Computer, Model 1103 A (Remington Rand Univac)

example of a large computer Fig. 3 shows the layout of the Univac Scientific (Model 1103 A). The cabinets of the rear row, from left to right, contain: Control Unit, Arithmetic Unit, part of the Input-Output Circuitry, and the Drum Memory. The latter also provides the basic Computer Clock. The second row has: Magnetic Tape Control, Power Supply and Control Panel, Magnetic Core Memory. The big cabinet on the right houses the cooling equipment. The four leftmost cabinets are the High Speed Printer and its associated equipment. On the platform we have the Card Control, Card Reader and Punch, Paper Tape Reader and Punch, Supervisory Typewriter. The front row shows five Magnetic Tape Units. On the desk in the foreground there is the Paper Tape and Magnetic Tape Preparation Equipment.

All units of a computer interact and cooperate very closely during an actual computation. Let us assume that by some auxiliary program a set of instructions as well as the operands have been placed in the memory and we want to execute this set of instructions. The operator manually enters the address of the first instruction on the control panel, then he depresses the start button. The control unit sends this address and a read signal to the memory. The first instruction is transferred into a register of the control unit. Upon completion of this transfer the instruction is examined to determine what steps have to be taken next. Let us assume the instruction calls for the multiplication of two numbers. It will contain a code for multiplication and the two addresses where the operands are stored in the memory. When the multiply code is detected, a clear signal is sent to the arithmetic unit which causes the result register, or accumulator, to be cleared of any previous information. Next, the address of the first operand and a read signal transfer the first factor from the memory to the arithmetic unit. Similarly the second factor is placed into another register there. The control unit then emits a multiply signal to the arithmetic unit and waits. The subsequence of operations for a multiplication is now performed. The desired product is formed in the accumulator. Upon completion the control unit receives a go-ahead signal and can now proceed to the next instruction. This is usually located at the next higher address in memory. Since the address of the old instruction is retained by the control unit, it merely need be increased by one. The next instruction will then be obtained and executed as described before.

Executing a set of instructions in the sequence in which they are stored in the memory is the normal or sequential execution. One of the major advantages of modern computers is the ability to depart from this sequence and proceed with any specified address instead. This is accomplished by the jump instructions. The execution of these instructions will place the new address into the control unit, so that the next instruction may be picked up properly. A jump may be unconditional or conditional, in the latter case it will occur only when a certain condition is met, e.g. a number being zero, or positive, one number larger than another, etc. Some jumps can be controlled by setting switches on the control panel. The conditional jumps enable the computer to make decisions between two alternatives. This is a very decisive advantage, and it contributes much to the flexibility of operations. Another advantage is the possibility of executing a series of instructions as many times as desired without storing them in memory more than once. A further important feature of modern computers is their ability to compose or modify instructions. The information contained in a cell of the memory is called a "word". It is either a number or an instruction. Since the internal language of computers consists only of numbers, all words have a numerical code. Instructions can therefore be used as operands in arithmetic and logical operations. This enables the programmer to write instructions which will manufacture or modify a program. Certain machine instructions are especially designed to make this task easy. These basic possibilities finally lead to translators, assembly programs, and compilers, which are treated in chapter 2.3.

2.13. Design Features

The diversified tasks which must be performed by the different parts of a digital computer may lead one to believe that the general design of such a machine is a very difficult matter. However, it turns out that only a small number of basic design features will determine the operational characteristics to a very large extent. Of course, a machine with perhaps several thousand tubes, diodes, or transistors will have a great variety of basic elements, and the elements of different machines will be of different design. Yet, all these elements perform essentially only one of two basic logical functions: that of making a decision or that of storing information. Consequently, it is possible to classify these elements into two categories regardless of the size or type of computer under consideration.

Decision elements are sometimes referred to as switching elements, gating circuits, or logical elements. Their behavior is most conveniently described in the language of Boolean Algebra. These elements are used to switch electric currents according to conditions inside or outside the computer. They perform a specific action only under certain conditions. Let us take an everyday example of this class of problems. Suppose we want the light X turned on if the switch A is turned on. The circuit, Fig. 4, is quite simple: the light is connected to the make-contact of the switch.

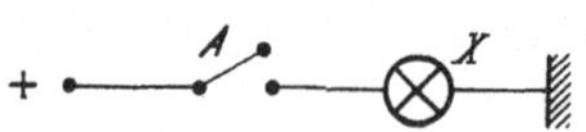

Fig. 4. Simplest Logical Circuit

We would say the light X is an indication for the presence of condition A, i.e. switch A is turned on. If we want an indication for two switches, A and B, turned on simultaneously, then we would need the circuit of Fig. 5a. This is the logical "AND" condition. Circuit *b* shows an indication for either A, or B, or both switches turned on. This is the logical inclusive "OR" condition. Circuit *c* gives an indication for switch A not turned on. We realize that the circuits give an indication for the presence or absence of certain specified conditions.

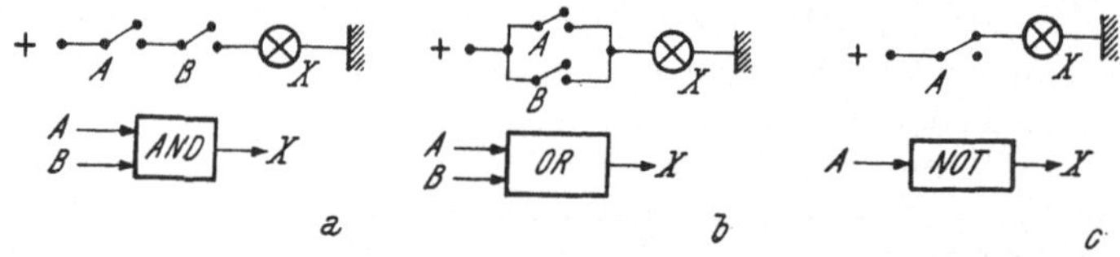

Fig. 5. Some Basic Logical Circuits and their Symbols

In an electronic computer, there are normally no switches in the usual sense. The presence or absence of conditions is represented by high or low potentials, by the presence or absence of electric pulses, or by their polarity. The same is true for the light bulb, whose condition is represented in the same manner. The circuits performing these tasks work electronically. Disregarding their design, it is customary to show only the symbols, as in the lower part of Fig. 5. From a mathematical viewpoint the quantities A, B, and X are considered as variables. They can only assume two distinct values, denoted e.g. by 0 and 1. The variable X is said to be a (logical) function of A and B. Using only the three circuits AND, OR, NOT, as elements, every conceivable combination can be realized. When this is the case, the corresponding logical functions are said to form a "complete set". The NOT is the only possible function of one variable. The OR and AND are functions of two variables, of which there are sixteen altogether. It can be shown that there exist a few complete sets of only two functions, one the NOT, the other selected from the sixteen, e.g. OR-NOT or AND-NOT. The circuits for two such functions can be designed so that they are identical except for one single connection, so that the complete logical circuitry of a computer could be based on one single basic electronic unit.

By means of logical circuits, the whole operation of a computer is reduced to simple yes or no decisions. For example, the next instruction has to be obtained from memory as soon as the present one is executed. A logical circuit would decide whether or not all conditions are present to indicate the finished execution of the present instruction. If the circuit decides yes, then a signal at the output would initiate the acquisition of the next instruction. Similar circuits initiate the multiply operation if all conditions are present which indicate that particular operation.

Storage elements are used to hold information. They are found not only in the memory of the machine but in any place where information must be retained for longer or shorter periods of time. We have already seen that the arithmetic and the control units need storage devices. Storage of information can be static or dynamic. A static device has two or more stable states, it can remain in either of them indefinitely. The state can be changed by electric signals. The simplest and most reliable storage elements have only two stable states; this feature makes the binary number system so attractive for digital computers. A widely used memory element is the magnetic core, a tiny ring of magnetic material which can be permanently magnetized in one direction or the opposite, just as one end of a magnet is either a north or a south pole. A row of such cores can be used to store a number. Assume we have the binary number 10111. We use five cores to represent the five bits of the number. All cores which have to store a "zero" we set to one stable state, all cores representing a "one" to the other state. If the stable states do not change in time, the machine can "remember" the number indefinitely. The dynamic storage elements do not have certain static conditions, but utilize the existence or nonexistence of certain dynamic states. An example for such a dynamic element would be a delay line according to Fig. 6. If no information is stored, the system is at rest, and there is no output at any time. To store information, one or more pulses are applied to the input. The pulses travel along the delay line and appear at the output after a certain time. By way of the amplifier, they are again introduced to the delay line, so that they keep circulating indefinitely. The stored information can be read at the output only at certain instants. This requires a delicate synchronization of all internal computer operations. The length of the delay and the time between pulses determine the number of pulses which can be stored. Short delay lines are often purely electrical. Longer delays use liquids or solids, like mercury, or quartz. The physical effect of magnetostriction has been used successfully to build delay lines. Sometimes, a track on a magnetic drum is used to generate the necessary delay.

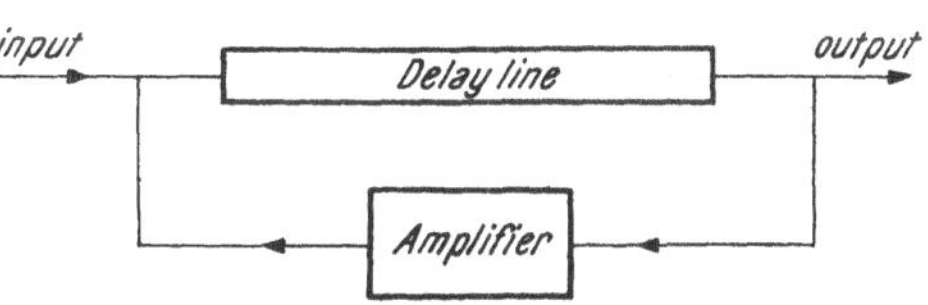

Fig. 6. Dynamic Storage Element

Information is transferred or processed, in a computer, usually in units corresponding to one computer word. In a serial memory, the bits of a word must be handled in a serial fashion, one after the other. In a parallel memory, all bits of information are available at any time. One can therefore classify computers as serial and parallel. Serial machines handle the digits of a word sequentially, one digit at a time, while parallel machines handle all digits of a word simultaneously. Suppose one word shall be transferred from the memory to the arithmetic unit. In a serial machine, the control unit will connect the two units by one line just for the time it takes to transfer that word. If the word has e.g. 36 pulses, the transfer will take 36 pulse times. In a parallel machine, the control unit would establish 36 connections, one for each digit, so that they can be transmitted all in one pulse time. Arithmetic and logical operations are organized in a similar manner. The serial machine would add, e.g. just like a human, i.e. start with the least significant digits and proceed digit by digit up to the most significant ones. The parallel machine would add all digits simultaneously. It can be seen that the parallel computer is much faster than a serial one, other things being equal; however, a serial computer needs less hardware and is, therefore, cheaper to build.

The two types of computer require somewhat different logical circuits. Let us explain this for the arbitrary example of command selection. An add command could, for instance, be identified by the three conditions *A 1*, not *A 2*, and *A 3*. A single AND circuit and a NOT circuit, as in Fig. 7, would suffice to detect the presence of these three conditions in a parallel machine. Its output can be used to initiate the add sequence. The equivalent procedure is more complicated in a serial machine, since the three conditions are available only serially, say at the times t_1, t_2, t_3. The code for addition would be a series of three pulses, the first and third are high, the second is low. The computer must generate timing pulses at each of the three pulse times on separate lines, so that the individual pulses can be detected. The circuit is shown in Fig. 8[1].

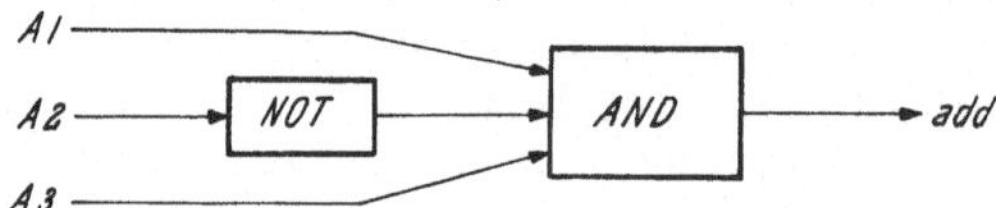

Fig. 7. Command Selection, Parallel Computer

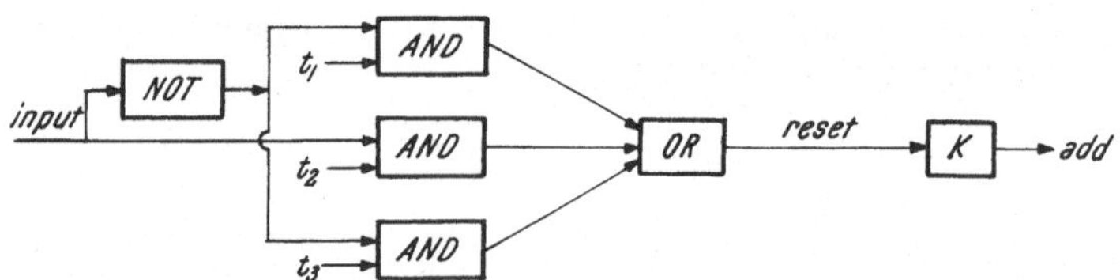

Fig. 8. Command Selection, Serial Computer

A storage element *K* is initially set to the "1" state. If it remains there it will later indicate addition. *K* is connected to an OR circuit in such a way that an output of the OR circuit at any time will reset *K* to zero. The three AND circuits can have an output only at times t_1, t_2, or t_3, respectively, since the timing pulses are connected into them. At time t_1 only the first AND circuit may have an output. This will happen if and only if the first pulse, *A 1*, is low, i.e. if the first pulse does not correspond to the add code. At the remaining times the other two pulses are tested in the same manner. In this way the storage element *K*

[1] This circuit has more elements than the previous one. This does not invalidate the earlier statement that a serial computer is more economical in hardware than a parallel one.

will remain in the "1" state only if all three pulses are correct. The output of K can then be used to initiate the add routine.

It is worth mentioning that there are computers which are neither truly parallel nor truly serial in nature. These mixed machines often are decimal, using several bits for each decimal digit (see Chapter 2.2). The bits of each decimal digit are handled in parallel, but the decimal digits serially.

The logical operations in a computer with so-called *AC* operation require the use of pulses, i.e. momentary rises or falls of potentials or currents. On the other hand, in a *DC* machine, all logical conditions are represented by potentials or currents which remain unchanged as long as a condition is present. Probably no existing computer is a true *AC* or *DC* machine, but will use both types of circuits.

Another design feature of digital computers is denoted by the terms synchronous and asynchronous. In a synchronous machine, all internal operations are in synchronism with the computer clock. The duration of all operations is fixed and can be expressed in multiples of clock pulses. In an asynchronous machine, all units are more or less independent in their operation. Each operation is not governed by the clock rate, but proceeds at the fastest possible speed. As soon as one operation is finished, the unit involved sends a ready signal to the control unit, which then initiates the next operation. Both methods have their advantages and disadvantages. The well defined time relationship in synchronous machines results in relatively clear conditions which facilitate maintenance and trouble shooting. Asynchronous machines do not have this desirable feature, but they are somewhat faster in operation, other things being equal.

An important feature in the design of a computer is the layout of its memory. There is actually no one optimal design, since the intended application of the computer enters into the picture. We have seen earlier (Chapter 2.12) that the total memory is divided into many cells. Each cell has an address for identification, and it can store a certain amount of information called a computer word. The capacity of a memory may be many thousands of words. During computation, the control unit must be able to communicate with all words, i.e. there must be the possibility of reading information without destroying it, and of recording new information. If the words can be handled individually in arbitrary sequence, the memory is said to have random access. Some memories permit the transfer of information only in larger quantities, called blocks or unit records, which vary in size between a few and a few hundred words. The ideal memory, from the programmer's standpoint, should be large, have random access and a short access time. This gives the programmer the greatest flexibility for writing his programs.

The realization of such an ideal memory turns out to be very expensive, so that large computers use several types of storage. Before we describe the most common types presently in use, a brief outline of the historical development may be proper. The early machines used electronic tubes for their small memory. One tube can store one bit of information by being either in the conducting or cut-off state. Although access times can be made quite short, larger memories require such a huge number of tubes that a tube memory is practically prohibitive. A small modern computer has a storage capacity of around 40,000 bits! The next step in the historical development was the acoustical delay lines. Information is stored in the form of acoustical impulses traveling through an elastic medium, like mercury and quartz. The pulses are picked up at the end with a transducer, converted to electrical energy, amplified and re-inserted at the front end of the line, so that they circulate continuously. The physical effect of magnetostriction has also been used in this manner. The access to information is serial in nature, which results in a relatively long access time. Engineering difficulties, due to thermal change of the propagation speed and to thermal expansion of the line itself limit the storage capacity. A much larger capacity, better reliability, and a lower price were obtained with magnetic drum memories. The access is still serial in nature, but one drum can have many recording channels in parallel, so that the access time will remain essentially the same when the storage capacity is increased. Up to the present time magnetic drums are used frequently as the main memory of medium speed computers, and as secondary storage for large computer systems.

The need for shorter access times resulted in the adaption of the cathode-ray tube for storage purposes. The screen of such a tube can be charged electrostatically by a focused electron beam. These charges, representing the information, will normally dissipate after a short time; however, they can be sustained permanently by an automatic regeneration process. Since the whole operation is completely electronic, access times are short. By using one tube for each bit position of all computer words, all bits of a word can be transferred simultaneously, which results in high operating speed. Electrostatic memories have been in use quite extensively. Due to difficulties in adjustment of operating voltages, tube imperfections, aging, and other engineering and maintenance problems, they have practically been abandoned in favor of the magnetic core memory. Magnetic cores are extremely reliable; they do not need regeneration to retain information. Their small size assures a high storage capacity per unit volume. The logical circuitry is commonly laid out for parallel access, and the access times are only a few microseconds. Engineering research is continually trying to build even better storage devices. The main objectives of these endeavors are: 1. reduce access time; 2. reduce size; 3. reduce operating power level; 4. increase reliability; 5. reduce effects of environmental conditions; 6. increase life-time; and last but not least: 7. reduce the cost.

Modern large computer systems have a fast random access memory of limited capacity which is supplemented by a large capacity memory with slower access. Then there are devices for input and output of data, i.e. the external memory. To illustrate the characteristics of different designs we will describe the three types of storage most commonly used in computers today.

Magnetic Core Storage: The magnetic cores are physically arranged in a two-dimensional array, or matrix. For example, a 100 bit memory would have the hundred cores arranged in ten rows and ten columns. Each of the possible addresses, in this case 00—99, can then be defined as the intersection of a row and a column, the ten's digit could designate the row, the unit's digit the column. There are wires, representing the rows and columns, which are energized for the reading from or recording in a certain core. The cores are placed at the intersection of these wires, and a third wire is threaded through all cores for the sensing of information. This simple example represents a memory of 100 words, each having only one bit. For the storage of words, each N bits long, N such matrices are stacked up, so that we get a three-dimensional array for the complete core memory. The search for a particular word proceeds simultaneously on the rows and the columns of all the matrices. The access time is equal for all words. Words may be referenced in random sequence. Since the whole process is completely electronic, short access times can be realized. Fig. 9 shows such a magnetic core matrix in the center, surrounded by the associated circuit elements.

Fig. 9. Cabinet with Magnetic Core Memory, Univac Scientific (Remington Rand Univac)

Magnetic Drum Storage: The storage element used here is magnetized spots on a ferromagnetic surface. Imagine we replace the two-dimensional core matrix by a sheet of magnetic material, with 100 spots, arranged again in ten rows and ten columns. We then paste this sheet on the surface of a drum, such that the rows are parallel on the axis, and the columns are parallel circles on the circumference. The drum is rotated at a constant speed. Over each column we place a so-called read-write head, a device for reading and recording the information All the bits stored in a column will pass under their corresponding head once every revolution. The address of a bit is still designated by a row and a column. Each column corresponds now to a particular head, whereas each row is defined by an angular position on the drum. The search for a bit consists of selecting a head, and of energizing it when the drum is in the right position. It can happen that at the instant the search starts the information is just past the head and will be available next only after one full revolution. The access time is therefore no longer constant, a fact the programmer must take into consideration. The arrangement of the information in actual drum memories depends on the type of logical operations of the computer. In serial machines each column, or track, contains a group of full words, recorded sequentially. Parallel machines have as many tracks as there are bits in a word, so that all bits can be handled simultaneously. The logical circuitry associated with the drum can be laid out such that individual words may be referenced in arbitrary sequence, so that we have random access. The other possibility provides only the reference to blocks of information, which is not quite so desirable from the programmer's standpoint.

Magnetic Tapes: The format of storing information is again of the matrix type. In the dimension across the tape there are only a few bits, usually between six and twelve. The other dimension contains as many bits as the length of the tape will permit. Since the tape is open-ended, the tape mechanism is built to move the tape in both directions past the read-write head. The access to information is essentially sequential, and long access times are involved. The advantages of magnetic tapes are their low price, the practically unlimited storage capacity, and the possibility of storing large amounts of information off the computer by removing recorded tapes from the machine.

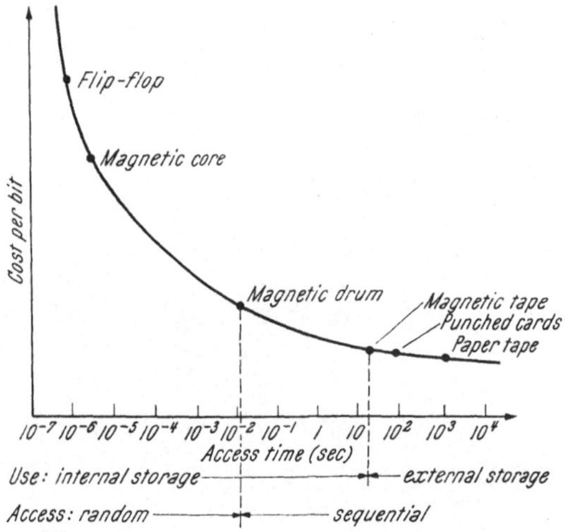

Fig. 10. Characteristics of different types of Memory

The general characteristics of the different types of storage are graphically illustrated in Fig. 10. The graph gives only the typical relations between the properties which must be considered for the design of a computer. Most computers have more than one type of memory to keep the total cost within practical limits. It is the programmer's task to make the best use of the different parts of the total memory.

After having discussed the basic elements of logic and storage, we proceeded directly to the overall organization of the memory, taking the word as the smallest unit. What remains is the structure of a word, that is, what does the code for an instruction or for a number look like. The coding of numbers may be accomplished in different number systems, there are several possibilities for the representation of negative numbers, etc. An instruction code will specify an operation and one or more addresses of operands. The discussion of these topics requires some familiarity with number systems and with programming, and we shall defer them until we get to these topics in the following chapters.

Physical Layout: The design features mentioned so far were concerned with the logic capabilities of a computer. Another aspect, equally important, is the use of sound engineering principles. The objectives here are utmost reliability, ease of maintenance, and ease of tracing malfunctions once they occur. We have already seen (Fig. 3) that a computer is built as an assembly of different cabinets. The wiring inside these units should be well organized and labelled. Color coding of the wires, clear numbering or other identification of terminals and connections, together with well-drawn circuit diagrams, are almost essential details. Fig. 11 shows a well wired computer cabinet. Experience has shown that it is good practice to mount those circuit components which are subject to wear on separate chassis. If the chassis are built so that they can be removed

Fig. 11. Cabinet of the Univac Scientific, showing the Wiring (Remington Rand Univac)

easily, they can be tested individually. As soon as a malfunction has been traced back to one of these chassis, or plug-in units, it can be replaced by a good one, so that the computer can continue operation without much delay. The bad chassis will be inspected and repaired off the machine. Fig. 12 shows a plug-in chassis of the Univac Scientific. A number of components, especially tubes, transistors, diodes, show a gradual decline in performance. These deteriorating parts can be detected by regularly performed tests. A replacement is possible even before any computer malfunction occurs. To obtain an optimum in reliability of a computer, good engineering design and well designed tests must go hand in hand.

Although most modern computers contain the basic units we described, and are therefore similar in nature, there are typical differences in the layout dictated by the intended application. A general purpose computer, as the name implies, is not particularly designed for any one application, whereas a special purpose machine may be built to do one specific job only. This may go so far

Fig. 12. Typical Plug-in Unit of a Computer (Remington Rand Univac)

that the complete program is built into the hardware and cannot normally be changed. Examples of this type are guidance computers for ships or airplanes, and some small business type computers. The capabilities of other special purpose computers are not restricted to one specific problem, rather their design is aimed at a certain field of application. Let us quote a few commonly used types of computers together with their main characteristics:

A *scientific computer* is probably closest to a general purpose computer, since the desired calculations are of a large variety. It shows great flexibility and speed in arithmetic and logical operations. The memory is of medium size, no special effort is made to obtain very high speed for input and output. The field of application is the solution of all kinds of mathematical or engineering problems. A *business computer* is used mainly for accounting and bookkeeping problems. It offers rather elementary arithmetic. The number system will usually be decimal, and special codes common in the business field can be handled. There is much emphasis on outputting directly onto various pre-printed forms, like statements, paychecks, etc. The automatic checking features are extensive. Punched cards are used to a great extent, this is to facilitate the operation of other business machines together with the computer. A *file computer* has the main purpose of storing and updating large files of information, for example, store inventories, or catalogues for large libraries. The arithmetic operations are limited whereas the memory is very large. The main emphasis is on fast location and transfer of data. Special instructions allow the extraction or correction of a single item in a file. The length of a word, or of a file item, is sometimes no longer fixed but may be specified by the programmer. The last two types of computers, needing only very little arithmetic computations, are also suitably called *data processors*.

2.14. New Concepts

For as long there are digital computers in existence, there will also be constant efforts to improve their performance. At present, the main trend is toward greater capacity and speed, higher reliability, smaller size, less power consumption, and more independence from the environment. All these efforts can be considered as improvements of the present concepts, even though new electronic components or new physical principles are used. However, in addition to these improvements, some efforts can be seen which use new logical concepts to increase the capabilities of computers.

Let us try to explain the ideas behind these new layouts. During a normal operation, a computer has to spend a considerable amount of time on rather trivial operations, like the transfer of information, or the handling of inputs and outputs. These operations are simple in nature and could just as well be performed by a device of much lower capability and hence of much lower cost than that of the computer. With the usual layout, a computer can perform only one operation at a time and must therefore spend its valuable time on these simple tasks. By adding an auxiliary data handling device to the computer, the situation can be improved. If this device can work independently from the computer, it will free the computer from these simple tasks, and its inexpensive time is substituted for expensive computer time. Since the two can, to a degree at least, operate simultaneously, the speed of the total system will be increased more than the price, i.e. the system is more efficient. In real-time application the increase in speed alone may be the decisive factor for the usefulness of the computer system.

The following remarks are concerned with the layout of some systems in this category. Some of them are presently in operation, others are in the planning stage.

IBM 709 Computer (Fig. 13):

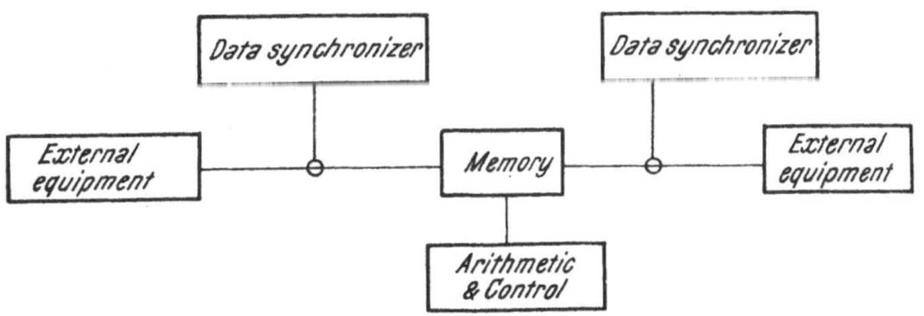

Fig. 13. Block Diagram of the IBM 709

Arithmetic and control together with the memory contribute what might be called a normal computer. Inputs and outputs are controlled by an auxiliary device, a data synchronizer. In effect, this synchronizer may be considered as an auxiliary computer which controls the exchange of information between external devices and computer. It also serves as a buffer with the effect of reducing or eliminating computer waiting times. The capabilities of this auxiliary computer are sufficient for the arranging of information into the proper format, but not for any arithmetic operations. Up to three data synchronizers can be connected to the system. The program for these auxiliary computers is stored in the main memory, so that the main program can change them if necessary.

Remington Rand LARC Computer (Fig. 14):

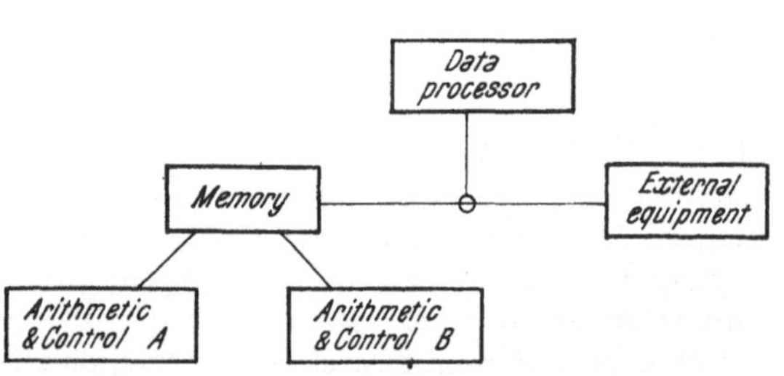

Fig. 14. Block Diagram of the Remington Rand LARC

This system consists of two main computers sharing the memory with an auxiliary computer, the data processor. The two computers can work completely independent on different problems, or together on one. The data processor is again in effect a computer with sufficient capability to handle input and output for both main computers.

Sylvania MOBIDIC Computer (Fig. 15):

The auxiliary device for this computer is not so elaborate as in the two previous systems. It is (no computer, but) essentially only one register. In spite of its simplicity, the device is quite effective. Inputs to the system are routed to those memory cells whose addresses appear in the real time address register. This transfer of information is automatic and does not require the assistance of the computer. The real time address is augmented for every input so that incoming information goes to consecutive cells. In addition, the computer can change the real time address if desired.

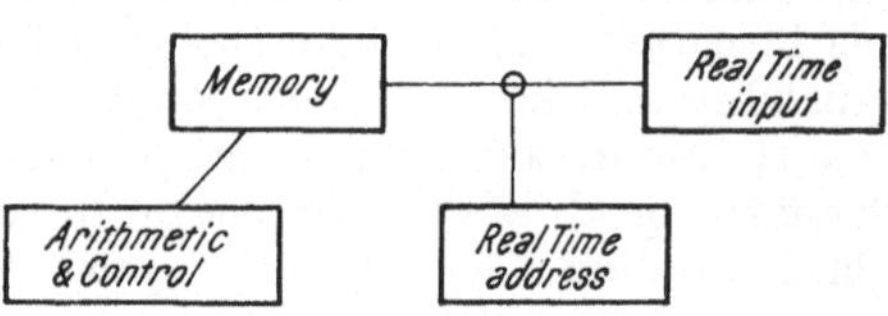

Fig. 15. Block Diagram of the Sylvania MOBIDIC

AFMDC Real Time System (Fig. 16):

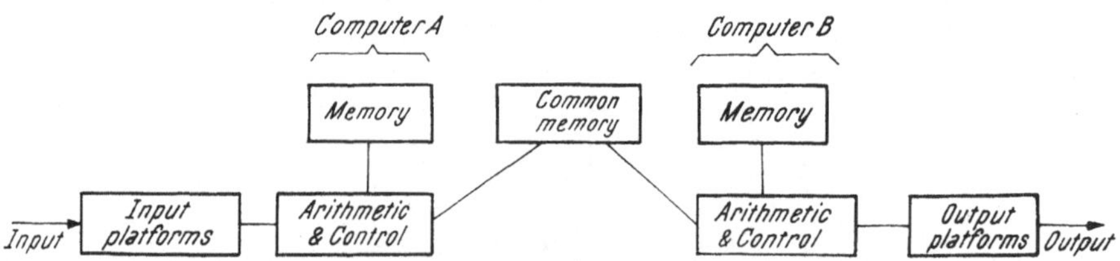

Fig. 16. Block Diagram of the Real-Time System of the Air Force Missile Development Center

This system is built around two identical computers. The flow of information in between them and on inputs and outputs is mechanized so that the computers can concentrate on actual computations. There are three types of information buffers: the Loading Platforms, the Common Memory, and the Output Platform. Together with the internal memories of the computers they constitute an overall memory. The input platforms will accept information from different sources at different rates of input. Because of the finite capacity of the loading platforms, new information overrides old information, but the computer has an arbitrary access to the last sixteen values of every information source. The output platform can delegate information to various external output devices. Both computers can simultaneously work on different calculations. A supervisory program, necessary to govern the flow of events of the overall system, may be programmed for either computer.

2.2. Number Systems

2.21. Principal Concepts

The art of counting, writing numbers, and performing the four basic arithmetic operations of addition, subtraction, multiplication, and division has been developed by mankind over a period of several thousand years. Every individual repeats this evolution process in just a few years as he goes through his formal education. This process begins with the positive integers and their arithmetic. Later on the number concept is gradually expanded to include fractions, negative numbers, and finally, irrational, transcendental, complex numbers, and vectors.

The most important achievement in the development of science has undoubtedly been the invention of our decimal number system. The counting procedure in units of ten is generally believed to stem from the fact that man has ten fingers. In a very few cases people have counted in units of five or twenty, which corresponds to only one hand, or both hands and feet. The expression of physical quantities in units not related to each other by some power of ten, as for instance second, minute, hour, day, week, for time, or mil, inch, foot, yard, fathom, for distance should not be interpreted as constituting number systems, as all these units are counted decimally. The number ten, used as the base of our number system, however, is not in itself a decisive factor for its usefulness. It has probably been in use for more than five thousand years. The main use of numbers in those early times was for plain counting and keeping records of quantities, rather than to perform any arithmetic operations. The numeration methods were thus designed solely for these purposes. With the development of trade and science these old numeration methods became more and more inadequate. In spite of this need for a better system it took a remarkably long time before an adequate number notation was invented. The Greeks and Romans, who had achieved a rather high development in science, did not succeed in this endeavor. Just imagine performing simple arithmetic with Roman numerals, like dividing MMDXLVI by CCIX, using Roman numerals only! As little as five hundred years ago simple operations like multiplication or division of large numbers required the service of an expert. Today every ten year old child can do them. The explanation for this fact is not higher intelligence of our children, but a better number notation.

There are two decisive factors, or inventions, which made this possible: the principle of position together with the numeral zero. The principle of position consists of giving a numeral, or digit, a value which depends both on the symbol and on its position in the whole number. Thus, the digit 5 has a different value in the three numbers 125, 152, and 507. In the first case it has its original basic value five, in the second its value is fifty, or five times ten, and in the last five hundred, or five times ten times ten. It will happen that some positions in a number are empty. If they were simply left out there would be no difference in notation between, say, two hundred four and twenty four. There the numeral zero serves to fill the gap. We write 204 if there are two hundreds, no tens, and four units. These two concepts now make arithmetic quite easy. All arithmetic operations on numbers of any size reduce automatically to operations on the ten digits 0 through 9. All that is necessary is to memorize an addition table and a multiplication table, each consisting of ten times ten, or a hundred values.

In a commonly used format these tables are given below:

Table 1. Decimal Addition Table

	0	1	2	3	4	5	6	7	8	9
0	0	1	2	3	4	5	6	7	8	9
1	1	2	3	4	5	6	7	8	9	10
2	2	3	4	5	6	7	8	9	10	11
3	3	4	5	6	7	8	9	10	11	12
4	4	5	6	7	8	9	10	11	12	13
5	5	6	7	8	9	10	11	12	13	14
6	6	7	8	9	10	11	12	13	14	15
7	7	8	9	10	11	12	13	14	15	16
8	8	9	10	11	12	13	14	15	16	17
9	9	10	11	12	13	14	15	16	17	18

Table 2. Decimal Multiplication Table

	0	1	2	3	4	5	6	7	8	9
0	0	0	0	0	0	0	0	0	0	0
1	0	1	2	3	4	5	6	7	8	9
2	0	2	4	6	8	10	12	14	16	18
3	0	3	6	9	12	15	18	21	24	27
4	0	4	8	12	16	20	24	28	32	36
5	0	5	10	15	20	25	30	35	40	45
6	0	6	12	18	24	30	36	42	48	54
7	0	7	14	21	28	35	42	49	56	63
8	0	8	16	24	32	40	48	56	64	72
9	0	9	18	27	36	45	54	63	72	81

Subtraction and division require no extra tables, since the two tables can be used backwards for these purposes. Due to the fact that both addition and multiplication are commutative operations, i.e. $a + b = b + a$ and $ab = ba$, the two tables have only fifty values each, which must be memorized.

Since this our normal decimal number system appears absolutely adequate for all practical purposes, why should we not just build electronic computers based on it, as has been done successfully with automatic desk calculators? This question can be answered symbolically by saying that an electronic computer has only two fingers as compared to the human ten. There are in fact two main reasons for not choosing the decimal system in computers.

A mechanical desk calculator uses wheels or disks to indicate digits. Each wheel has the ten digits 0 through 9 engraved on its circumference. It can rest in any of ten positions, thereby showing one of the digits through a window in the front panel. Electronic computers do not use mechanical wheels, because mechanical devices operate too slowly, but rather electronic devices, e.g flip-flops, or magnetic cores. Even electric relays are being used less and less, because they involve mechanical motion and cannot exceed certain speed limits. Purely electronic devices are capable of tremendous speed but it is difficult to provide ten different stable states. There are basically only two states: on and off, high and low, positive and negative. We may also associate them with the numbers 0 and 1. In analogy to the digit wheels of the desk calculator, whose ten positions correspond to the base ten, or decimal number system, the two states of electronic devices would suggest a number system with the base two, or binary numbers. Indeed, this is the system best suited for electronic computers.

In the binary system the counting process starts as usual with 0 and 1. Now all symbols are already exhausted, there is no 2. The next number, two, is made by starting over with the first symbol 0 in the last position and writing a 1 in the next higher position to the left. Two is therefore written as 10 in binary. A list of binary numbers may be found in Table 5; the binary number system is treated in more detail in Chapter 2.24.

Another reason for not using the decimal system in computers is the size of the addition and multiplication tables, which must be incorporated into the logic of the machine. With 200 possible cases to be determined the circuitry becomes quite complicated. A number system with base b requires two tables with $2\,b^2$ entries, which amounts to 200 for the decimal system, as we have seen earlier. A lower value for b results in fewer values and consequently is simpler to mechanize in a computer. The simplest possible case is $b = 2$, which again brings us to binary numbers. The two tables have now only eight values, as shown below:

Table 3. Binary Addition Table

	0	1
0	0	1
1	1	10

Table 4. Binary Multiplication Table

	0	1
0	0	0
1	0	1

The advantages of the base two are economy of symbols (there are only two of them), and tremendous simplicity of operations. The drawback is its lack of compactness. For example, the decimal number 9013 would be expressed in binary by 10001100110101. It is very hard to memorize such a binary number even for a short time. For human usage compactness is quite an important factor and the binary system is definitely inferior to the decimal system in this respect. For automatic computers the lack of compactness is of no great consequence. The binary system is thus optimal, in that it assures a minimum number of computer components and maximum possible speed at the same time. It should be mentioned here that by choosing the binary system, only the number base was changed from ten to two. The principle of position and the zero are retained, thus still assuring the benefits which derive from them.

The binary number system is described in more detail in chapter 2.24. Conversion of numbers from one system to the other is treated in chapter 2.25. The reader may skip the next two chapters without loss of continuity.

2.22. Fixed-Point Numbers

Numerical calculations, in isolated cases, are restricted to integers only. This is the case, for example, if dollars and cents, or quantities of items have to be computed. In general, however, engineering and scientific, as well as business type problems, deal with rational, irrational, and transcendental numbers. By their very nature all digital computations can be done in rational numbers only. How can this difficulty be resolved? Every number can be represented uniquely in any digital number system, be it base ten or two. Most rational numbers, and all irrational and transcendental numbers, have a digital form with an infinite fractional part. These can therefore never be exactly described by a finite number of digits. In practice all such numbers are truncated after a suitable number of places, depending on the required accuracy. This replacement of infinite numbers by rational numbers of finite length must necessarily be done for all numerical calculations, whether computers are used or not. The results obtained are consequently also only approximations to the true values. For most practical cases a number size of ten decimal digits has proven to be adequate. Most computers and desk calculators have about this size. Information theory tells us that the information, I, contained in an n-digit decimal number is:

$$I = \log_2 10^n = 3.32\, n \text{ bits}$$

A binary number with m bits consequently carries the information:

$$I = \log_2 2^m = m \text{ bits}$$

The binary computer equivalent to a ten-digit decimal machine must therefore have a number length of 34 bits. Most computers have between 35 and 42 bits in a number. If computations are carried through with this number length, i.e. each number occupies one cell in the memory, one speaks of single precision. Occasionally, the accuracy thus obtainable is insufficient and one has to combine the contents of two cells to represent numbers of double length. Since operations on double length numbers are normally not built into the computer logic, the operations have to be programmed.

Having explained the reasons why all computations must be performed with rational numbers of a finite, definite length, we can proceed now to show how numbers of arbitrary magnitudes are fitted into the computer. For illustration purposes we will take a decimal computer with numbers four digits long plus sign. All conclusions derived here can be applied equally well to binary machines.

The numbers we have to deal with in calculations are either integers, pure fractions, or they are mixed numbers with both an integral and a fractional part. Let us consider machine numbers to be integers. Although this assumption is somewhat arbitrary, it comes close to what one would do with a desk calculator. To get correct results care must be taken to keep track of the position of the decimal point. In hand computing this is done manually by observing a few simple rules. When using a desk calculator the procedure is essentially the same. Instead of writing the decimal point where it belongs, mechanical indicators are manually set on the different registers of the calculators to make the correct copying of the results easier. The setting of these decimal point indicators does in no way affect the operation of a desk calculator. The same is true for electronic computers. Here it is the programmer who must keep track of the decimal point. If the numbers do not fit into the computer as they are, they have to be scaled first. This means multiplying them by a suitable power of ten before they are entered into the computer. A few examples will show this:

Example 1. Compute 1.66 + 0.234. Both numbers are multiplied by 10^3.

Manual procedure:		Computer:	
	1.66		+ 1660
	+ 0.234		+ 0234
	1.894		+ 1894

Example 2. Compute 166,000 + 23,400. Both numbers are scaled down by multiplying them by 10^{-2}.

Manual procedure:		Computer:	
	166000		+ 1660
	+ 23400		+ 0234
	189400		+ 1894

In addition and subtraction the decimal point location is the same for the operands and the results. It may be even outside the actual computer numbers, as the second examples shows. The procedure is not quite so simple if multiplication or division is involved. The product of two four-digit numbers has in general eight digits, the first can be zero. For further computations only four digits can be used and have to be properly chosen from the eight.

Example 3. Compute $1.66 \times 0.234 + 0.15$.

Manual procedure:		Computer:	
	1.66×0.234		1660×0234
	332		00000
	498		03320
	664		04980
			06640
	.38844		+ 00388440
	+ .15		
	.53844		
			+ 3884
			+ 1500
			+ 5384

In most computers the results of a basic operation are formed in a register of double length. Without special programming effort either the lower half or the upper half of this register is carried on for further computations. The computers are called integral and fractional respectively. The distinction is somewhat artificial, because all computers allow the programmer to select any desired single length number from this double register. In our example the center four digits must be chosen. Note that the decimal point is located in different places for the operands, the product, and for the final result. It is important to notice that the computer, just as in the case of the desk calculator, does not know where the decimal point is; the programmer has to keep track of it.

Large computations require frequent rescaling of numbers to keep them properly positioned within the range of a computer number. If a number is beyond the capacity of a computer register it is said to overflow. It must be scaled down lest the most significant digit or digits are lost. On the other hand, it can happen that numbers are scaled down too far, they then have too many leading zeros and too few significant digits. The important fact is that each quantity has its own defined decimal point, which is stated or fixed by the programmer. This type of computation is commonly referred to as fixed-point arithmetic. In some cases the task of scaling puts a rather heavy burden on the programmer. It may be difficult or even impossible to estimate the size of all intermediate or final results with reasonable accuracy. To detect overflows, most computers have an automatic test or alarm built in, alerting the programmer to the need of rescaling his problem. Loss of significance can be seen by looking at intermediate and final results. They will have most, if not all, leading digits equal to zero.

2.23. Floating-Point Numbers

The difficulty of scaling in fixed-point arithmetic has led to the development of the so-called floating-point notation. The normal decimal notation of numbers becomes clumsy when the numbers are very large or very small. One usually then resorts to the scheme of splitting up the numbers into two factors, one an ordinary decimal number, the other a power of ten. Thus, for instance,

$$N = +\,1{,}230{,}000{,}000{,}000 = +\,0.123 \cdot 10^{13}$$

or

$$M = +\,0.000{,}000{,}000{,}012{,}3 = +\,0.123 \cdot 10^{-10}$$

The last notation is very compact but still contains all the necessary information. The number N can of course be written in various other ways, e.g. $1.23 \cdot 10^{12}$, or $0.0123 \cdot 10^{14}$. If we agree to write the first part always with the point at a definite place, say in front of the first non-zero digit, we no longer have to write the point at all. Secondly, if we know the number base, it is only necessary to write down the exponent. Both values have a sign associated with them. We thus get

$$N = +\,123 + 13 \qquad M = +\,123 - 10$$

This is the floating-point notation. The first number is the magnitude, a pure fraction always equal or larger than 0.1. Sometimes it is called the mantissa, actually a misnomer. The last number is the exponent. One can look at this notation as the magnitude giving the digit configuration, and the exponent telling where the decimal point ought to be. The advantage of this notation is that no zeros have to be carried along, they convey only very little actual information. The assignment of the available digits of a computer number to fit floating-point is governed by practical experience. Some balance has to be found between the number of significant digits (magnitude) and the maximum possible range (exponent). For a ten digit computer eight digits might be assigned to the magnitude and two for the exponent, plus provision for the two signs. For binary machines with a word length of 36 bits a customary assignment is 27 bits for the magnitude, 7 for the exponent, and 2 for the signs. The range of numbers which fits into this latter scheme is between 10^{-38} and 10^{+38} in absolute value. This range is so big that it is hardly ever necessary to scale the numbers at all.

This extremely helpful advantage for the programmer is gained at a price, however. The arithmetic, and consequently the computer logic and circuitry, are more complicated than for fixed-point numbers. Both magnitude and exponent have to be handled separately. The computer will cost more and the speed of operations is reduced by a sizeable factor. The time saved in programming will often more than offset the slower computing speed. So the floating-point is a highly desirable feature, especially for scientific calculations. Most modern large scientific computers have the floating-point built in. On others subroutines must be written to simulate these operations.

2.24. The Binary Number System

Every number system has as many different symbols as its base indicates. The counting process goes through these symbols in order, as soon as all symbols are exhausted, the sequence repeats and one is added to the symbol to the left. Applying this basic rule to systems base 10, 2, and 8, we get Table 5.

The octal numbers are quoted here, because they are often used as a shorthand notation for binary numbers. A look at the binary sequence shows that there are precisely eight possible combinations of 3 binary digits or bits. If we arrange a binary number in groups of 3 bits, we can then denote each group by one of the numbers 0 through 7. For example, the binary number 110,100,111,010,001 can be written 64721, which is its octal equivalent. The advantage is compactness, and the procedure to go from one notation to the other is trivial.

Table 5. *Binary and Octal Numbers*

Decimal	Binary	Octal
0	0	0
1	1	1
2	10	2
3	11	3
4	100	4
5	101	5
6	110	6
7	111	7
8	1000	10
9	1001	11
10	1010	12
11	1011	13
12	1100	14
13	1101	15
14	1110	16
15	1111	17
16	10000	20
17	10001	21

One can just as well partition a binary number in groups of four each. Then 16 symbols are needed; usually the ten digits 0—9 and the six letters A—F are taken. In this hexadecimal notation our example above would be 110,1001,1101,0001 = 69D1. This rather strange looking notation has been used on some early computers but is now gradually being abandoned in favor of the octal notation.

In mathematical computations we are not only concerned with cardinal numbers, but have to handle negative numbers and fractions as well. The most natural way of denoting negative numbers is to place a minus sign in front. This is done in a great number of computers. Preceding the magnitude of a number is an extra sign-bit, for positive numbers this is zero, for negative numbers it is one. This procedure is exactly the ordinary mathematical notation. However, this implies that the sign of two numbers has to be examined before an arithmetical operation can be performed. Suppose we want to add two numbers. If both signs are equal we must add, if they are different we must subtract. We also then have to subtract the smaller one from the larger one, and finally decide whether the result is positive or negative. For illustration, let us take binary numbers with 6 bits and sign.

Example 1. $x = a + b$, $a = 29$, $b = 10$.

In Decimal:		In Binary:	
	+ 29		0 011101
	+ 10		0 001010
	+ 39		0 100111

The binary operation is straight addition through the whole number including the sign bit.

Example 2. $x = a + b$, $a = -29$, $b = -10$.

In Decimal:		In Binary:	
	— 29		1011101
	— 10		1001010
	— 39		1100111

The binary addition extends not over into the sign bit, which has to be considered separately.

Example 3. $x = a + b$, $a = +29$, $b = -10$.

In Decimal:		In Binary:	
	$+\ 29$		0 011101
	$-\ 10$		1 001010
	$+\ 19$		1 010011

Both processes are actual subtractions now.

The decision whether to actually add or subtract has become such a deep-rooted habit, that one would hardly try a way to avoid it. But there exists a notation for negative numbers which makes the process of addition unique regardless of the sign of the numbers. For the binary system this is the one's complement notation, for the decimal system it would be 9's complements. One gets a negative binary number from a positive one by replacing all zeros by ones and all ones by zeros, a process called complementing. Thus if $+29$ is 0011101 in a computer, -29 would be 1100010. A straightforward addition process through the whole number may result in a carry from the most significant bit, this carry must be added to the least significant bit to get the correct result. This is called the end-around carry. The one's complement notation of negative numbers does not change our example 1 above. For example 2 we get:

In Decimal:		In Binary:	
	$-\ 29$		1100010
	$-\ 10$		1110101
	$-\ 39$		1 1010111
			1
			1011000

The binary operation is straightforward addition through the whole number, including the sign bit. The final result is actually -39 as can be easily seen when complementing it to get $0100111 = +39$.

For example 3 we get:

In Decimal:		Binary:	
	$+\ 29$		0011101
	$-\ 10$		1110101
	$+\ 19$		1 0010010
			1
			0010011

We see that this result was obtained by the same addition process, and a decision whether to really add or subtract is no longer required.

The last example shall also be shown on 9's complements for a calculator of 4 digit length. The number 29 would be 0029, $+\ 10$ hence 0010, and $-\ 10$ 9989. Addition and end-around carry then yield:

$$\begin{array}{r} 0029 \\ \underline{9989} \\ 1\ 0018 \\ \underline{1} \\ 0019 \end{array}$$

which is the correct result. It is of course hopeless to tell people to henceforth write negative numbers in 9's complements, just to save them the decision between adding and subtracting. But automatic computers do not have to learn any new rules, nor for that matter give up old deep-rooted habits. They can be built on any system.

The advantage gained by adoption of the binary number system for a computer is simplicity and elegance of operations, minimum number of computer elements, and great speed. The difficulty now is that the human operator still wants to quote his problems and get his answers in the normal decimal manner.

This requires the conversion of numbers from decimal to binary (or octal) and vice versa. Since these operations are of a mechanical nature, they can best be performed by the computer itself. We will describe algorithms suited for manual conversions in the next chapter. Input of numbers into the computer is usually accomplished by punched cards or by teletype tape. Output is by means of card punching machines, typewriters, printers, or teletype punches. The speed obtainable with these operations is dictated by mechanical considerations. It is relatively very low as compared to the internal computing speed of computers, which is governed by electronic considerations. This fact makes it possible to convert numbers so fast that there is time enough to convert one number and still be ready for the next one while the mechanical equipment is running at maximum speed. An example might best illustrate the possibilities. The Univac Scientific computer has a line printer which can print up to ten lines per second. When eight decimal numbers of ten digits each are to be printed on each line, the conversion of the binary machine numbers is so fast that the printer can still run at full speed. Thus it can be seen that an internal binary number system does not involve a sacrifice in speed of operation, if, as usual, input and output are both decimal.

This argument does not stand up for medium size computers having a (mechanically moving) magnetic drum as the main memory. These machines are therefore often built with the decimal number system. Decimal codes used in computers are treated in chapter 2.26.

2.25. Conversion Between Decimal and Binary Numbers

Since many computers are using binary numbers internally, it is necessary to convert numbers from one base to the other. As already mentioned, an economical way to write binary numbers is the octal notation, simply arrived at by grouping the bits of a binary number in sets of three and writing them as the numerals 0—7. We can therefore restrict our algorithms to the conversions between octal and decimal numbers.

In ordinary decimal notation an arbitrary number N is written as a series of digits

$$N = d_n\, d_{n-1} \ldots d_2\, d_1\, d_0 \cdot d_{-1}\, d_{-2} \ldots d_{-m}$$

where the d's are any of the digits 0 through 9. The position of a digit relative to the decimal point determines its actual value

$$N = d_n\, 10^n + d_{n-1}\, 10^{n-1} + \ldots d_2\, 10^2 + d_1\, 10 + d_0 + d_{-1} \cdot 10^{-1} + + d_{-2}\, 10^{-2} + \ldots d_{-m}\, 10^{-m}$$

The same number N can be expressed in any other number base, for example 8. Choosing the letter c for any of the digits 0 through 7, we have

$$N = c_p \cdot 8^p + c_{p-1}\, 8^{p-1} + \ldots c_2\, 8^2 + c_1 \cdot 8 + c_0 + c_{-1}\, 8^{-1} + c_{-2}\, 8^{-2} + \ldots c_{-q} 8^{-q}$$

As any number is uniquely defined by its digits, it follows that all octal digits can be determined from the decimal digits and vice versa. The number of fractional digits is usually different in both cases, certain rational numbers N will result in finite fractions in one system and in infinite periodic fractions in the other. So, for $N = \frac{1}{10}$ we have in decimal 0.1 and in octal .063146314 . . . Irrational and transcendental numbers are of course infinite in any system with a rational base.

The algorithm for conversion is different for integers and for fractions, it also depends on the direction of conversion, i.e. decimal to octal, or octal to decimal. Thus, we have the following four cases:

1. Integer conversion from decimal to octal: Let us illustrate the process by taking a four-digit decimal number:

$$N = d_3\, d_2\, d_1\, d_0 = d_3\, 10^3 + d_2\, 10^2 + d_1\, 10 + d_0 \tag{1}$$

We seek the corresponding octal digits c for the same number N:

$$N = c_4\, 8^4 + c_3\, 8^3 + c_2\, 8^2 + c_1\, 8 + c_0 \tag{2}$$

The division of N by 8 will yield an integral quotient q_0 and a remainder r_0, where $r_0 < 8$. Doing this on both equations, we get

$$\frac{N}{8} = q_0 + \frac{r_0}{8} = c_4\, 8^3 + c_3\, 8^2 + c_2\, 8 + c_1 + \frac{c_0}{8}$$

Equating the integral parts and the fractions separately, we have

$$q_0 = c_4\, 8^3 + c_3\, 8^2 + c_2\, 8 + c_1$$
$$r_0 = c_0$$

The remainder r_0 is seen to be the last octal digit c_0. Repeating the process by dividing q_0 by 8 we get a new quotient q_1 and a new remainder r_1, the latter is our second octal digit.

$$\frac{q_0}{8} = q_1 + \frac{r_1}{8} = c_4\, 8^2 + c_3\, 8 + c_2 + \frac{c_1}{8}$$
$$q_1 = c_4\, 8^2 + c_3\, 8 + c_2$$
$$r_1 = c_1$$

This process is continued until nothing is left. A convenient arrangement of the numbers is the following:

N	
q_0	c_0
q_1	c_1
q_2	c_2
q_3	c_3

Example 1. Convert $N = 5432_{10}$ to octal.

5432	
679	0
84	7
10	4
1	2
0	1

$$5432_{10} = 12470_8$$
$$= 1{,}010{,}100{,}111{,}000_2$$

The binary notation follows immediately from the octal notation by inspection. The process applies in general to any bases a and b, so we have:

Rule 1: To convert an integer N (base a) to base b, divide N by b and set aside the remainder. Divide the integral part of the quotient by b and set aside the remainder. Keep doing this until the quotient becomes zero. Then the remainders in reverse order are the digits of N to base b. The divisions must be performed in base a arithmetic.

2. Integer conversion from octal to decimal: Here again the equations (1) and (2) apply, only now the c's are known and the d's sought. Rule 1 may be used, however, we now need to divide in the unfamiliar octal arithmetic. Division should be by 10, which is 12_8. A way around this difficulty is the direct evaluation of equation (2) term by term. We use a table of values of powers of 8.

n	8^n
0	1
1	8
2	64
3	512
4	4096
.	.
.	.
.	.
.	.

Example 2. Convert $N = 12470_8$ to decimal.

$$N = 1\times 8^4 + 2\times 8^3 + 4\times 8^2 + 7\times 8 + 0\times 1$$
$$= 4096 + 2\times 512 + 4\times 64 + 7\times 8 = 5432_{10}$$

A slightly different approach can be taken when rewriting equation (2) as

$$N = \{[(c_4 \cdot 8 + c_3)\, 8 + c_2]\, 8 + c_1\} \cdot 8 + c_0 \tag{2a}$$

Our example is then:

$$1\times 8 + 2 = 10$$
$$10\times 8 + 4 = 84$$
$$84\times 8 + 7 = 679$$
$$679\times 8 + 0 = 5432$$

This scheme is known as synthetic multiplication, the numbers are usually arranged as follows:

	1	2	4	7	0
	—	8	80	672	5432
× 8	1	10	84	679	5432

We can summarize this procedure as

Rule 2. To convert an integer N (base a) to base b, multiply the first digit by a, then add the second digit to the product. Multiply the sum by a and add the next digit. Keep doing this until the last digit is added. The final sum is N to base b. The operations must be carried out in base b arithmetic.

3. *Fraction conversion from decimal to octal:* The basic equations are now

$$N = .d_{-1}\, d_{-2}\, d_{-3}\, d_{-4} \ldots$$
$$N = d_{-1}\, 10^{-1} + d_{-2}\, 10^{-2} + d_{-3}\, 10^{-3} + \ldots \tag{3}$$

and

$$N = .c_{-1}\, c_{-2}\, c_{-3}\, c_{-4} \ldots$$
$$N = c_{-1}\, 8^{-1} + c_{-2}\, 8^{-2} + c_{-3}\, 8^{-3} + c_{-4}\, 8^{-4} + \ldots \tag{4}$$

Multiplication of N by 8 results, in a number which can be written as

$$8\, N = i_1 + f_1 \tag{5}$$

where i_1 is an integer, and f_1 a pure fraction. Multiplying equation (4) also by 8 gives

$$8\, N = c_{-1} + c_{-2}\, 8^{-1} + c_{-3}\, 8^{-2} + c_4\, 8^{-3} + \ldots \tag{6}$$
$$= c_{-1} \cdot c_{-2}\, c_{-3}\, c_{-4} \ldots$$

The integral part is c_{-1}. We have actually only moved the octal point one place to the right. Since (5) and (6) are equal, it follows immediately that

$$i_1 = c_{-1}$$

Repeating the multiplication by 8 with f_1 yields a new product $i_2 + f_2$, where $i_2 = c_{-2}$ is the second octal digit.

A convenient scheme for practical computation is:

$$\begin{array}{c} N \\ i_1 . f_1 \\ i_2 . f_2 \\ i_3 . f_3 \\ \vdots \end{array}$$

Example 3. Convert 0.171875_{10} to octal.

```
0.171875
1.375000
3.000          0.171875₁₀ = 0.13₈
                          = 0.001,011₂
```

$$0.171875_{10} = 0.13_8 = 0.001{,}011_2$$

In most cases the result is an infinite fraction.

Example 4. Convert 0.5432_{10} to octal.

```
0.5432
4.3456
2.7648
6.1184
0.9472
7.5776
 etc.
```

$$0.5432_{10} = 0.42607\ldots_8 = 0.100{,}010{,}110{,}000{,}111\ldots_2$$

This process also applies in general to any bases a and b, so we get

Rule 3. To convert a fraction N (base a) to base b, multiply N by b and set aside the integral part of the product. Multiply the fractional part of the product by b and set aside the integral part. Continue doing this until the new fraction becomes zero or until enough digits are generated. The integers set aside, in proper order, are the digits of N to base b. The multiplications must be performed in base a arithmetic.

4. Fraction conversion from octal to decimal: This case can be solved by using Rule 3. Then octal multiplication has to be used, the multipliers being 10_{10} or 12_8. This is not quite so difficult as the octal division. An example will show this.

Example 5. Convert 0.13_8 to decimal.

0.13 × 12	0.56 × 12	0.14 × 12	0.70 × 12	0.60 × 12	0.40 × 12
13	56	14	70	60	40
26	134	30	160	140	100
1.56	7.14	1.70	10.60	7.40	5.00

The integral parts of the products, written in decimal, are the desired digits.

$$0.13_8 = 0.171875_{10}$$

An alternate way of conversion uses a table of powers of 8^{-n} expressed in decimal and evaluates equation (4) term by term.

n	8^{-n}
1	0.125
2	0.015625
3	0.001953125
.	.
.	.
.	.

Doing example 5 this way we get

$$\begin{aligned} N &= 1 \times 0.125 + 3 \times 0.015625 \\ &= 0.125 + 0.046875 = 0.171875_{10} \end{aligned}$$

The same result may be obtained, if a table of negative powers of 8 is not available, by using synthetic division. Equation (4) is then rewritten as

$$N = \left\{\left[\left(c_{-4}\frac{1}{8} + c_{-3}\right)\frac{1}{8} + c_{-2}\right]\frac{1}{8} + c_{-1}\right\}\frac{1}{8} \tag{4a}$$

One has to start with the rightmost digit first. The scheme for our example would be

	3	1	
	—	0.375	0.171875
: 8	3	1.375	

The general rule is then:

Rule 4. To convert a fraction N (base a) to base b, divide the last digit by a. Add the digit next to the left and divide the sum by a. Continue this until all digits are used up. The final quotient is N to the base b. The operations must be carried out in base b arithmetic.

2.26. Binary-Coded Decimal Numbers

As explained previously, the logical building blocks used in electronic computers are basically bistable elements, they are ideally suited for the binary number system. For some computers it is nevertheless desirable to use decimal numbers. One has then to construct combinations of binary elements to represent decimal numbers.

We have seen that three bits represent eight different combinations or numbers. The representation of the ten decimal digits, therefore, calls for at least four bits per digit. Four bits now describe sixteen cases of which only ten are needed. One can theoretically choose any ten out of the sixteen combinations and associate them with the ten decimal digits. Theoretically, there are $16!/6! = 29 \cdot 10^9$ possibilities, the number of variations of sixteen elements taken ten at a time. Out of this huge number only very few lead to reasonably simple circuitry for handling the arithmetic operations. Some codes are distinguished by the fact that each bit has a definite value or weight. The first two codes in Table 6 are of this type, the name given to these codes is just the weight of the bits in order. The 8421 code is a straight-forward representation

Table 6. *Four-Bit Decimal Codes*

Binary Code	Assigned Decimal Digit			
	8421	2421	Excess 3	2-out-of-5
0000	0	0		
0001	1	1		1
0010	2	2		2
0011	3	3	0	3
0100	4	4	1	4
0101	5		2	5
0110	6		3	6
0111	7		4	
1000	8		5	7
1001	9		6	8
1010			7	9
1011		5	8	
1100		6	9	0
1101		7		
1110		8		
1111		9		

of the digits by the ordinary binary numbers. The 2421 code results, if the first bit carries a weight of two. The code is ambiguous since e.g. the number 2 could be 0010 and 1000. The generation of the six codes not assigned must be artificially prevented in a computer. The third code has no particular weights for the bits, it is made by adding three to the true binary representation of the decimal digits. The last code is actually an abbreviated 5-bit code. We will come back to it in chapter 2.27. The second and third codes have two features in common, which make the logic circuits for arithmetic operations relatively simple. First, the 9's complement of any digit is obtained simply by complementing the corresponding binary codes. This property is very helpful, as we have seen in chapter 2.24 for binary numbers. The second property is that the addition of any two digits will produce a carry into the code to the left, if the corresponding decimal digits produce a carry when added.

Six possible combinations are not used in each system. These can therefore never occur during computations as long as the computer works properly. A computer can have automatic checks on such illegal codes and give an alarm should they occur. The last two codes have the additional property that numbers consisting of all zeros or all ones are illegal. This is sometimes helpful for detecting machine errors.

2.27. Redundant Number Codes

Any normal English text contains more letters or even words than would be necessary to convey its information content. This redundancy makes the text longer than necessary, but it also enables us to understand it, even when some letters are unreadable or when spelling mistakes have been made. In contrast to this our number notations are not redundant. If any one digit is wrong in a number we can never tell what the correct number should be. To avoid any doubts, numbers are often quoted twice in different ways of writing, especially when they mean dollars and cents. The principle of redundancy can well be applied to number codes. One or more digits are added to the number. They must be derived in some defined logical manner from the original number. Any such redundant number can then be checked for errors; in some cases it is even possible to correct errors.

The simplest redundant code is used quite frequently for recording information on magnetic tape. The essential information is usually recorded in groups of six bits across the tape. In the process of recording a seventh, redundant bit is also put on the tape. It is determined in such a way as to make the total number of ones always an odd number, whence the name parity bit. Table 7 shows a few examples:

Table 7. *Code With Odd-Even Check Bit*

Information	Check Bit	Redundant Code
000000	1	0000001
000001	0	0000010
010101	0	0101010
010111	1	0101111

Every possible code has at least one bit equal to one; this fact can be utilized in the computer to make a decision between an intended all-zero information code and no information at all.

Experience has shown that magnetic tapes have occasionally small bad spots in the magnetic film. It also happens that some tiny dust particle gets under the read- or write-head of the tape recorder, so that a bit may get lost. These cases can easily be detected automatically by the machine. If no parity error was detected one can be reasonably sure that the information was read correctly. The parity bit is discarded as soon as the information enters the memory of the computer. This simple parity check is not a complete error check, since two bits dropped or added simultaneously cannot be detected.

Another example of redundancy codes is the 2-out-of-5 code, used to represent decimal digits. It has five bits, as shown in Table 8. Any one of the five bits can be considered the redundancy bit, the other four are still unique. Usually the last one is taken as redundant, and only the first four form the original code, see Table 6. The full five-bit code makes use of the fact that there are exactly ten possible combinations to select two out of five elements. Each code has exactly two 1's. This fact can be used for automatic error checking.

Table 8. *Redundant Decimal Codes*

Decimal	2-out-of-5	Biquinary	Condensed Biquinary
0	11000	0100001	00110
1	00011	0100010	00011
2	00101	0100100	00101
3	00110	0101000	01001
4	01001	0110000	01010
5	01010	1000001	01100
6	01100	1000010	10001
7	10001	1000100	10010
8	10010	1001000	10100
9	10100	1010000	11000

The biquinary code uses as many as seven bits to represent the decimal digits. As the previous code it also has two 1's. In addition it is a weighted code, the weights being 5043210, as can be seen from Table 8. The large redundancy allows the detection of multiple errors. The code is employed in a widely used computer of medium size and speed (IBM 650). All numbers passing through certain points in the computer are automatically checked for errors. For storage of numbers in the main memory, a magnetic drum, a condensed five bit code is used for economy as given in the last column of Table 8.

In general, the possibilities of detecting and correcting faulty codes increase with the number of redundant bits. So does the cost of the computer, since these extra bits must be stored, generated, and checked. The opposite approach to build a reliable computer is to use no redundancy at all. This reduces the number of electrical components in a machine, and thereby the chance of machine malfunctions. This philosophy was used in another computer of comparable size (Electro Data), also in wide use. There are arguments for and against each of the two approaches. At the present time no final judgment can be made. For scientific computers the recent improvements made in components favors a trend toward non-redundant machines. One of the main self-checking features not likely to be abandoned is the use of the odd-even check bit for storing information on magnetic tape. To insure proper working, regularly scheduled comprehensive test programs are run under marginal operating conditions, normally once a day. If no malfunctions are detected in these tests, the computer is returned to normal conditions and will perform very reliably for the rest of the day. Any desired checks on the correctness of results can always be incorporated in the program. Computers for business type problems, also called data processors, demand a very high degree of reliability for each single number. To be able to adjust the number of checks to the type of problem or to the disgression of individual users, some companies have incorporated a minimum of automatic checks, providing at the same time an easy way to program a variety of additional checks.

2.28. Residue Number Systems

In conclusion of the discussion of number systems we will briefly describe a system based on a quite different concept, which is very interesting, if possibly of no great practical value. In the last chapter we introduced the idea of redundancy bits, which are derived in some simple logical manner from the number itself. If the number of these redundant bits is large enough, they can uniquely identify the number itself. So one could actually omit the original number altogether, and use the redundant information alone.

One such system shall be described shortly here, using decimal notation for simplicity. If we divide any integral number N by an integer a we get a quotient and a remainder at most equal to $a - 1$. This remainder, or residue, is the number N expressed modulo a. Taking several values for a we get several residues. By choosing prime numbers for a, N can be uniquely expressed by its residues. For example, taking the first four prime numbers: 2, 3, 5, 7 will give the following Table 9:

Table 9. *Residue Table*

N	Residues				N	Residues			
	$a = 2$	3	5	7		$a = 2$	3	5	7
0	0	0	0		8	0	2	3	1
1	1	1	1	1	9	1	0	4	2
2	0	2	2	2	10	0	1	0	3
3	1	0	3	3	11	1	2	1	4
4	0	1	4	4	12	0	0	2	5
5	1	2	0	5	13	1	1	3	6
6	0	0	1	6	14	0	2	4	0
7	1	1	2	0	15	1	0	0	1

The number 5 would be denoted by 1205, where $5 = 1 \bmod 2$, $5 = 2 \bmod 3$, $5 = 0 \bmod 5$, and $5 = 5 \bmod 7$. The notation is unique until it finally repeats after $2 \times 3 \times 5 \times 7 = 210$, which again would be denoted as 0000. The arithmetic operations with these numbers differ of course quite drastically from the usual ones. Addition is accomplished by adding the corresponding residues and expressing these sums again by their residues. For example:

$$\begin{array}{r} 4 = 0144 \\ +\,6 = 0016 \\ \hline 10 = 0103 \end{array}$$

$0 + 0 = 0 \bmod 2$, $1 + 0 = 1 \bmod 3$, $4 + 1 = 0 \bmod 5$, and $4 + 6 = 3 \bmod 7$.

Addition and subtraction can be mechanized relatively easily. Multiplication in the residue system is effected by obtaining the modulo product of corresponding digits. Since no carries or repeated additions are involved, multiplication is faster than with ordinary binary numbers. The main difficulties of the system arise in the division process, the detection of overflows, and in the determination of the correct sign of a subtraction operation.

In an electronic computer the residues will be represented in binary. For our example, we would need 1 bit for the first digit, 2 bits for the second, 4 for the third, and 4 for the fourth, altogether 11 bits. In straight binary notation, only 8 bits are necessary. A computer using the residue system therefore will have more components than if the ordinary binary number system were used. By adding one or more residues the system can be made redundant and error detecting or error correcting procedures can be employed.

Up to the present, no computers have been built with this number system. Only small laboratory models exist, used to explore the possibilities of the system.

2.3. Programming

2.31. Introductory Remarks

Any problem in numerical computation, regardless of its complexity, is solved in practice by breaking it down to a combination of a rather limited variety of elementary computing steps. Analytical expressions, even those like square root, trigonometric functions, or integration, eventually reduce to the four fundamental rules of arithmetic. Even those can be in turn considered as to consist of nothing but repeated addition or subtraction of the ten numbers zero through nine. It is only a matter of convenience what to consider an elementary operation and what a complex one. For hand calculations everybody draws his own line. What he does by mental arithmetic can be considered basic; as soon as he needs pencil and paper or other resources he performs complex operations. With digital computers the situation is quite the same. As explained in chapter 2.1 a computer has the ability to perform a variety of relatively simple operations. These are of an arithmetic, logical, or mechanical nature. They have to be so chosen that any desired calculation may be performed. Another necessary requirement is the ability of receiving problems and delivering results in a manner easily intelligible to the human being.

The designer of a computer faces the problem of properly selecting a set of basic operations, or instructions, as they are called also. His decision will of course depend on the intended application of the machine. However, he has to take into consideration other factors as well, such as complexity of the circuitry, speed of operation, reliability, and cost. Let us demonstrate the problem for a general purpose, or scientific, digital computer, whose application is the solution of mathematical and engineering problems. In the early state of the art there was a tendency, if not the only possibility, to keep the set of instructions to a minimum. The SWAC (National Bureau of Standards Western Automatic Computer), for instance, did not have a divide instruction. Each division, therefore, had to be accomplished by a combination of additions, subtractions, multiplications, and some logical instructions. On the other hand, machines do exist which have a built-in square root instruction. In the first case the amount of hardware of the computer is kept small, in the latter the number of instructions needed for a certain computation is a minimum. This little example shows a basic rule. A computer constructed to make programming very easy is bound to be big, complicated, and expensive, whereas the ideal machine from the engineer's standpoint will be simple, rather small, reliable, and cheap, but it will require much more programming effort. Any computer must therefore necessarily be a compromise between these two extremes. The term "programming" denotes the method of how to use a computer, it is more precisely defined later in the text.

Let us for a moment return to our analogy of the man and his mental arithmetic. There the difference between a small and a large repertoire of basic operations is a matter of education and mental ability. It can be described by adjectives such as stupid, clever, proficient, expert etc. For assessing the usefulness of a human computer other things have to be considered, mainly speed, reliability, and his salary. The same aspects also apply to computing machines, if not in the same proportions. Speed and reliability are far beyond human capability. The increase in complexity of basic operations is not nearly so spectacular due to the rapidly rising complexity and cost of the computer.

Modern electronic digital computers resemble each other very much in their set of basic operations. Barring any drastic technical developments, this picture is not likely to change much in the near future. A short survey of the present instruction repertoire of computers will therefore be in order. The instructions are divided into five groups. The first two are of an arithmetic nature, the next two are logical, and the last is mechanical. The distinction is naturally somewhat arbitrary.

Group I. The *arithmetic* instructions will perform the following operations:

1. Addition, $(a + b)$ [a, b, c, denote numbers]
2. Subtraction, $(a - b)$
3. Multiplication, $(a b)$
4. Division, (a/b)

Large machines often have in addition:

5. Inner Product, $(a + bc)$
6. Polynominal Multiplication, $(a + b)\, c$

These operations are ordinarily performed in fixed-point (or stated-point) arithmetic, just as any desk calculator does it. Large machines may have provisions for arithmetic with numbers in the so-called floating-point notation (cf. chapter 2.2, number systems).

Group II. The *transmissive* instructions will move information inside the computer memory from one place to another. They will sometimes also perform simple arithmetic operations such as reversing the sign or taking the absolute value of a number.

7. Transmit a word within the memory.

Group III. The *decision-making* instructions, interchangeably called jump, test, or sense instructions, serve to decide between two alternatives in a computation sequence by examining these conditions:

8. Equality, $a - b = 0$, $(a - b \neq 0)$
9. Magnitude, $a - b > 0$, $(a - b \leqslant 0)$
10. Zero, $a = 0$, $(a \neq 0)$
11. Sign, $a \geqslant 0$, $(a < 0)$

The conjugate condition is put in parentheses. The two conditions are, of course, mutually exclusive and, together they comprise all possible cases. Also in this group belong instructions which look at some mechanical condition, like the setting of switches etc.

12. Physical condition.

Group IV. The *logical* instructions perform some other logical operations, as:

13. Logical sum, logical product.
14. Extract or replace certain portions of a word.
15. Shift a number up or down a desired number of places.
16. Change the notation of a number, e.g. from stated point to floating point, or from one number system to another.

Group V. This group, the *external* instructions, have to do with the external equipment. The term denotes devices connected with the computer proper but not considered an integral part of it. In this category we find typewriters, line printers, teletype machines, punch card equipment, magnetic tape recorders, graph plotters, photographic cameras, etc., in all sorts of combinations. Accordingly, the instructions vary considerably from computer to computer. Their functions can briefly be summarized as:

17. Receive information, or input.
18. Produce information, or output.
19. Conserve information, or storage.

Most of the above mentioned operations require more than one machine instruction. The actual number of instructions of a computer is also influenced by its internal design, especially by the command structure. Multiple-address machines do not need as many instructions as single-address machines. The actual repertoire of existing computers varies roughly between 30 and 120. With general purpose or scientific computers the emphasis is more on the arithmetic instructions, whereas business type computers have a larger variety of instructions in groups II and V.

The flow of events inside the computer's circuitry is governed by the so-called control unit. Besides taking care of the details necessary to perform all the individual instructions, the control unit will also determine the sequence in which the instructions are to be executed. In other words, after the execution of each instruction a decision is made which one to execute next. Older computers were given one instruction at a time, for example by means of punch cards. As a card was read in, the instruction punched in it was executed, then the next card was read, etc. So one card after another went in until finally the whole problem was done. A computer of this type is the IBM Card Programmed Calculator (CPC). Modern machines employ a different principle. They are able to store the whole set of instructions for a given program in their memory. The normal order of execution is the sequence in which they have been recorded. However, subject to conditions found by the decision instructions the ordinary sequence may be departed from. Another characteristic is the possibility of changing an instruction during computation automatically. These features have resulted in a vast increase in speed and flexibility of operation. All modern computers possess these features and therefore are sometimes referred to as stored-program computers with the ability of instruction modification.

We now have an idea of what the computer hardware can do. We have a calculating tool of great speed and accuracy, something like a super desk calculator. The following chapters will show us the methods developed to use this tool skillfully for the solution of problems.

2.32. Definition and Scope of Programming

Given a certain computer with its set of instructions, how can we make it solve a certain mathematical problem? To close the gap between the formula and the machine, it is obviously necessary to break down the problem into progressively smaller steps, until finally there is nothing left but machine instructions. Having done so we need some means of directing the machine to perform these hundreds or thousands of instructions in precisely the correct order. This task, called programming, includes all the steps necessary from the initial mathematical statement of a problem to its final solution, say a table of results printed on paper. The major steps involved are:

1. Analysis: Selection of a suitable numerical method.

2. Flow Charting: Breakdown into small computing steps and arranging these in logical order.

3. Coding: Generate a set of instructions, the computer program, in a form acceptable to the machine.

4. Checkout, Debugging: Prove that the program will actually solve the given problem.

5. Error analysis: To establish whether or not the results fulfill the required accuracy limits.

6. Optimization: Among different possible approaches to the problem find the most economical one, judging by some appropriate criterion like actual computing time, or overall elapsed time.

Not all steps have to be done for each problem, nor have they to be done in the given order.

A few computers may be used for one single purpose only. However, the vast majority have to solve a variety of problems every day. Programming, therefore, in the general sense, as contrasted to coding, will concern itself with the over-all or long time efficiency of computer operation. This means the planning and implementing of an operating system, aimed at facilitating an easy and fast change from one problem to another. In the first place programming means writing programs in an optimum and efficient way. Certain small or larger computational steps have a tendency of occurring repeatedly in different problems. The operational system should provide for these steps to be available as ready-made building blocks and thus simplify the necessary coding for each problem as much as possible.

There is no need to discuss points 1. and 5. in any detail, the procedure arises directly from the given problem. Point 6., the optimization, makes use of the results of other steps plus a detailed knowledge of computer characteristics. It is an effort to make computation as fast and cheap as possible. The following chapters will consequently be concerned with flowcharting, coding, and debugging.

2.33. The Mechanics of Automatic Computation

The programmer does not have to know every detail of the basic operations inside the computer. For example he need not be concerned about the multiplication algorithm as long as he knows what the product of two numbers will be. What he must know, however, is how the machine gets the numbers to calculate with, and how after the execution of an instruction the next one is determined and found.

To understand, how the program, the numbers, and the actions of the machine mesh together, let us take a very simple example. The problem shall be to compute

$$Y = AX + |B|$$

with $A = 25$, $X = -3$, $B = -10$. Imagine we take a chest of drawers numbered in natural order 1, 2, 3, ... as shown in Fig. 17.

1 Copy from (11)	6 Add (14)	11 + 25
2 Multiply by (12)	7 Type out	12 — 3
3 Store in (14)	8 Stop	13 — 10
4 Copy from (13)	9 Change sign	14
5 If negative, go to (9)	10 Go to (6)	15

Fig. 17. Chest of Drawers Computer

Suppose somebody placed notes in the drawers with remarks written on them, as indicated. We will now ask a man to compute our problem without telling him what it is. We simply give him pencil, paper, and a typewriter, then we tell him to observe the following simple rules by the letter.

a) When given the go-ahead signal, look into drawer 1.

b) Do what the content of the drawer demands.

c) Then go to the drawer with next higher number, unless instructed otherwise.

d) Numbers in parentheses denote drawer numbers.

e) Write each result on a new working sheet, discard the old one. Similarly, when putting a note in a drawer, throw away any old one, which may be there.

f) A number implicitly referred to is understood to be the one on the latest working sheet.

The sequence of events which will occur is illustrated in Table 10 below.

Table 10. *Computing Sequence*

Action A	Action B	Number on work sheet
Look in drawer 1	Write + 25	+ 25
Look in drawer 2	Multiply by — 3	— 75
Look in drawer 3	Work sheet to drawer 14	—
Look in drawer 4	Write — 10	— 10
Look in drawer 5	Decide to go to drawer 9	— 10
Look in drawer 9	Reverse sign	+ 10
Look in drawer 10	No action	+ 10
Look in drawer 6	Add — 75	— 65
Look in drawer 7	Type out — 65	— 65
Look in drawer 8	Stop working	— 65

The final result typed out is the correct answer to our problem, although the man doing all the work has no knowledge of it. The same computation with other values of A, B, X, may be accomplished by simply changing the contents of drawers 11, 12, 13, the others remain unchanged.

Certainly, this is not a very efficient way to compute such a simple problem. This example shows, however, that the man doing the computing need not be very bright. He has to perform a rather boring and automatic job, which consequently can be done better and faster by a machine. The example was chosen because it demonstrates the operation of a digital computer. The chest of drawers is the memory, the drawers being the individual cells or registers. The drawer numbers are the addresses. The man performs the tasks of arithmetic, input, and output (Actions B) as well as the sequence control (Actions A). His work sheet corresponds to a special memory cell called accumulator. In the example part of the memory is used for the program, drawers 1—10; and another for the numbers or data, drawers 11—15. Each instruction references one drawer number only. A computer whose instructions specify one address only are called single-address machines. There exist computers with up to four addresses per instruction. The technical advantages or disadvantages connected with the number of addresses in an instruction are not very pronounced, unless the number is large. A guiding factor for the choice is that most machines have only one definite word length serving for both numbers and instructions.

To illustrate programming procedures we have to select a computer with its set of instructions. Since the basic principles involved can best be shown on a one-address machine, we chose a model of that type. It will have only the instructions necessary for the purpose of this book.

Before we go into the details of coding, it may be appropriate to explain the most commonly used technical terms in this field.

Computer, Machine: Electronic digital stored program computing machine.

Control: That portion of the computer directing the sequence of operations.

Cell, Register: A device capable of retaining, temporarily or permanently, a certain amount of information. Each cell is identified by a number, called its address.

Memory, Store: All cells considered as a whole.

Address, Location: Identification of a cell.

Accumulator: A special register found in some computers, used for arithmetic.

Word: The information contained in a cell.

Number: A word representing a number.

Instruction, Command: A word representing an operation.

Scaling: Multiplication of a number by a known factor, to better fit it into a cell.

Initialization: Setting up the initial conditions of a program necessary to start computation.

Modification: Change, especially of addresses.

Temporary Storage or Working Space: A portion of the memory set aside for temporarily keeping intermediate results.

Loop: A section of a program to be executed repeatedly.

Routine, Subroutine: Another name for a (short) program.

2.34 Absolute Coding

Now let us proceed to define our fictitious computer.

Number System: All numbers will be represented in the machine in the binary system, one bit for the sign and 15 bits for the magnitude. All numbers are treated by the machine as true fractions.

Word length: 18 bits or 6 octal digits.

Word structure: A word may contain a number or an instruction in the following manner (Fig. 18).

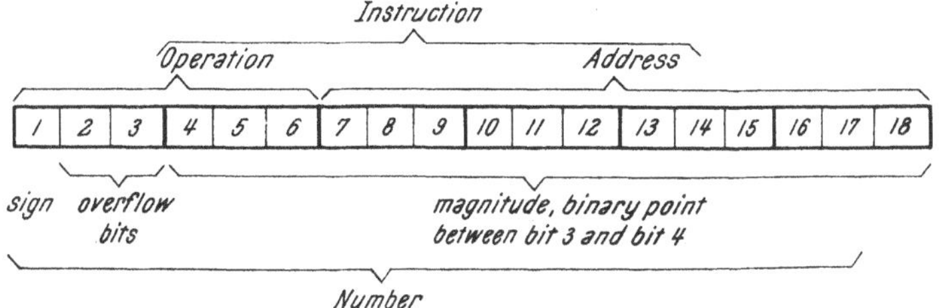

Fig. 18. Word Structure of Fictitious Computer

Storage: Memory of 2048 individually accessible cells, with octal addresses 0000—3777.
Accumulator: One cell, octal address 5000.
Zero: Special cell, address octal 4000, contains always zero.

Instruction Repertoire (Table 11):

Note, A stands for Accumulator, parentheses, ( ), denote "content of", X is an arbitrary address, quoted in an instruction.

Table 11. *Instruction Repertoire of Fictitious Computer*

Operation Code (octal)	Name of Operation	Description of Operation
10	Pick	(X) transmitted to A, short: $(X) \to A$ previous (A) ignored and destroyed
11	Add	$(A) + (X) \to A$
12	Add absolute	$(A) + \|(X)\| \to A$
13	Subtract	$(A) - (X) \to A$
14	Multiply	$(A) \cdot (X) \to A$
15	Divide	$(A) : (X) \to A$
16	Store	$(A) \to (X)$ (A) preserved
17	Store Address	Bits 7—18 of A transferred to X; (A) and bits 1—6 of X preserved
20	Shift down	Shift (A) X bits right
21	Shift up	Shift (A) X bits left
		Last two instructions affect only bits 2—18, bits shifted out are lost
22	Jump	Take next instruction from cell X
23	Plus Jump	If $(A) > 0$, jump to X
24	Zero Jump	If $(A) = 0$, jump to X
25	Overflow Jump	If (A) has overflow, bits 2 and 3 not both zero, jump to X
26	Stop	Stop computing. Machine will halt
27	Print	Print (X) as a decimal fraction
30	Read	Read a decimal number from a punch card, convert to binary, and store in cell X

The product or quotient of two numbers of finite length are of double this length, we shall assume that the computer will produce a rounded single-length number. If an operation requires two operands, the second one is understood to be in the accumulator. The programmer must take care that it is there at the right time. If scaling is not properly done, results may be larger than 1, this can happen on Add, Subtract, and Divide. In this case one or both overflow bits equal 1. In some instructions the "address" is no real address: in the Shift commands it will be interpreted as the number of shifts wanted. The Stop instruction does not need an address, so any address there has no significance.

Our computer has provisions for reading and printing decimal numbers, which means that the necessary number conversions binary-decimal and decimal-binary are built into the hardware. No provisions are made for reading binary (or octal) information, the notation of an absolute program. So let us assume that there is some way of getting a program into the memory.

We are now ready to code a simple example. Let us try to generate a program which can be directly interpreted by the computer, or, in other words, which is written in machine language. The only expedient we will use is octal notation, which as we know is only a shorthand notation for binary numbers. The program made in this fashion is called an "absolute program" and the procedure consequently known as "absolute coding". For an example we take the following problem:

Given 10 numbers X_1, X_2, ... X_{10}, punched on cards, compute and print the sum of all positive numbers in the set. Assume that no overflow occurs.

Before writing down the actual instructions it is good practice to first think about the problem and decide what operations are required in logical order. The result, a logical diagram or flow chart, would then look like this:

Flow Chart A:

Read X_1 and store at address 0100
Read X_2 and store at address 0101
.
.
Read X_{10} and store at address 0111
Set sum cell equal to zero

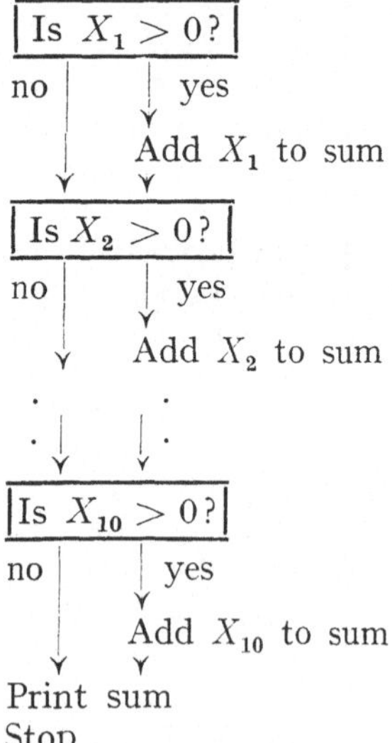

Programs are usually written in tabular form. The first column contains the address or location of the instruction, then follow the operation code and the address. At the end of the line there is room for remarks. These are for the benefit of the programmer only and do not enter the machine. Assigning cell 0000 for the first instruction, cell 0100 for X_1 and cell 0200 for the sum, we will get the following

Program A

Location	Operation Name	Operation Code	Address	Remarks
0000	Read	30	0100	Read and store X_1
0001	Read	30	0101	Read and store X_2
0002	Read	30	0102	
0003	Read	30	0103	
0004	Read	30	0104	
0005	Read	30	0105	
0006	Read	30	0106	
0007	Read	30	0107	
0010	Read	30	0110	
0011	Read	30	0111	Read and store X_{10}
0012	Pick	10	4000	Set $(A) = 0$
0013	Store	16	0200	Sum = 0
0014	Pick	10	0100	X_1 to A
0015	Plus Jump	23	0017	If pos., go to 0017
0016	Jump	22	0021	Jump to 0021
0017	Add	11	0200	Add sum to X_1
0020	Store	16	0200	Store new sum
0021	Pick	10	0101	X_2 to A
.	.	.	.	
.	.	.	.	
0071	Pick	10	0111	X_{10} to A
0072	Plus Jump	23	0074	If pos., go to 0074
0073	Jump	22	0075	Jump
0074	Add	11	0200	Add sum to X_{10}
0075	Print	27	5000	Print final sum
0076	Stop	26	0000	Stop

This program is written in a very simple straightforward manner. It will be noted that the same commands repeat for each X_i, only some addresses differ every time. This suggests writing the commands only once and execute them as often as needed. The portion of a program to be repeatedly executed is called a loop. The programming task is now a little more complicated. We have to secure the proper addresses for the first execution, this is called initializing. After each execution some addresses must be changed or modified for the next one. Also, the number of executions must be kept track of by counting or tallying, sometimes called indexing. This enables us to leave the loop and continue computation in normal fashion. Let us summarize what must be done in a few words:

Initialize, compute, Modify, tally, test for end.

Using this technique, except for input, we arrive at

Flow Chart B:

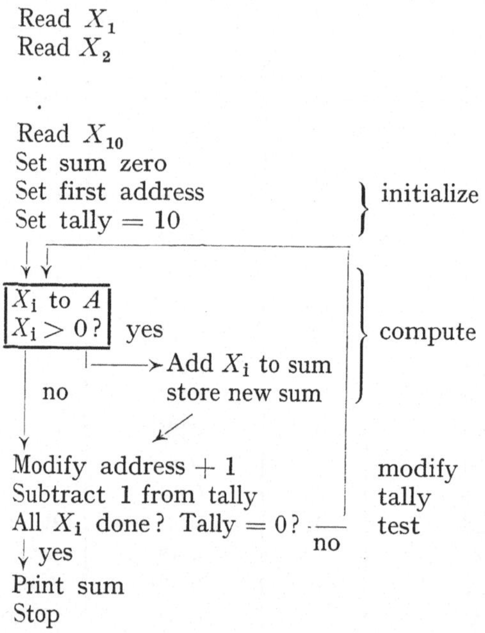

```
Read X1
Read X2
.
.
Read X10
Set sum zero
Set first address                        } initialize
Set tally = 10

[Xi to A  ]
[Xi > 0 ? ] yes                          } compute
   |      ---> Add Xi to sum
   no          store new sum

Modify address + 1                         modify
Subtract 1 from tally                      tally
All Xi done? Tally = 0? --- no             test
   yes
Print sum
Stop
```

Now the absolute program can be written easily. Using address 0201 for the tally, we get

Program B

Location	Operation	Address	Remarks
0000	30	0100	Read X_1
1	30	0101	Read X_2
2	30	0102	
3	30	0103	
4	30	0104	
5	30	0105	
6	30	0106	
7	30	0107	
0010	30	0110	
11	30	0111	Read X_{10}
12	10	4000	$(A) = 0$
13	16	0200	Sum = 0
14	10	0000	First address to A
15	17	0020	First addr. to pick-cmd
16	10	0037	$(A) = 10$
17	16	0201	Tally = 10
0020	10	(0000)	X_i to A
21	23	0023	X_i positive?
22	22	0025	Jump
23	11	0200	Add sum to X_i
24	16	0200	Store new sum
25	10	0020	Pick-cmd to A
26	11	0036	Modify + 1
27	17	0020	And store new address
0030	10	0201	Tally to A
31	13	0036	Subtract 1
32	16	0201	Store new tally

Location	Operation	Address	Remarks
33	23	0020	Tally still positive?
34	27	0200	Print final sum
35	26	0000	Stop
36	00	0001	Constant 1
37	00	0012	Constant 10
0200			Sum
0201			Tally

The address in the instruction at location 0020 is put in parentheses to indicate that it will change during computation. The value 000 written there has no meaning since the program itself will provide the correct first address with instructions 14 and 15. Similarly, cells 0100 through 0111, and 0200, 0201 may contain any information prior to the start of computation.

This program is only half as long as the first one. However, this advantage has been gained at the expense of an increased total number of instructions to be executed, or computing time. One might be inclined to think that there is no better approach to this simple problem, but there are still two ways of improving it. First we take advantage of the "Add Absolute" command. Since $X + |X| = 2X$ for positive X, and $X + |X| = 0$ for negative X, we can perform these two additions with all X_i regardless of sign. This eliminates testing each number before adding. The final sum is twice the desired one, and must therefore be divided by two. This is best done by shifting it down one bit. The second improvement consists in adding the numbers as soon as they are read in, rather than store them all in the memory before computing. With this we arrive at

Flow Chart C:

Set sum zero
Set tally = 10
Read X_i to A ←
Add $|X_i|$
Add result to sum
Store new sum
Tally −1
All done? — no (back to Read X_i to A)
Divide sum by 2
Print sum
Stop

Program C

Location	Operation	Address	Remarks
0000	10	4000	$(A) = 0$
1	16	0200	Sum = 0
2	10	0021	10 to A
3	16	0201	Tally = 10
4	30	5000	X_i to A
5	12	5000	Add $\|X_i\|$
6	11	0200	Add sum
7	16	0200	Store new sum
0010	10	0201	Tally to A
11	13	0020	Subtract 1
12	16	0201	Store new tally
13	23	0004	All done?
14	10	0200	Sum to A
15	20	0001	Shift down 1 bit

Location	Operation	Address	Remarks
16	27	5000	Print final sum
17	26	0000	Stop
0020	00	0001	Constant 1
21	00	0012	Constant 10
0200			Sum
0201			Tally

Which of the three programs is now the best one? One criterion is the memory space, the number of cells, required. On large problems it may well occur that the whole program cannot be stored in the available memory, necessitating a break-up into sections. A short program is desirable for another reason also, the number of errors made in writing it will roughly be proportional to its length. The other criterion is of course the computing time needed by the machine. From an overall point of view the time needed to write the program enters into the picture. Let us compare our three programs on these counts. To arrive at the execution time, we will assume that all instructions take an equal amount of time, so we have to count the total number of instructions executed to get a relative value of the total time.

Program	A	B	C
Space needed	74	44	20
Execution time	48	125	88

We at once can discard program *B*, as *C* is better than that on both counts The final decision is then between *A* and *C*, Which one should be taken, depends on how important time is as compared to memory space.

2.35. Library Systems, Subroutines

The great variety of problems which nowadays is solved on automatic computers is commonly divided into two classes, scientific and business type problems. In business application a computer is normally used for one main purpose only. This may be an accounting and billing, or an inventory problem. The distinguishing feature here is the large amount of data and the relatively simple type of arithmetic to be done. Once the program is written and checked out, no more programming is necessary except possibly for improving the efficiency of the program. The effort needed to write a program is only of secondary importance, the efficiency of the program itself being the decisive factor. In scientific applications the situation is quite different. Here new problems come up almost every day and require new programs. A close look at these problems, however, reveals that quite a number of partial computations occur over and over. The incessant rewriting of those partial computations can be avoided by using the subroutine concept. Let us explain this by an example.

Take the ordinary sine function, it will certainly occur many times in all sorts of problems. A separate, self-contained program is now written with the sole purpose of computing $Y = \sin X$ for any given X. This little program is stored permanently in the computer and thereby made available to all programs at any time. Being at the command of any general or "main" program, we will call our sine program a subprogram or a "subroutine". The procedure of using the subroutine is now rather obvious. If the main program gets to a point where $\sin X$ is wanted, it will supply the value of X in a designated location, and then transfer control to the subroutine itself, by a jump instruction. The subroutine will now compute the desired Y and transfer control back to the proper place in the main program. The advantage of this system can be seen immediately. The programmer need no longer worry about a sine routine. He only must provide the proper connection or linkage with the subroutine. Another advantage is that only one sine routine is necessary even if $\sin X$ is required at several places in the main program. This saves space in the computer's memory. Fig. 19 shows the logical connections between main program and subroutine for two references.

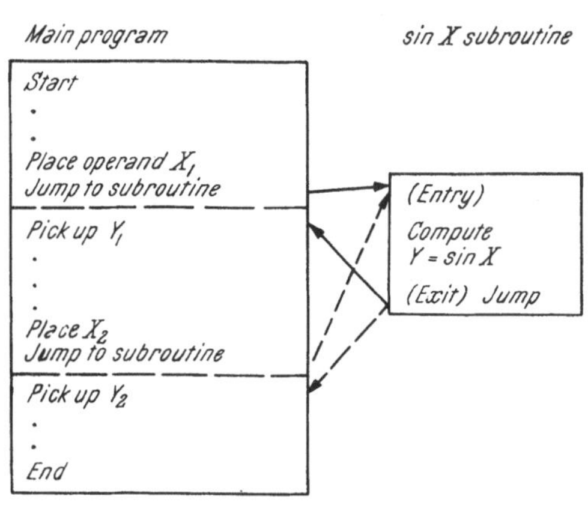

Fig. 19. Subroutine Linkage

The actual location of the subroutine is of no concern as long as the main program knows where to find it. It is therefore customary to store it outside of the main program, e.g. at the end of it.

Each computer installation will have a number of such subroutines to fit their needs. All are handled in the manner just explained and stored together in a subroutine library. An average library may contain from 20 to 100 routines. The function subroutines have sin X, arcsin X, tang X, $\sqrt{X}$, e^x, log X etc. All operations involving input and output of data with their necessary number conversions belong there. Depending on the type of problems to be solved, subroutines are made for numerical integration, curve fitting, data smoothing, statistical procedures and the like. To summarize the advantages, the main programs become shorter and are easier to write, no errors will occur in the subroutine part of the computation, since the subroutines are very carefully checked out. Memory space is saved, since each subroutine has to exist only once.

There is another kind of library routines which is necessary for an efficient operation of a computer. They are called service routines, and are designed to help the operator, i.e. the man sitting at the machine, perform various tasks. In this category belong routines to load programs into the computer, memory dumps, alarm prints, and routines to check proper operation of the computer. Others help the programmer to find errors in a program during the checkout or debugging phase. These so-called debugging routines will indicate automatically certain logical or typographical errors made in programming.

At the end of the line in this direction are the job monitoring or operational programs. These work on a higher level, directing the operations of a computer over a longer period of time. After one job is finished, the job monitor takes over automatically, selects and starts the next job immediately. The final goal is the "one button" computer. All programs and data for a day's work are prepared off the computer. The operateur puts them on in the morning, then hits the "one" start button. Computation then goes on without interruption. Should a situation arise, which requires human intervention, the computer will stop after having typed out the necessary directions for the operator.

2.36. Relative and Symbolic Coding

The absolute programming procedure described above is far from ideal. In large problems it is difficult to assign suitable addresses to the instructions, constants, and working cells, because the required space is not known in advance. The result may be an overlap of addresses, necessitating rewriting of the program, or it may be unused spaces within the program, a rather wasteful use of memory space. Provided this difficulty has been successfully overcome for a particular program, the same trouble arises again, if any changes have to be made. These may be necessary to eliminate errors in the program or because the problem itself has changed. Another undesirable feature of an absolute program is that it consists of nothing but numbers, which as such do not suggest any particular meaning to the reader. It is therefore hard to analyse an absolute program and find out what it actually will compute. The ordinary human mind is not accustomed to attach specific meanings to numbers, but is rather used to think in terms of the ordinary English (or other) language.

An important step to make programming easier and more readable, is the system of "relative coding". Here two things are accomplished which go beyond absolute coding. The program is divided into several sections, or regions, whose length need not be known in advance. The first word in each region is given an address, all other addresses within that region are noted with respect to this first one. A program can now be written rather straightforward. The second step is the assignment of names, or symbols for the region addresses. For example, the working space can be named WS, the individual addresses in this region would then be WS 1, WS 2, . . . etc.

To illustrate the procedure let us rewrite our Program *C* in relative notation. We select 3 regions as follows

R for the instructions
S for the constants
T for the temporary working cells.

Choosing the letter *A* for the accumulator, address 5000, and *Z* for the zero cell, address 4000, we will get

Program C, relative notation.

Loc.	Op.	Addr.
R 1	10	Z
R 2	16	T 1
R 3	10	S 2
R 4	16	T 2
R 5	30	A
R 6	12	A
R 7	11	T 1
R 8	16	T 1
R 9	10	T 2
R 10	13	S 1
R 11	16	T 2
R 12	23	R 5
R 13	10	T 1
R 14	20	0001
R 15	27	A
R 16	26	0000
S 1	00	0001
S 2	00	0012
T 1		
T 2		

(Remarks omitted, since they are identical with Program C)

The reader will notice, that the complete program can be written without knowing in advance how many locations are needed in each region. After writing one has only to count the number of cells in each region and assign one absolute address to each region, such that the complete program will be in one continuous area of the memory. Since this process completely defines all addresses in the program, the process of transcribing it to absolute notation is fully automatic and hence can be mechanized by the computer itself. One has merely to write a so-called assembly program. This will read the relative program and produce an absolute version. The advantages are speed, accuracy, and the elimination of clerical errors.

The regional coding system proved to be such an advantage, that further developments in this direction were greatly encouraged. The aim was to relieve the programmer of every phase of the programming work, which was of an automatic nature and could therefore best be done by the computer itself. At the same time it was desirable to keep the original program as close to ordinary English and to standard mathematical notation as possible.

Let us examine then which of the phases of relative coding could possibly be mechanized.

1. After assigning a starting address for a region, the number of commands in that region must be counted to find the proper address for the next region. This is automatic.

2. It is not necessary to have all the locations written down, (R 1, R 2, R 3, . . .). The only one ever needed by any instruction is R 5 (needed in R 12). For this reason the separation of a program into several regions appears to be rather arbitrary. It would be much better to assign names, or location symbols, only to those instructions which are referenced elsewhere in the program. A suggestive name or symbol will greatly help to increase the readability of the program. The conversion of such a program can still be done correctly by the computer.

3. The operation code numbers can be replaced by letters, e.g. *AD* for add, *PR* for print, etc. The programmer will memorize these much more easily than octal numbers. The machine can be programmed to substitute the proper numbers.

4. Constants written in actual machine notation are not very recognizable, the number π e.g. will look rather unfamiliar in octal notation. Besides, to get the octal numbers they have to be manually converted from the originally given decimal numbers. Suppose we write in the operation column a *D*, followed by the decimal number in the address field. The machine can be programmed to inspect this operation and, upon finding a *D*, treat the rest of that instruction as a decimal number, namely, convert it to its binary equivalent automatically. As "*D*" is not one of the machine instructions, it is called a "pseudo-instruction", it will not appear in the final absolute version of the program.

A system making use of the above mentioned items is called "symbolic coding". The notation used in writing a program is the symbolic language. A program which will interpret a symbolic program and produce an absolute version of it is commonly called a compiler. Writing a program in symbolic language is much easier than in the previous notations. The bulk of the work has been shifted to the compiler, i.e. to the computer. The compiler may be a rather complicated program. Some existing compilers have taken as much as several man-years to complete. However, since this has to be done only once, the final result is still a vast saving in programming time.

As before, we shall take our Program *C* as an example. The symbols chosen are easily understood and need no further explanation.

Program C, Symbolic Notation.

Loc.	Op.	Addr.
START	PK	Z
	ST	SUM
	PK	TEN
	ST	TALLY
LOOP	RD	A
	AA	A
	AD	SUM
	ST	SUM
	PK	TALLY
	SU	ONE
	ST	TALLY
	PJ	LOOP
	PK	SUM
	SR	0001
	PR	A
	HT	0000
ONE	D	1
TEN	D	10
SUM	—	—
TALLY	—	—

Addresses may also be stated by combining symbols with numbers, e.g. LOOP + 1 would be instruction following LOOP. The advantages of symbolic coding can be easily imagined. One major point is that a program now looks much more like ordinary English and is therefore much easier to write and check. In addition, the programmer has no longer to worry very much about the binary representation of numbers inside the computer, because all he sees is decimal numbers, the conversions are done automatically.

One problem still remains for him. He must scale his numbers properly. All numbers, including intermediate results during computation must be neither too large in the machine (overflow) nor too small (loss of significance). This, however, can be greatly facilitated by using floating point arithmetic. Here the range of numbers which can be held is very large, e.g. from 10^{-38} to 10^{+38}. Due to normalization always about 8 significant digits are carried through the computation. The Floating point arithmetic can either be programmed or it is built into the hardware of the machine.

2.37. Algebraic Compilers

The idea which lead to symbolic coding can be pursued still further. In symbolic coding there is usually a one-to-one relationship between symbolic and absolute program. This means that for each line of symbolic coding one absolute machine instruction or number will be generated.

In an algebraic system a line of coding, or statement, is more complex and has to be implemented by a series of absolute machine instructions. The process of translation or compilation will, of course, be much more complicated. The compiler program will have to be much more sophisticated, and it will take a longer time to generate the absolute machine program. The big advantage is now, that statements can be written which look almost like ordinary algebraic notation. The machine programs generated in this manner may not be optimal with regard to execution time or memory space, but this is more than offset by the simplicity of the symbolic program and the saving in programming time. Especially for one-shot problems, there results quite a saving in the elapsed time between the statement of a problem and its final solution.

The process of compiling is very complicated and time-consuming. To translate a statement takes approximately 1 to 10 seconds on high speed computers like the IBM 704 or the Remington Rand 1103 A (Univac Scientific). An algebraic compiler therefore is practically prohibitive, time-wise, for low and medium speed computers with clock pulse rates up to 100 kc/s. High speed computers now have about 1 mc/s clock rates. Considering the rate the technical development of computer components has been going on, one can expect computers to be ten times faster within a few years.

The rules and regulations according to which a program must be written to be correctly interpreted by a compiler, is called the language. With the high-level compilers presently in existence this language is quite remote from basic computer code. In fact, there is so little left which pertains to the particular computer, that it seems feasable to construct a language common to different computers. The compiler necessary to translate and interpret this language is naturally a different one for each computer.

A common language offers the great advantage of an easy exchange of programs between installations with different computers. An intermediate step toward exchange of programs without the necessity of reprogramming is to write small translators, which will take a program in language A and produce the same program in language B. Then the existing compiler for language B generates the absolute program needed.

The ideal solution to this problem is naturally a language which can be used for every computer. Much research is being done in this field. At present, negotiations are under way between American and European computer people to establish a common international language for scientific problems. This task, difficult as it is, is not impossible due to the fact that there exists a common notation for writing mathematical formulas throughout the whole world. This will serve as the basis for the design of the common language. The international algebraic language now being developed is known as ALGOL. Its basic specifications have been well defined. Compilers are already being written for several large computer systems so that experience may be gathered about its usefulness.

Let us assume for a moment that a common language exists. The next thing to do is to write a compiler for every computer. This requires a tremendous amount of work. Compilers which have been written have taken as much as 20 man-years to complete. No computer installation could possibly afford to invest so much work in a new compiler and throw away their old one, just to be able to exchange programs on a universal basis. A practical way out of this difficulty is to write several small compilers or translators which will translate the common language into the various existing symbolic languages. This task is much easier, since these translators have a much smaller scope. In general, one can establish various levels of languages, the common language would be at the top of the list, the absolute machine code at the bottom. Any compiler could then be designed to do only part of the work, like transforming a program to the next lower level, or possibly go down two steps. The hierarchy of languages is shown in Fig. 20. Here Unicode was chosen to represent a language used in an algebraic compiler, and the USE-language for the ordinary symbolic language (USE stands for Univac Scientific Exchange.) The list shows that more and more restrictions are added to a language as we go down the list.

Level	Language	Restricted to
1	Universal	—
2	Common	scientific problems
3	American	scientific, English language
4	Unicode	scientific, English, compilers accepting Unicode
5	USE-language	scientific, English, compilers, 1103, 1103A, 1105 computers
6	Abs. machine L.	scientific, English, compilers, 1103A computer

Fig. 20. Hierachy of computer languages.

To go from one computer to another, one can now use compilers which transform a program to lower steps, or one can first translate from one system to another on the same level. For example, let a program be given in Unicode language, which shall be used on an IBM 704 computer. One way is to use a compiler which will take the Unicode program and directly generate a 704 absolute program. The other way is to use a smaller compiler which translates from Unicode into Fortran language, on the same level, then use the existing Fortran compiler to get the absolute program. Quite a few compilers exist already which work in the levels 4, 5, 6.

Finding a common language for problems of a non-mathematical nature is very difficult. These problems, loosely named business type problems, can as yet not be stated in a precise notation which everybody will understand. It is therefore unlikely that these problems will be handled on a universal basis in the near future. The existence of the large computers, their ability to handle such problems, may well enhance the generation of such a common notation. In fact, there is a serious effort supported by a number of computer organizations to create a common business oriented language known as COBOL, which has already shown some promising results.

2.38. Optimum Compilers

Before we close this chapter, we have to point out some disadvantages of automatic coding. Consider the set of all different operations a computer can perform, this could be termed capability, or flexibility. Let us denote this set (N). If we have agreed upon a definition of the word operation we can, theoretically at least, find the set (N) for any given machine, if we know its structure in every detail. Different machines will have different sets (N), not only in number, but also in kind. In other words, machine A may have fewer operations (N_1) than machine B (N_2), but it still may have some features which the larger machine B does not have. In mathematical terms, the two sets (N_1) and (N_2) are of different size, and they overlap, as shown in Fig. 21.

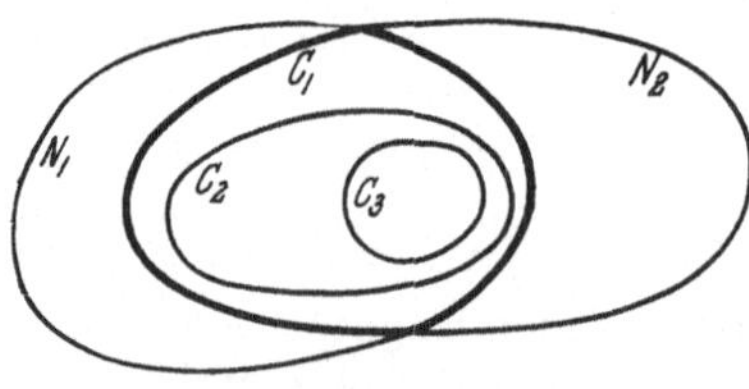

Fig. 21. Capabilities of Computers and Compilers

An ideal compiler compatible with both machines should allow the set (C_1) equal to the intersection of (N_1) and (N_2). By ideal we mean that the compiler allows all possible operations common to both machines. Due to restrictions imposed by the compiler language and other practical reasons a realistic compiler of this kind will have a smaller set, like (C_2). This means, of course, that we can no longer make optimal use of the capabilities of the computers, if we use the compiler as a programming device. A similar argument holds for a high level compiler, which will further restrict the number of possible operations, shown as (C_3). This is a natural consequence of the fact that such a compiler is primarily designed to make programming easy. To gain ease of programming we have to sacrifice some flexibility of operations.

Let us take an example. Most algebraic compilers perform all arithmetic in floating point notation. The reason for this is simply to relieve the programmer from the task of scaling his variables, which he would have to do in fixed point arithmetic. The possibility for fixed point arithmetic is preserved only to the extent necessary to compute indices and tallies, i.e. it is integer arithmetic for numbers up to five decimal places, for example. Using this compiler one can no longer compute any integer of more than five places, whereas the computer could do it to perhaps 10 or 12 places.

We are thus faced with a true dilemma. A real convenient compiler and full utilization of all computer operations are incompatible. A compromise can be made which is reasonably good on both counts. Practical experience, however, seems to point strongly to another solution, namely, to have two compilers for the same computer. The first one should be a rather lowlevel compiler, permitting the programmer all possible operations with the least difficulty in programming obtainable. It would use a symbolic language as described in chapter 2.36. The second one would be a high-level compiler, allowing formulas, logical relations, indexed variables, etc. Here the emphasis should be entirely on programming ease, with little regard to the efficiency of the absolute machine program.

The existence of both compilers will be most useful, if a translator program is made, which transforms programs from the algebraic language to the simpler symbolic language, which in turn is then translated into an absolute machine code (see 2.37). An example will illustrate this. Suppose we have a certain physical problem described by a set of mathematical equations. To test whether or not the mathematical model is adequate, numerical solutions have to be calculated and examined. If the results are satisfactory, many computations are desired, so that the ultimate machine program should be as good as the computer will permit. The fastest way for the validity test would be to program the problem with the high-level compiler, then translate down to absolute machine code (in two steps) and run the trial cases necessary for the test. After acceptance, the low-level version of the program can be taken as a starting point for further improvement of the program, since at that level full use can be made of all possibilities of the machine.

It should be emphasised that both types of compilers could be improved, if the design of computers and compilers went hand in hand. This fact is now being realized more and more, so that better computer systems can be expected in the future.

2.4. Capabilities and Limitations

2.41. Applications

The basic function of the digital computer, as the name suggests is computations with numbers. The word computation must be interpreted here in its widest sense. Besides arithmetic in its usual meaning, it includes operations in logic as well as information storage and retrieval. Every problem which can be reduced to logical operations can be solved on a digital computer. The operations and the symbols to which they are applied must only be defined clearly. The method of solution is not dictated by the nature of the machine but can be chosen freely by the programmer. Besides arithmetic he has at his disposal every method of numerical analysis, Boolean algebra, and statistics.

One could justly argue that all these methods existed long before computers were invented and that consequently the invention of automatic computers could not possibly be such a revolutionary achievement as it is frequently claimed to be. The basic idea of this argument is certainly true; however, it does overlook the very important practical significance of speed, reliability, and convenience. For comparison let us take a brief look at the technical developments in the field of transportation. The invention of the steamship, the railroad, the automobile, or the airplane did not provide man with means of reaching any point on the earth which could not previously be reached with sailing vessels or with horse and carriage. But these inventions did make transportation much faster, safer, and more convenient, and nobody will seriously deny their tremendous influence on human society. The situation is quite similar in the case of modern automatic computers. Due to highly increased speed and reliability, problems can now be solved economically which hitherto had been far beyond practical human capability. Many problems were practically unsolvable because they would simply take too long. Others defied solution because of the difficulty of avoiding human errors. A particular class of problems require a solution within a certain time, lest they are useless. One example is weather forecasting. If the analysis of today's weather picture necessary for the prediction of tomorrow's weather takes longer than a day, a prediction cannot be made at all. One way out is to simplify the analysis, which of course makes the prediction less reliable. The advent of high-speed computers has brought many such problems within the range of practical solution. Still, problems remain that are so huge as to surpass the capabilities of even the fastest computers, but the range of possibilities has been expanded tremendously so that the impact of computers on human society is already starting to change our way of life.

The type of problems suitable for solution with digital computers is often divided into two classes: scientific calculations and data processing. A short list of typical problems in each category, not claimed to be complete, will illustrate their wide scope.

Scientific problems are:

1. Evaluation of algebraic formulas
2. Numerical integration
3. Solution of differential equations
4. Linear programming
5. Strategic decisions
6. Automatic coding and deciphering
7. Language translation
8. Design of logical circuitry
9. Automatic control
10. Trajectories and orbits
11. Statistical procedures

In the data processing area we have:

12. Information storage and retrieval
13. Sorting and collating
14. Accounting, bookkeeping
15. Inventory control
16. Census and other statistics.

Not all of these problems must necessarily be solved on digital computers. Some of them could just as well, or even more conveniently, be handled by analog computers. An outstanding feature of the digital computer is, that every computation may be repeated as many times as desired and must give identically the same result each time if the computer works properly. This allows making a clearcut decision between a computer fault and an error in the program. For this reason digital computers are often used to verify solutions obtained with analog computers.

The first three items on the list concern mathematical problems, and solution methods can be found in standard text books on numerical analysis. It is worth pointing out that while the computer can evaluate any algebraic expression numerically, it cannot solve problems in analysis. One cannot program a computer to solve the general quadratic equation

$$x^2 + ax + b = 0$$

and come up with the result

$$x_{1,2} = -\frac{a}{2} \pm \sqrt{\frac{a^2}{4} - b}\,.$$

This remains the exclusive domain of the mathematician.

Linear programming is the problem of calculating an optimum operating procedure under given conditions and constraints. Examples are the calculation of an airline schedule, or the routing of freight cards of a railroad company. The general objective is to optimize a certain quantity. In the case of the airline it could be to find the minimum number of airplanes required to perform the desired service. A further example is to compute the most economical production schedule of a given number of factories, taking into account the geographical location and production capacity of the plants, the location of raw materials and consumer markets, shipping rates, etc.

Similar in scope are the strategic problems. As above, the object is making the best possible decision. But several factors make the task much more difficult. First, the facts are not all known and one must take an educated guess on those. Some information about the actual situation may even be completely wrong. Then there is an opponent whose interests are opposed to one's own, and who will therefore try his best to counteract as much as he can. These problems can be solved with the methods of the theory of games. The general area of investigation is often called Operations Research. The complexity of analysis and solution methods makes the automatic digital computer an ideal tool for such problems.

Physical problems are based on data which are determined experimentally and therefore contain errors. Since these errors are not known the true values cannot be determined. One has to use statistical methods to find best estimates. If the amount of data is so large that they cannot be obtained or computed on for practical reasons, one resorts to the method of taking samples. In order that a sample is representative of all the data it is necessary that the sample is taken completely at random. This means that the selection of the samples should not follow any rules or patterns. A digital computer can perform such sampling operations if it has a set of random numbers. A program for generating random numbers is, as any program, based on strict logical rules. It can therefore never generate truly random numbers. All programs for random numbers exhibit a period after which the series of the generated numbers repeats. This period can be made so large that the numbers are close enough to being random for all practical purposes.

An important class of applications of a digital computer is due to its ability to perform operations in logic. One application is the use of a computer to help make its own program. This was mentioned in some detail previously, see Chapter 2.37. Another is the use of the computer to design computer circuitry. The desired logic of the planned computer is expressed in Boolean algebra, the salient characteristics of all circuit elements to be used are stated in a similar manner. Then a program can be written which will compute the optimum circuit possible under those assumptions. The final design can again be simulated on a computer to perform a check on the expected behavior.

Finally, let us mention some recent research about the capability of computers to learn. The basic question here is, can a computer improve its own logic or program by using previous results? Investigations in this area are still in an early stage and it is difficult to predict any results.

2.42. Speed

The actual run of a problem on a digital computer consists of three distinct phases: input of program and data, computation, and output of results. The amount of work for each phase, taken absolutely as well as in relation to each other, varies from problem to problem. One can therefore not easily define the speed of a computer. Usually typical speeds or execution times are quoted for the individual operations. For arithmetic speed, the time needed for adding two numbers or the number of additions per second serves as a good guide. Slow computers will perform about 60 additions per second, fast machines can handle 25,000. The practical limit at present is about 250,000 additions per second. Multiplication and division take three to ten times longer. Data processing, or business type computations, require only little arithmetic, but involve the transmission of many data in the computer. A more useful speed for these machines is the time needed to obtain a desired item from memory. This so-called access time depends mainly on the type of memory. Magnetic drums have average access times of about 15 ms. Electrostatic devices and the more recent magnetic cores have from 2 to 10 μs. By far the longest time is needed to find an item on a magnetic tape, since it may involve moving a long tape past the reading head. There is no one typical access time, since it depends on several factors like tape speed, tape length, density of recording, etc. Access times range anywhere from 10 seconds to 3 minutes. The figures quoted are typical for general purpose computers somewhat higher speeds are obtained with special purpose machines.

The speed of input or output of data depends mainly on the type of mechanical equipment rather than on the internal circuitry of the computer. The three most commonly used media for both input and output are punched paper tape, punched cards, and magnetic tape. Teletype paper tape can be read by mechanical means at a rate of 10 characters per second. Theoretically, the rate of transmission of information should be stated in bits per second; it is common usage to use characters as a unit, a character being any print symbol, a number or letter. Most computers use six bits to represent a character. Reading of teletype tape with photoelectric devices is faster, a typical speed is 200 characters per second. Output on paper tape, that is the actual punching, varies between 10 and 100 characters per second. The second medium, probably the most widely used one, is punched cards. For average applications the speed of input or output is between 150 and 400 characters per second. Machines presently being developed may raise this rate by a factor of two or three. To save time, some computers have provisions for simultaneous reading and punching of cards. The reading of data by these machines requires their recording in a very rigid format, for which special expensive punching devices must be used. A more conventional and most common format of data is the typewritten sheet of paper. The desire to avoid the special punching process has prompted an extensive research, which has already shown very encouraging results. It is now possible to read printed numbers directly with photoelectric devices. This new technique is employed in automatic banking and accounting. The original checks or sales slips can now be directly processed by the computer; duplicates of the originals on punched cards or similar media are no longer necessary. Time is saved and human errors in punching are avoided. The third medium for recording data is magnetic tape. Typical speeds for both reading and writing are from 5,000 to 30,000 characters per second. The much higher speed of magnetic tape as compared to paper tape or cards is possible because most complicated start-stop type motions of mechanical parts are avoided, it is only necessary to move a rather light-weight tape past the reading or writing head at a constant speed. The density of recording can also be made much higher than on paper.

All these media need some special machinery to record data manually as well as to obtain printed copies of the output. This is done in off-line operation, i.e. the printing device is not connected to the computer. After having computed the results, the computer records them on a medium. This is then taken off the computer and placed on the printer to get the printed copy. Typewriters and printers may be connected directly to the computer, thus eliminating the medium altogether. This so-called on-line operation saves overall time, if not actual computer time. Small computers often use typewriters and output about 10 characters per second. Line printers will print a whole line across the page, about 120 characters, at one time. They produce about 200 characters per second. The most recent line printers now in use, usually designated as high-speed printers, will output in the order of 1200 characters per second. This is about the highest speed obtainable by using relays and mechanical print wheels as elements. By using the same technique as with magnetic tapes, i. e. reducing the mechanics to a continuous motion of the paper and producing the printing of the characters by some electronic procedure, speeds of 10,000 characters per second have been obtained.

It remains to say a few words about the speed with which programs can be entered into the memory of the computer. The time spent to record the program on the medium does not concern us here, since this is done only once. The input speeds are basically the same as quoted above. One can, however, record programs in more compact form by using octal or binary notation. Typical for this are punched cards. One card, using 72 columns, usually contains six decimal numbers, each with ten digits, a sign, and a decimal point. These will go into six computer words. When binary notation is used for the program, a card can hold 24 instructions, equivalent to 24 words in the memory. Thus, the loading of a program is generally faster than the input of data by a factor of 1.5 up to 4.

The design of an optimal computer system, i.e. the most efficient combination of basic computer, input and output equipment, depends a great deal on the type of problems to be solved. If large masses of data go in and out, while relatively little arithmetic computation is required, as is the case in data processors, the emphasis is definitely on fast input and output and short access time. On the other hand, if the bulk of the work are arithmetic calculations, as in many scientific problems, the internal computing speed is the dominating factor for design.

Great progress has been made in the last few years to increase the speed of computers, and new inventions and improvements are made continuously. Almost every facet of the design of a computer has some effect on its speed. The major factors are:

1. The basic computer components: diodes, flip-flops, amplifiers, relays, magnetic cores, etc.

2. The logical layout of the computer: serial or parallel, word length, binary or decimal number system, logic of control unit.

3. The type of instructions: number of addresses per instruction, automatic or programmed indexing, stated point or floating point arithmetic.

4. The type of memory: random access or block access, memory size.

5. Input and output equipment.

6. Programming, see chapter 2.34. This item is not under control of the designer.

To design a fast computer it is not sufficient to simply select the best components available. One must make a careful study of matching the various elements so that an overall optimum will result. Electronic components are faster than mechanical components by several orders of magnitude. In order to obtain good computer efficiency one often uses only the fastest mechanical equipment in direct connection with the computer. The slower mechanical devices are operated off-line if at all possible. This mode of operation will also reduce the probability of computer failures. An example is the output of data on magnetic tape; the printing takes place separately using this tape. Another method of increasing speed is to let several operations take place simultaneously. When information is needed from a magnetic tape, for instance, the control unit will initiate a search for that information. While the search is going on the computer continues with other activities. Another possibility is to separate the control unit into two largely independent sections, one of which governs the overall sequence of events and the arithmetic operations, the other takes care of input and output only. Even within the arithmetic section time can be saved by simultaneous operation. The execution of an instruction consists of different phases: obtaining the instruction, acquiring the operands, performing the actual operation, and storing the result. One can already obtain the next instruction while the present one is still being processed. This overlapping of certain phases in the execution of instructions can speed up the computer by a factor of 2 or 4.

Another feature worth mentioning increases overall computing speed by reducing the time for input of data. In normal operation input data have to be prepared manually before the computer can accept them. Modern electronic equipment makes it possible to measure these data automatically at their source, transmit them to the computer location, and convert them into a digital format acceptable to the computer. This eliminates completely any time consuming human handling of these data. If the computer has a special memory the data can be entered into it as soon as they arrive without interfering with any computations going on. The computer control unit can pick up the information whenever it needs it. Under certain conditions regarding speed of incoming data and amount of computation the data can be processed as fast as they come in and results are ready after a very short delay. This so-called real-time application allows the use of digital computers in closed loop control systems. Since speed is very important for this application computers are often built for a special purpose only, frequently with the whole program wired into the circuit. For further details on computers in control systems see chapter 6.

2.43. Accuracy

Before any results obtained with digital computers are accepted they must be checked for possible errors. Wrong results may be obtained for various reasons. To begin with, the mathematical or logical statement of the problem may be wrong or at least inadequate, the numerical method chosen may be insufficient, then the program may have errors. These error sources are always checked very carefully before a program is accepted for production runs. The remaining sources of errors depend partly on the type of the problem. Business type problems have only one correct result. Every result not quite correct is useless. An example is bank accounting. Each month the books are checked and must balance up to the last cent. When a computer is used for this job the same rules apply. Errors can occur only from erroneous input data or from computer malfunctions. The latter, if not prevented by automatic or programmed checks, can be traced by repeating the computation. The answers must repeat digit for digit.

For scientific calculations the question of accuracy takes on a different meaning. Besides the errors just mentioned, which can be traced without too much difficulty, there are others not so easily determined. They are either of a mathematical or of a physical nature. A purely mathematical problem has only one correct result, which is exact and unique. A computer cannot always compute this exact result. One reason is the limited number length, which causes a number to differ from the real value by as much as half a unit in the least significant digit or bit. The round-off errors of all numbers used in a computation effect the error of the final result. The final error must be calculated or at least estimated so that the accuracy of the computation can be stated. The round-off error can be reduced by better scaling, rearrangement of calculation steps, or by using multiple precision arithmetic. The other source of errors for mathematical problems is the replacement of an exact mathematical procedure by an approximate numerical method. For example, the evaluation of an integral must be done by some stepwise numerical method, like Simpson's Rule or the Runge-Kutta method. All these methods have a larger or smaller error due to truncation of infinite series. The truncation error must also be analyzed before a statement about the final accuracy can be made. The analysis of the influence of round-off and truncation errors combined can become very difficult for complicated calculations. One often resorts to statistical estimates or to calculations of special cases of the problem where the result is known a priori.

For physical problems additional error sources must be taken into account. The physical problem is described by a mathematical model which is used for the computation. This model can at best be a good approximation to the actual physical system, it will never be quite perfect. Furthermore, the input data are derived from some physical measurements and contain the errors inherent in them. All these error sources have to be carefully examined to find out whether the computation will yiels results within the required accuracy. Due to the presence of random errors it is not possible to compute the accuracy directly, one has to be satisfied with statistically determined confidence limits.

2.44. Conclusion

From the previous chapters it should have become apparent that the digital computer is by far the most versatile instrument for computations. Any problem which can be stated in mathematical or logical form can be solved. Only the size of the memory, that is the number of data which can be stored, puts a practical limit on the problem size. Present computers have a fast random access main memory with a capacity of 1000 to 32,000 words. This is often supplemented by a medium speed memory of 4000 to 32,000 words capacity, usually a magnetic drum. On top of that there are magnetic tapes which can be used for intermediate storage of large quantities of data, going into the millions. Despite this huge memory capacity there are still problems so large that they cannot be handled at all or at least not in a reasonable length of time. In these cases one can sometimes resort to statistical methods, random sampling of the data, etc. An exact result cannot be obtained, but one gets a statistical estimate.

In spite of the many capabilities of digital computers one basic limitation should not be overlooked. The digital computer cannot process continuous functions without error. Because of the finite length of machine numbers the set of all possible numbers is a finite set of rational values. This can only be an approximation, although often a very good one, to the infinite set of all real numbers. A continuous function must therefore necessarily be represented by a finite set of discrete samples. This generates two errors, one is the round-off error of the individual sample values, the other is caused by the sampling itself. The sampling theory states that under special conditions the complete continuous function can be exactly represented by its samples. In the general case, however, some information about the function is lost and this will cause an error. The second limitation originates from the first one and consists of the fact that many numerical methods, e.g. integration and differentiation, approximate an infinite number of infinitely small steps by a finite number of finite computation steps. In other words, the computer cannot duplicate exactly the mathematical process of taking the limit. One could be inclined to think that the analog computer might be superior in this respect as it can handle continuous functions. But there we are working with physical quantities whose measurement is always subject to errors. The overall balance is in favor of the digital computer, since it is possible to obtain any desired accuracy by suitably choosing the number length and the step size of the numerical method. An increase in accuracy necessarily entails an increase in computing time. In real-time applications one can only achieve a limited accuracy, as a certain computing time must not be exceeded. In these cases an analog computer could be the better choice.

Bibliography

Staff of Engineering Research Associates, "High-Speed Computing Devices". McGraw-Hill, New York, 1950.

—, "Faster than Thought, a symposium on digital computing machines". Pitman, London, 1953.

White, G. S., "Coded Decimal Number Systems for Digital Computers". Proc. I. R. E. *41*, 1450—1452, 1953.

Charnes, A., Cooper, W. W., "An Introduction to Linear Programming". Wiley, New York, 1953.

Williams, J. D., "The Compleat Strategyst". McGraw-Hill, New York, 1954.

Dantzig, T., "Number, the Language of Science". Macmillan, New York, 1954.

Locke, W. N., Booth, A. D., et al., "Machine Translation of Languages". Wiley, New York, 1955.

Chapin, N., "An Introduction to Automatic Computers". D. van Nostrand, Princeton, 1955.

Richards, R. K., "Arithmetic Operations in Digital Computers". D. van Nostrand, New York, 1955.

Booth, A. D., Booth, K. H. V., "Automatic Digital Calculators". Academic Press, New York, 1956.

International Business Machines Corp., "The Fortran Automatic Coding System for the IBM 704". IBM Publication, 1956.

Berkeley, E. C., Wainwright, L., "Computers, their Operation and Applications". Reinhold Publ. Co., New York, 1956.

Wilkes M. V., "Automatic Digital Computers". Wiley, New York, 1957.

Grabbe, E. M., "Automation in Business and Industry". Wiley, New York, 1957.
Livesley, R. K., "An Introduction to Automatic Digital Computers". Cambridge University Press, 1957.
McCracken, D. D., "Digital Computer Programming". Wiley, New York, 1957.
Remington Rand Univac, Unicode, "Automatic Coding for Univac Scientific". Remington Rand Publication, 1958.
Phister, M., jr., "Logical Design of Digital Computers". Wiley, New York, 1958.
Jeenel, J., "Programming for Digital Computers". McGraw-Hill, New York, 1959.
Garner, H. L., "The Residue Number System". Trans. I. R. E., *EC-8*, 140—147, 1959.
Gschwind, H. W., "A Real Time Data Assimilator". Comm. Ass. Comp. Mach. *2*, 33—36, 1959.
Perlis, A. J., Samelson, K., "Report on the Algorithmic Language". ALGOL etc. Numerische Mathematik *1*, 41—60, 1959.
Leiner, A. L., et al., Pilot A new Multiple Computer System, Jour. Ass. Comp. Mach. 6, 313—335, 1959.
Naur, P., "Report on the Algorithmic Language ALGOL 60", Comm. Ass. Comp. Mach. *3*, 299—314, 1960.

Chapter 3

Analog Computers

By

Martin G. Jaenke (Dr.-Ing.)

(Chief, Simulation and Computation Division, Air Force Missile Development Center, Holloman Air Force Base, New Mexico, USA)

With 49 Figures

3. Analog Computers

3.1. Basic Philosophy

It is quite possible to analyze and compare critically and quantitatively computing machines of different types with the purpose of making an optimum decision for their selection. The procedure is well known: define purpose and requirements of application, investigate capabilities and limitations of the machines, study the problems of operation and maintenance, investigate the cost situation, finally weigh all these factors carefully one against the other and make the decision. However, in many cases it will be very difficult and even impossible to define all these factors clearly and quantitatively and the successful analyst will have to rely on his intuition. And, of course, this intuition must be based on his knowledge and understanding of the working principles of the computing machines. The attempt to provide such an understanding in this book may be facilitated by the fact that the available space is restricted. This allows to concentrate on the essential characteristics, to point them out bluntly and even to accept the dangers of over-statements, if they help to form a clear basic concept. The complexity and flexibility of modern large scale computers justify such an approach even more. A sound judgment in problem fringe areas can be based only on a clear basic concept.

This chapter deals with "Analog Computers". In starting to form a concept it seems to be fruitful to take into consideration that such a machine basically is not really a "computer". This is certainly justified, if "computation" is understood as a process of finding a mathematical solution for a mathematically formulated problem. Of course, an analog machine solves problems, primarily such problems which originate in the world of physical reality. But this is achieved by substituting the physical process under study by another equivalent, analogous physical process. This then allows to observe and to measure the quantities of interest in their reaction to given disturbances and to reinterpret this analogous information in terms of the original problem. So then, instead of being a computer the analog machine is rather an "experimental kit", consisting of a collection of physical operational elements, which have to be combined properly in order to establish the analog process, or, as it is frequently called, to "simulate" the original process. This can even be done if a mathematical description of the process is not available, provided, of course, that the physical meaning of the problem is fully understood and that the characteristic constants of each elementary process are known.

In such a simulation it is possible to use parts of the original physical process under study directly without simulating them. It is only necessary to convert the variables fluctuating between the parts of the system, the original and simulated ones, to proper form, which in most cases is not difficult. This is an important feature of analog techniques. The main reason for doing it is that it is frequently important to incorporate the exact characteristics of a subsystem in the study of a problem whose exact analytical description is not obtainable. And, conversely, analog techniques are by their very nature most adequate to provide correction or control functions in a complex technical-physical process, as for instance in automation problems.

The heavy emphasis on the physical nature of analog techniques was quite useful to furnish the understanding of their basis principles. On the other hand it was quite certainly an overstatement to deny analog machine the character of a computer. It was said that it is not necessary to have a mathematical description of the process to be investigated. But this of course does not exclude the possibility to "mechanize" on the analog machine a process which is known only by its mathematical description and to find the desired solutions. Actually, this is the normal procedure, but is does not invalidate what was said above. After all, the mathematical formulation of a physical process is only a special form of a "shorthand" description. Quite certainly, any mathematical relation can be solved on the analog machine, provided, and this is important to note but easily understandable, that the described situation is physically realizable. So, the analog computer is a computer after all.

The discussion concentrated so far on the second word of the title, the "computer". The "analog" certainly was clarified at the same time. In this connection, it may be of interest to note how computer concepts and terminology reflect on the technical language. It becomes more and more common usage to talk about "analog" or "digital" information. The meaning is clear. Analog information is the result of a measurement of a variable in its continuous functional form, as it is encountered in the original physical processes and, of course, on the analog computer. This is in contrast to "digital" information which means presentation of the functions as a table of numbers or a sequence of samples as it is required for the treatment on a digital computer.

It seems to be important to point out that the analogy is basically in the "system", the one under study and the one representing it on the computer. This, of course, leads to analogy of the variables.

To avoid misunderstandings, a clear definition of terminology is in order. The meaning of "system" and "variable" can best be described by an example. If the reaction of a mass to the application of a given force is investigated, the mass is the physical "system" under study. The forces, acceleration, velocity, and position are the "variables". Specifically, the force which disturbs the mass is the input variable, input function or forcing function and the others describing the reaction of the system, are the output variables, output functions or the solutions.

Thus, the analog computer is a collection of physical components used in proper combination as substitutes for the actual physical system under study. The understanding of this basis feature immediately leads to the cognizance of its basic limitations. The physical components of the computer are of technical form and any technical component is of finite quality. The attempt to improve their quality results in an unproportionally high increase in cost if certain limits are approached which are given by the state of technology. An analog computer of reasonable cost, accordingly, is of finite accuracy. It is not the instrument to look for if high-precision computations are required. But it is certainly preferable if the engineer or physicist looks for an instrument which not only gives a formalistic answer to the questions he asks but which provides a physical entirety, intimately related to his problem. It allows the study of every detail of his problem under any desired configurations in a direct, experimental way.

3.2. Components of Analog Computers

3.21 Required Components

In order to perform an analog computation, it is necessary to have sufficient physical elements, components, at hand, sufficient with respect to diversity and number. First it has to be discussed what kind of components are required. It certainly is wise to make the processes performed by the components as fundamental as possible. This yields highest flexibility and convenience in operation and maintenance. Now, since physical problems basically are described by differential equations, a collection of components has to be defined which is necessary and sufficient to simulate differential equations on the computer. In their fundamental form they are ordinary, linear and have constant coefficients. The components used for the solution of this type of equations are called "linear". Such equations are of the following form:

$$a_n \frac{d^{(n)} y(t)}{dt^n} + a_{n-1} \frac{d^{(n-1)} y(t)}{dt^{n-1}} + \dots a_0 y(t) = x(t) \tag{1}$$

It is obvious that one of the basic processes required is addition. In order to use the adders also for the inverse process, subtraction, it is required to have sign changers. Since the derivative terms contain real coefficients, devices are needed which change the amount of a variable by a defined, fixed ratio. This ratio may be smaller or larger than one, and the techniques employed may be different in these two cases. In this general state of the discussion the devices will be called attenuators and amplifiers, respectively. Then, of course, it is necessary to perform differentiation processes. But pure differentiation processes with sufficiently ideal characteristics are difficult to realize while it is comparatively easy to perform adequate integrations with physical components. Consequently, integrators are provided as important linear components in practical analog computers. It is then necessary to replace prescribed differentiations of one variable by integrations of others. This reorientation of procedures is not difficult and will be seen to fit very well in the general concept of analog computation.

Table 1

Adder
Sign Changer
Attenuator
Amplifier
Integrator

In review, the basic components required to solve ordinary linear differential equations, the "linear" components, are compiled in Table 1.

The more important and more general problem is the solution of ordinary non-linear differential equations, or such with varying coefficients. This field, which is so difficult to handle by analytical methods is the natural and prominent application area of analog computers. Referring to (1), the necessity is seen to provide facilities to make the coefficients, a, variable and control their magnitude by functions either of the independent variable, time, or of any dependent variable. The basis component for the purpose could be called a "variable coefficient device", it is normally called a "multiplier". It is a unit whose relation between input and output, α, is controlled by a third variable:

$$\begin{aligned} z &= x \cdot \alpha \\ \alpha &= K \cdot y \\ z &= K \cdot x \cdot y \end{aligned} \tag{2}$$

Such a component is of tremendous importance and flexibility. It is easy to see that it not only can be used as variable coefficient device and multiplier, but as an instrument to establish a wide family of functions of variables. If the same variable is used as input and for coefficient control, the output will be proportional to its square. By properly sequencing such multipliers, any integer power of a variable can be generated. Thus, all functions which can be represented by power series can be mechanized on the analog computer by a proper combination of multipliers, adders, sign changers, and attenuators.

However, in practical physical problems, many functions are known only empirically and no mathematical description is available. In order to mechanize such functions by the process indicated above, it is necessary to find a power series approximation, which frequently is quite tedious. Also, this type of mechanization is expensive, because a great number of individual components is required. So, another basic non-linear computing component was created which is known as "function generator". It is mainly applied in such cases, where the function is known only by graphical representation. The function generator is empirically adapted in such a way that its output matches as closely as possible the graphically defined function. Of course, such a function generator can be used in cases also where the functions are mathematically defined. But again the method to set it up in such cases is the same, namely, empirical matching against a graphically presented information.

Despite the fact that the non-linear components described so far are basically sufficient to cover all requirements, there is a tendency to provide special functional devices. The reason for this is that some functions are used very frequently and that it is convenient to have them directly available. Additionally, a component designed for a special purpose is usually more accurate than a general purpose device. The most important example in this class is the sine and cosine function generator. Built in proper combinations it allows to resolve vectors between different coordinate systems. Such a combination is known as a "resolver".

Another function which is frequently encountered is the logarithmic function and its inverse. Despite its importance and its obvious advantage in performing multiplication processes, no commerical element which basically produces this function with sufficient accuracy is available. In Table 2, the basic non-linear components are compiled:

Table 2

Multiplier
Function Generator
Resolver

3.22. Possibilities of Realization

The computation processes to be performed in the components listed in Table 1 and 2 can be of different physical nature. The principal disciplines of physics for the realization of the analogous processes are mechanics and electricity. But there is no limitation to any specific discipline. So, for instance, optical and hydraulic processes are frequently employed, specifically in special purpose applications. Historically, analog computation started with mechanical tools. Since many of the mechanical components are still of practical interest it is worth while to explain them in some detail.

Fig. 1. Differential Gear (Librascope, Inc.)

3.221. Mechanical Processes. Depending on the form of the mechanical variables, rotational or linear displacements or their derivatives, the basic operations are performed in a straight forward manner by gear trains, differential gears or linkages. Fig. 1 and 2 show practical examples of such components. The most important and versatile mechanical component is the "ball-disc integrator". Its principle is shown in Fig. 3. A disc (1) is driven by the input quantity x. The balls (2) couple its motion to cylinder (3), which performs the motion z. If y is the distance of the balls from the center of the disc, the relation holds:

$$z = K \cdot x \cdot y \tag{3}$$

In order to make it a multiplier or variable gain device, the distance, y, must be changeable in accordance with the respective variable. Using the device in this form of course is equivalent to a gear train with changeable gear ratio.

Fig. 2. Precision Addition-Subtraction Linkages (Librascope, Inc.)

In order to use the instrument as an integrator, its input shaft position, x, must be made proportional to the independent or integration variable. Then the relation holds:

$$dz = K \cdot y \cdot dx \tag{4}$$

It is a definite advantage of this integrator, that x can represent any arbitrary independent variable. It is not necessarily restricted to integrations with respect to time, as is the case with many other physical integrators. Fig. 4 shows such a ball-disc integrator.

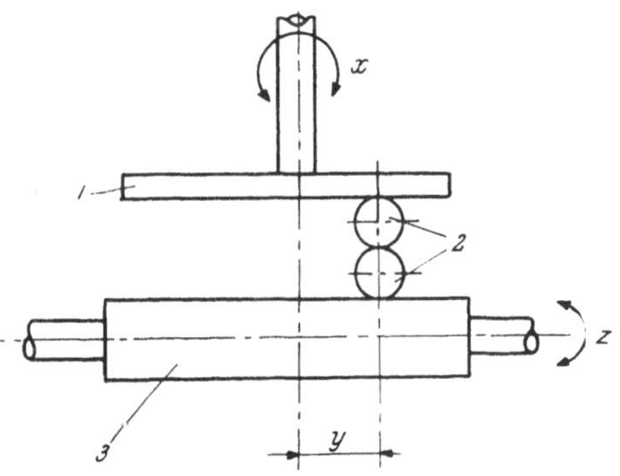

Fig. 3. Principle of the Ball-Disc Integrator

Mechanics provide a very adequate possibility to generate arbitrary functions in form of the cam shaft device. A basic example is shown in Fig. 5. Disk (1) rotates around shaft (2) in accordance with the variable, x. A feeler pin (3) is pressed against the circumference of (1) and will assume the position, y. The radius r of (1) is made proportional to the desired function $f(x)$, and one obtains:

$$y = K \cdot f(x) \tag{5}$$

The sine and cosine functions are easily and accurately representable by measuring

Fig. 4. Ball-Disc Integrator (Librascope, Inc)

the rectangular coordinates of a point on a rotating disc. Fig. 6 shows a practical component. With x being the rotational positioning of the input shaft and y the linear excursion of the output element it yields the function:

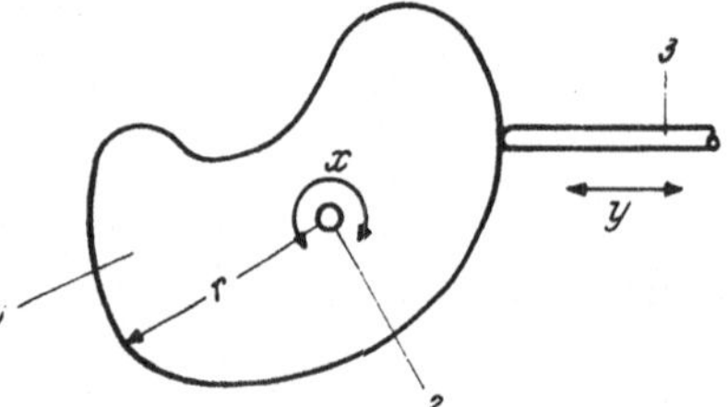

Fig. 5. Principle of the Cam Shaft Function Generator

$$y = K \cdot \sin x \tag{6}$$
$$\text{or } y = K \cdot \cos x$$

depending on the definition of the reference position.

In the discussion of these mechanical computer components it was seen that their input and output variables are either angular or linear positions or their derivatives. So an additional component is required which permits easy conversion between these two definitions. This is the rack and pinion device, which is shown in Fig. 7. Its operation is evident.

3.222 Electrical Processes. The electrical elements and processes used for linear operations are the following:

Adding: Resistor networks following Kirchhoffs law.
Sign Changing and Amplifying: Amplifiers.
Attenuating: Potentiometers.

It has to be noted that for all the purposes above transformers with proper winding ratios can be used if AC voltages or currents represent the variables in the analog process.

Integrating: The voltage-current relations on condensers or inductances.

The non-linear operations are performed as follows:

Multiplication: Natural electrical multiplication processes, such as the amplification of a variable-μ-tube, are too inaccurate for most purposes. The simplest device in practical use are potentiometers, the shaft position of which is made proportional to one of the problem variables. However, it has to be noticed, that shaft position is of mechanical form and so an additional device is needed to produce such a mechanical variable from an electrical quantity (voltage or current), which, of course, is the standard form of the variables in an electrical computer. Such transformation devices are known as servo mechanisms. The implications of this electro-mechanical conversion will be discussed later.

Fig. 6. Sine-Cosine Mechanism (Librascope, Inc.)

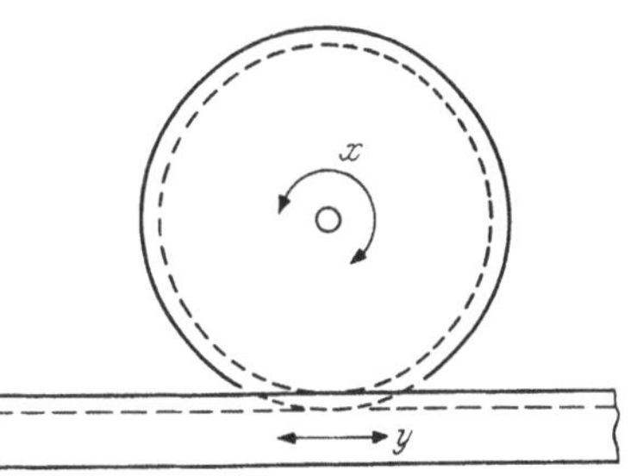

Fig. 7. Principle of the Rack and Pinion Drive

Purely electrical multipliers make use of rather complicated processes. One important class might be called modulation multipliers. In these an auxiliary carrier wave is modulated in sequence by two different modulation processes, e. g. amplitude and frequency modulation or pulse amplitude and pulse width modulation. The modulating voltages are proportional to the two input variables. The desired product is attained by an adequate demodulation process.

The other important class might be called square law multipliers. They are based on the following mathematical relation:

$$z = x \cdot y = \frac{1}{4}\left[(x + y)^2 - (x - y)^2\right] \tag{7}$$

The square law functions required in this process are produced by function generators as described later.

So, purely electrical multipliers in their present form are complicated devices, as will become even more evident later when details will be discussed. However, considerable effort is employed to develop methods which are based on more fundamental processes. The most promising approach seems to be the Hall effect multiplier. The Hall effect is the change of conductivity in a semi-conductor produced by the influence of a magnetic field.

Function generation: There is a wide variety of fundamental approaches and specific solutions. The most important class is characterized by a straight line approximation method. The function which is graphically represented is sub-divided in a number of sections in such a way, that the value of the function within these segments can be approximated by straight lines with a minimum of error. There are two basic approaches to mechanize this type of function generator: The first uses a potentiometer which is subdivided by a number of taps.

These taps are shunted by fixed resistors in such a way, that the desired train of straight lines with its break points and slopes is represented as closely as possible as a function of the shaft position of the potentiometer. The process of evaluating the necessary shunting resistors is tedious, since the interaction of the shunts and loading reactions have to be considered. However, practical set-up methods have been developed which facilitate the task and, once established, the function can be relied on to remain in the desired form. These devices are known as servo function generators, they are again of electro-mechanical form, a fact which has to be kept in mind for later discussions. The other fundamental approach to mechanization is purely electrical. Here, diodes are used, the conductivity of which is adjustable by setting a bias voltage to obtain the desired breakpoint of the function segment and by inserting a proper circuit resistor to achieve the desired slope. The output voltages or currents are summed to get the overall function. These devices are known as diode function generators. They are more flexible than servo function generators, since they are not restricted to a fixed length of the segment. But a function once established may change due to variations of the characteristics of the diodes.

The other important fundamental class of function generators may be called "curve followers". They are characterized by the capability of translating directly a graphically given function into electrical information. One basic approach to achieve this is known as "Photoformer".[1]

Its working principle is shown in Fig. 8.

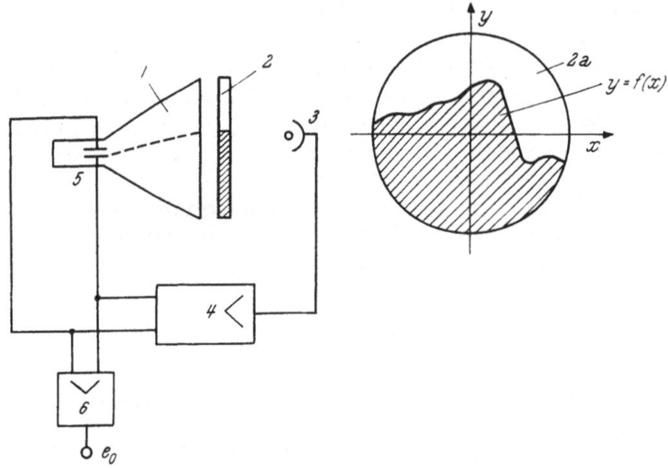

Fig. 8. "Photoformer" Function Generator

The beam of a cathode ray tube (1) is swept across the screen by a voltage which is proportional to the variable x. A mask (2) is put in front of the cathode ray tube (1). This mask carries the function information as the border line between a translucent and an opaque zone, as shown in the front view (2a). A photo cell (3) measures the light intensity on the screen of the CR tube, its output is amplified in (4) and fed to the vertical deflection plates (5). Now at any given horizontal position of the electron beam the closed loop mechanism (2) thru (5) will keep the electron beam just on the borderline between the translucent and

[1] Produced by Midcentury Instrumatic Corp.

opaque zone on (2). The vertical deflection voltage which is necessary to achieve this is amplified in (6) and represents the function value in electrical form.

Other fundamental approaches to function generation are electro mechanical. Their common feature is to present the function by a medium of finite electrical conductivity and to have electrical sensing devices follow this medium. Fig. 9 shows the basic principle of one typical approach.

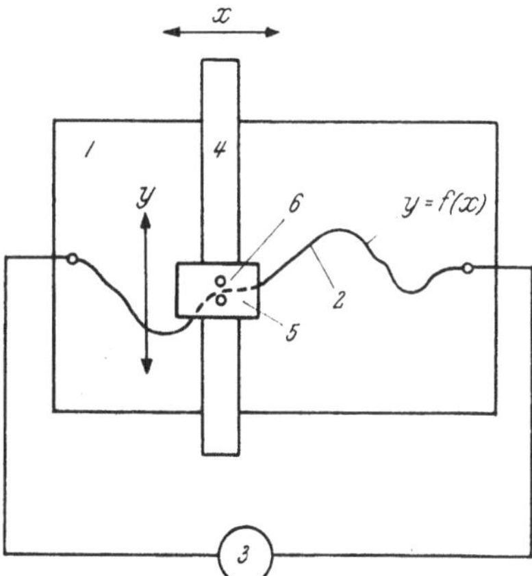

Fig. 9. Principle of Electro-Mechanical Curve Follower

The given function is plotted on a sheet of paper (1) by a trace of conductive ink (2). This conducting trace is connected to a high frequency generator (3), so that a high frequency magnetic field will be built up around the trace. A sled (4) is moved across the paper plane by a servo in such a way that its position corresponds to the value of the input variable, x, of the process. A carriage (5) is moved along the sled by another servo system. Its position on the sled is controlled by a pair of balanced pick-up coils (6), zeroing the combined output voltage induced by the magnetic field of the trace. The position, y, of the carriage is measured electrically and the respective voltages are proportional to the given function of x. Fig. 10 shows a practical instrument of this type which can be used as function plotter and as a curve follower.

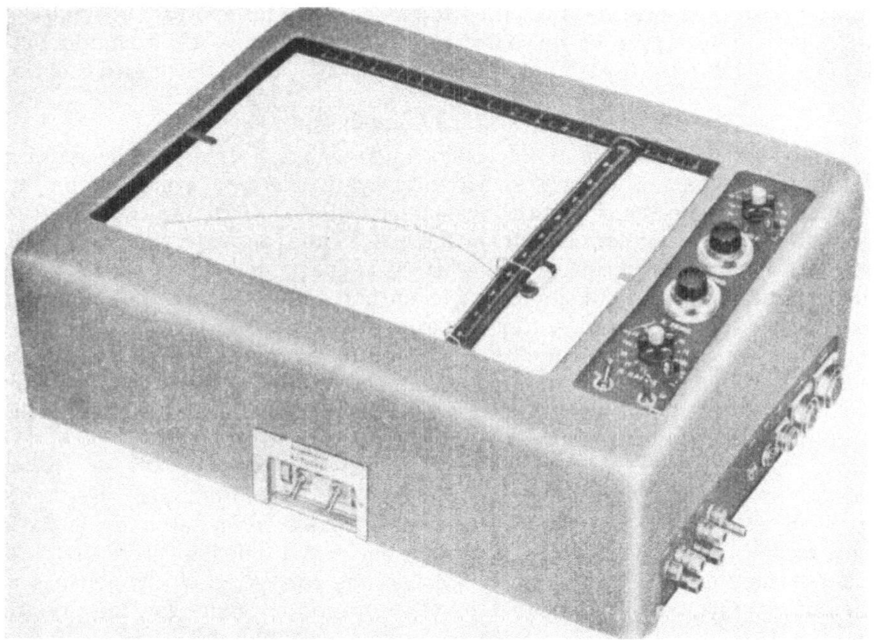

Fig. 10. Combined Curve Follower and Function Plotter (F. L. Moseley Company)

The obvious complexity of all the approaches in electrical function generation indicates that there is as yet no ideal solution. Research and development work continues to establish better methods.

Concluding this discussion of electrical function generators it is pointed out again that they may also be used for the generation of functions which are analytically defined. One practically important example is the use of the function x^2, mechanized by diode function generators in the square law multipliers mentioned above. Another example is the use of the functions $\sin x$ and $\cos x$, again mechanized by diode function generators, as basic functional elements in fully electronic resolvers.

Resolvers: Besides the fully electronic approach to the generation of sine and cosine functions, which was described above, primarily electro-mechanical methods are in practical use at the present time. One type, the "synchro", makes use of a natural process of generating sine or cosine functions. It is the voltage induced in a coil, the axis of which has different angular positions in a homogeneous alternating magnetic field. The input variable again is angular shaft position of the synchro and a servo is required to make it proportional to the original electrically defined variable. The output variable is an ac voltage. This is inconvenient and requires special conversion devices in computer installations in which dc voltages are the general variables.

Another type uses potentiometers which carry a winding shaped in such a way as to make the electrical output proportional to the sine or cosine of the shaft position. Again the mechanical shaft position of the potentiometer is the input variable and a servo is required to produce it. This approach is related to the cam-shaft technique of mechanical function generators, the common basic idea being to fabricate an element of specific shape adapted to the desired function.

3.23. Critical Comparison

In the previous discussions of possible approaches to establish the required basic analog computing processes a critical evaluation was avoided. This will be done now, employing certain evaluation criteria which are important to justify the selection of components or methods. Thus, an understanding of why the art of analog computing stands where it is today and the formation of an independent opinion about its probable further course can be developed. In addition, it may help a prospective user of analog equipment to judge independently the proposals of manufacturers. He quite certainly has a considerable freedom to combine components in a way he thinks best or which fits optimally his specific purposes. To give characteristic examples for this trend it might be mentioned that one important Analog Computer installation in the USA uses nearly exclusively servo-multipliers to generate functions based on power series approximations. Another large and important installation uses only curve-followers for this purpose. This is interesting insofar as the common trend seems to be to use diode function generators and servo function generators. And it is not unusual to find computer installations consisting of components of different manufacturers, composed to yield optimum results for the specific purposes. However, the task to make on optimum selection should not be underestimated. The large variety of basic approaches, and the modifications of different manufacturers, confront the prospective user with a task of considerable magnitude.

Important points of view for critical comparison are the following: Accuracy, Flexibility, Reliability, Maintenance, and Cost. Others can be thought of, but even of the list above, only the first three items are considered to be fundamental and general enough to be discussed in more detail within the restricted space of this book. The two last items are too closely related to the situation of the individual user to be the object of a general discussion.

3.231. Accuracy. Accuracy has two aspects, the static and dynamic accuracy. Since in very many cases one of them can be traded against the other within certain limits by different emphasis in design or different modes of operation, an attempt will be made to define quality figures which comprise both aspects. This will not only facilitate the selection of adequate analog components, but may help to compare quantitatively analog to digital processes.

Any active component may be considered as a dynamic system, i. e, it does not react infinitely fast. Then the static accuracy will be defined by the errors in steady state gain coefficients and the dynamic accuracy by the magnitude and the phase shift of the frequency response function describing such a system. Now, both steady state gain and frequency response will be affected by another error source, namely the interaction of components. This problem area will be discussed first. Interaction is defined as the change of the characteristics of one component if either its output or input side or both are connected to other components. To be able to control this phenomenon is, of course, important. In setting up an analog computing process, one must be absolutely free to combine the components in any way as it is prescribed by the problem without being forced to consider a possible change of the properties of one individual component by connecting it to other ones. Fundamentally, electrical components in their basic form as described above will be much more sentitive to such interaction effects than mechanical ones. It is quite obvious that the characteristics of a summing network, of the charging process of a condenser or the calibration curve of a potentiometer will depend quite severely and systematically on the respective feeding and loading situation. However, the electronic art provides an element which practically eliminates the systematic interaction difficulties and has other important advantages in addition. This is the high-gain amplifier with feedback control, or, as it is frequently called, the operational amplifier. It has an input impedance which tends to infinity and an output impedance which tends to zero, both tendencies depending on the efforts expended in design and cost. It is the ideal element, to decouple or unload the individual computing components and the margin between input and output is large enough to require little care from the operator to avoid interaction errors. The high-gain amplifiers have other significant advantages, which will be discussed later. Since practically each electrical computing component is sensitive to interaction, a large number of operational amplifiers will be required in a computer installation. So, despite the fact that these amplifiers are not computing components in a strict sense but merely auxiliary though indispensable devices, they are the major basic elements of electrical analog computers. This is very clearly demonstrated by the fact that computer installations are mostly described in a short form by the number of operational amplifiers they contain. This gives a very close information of the overall capability of the installation. And the emphasis on the amplifiers is understandable from the standpoint of cost, too. Very clearly these high quality amplifiers constitute one of the main cost elements and exceed significantly in this respect the actual basic computing components such as resistors, capacitors and potentiometers.

Similar interaction problems are encountered in mechanical computers. They seem to be not so severe at first glance, since the components are rigidly connected and the combination of an increasing number of components primarily results in an increasing power requirement on the driving source. However, friction, mass, and elasticity lead to increasing static and dynamic errors caused by interaction of components. But an element similar in scope to the high gain amplifier of electrical computers helps to prevent interaction errors. This is the torque amplifier. Its principle of operation is to position an output shaft by providing the necessary torque from an extraneous power source without loading the input shaft.

After elimination of interaction influences the remaining sources for static errors are the following: Limited quality of components, environmental effects, and operational limitations. The quality of the components depends on the design and the efforts and costs of the manufacturing process. The difficulties and problems are about equally distributed between mechanical and electrical components. To manufacture highly precise resistors, capacitors, or potentiometers can be considered to be equally difficult as cutting, grinding, and mounting precision gears. But there is a serious error source in the high gain amplifiers of electrical computers. This is amplifier drift, the phenomenon that the amplifier delivers a finite output with a zero input. This drift is specifically dangerous if the amplifier is used to unload a capacitor in an integration process. Then the undesired output builds up with time and can cause considerable computation errors. It is therefore the most important concern of the amplifier designer to reduce this drift to a minimum and the necessary techniques contribute significantly to the cost of the unit. Though ingenious techniques were developed, this drift remains a significant problem in electrical computing processes.

The main environmental effects are temperature and aging influences. Again electrical components are basically inferior with respect to temperature. But the use of "ovens", temperature controlled chambers, allows to eliminate these effects to any practically sensible degree at reasonable cost. The aging influences are more difficult to grasp and to define quantitatively. Of course, it is comparatively well known what to expect and how to cope with the aging of vacuum tubes. But the aging properties of passive electrical components and their relation to loading or temperature cycles are only empirically known. The necessary pre-aging processes significantly reflect on the cost of the products. With mechanical components, aging mainly leads to wear of the parts. And this depends clearly on the quality of manufacturing and frequency of use so that a general appraisal is hardly possible.

Operational limitations are unavoidable, since all of the computer components are of physical-technical nature. Upper limits are given by the maximum capability of an element, such as saturation in an amplifier or maximum permissible excursion in mechanical devices. Lower limits are given by backlash and friction effects in mechanical and the "noise" in electronic components. Of course, all these quantities defining the lower limit are under a certain control; they depend again on the care and cost of the manufacturing process. But they will always be finite and can cause considerable errors if the problem variable is small. But these operational errors can be mitigated by the computer operator. He must program the computer process in such a way that the magnitude of the computer variables remains sufficiently large with respect to the lower limits and sufficiently small with respect to the upper limits in order to obtain a certain desired accuracy. This "scaling" of variables is the most intricate task of the operator in the otherwise simple process of setting up an analog computation. These aspects will be discussed in detail later.

Similarly, limitation effects can cause dynamic errors. A servo, for instance, is capable only to operate at a maximum velocity or acceleration. If the given function of the simulated variable calls for higher instantaneous values, the servo will momentarily not be able to follow the function and so cause dynamic errors. But these errors are mainly restricted to servo system and do not show in other elements. Again they can be avoided or sufficiently reduced by proper care in the "scaling" of the computer. But the important dynamic errors are caused by linear effects. It is easiest to explain them by the fact that a physical device is not able to perform a jump but always will react to a jump in its excitation function by following a certain transient. This behavior is reflected by the frequency response or transfer function which describes in detail how the output variable of a system differs in amplitude and phase from the input, if the latter is of sinusoidal form. A physical system will only react to frequencies up to a certain limit and a defined phase shift is associated with such a finite passband. Any frequency beyond this limit which may be contained in the spectra of the variables of the problem under study will be suppressed and the variables will be distorted. The phase shifts of the individual components combined in the problem simulation will add, and, if the number of components is large, a considerable total phase shift may result. This is particularly dangerous if the components are arranged in a "closed loop" fashion, which is frequently the case. If the total phase shift within such a loop attains the value of 180°, the loop will become unstable and the simulation of the problem will be impossible. But again, the operator can mitigate the effect of dynamic component errors by proper scaling, in this case of the independent variable "time". He can define arbitrarily what one second of the events happening on the computer should mean in terms of the time history of the problem. In doing so, he can reduce the frequencies in the spectra of the computer variables. But he must be consistent in his definitions. If any empirical input functions of time are given, he must feed them into the computer at the selected time scale, he must define the coefficients of his integrators correctly and finally interpret the output information accordingly. In doing all this, he changes the requirements with respect to the frequencies to be handled by the computer and so has a tool to reduce the influence of the dynamic component errors systematically. But of course there are disadvantages connected with this re-scaling of time. Disregarding the change in required computer operation time, there is still the sacrifice of the "real-time" capability, the capability of the Analog Computer to present the events of the problem under study in their original historical sequence. This may be unimportant in a great number of practical cases and actually "time scaling" is frequently used. But it is important if original components of the process under study are to be incorporated in the simulation process, a feature which makes Analog Computers so attractive for technical evaluations. In consideration of its significant influence, the phase angle of a component is used to describe quantitatively, or to specify, its dynamic accuracy.

Concluding this discussion on basic errors of Analog Computer components, an attempt will be made to provide a quantitative information on the errors actually encountered. Fig. 11 is a quality field, in which the horizontal axis represents the 1°-degree frequency, f_1, defined as the frequency at which a phase shift of 1° should not be exceeded. The vertical axis represents the static accuracy, A, defined as the inverse of the static error, which in turn is expressed as a fraction of the maximum value the computer variables may attain without limiting distortions. The diagonal lines are the lines of equal products, $A \cdot f_1$, which can be considered as quality figures. The field is divided horizontally into two distinct zones, the dynamic range of servos, the essential element of all electro-mechanical components, and the dynamic range of fully electronic devices. Vertically, upper limits for static accuracies of various components are indicated.

This was done with some hesitation, because these limits depend very clearly on the state of manufacturing techniques. The smaller areas, *A* to *D*, describe roughly the present quality status for different important components. One

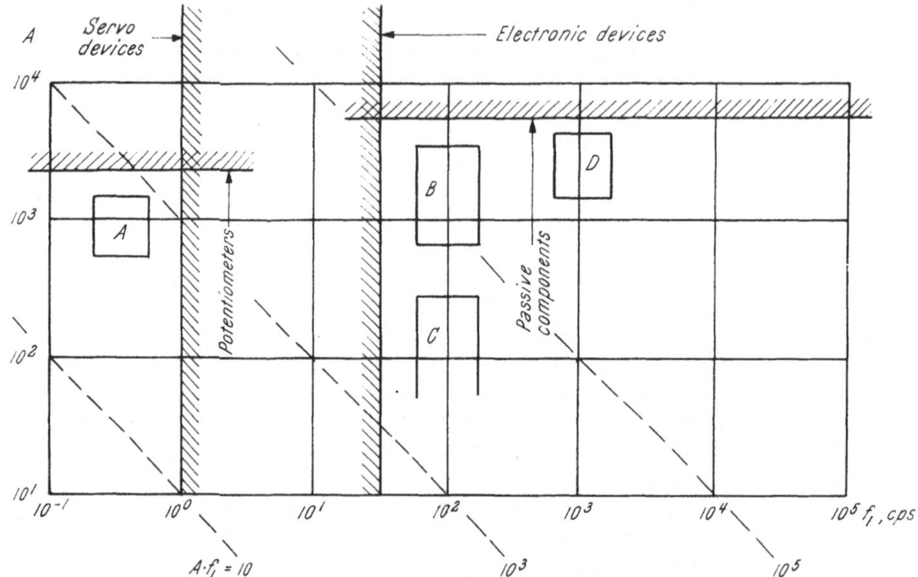

Fig. 11. Quality Field of Analog Computer Components
A: Electro-mechanical components (servo-multipliers and resolvers)
B: Electronic Multipliers
C: Diode Function Generators
D: Operational Amplifiers and Integrators

comment has to be made with respect to diode function generators. Here the upper accuracy limit describes the errors caused by the drift of the elements. Higher errors (lower accuracy) may be encountered if the straight-line approximation of the desired function is inadequate.

3.232. Flexibility. Considerations of flexibility are discussed here because the main interest will concentrate on computers which can be used in an easy way to solve equations of any kind. They are usually called "general purpose" computers. They are in contrast to "special purpose" computers, which are designed in an optimum way to solve one particular set of equations and cannot be used for different problems. Now the requirements for a general purpose Analog Computer are first that a sufficiently large number of sufficiently diversified components is available to solve the equations of the anticipated type. The second important requirement is flexibility, the possibility to combine the components for the computing process in an easy, reliable and clear way. In this respect the electrical computer is obviously superior. The means of combining components are electrical connections, which are easily established and which can be clearly organized. In addition, electrical switching techniques give the possibility of introducing automatic or semiautomatic features. On the other hand, these nonpermanent electrical connections are subject to the well known contact problems. But this depends to a wide extent on the quality of the manufacturing process. These properties of an electrical computer stand against the problems of interconnecting mechanical components, which quite obviously is not as easy. It should be mentioned that in this respect electro-mechanical components are identical to electrical ones. The input variable, which positions the servo, is of electrical form and so is the output variable, taken from a potentiometer or a synchro.

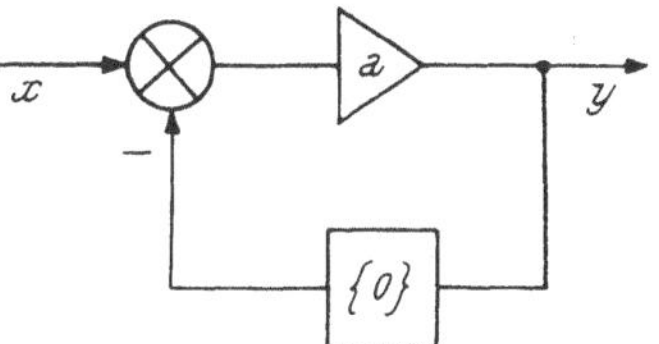

Fig. 12. Process Inversion by Feedback Around High Gain Amplifier

In this discussion of flexibility one important property of the electrical computer must be pointed out. The most fundamental of its components, the high gain amplifier, provides the possibility of inverting computation processes by employing the feedback principle. Fig. 12 shows the block diagram of such a basic setup.

With, a, being the gain of the high gain amplifier, $\{0\}$ representing an operation performed on the output variable, y, and the result of this operation being subtracted from the input variable, x, the following equation holds:

$$\frac{y}{a} + y\,\{0\} = x; \quad y = \frac{x}{\{0\}} \quad \text{far } a \to \infty \tag{8}$$

So, the inverse operation is performed on the input variable with sufficient accuracy, if the gain of the amplifier is sufficiently high. This property is preferably used to convert multipliers into dividers, but is applicable for any other process. It is certainly an important principle to use available components efficiently and economically.

3.233. Reliability. Mechanical processes are certainly more reliable than electrical ones. The difficulties to maintain reliable operation of large and complex electronic installations are well known. But if the vast experience gathered in the various fields of electronics and communications is intelligently applied to electrical analog computers, if their components are of sufficient quality and if a strict preventive maintenance schedule is kept up, a quite satisfactory reliability is achievable.

3.234. Conclusions. Comparing the advantages and disadvantages of the different components, it is evident that it is not easy to make a final decision. However, the actual development of analog computation indicates a preference of the electrical computer. This is, to a certain extent, surprising because the electrical computer can operate only with the independent variable, time, while the mechanical computer is free in this respect. The reason for this practical preference is probably the favorable combination of adequate static and dynamic accuracy and the high degree of flexibility of the electrical computer. This last argument is particularly important for general purpose applications. In special purpose applications, expecially where high static accuracy and reliability are required, mechanical computers are quite frequently encountered. Since the purpose of this book can only be to discuss general purpose computers, the further discussion will concentrate exclusively on electrical computers.

Of the many possible forms of electrical computers it is primarily the so called *DC* Analog Computer which is of the highest practical interest. In this type, the problem variables are represented by *DC* voltages. Other forms are *AC* computers, but they are used mostly for special purpose applications. In such a case additional components, modulators and demodulators, are needed to convert freely between *DC* and *AC* voltages as representation of the problem variables.

One interesting form of electrical analog computers has to be mentioned, namely, the repetitive computer. In this type of computer the solution of the problem, which is restricted to a finite time interval, is repeated at a high rate, high enough to be presented on a normal electronic oscilloscope. This can be done by using a proper time scale. Of course, special components have to be designed for this purpose to meet the extremely high dynamic requirements. Computers of this type are primarily used to find qualitative quick problem solutions. They are also advantageous to find quickly a large sample of solutions in statistical investigations. However, the high precision, real-time, *DC* computer is considered representative of present day analog computation. All further discussion will therefore concentrate on this specific form of Analog Computer.

3.24. Components of the DC Analog Computer

3.241. The High Gain Amplifier. It has already been pointed out that the high gain amplifier is the most important building block in *DC* analog computation. By its very action it serves to make all computing processes more accurate and independent from each other. But to be able to do this the high gain amplifier must be able to meet a set of very stringent requirements. They are the following:

a) Extremely high gain. Gain values up to the order of 10^8 are common in modern amplifiers.

b) Minimization of Drift. Drift is a complex combination of influences from different sources, but it is common practice to refer to it as being originated at the grid point of the first tube. It is possible today to obtain drift values of 100 microvolts, or smaller, in one 8-hour period, in an amplifier configuration with an effective gain of 1. In an integrator, the drift can be kept smaller than 0.1 V per hour.

c) A wide pass band extending from zero frequency to sufficiently high frequencies. The high frequency limit depends on the way of operation. It is usual to define it for feedback conditions which would reduce the effective gain to 1. Under such conditions the frequency response of modern amplifiers is flat within 1 *db* and does not exceed a phase shift of 1° up to more than 10 *KC*.

d) Stability under all foreseeable feedback and loading conditions. This requirement is fundamental but is difficult to meet. The means to provide stability are proper compensation networks, the tolerances of which must be carefully considered.

e) Minimization of noise. Great care must be taken to reduce the effective noise to its theoretical minimum. Values achieved in modern amplifiers are less than 10 microvolts rms, referred to the grid of the first tube.

f) Sufficient output power. Modern amplifiers are capable of delivering 20 mA at the peak value of the output voltage, namely, 100 volts.

There are two basic operational principles which can be used in the design of a *DC* amplifier. One is the direct coupling principle. This design is sensitive to drift. Improvements are made by using bridge balance circuits and stabilized power supplies. The other is the auxiliary carrier principle in which the original *DC* variable is modulated on a carrier, amplified, and demodulated. This principle is essentially drift free, since the drift components originating in the amplifier itself are outside the pass band of the system, but there are limitations with respect to the frequency range of the variables. Obviously, the frequency of the variable must be small with respect to the frequency of the auxiliary carrier and the carrier frequency must be selected in such a way that adequate precision modulators and demodulators can be made available. Modern amplifiers use a combination of both principles as shown in Fig. 13. Here (1) is the direct coupled part, (2) is the *AC* amplifier part, (3) and (4) the modulator and demodulator, including the auxiliary carrier source, (5) a coupling stage, (6) are blocking capacitors which prevent DC currents from passing in and out from the AC amplifier, and (7) is a filter to eliminate the ripples after demodulation. Normally (1) has a gain of 10^5 and (2) a gain of 10^3. So the total gain at DC and low frequencies is approximately 10^8 and at higher frenquecies about 10^5. The sensitive parts in such an amplifier are the modulator and demodulator. The modulator must be free from spurious offset voltages and must be well shielded to avoid induction of carrier components which would yield unwanted demodulation products. The best components which are presently available are mechanical devices. They are either vibrating relays, so called choppers, or rotating mechanical switches which can be used in common for a group of amplifiers. Normally, carrier frequencies around 100 cycles are used in the chopper system and frequency lower than 10 cycles for the rotation switch system. Fig. 14 and 15 show examples of practical amplifiers.

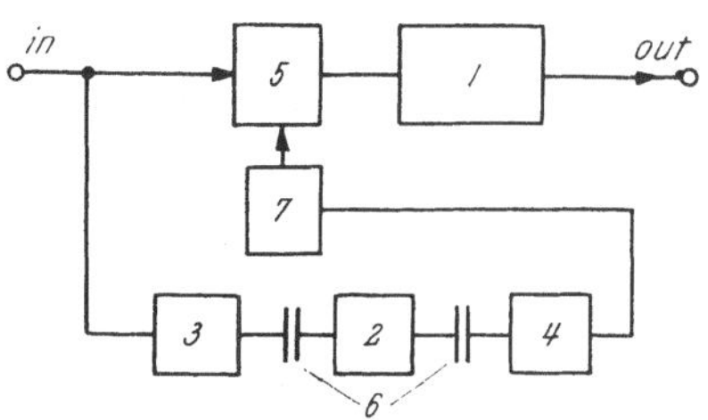

Fig. 13. Block Diagram of High Gain Amplifier

It was already pointed out that these high gain amplifiers are operated in a feedback arrangement to perform the desired computation processes. Fig. 16 shows the basic arrangement. The triangular symbol represents the high gain amplifier with gain, a, as it was described in the block diagram of Fig. 12. The $\{0\}$ represent admittances which operate on the input and output voltages and produce the currents, i_i and i_f. The outputs of the two operational networks are connected to the input point of the high gain amplifier or the "summing point". Due to the high gain, the voltage, e', which is required to produce the desired output voltage, e_0, is very small. In approximative descriptions of the process it is normally assumed that e' is equal to zero, or, that the two currents, i_i and i_f, which flow to the summing point, are equal. Based on such an approximation, equation (9) describes the input-output relation for the overall combination.

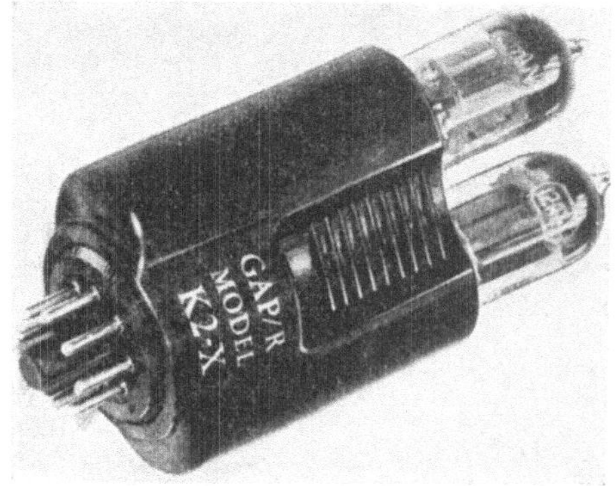

a

b

Fig. 14. Versatile High Gain Amplifier (George A. Philbrick Researches, Inc.)
a) DC Amplifier Part
b) AC Amplifier Part with Chopper

$$\begin{aligned} e' &= 0 \\ i_i + i_f &= 0 \\ e_i \{0_i\} + e_0 \{0_f\} &= 0 \end{aligned} \qquad \frac{e_0}{e_i} = -\frac{\{0_i\}}{\{0_f\}} \tag{9}$$

It is seen that this input-output relation is defined only by the operational networks. The sacrifice in effective gain is traded for an increasing independence on the properties of the amplifier itself. This in turn explains why the in-

Fig. 15. Dual High Gain Amplifier with Common Chopper (Donner Scientific Company)

put-output relation of such a feedback device is practically independent of the loading conditions. Despite the reduction of gain of the amplifier itself due to finite loads, the effective gain of the complete circuit is practically not affected.

In consideration of the feedback properties the discussion of the main linear computing components can concentrate on the properties of the operational admittances.

In the cases of sign changer, adder, and amplifier the admittances are of the form $\frac{1}{R}$ (see Fig. 16, b and c). So, the overall gain is described by the equation:

$$i_f + \Sigma i_i = 0$$

$$e_0 = - R_f \, \Sigma \frac{e_i}{R_i} \tag{10}$$

For the sign changer the two resistors are of the same value, usually about one Megohm. In the case of the amplifier the two resistors are selected in such a way as to yield the desired gain factor.

In all these cases the accuracy is defined by the properties of the resistors. The techniques to build precision resistors at reasonable cost are quite advanced. They are of the wire wound type, have small capacitances and small inductances. Temperature influences are kept under control by making the temperature coefficients of the resistors as equal as possible. In addition, these resistors are normally mounted in a temperature controlled environment, the "ovens", where temperature is kept constant within small tolerances.

Aging effects are greatly reduced by subjecting the resistors to a number of temperature and load "cycles" before they are built in.

With all these precautions it is now possible to keep the long term error in resistance smaller than 10^{-4} of the nominal value.

In integrators, the feedback admittance is of the form ωC (see Fig. 16d).

$$C \frac{d e_0}{dt} + \frac{e_i}{R_i} = 0;$$

$$e_0 = - \frac{1}{C R_i} \int e_i \, dt + e_0(0) \tag{11}$$

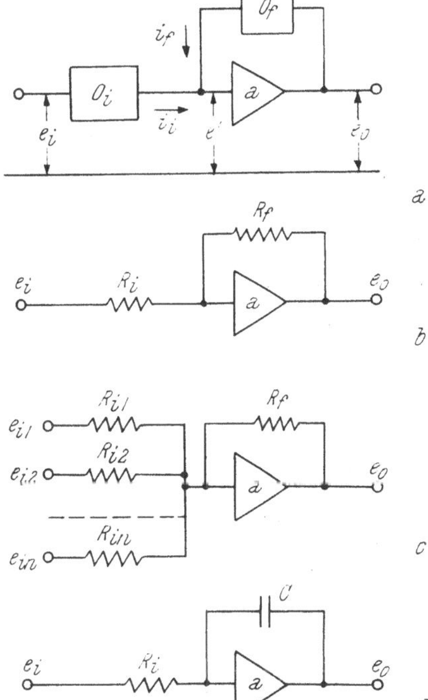

Fig. 16. Operational Combinations with High Gain Amplifier

a) Basic Principle
b) Operational Amplifier, Sign Changer
c) Summer
d) Integrator

To build highly precise capacitors is extremely difficult. However, by mounting the capacitors in a temperature oven and by subjecting them to temperature and load cycles before installation, the errors in capacity can be reduced to smaller than 10^{-4} of the nominal value. But there is an additional requirement for these capacitors, namely, an extremely high leakage resistance. In performing a computation process it is frequently required to "hold" the computation for a certain time in order to study and to read out the previous results. During such an interval the capacitor must maintain its charge within a very high degree of accuracy. Discharging influences originating in the connected circuitry are compensated by the feedback action. But the internal discharge of the capacitor must be kept within required tolerances.

3.242. Attenuators. Potentiometers are used to establish coefficients smaller than 1. They are normally of the multi-turn type and have high linearity and high resolution. However, they operate into finite loads and the loading reactions have to be considered in order to establish the coefficients with the required accuracy. To reduce such loading effects, the output of a potentiometer is usually connected to the input of an operational amplifier. But since the input impedance of an operational amplifier is finite (see Fig. 16), a high accuracy adjustment of a coefficient potentiometer must be performed under given load conditions. This is done by connecting the potentiometer and its load to a high precision bridge network into which the desired coefficient value is preset.

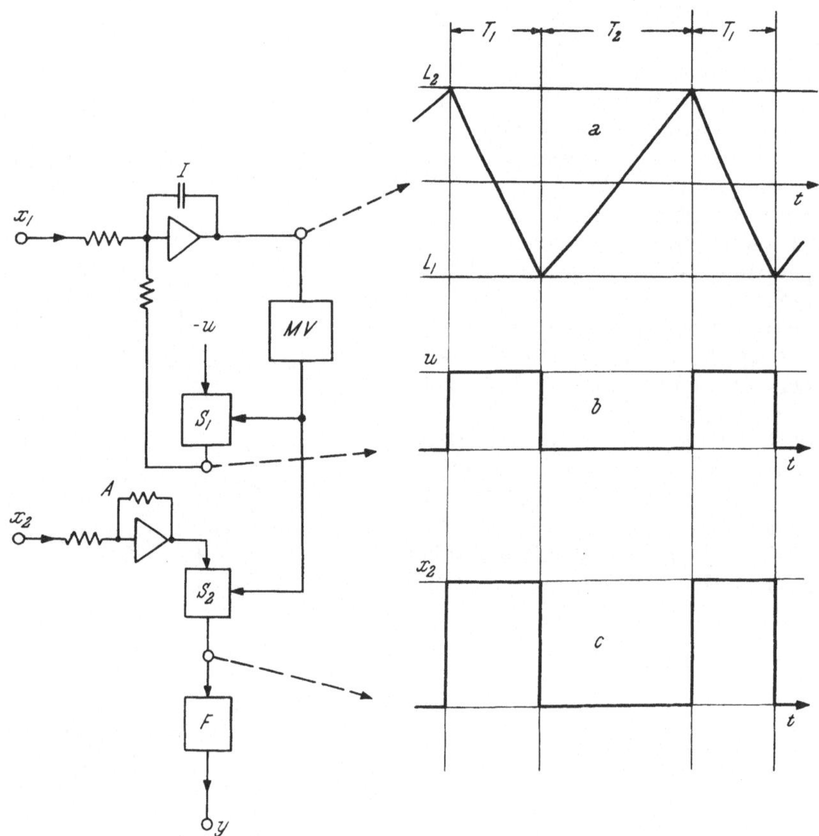

Fig. 17. Time Division Multiplier. Basic Block Diagram and Waveforms

3.243. Time Division Multiplier. The time division multipliers belong to the class which was formerly identified as modulation multipliers. Specifically, they make use of pulse width and pulse amplitude modulation. The block diagram in Fig. 17 shows the basic principles in a simplified form. It is convenient to begin the explanation with the waveform, (*c*), which is a pulse train of an amplitude which is proportional to one of the input variables, X_2. It is width-modulated by a factor, $\frac{T_1}{T_1 + T_2}$, which, in turn, is proportional to the other input variable,

X_1. The width modulation is achieved by the action of the electronic switch, S_2, which is open in one of the two stable states of the multivibrator, MV. The switching sequence is generated in a loop consisting of integrator, I, multivibrator, MV, and electronic switch, S_1. Wave (a), the integrator output, rises during the time interval, T_2, from the level, L_1, at which MV closes the switches, S_1 and S_2, to the level, L_2, at which MV opens the switches. During this interval only the input variable, X_1, is feeding into the integrator, therefore

$$T_2 = K \cdot \frac{1}{X_1} \tag{12}$$

During the time interval, T_1, the auxiliary constant voltage, $-u$, is connected to the integrator input in addition to X_1 so that

$$T_1 = K \cdot \frac{1}{u - X_1} \tag{13}$$

From (12) and (13) it is found

$$\frac{T_1}{T_1 + T_2} = \frac{X_1}{u} \tag{14}$$

The average value of wave (c), designated as $\bar{c}$, consequently is

$$\bar{c} = \frac{X_1 X_2}{u} \tag{15}$$

It is proportional to the desired product and it is only necessary to remove the ac-components of wave (c) by the low pass filter, F, in order to obtain the output, Y. This filter must be designed to suppress the ac-components sufficiently in order to get a ripple-free output. On the other hand, its pass-band must be wide enough to provide sufficient dynamic accuracy of the multiplier. Most multipliers provide the "slaving" feature for economic reasons. If a number of products have one variable in common, then the circuit producing the switching sequence, (I, MV, S_1), is used commonly to control the switches S_2.

Present multiplier designs use pulse repetition frequencies, f_r, between 10 KC and 20 KC which allows adequate filters with a phase-shift of about one degree at 100 cps. It will be noted that this carrier frequency, f_r, to which the modulation processes are applied is not of constant value:

$$f_r = \frac{1}{T_1 + T_2} = \frac{X_1 (u - X_1)}{K \cdot u} \tag{16}$$

This variability is of no consequence, as long as a certain minimum value of f_r given by the filter characteristics and the ripple requirements for Y is provided. But this can be achieved only if an additional auxiliary voltage is introduced which prevents f_r from becoming too small for small values of the variable x_1. Furthermore, this auxiliary voltage makes a "four quadrant" operation of the multiplier possible. However, it gives rise to undesired product terms, which have to be eliminated by proper compensation. So, the final component is an intricate device and its detailed description would exceed the scope of this book.

The high accuracy goal (about one part in 10,000) imposes high quality requirements on the parts of the multiplier. Specifically, the switching techniques in the multivibrator and the electronic switches present difficulties. Switching levels must be extremely well defined and constant and the transient times of the switches must be extremely short. But the electronic time division multipliers, which are presently available from different manufacturers, are of high quality and reliability and constitute important and valuable computer components. Fig. 18 shows a practical electronic multiplier. The economy of

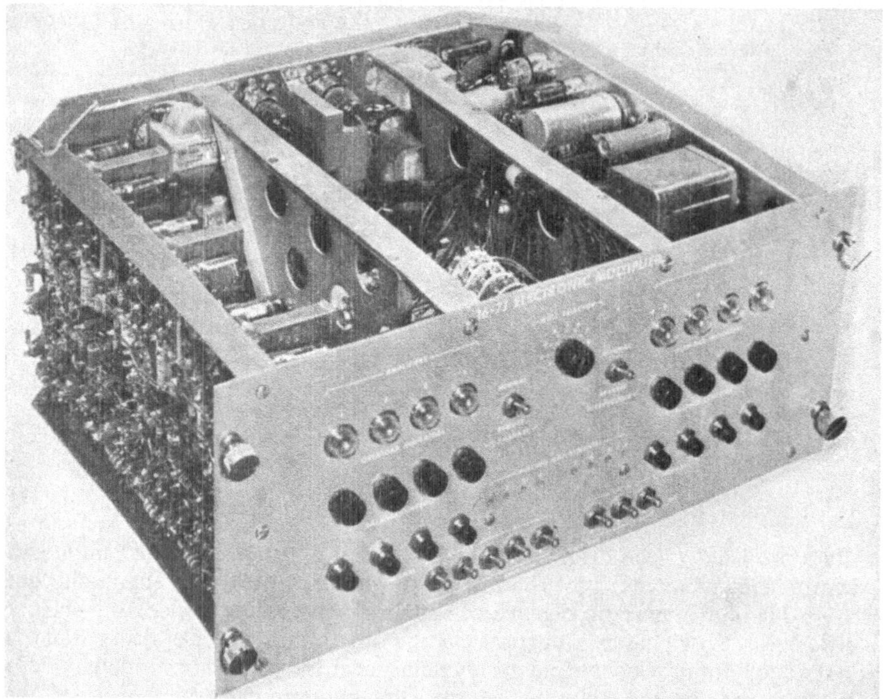

Fig. 18. Electronic Time Division Multiplier (Electronic Associates, Inc.)

most commercially available components is increased by making the built-in high gain amplifiers available for other computation purposes if the multiplier is not needed.

3.244. Diode Function Generator. The basic property of diodes, namely, to be conductive in certain voltage ranges and non-conductive in others, makes it possible to establish a great variety of functions consisting of straight line segments. Fig. 19 shows a basic functional element. It has to be pointed out, that the configuration shown was selected because it is well suited to demonstrate the basic concepts of diode function generation. It is not optimal and in fact has many practical disadvantages.

If in Fig. 19a a signal input voltage, X, is applied from a low impedance source, an output current, Y, can be drawn if the following condition is met:

$$X \geqq E \frac{r_1}{r_2} \tag{17}$$

E is the bias voltage source and voltage $X_B = E \frac{r_1}{r_2}$ is called the breakpoint voltage. Already such a single diode element is of interest, since it allows to simulate functions of practical importance. One is the so called "dead space" function. Its character and its mechanization is shown in Fig. 19b. The other one is the "limiting" or "saturation" function, its character and mechanization is shown in Fig. 19c. It will be noted, that in both cases the same diode element is used. In Fig. 19b it is placed in the input path of an operational amplifier and in Fig. 19c in the feedback path. In Fig. 19b an input current to the summing point can flow only if $X > X_B$ and only under this condition a finite output voltage is obtained. In Fig. 19c an additional feedback current flows if $Y > Y_B$. Under this condition the feedback resistor, R_f, is shunted by the impedance of the diode. Since this is normally very small with

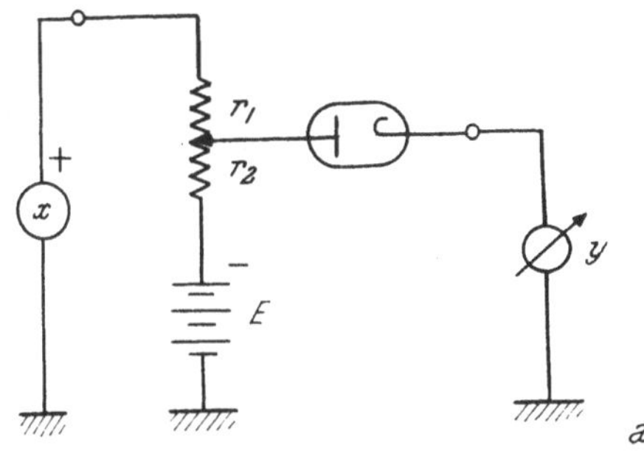

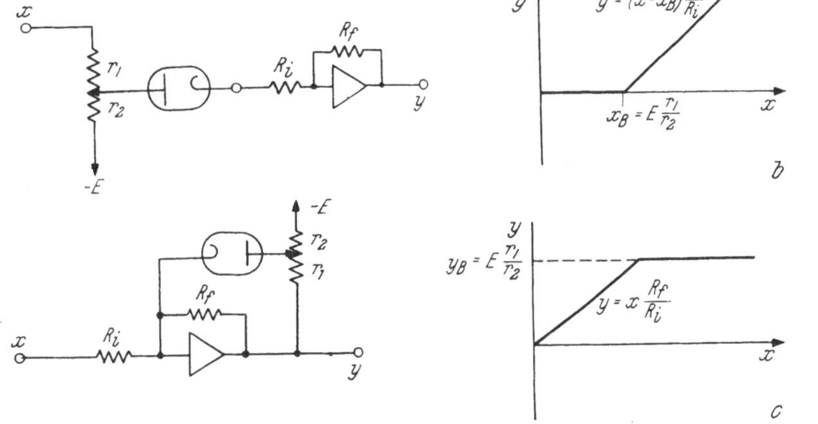

Fig. 19. Diode Function Element

a) Basic Principle
b) Applied to Simulation of "Dead Space" Function
c) Applied to Simulation of Saturation Function

respect to the input resistor, R_i, the effective gain of the amplifier approaches zero. The possibility of generating these two different functions with the same functional element is another example of the operational flexibility provided by the high gain amplifier.

The functions discussed so far have a single breakpoint and only a single diode element is necessary to simulate them. If a multitude of such diode elements is properly combined, it is possible to simulate functions with many breakpoints connected by straight lines. Such an arrangement, properly known as Diode Function Generator, is shown in Fig. 20, again in a severely simplified form. Here, n diode elements are connected in parallel. Each of them has a potentiometer to adjust its individual breakpoint and a variable resistor to adjust the individual current flowing into the summing point of the amplifier. An example for the synthesis of a function is worked out in Fig. 20 and is essentially self-explanatory. It has to be noted that the capability of the simple device shown is restricted to operation with positive input voltages and to positive slopes of the function. The extension to operation with negative inputs and negative slopes is considered as a routine design problem. The practical solutions are of great variety and their presentation would exceed the scope of this discussion.

The functions which can be generated with the Diode Function Generator consist of straight line segments. Since most functions to be simulated are contin-

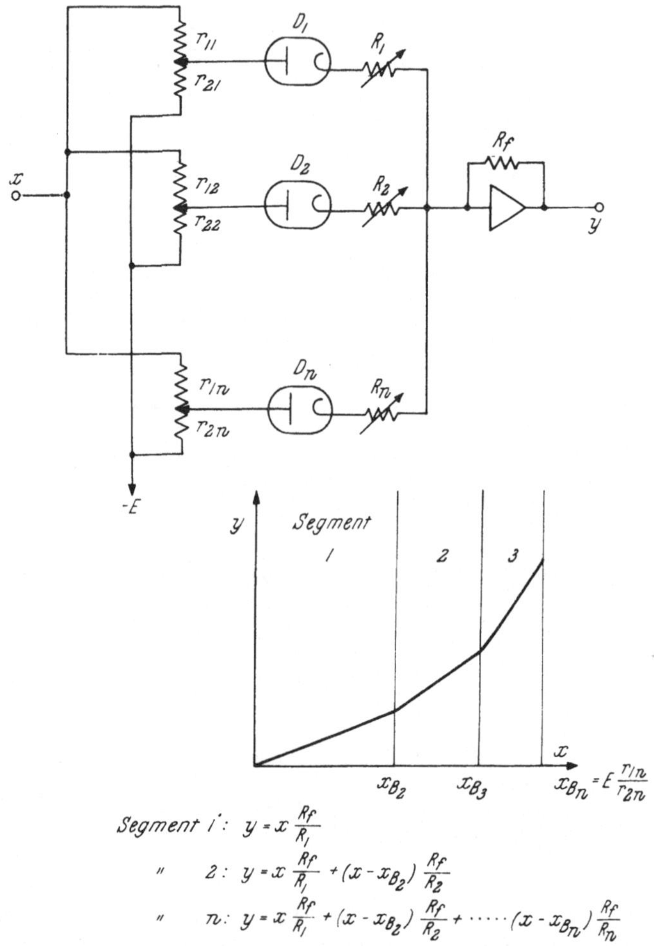

Fig. 20. Principle of Diode Function Generator

uous it is only possible to approximate them. The first step in any simulation then has to be a decision how to distribute the available diode segments in an optimum fashion. Practical function generator units consist of about 20 segments which can be considered to be sufficient for most purposes. Quite definitely a wide variety of empirical functions in technical problems are defined and known only to a limited degree of accuracy. Thus, limitations in the means of approximating such functions are really not too severe. What counts is a sufficient stability of a function which is once established. This is important in order to obtain repeatable solutions of a problem. It is specifically important in statistical investigations, where a great number of computer runs has to be performed and erratic contributions to the variance of the answer have to be kept at a minimum.

The repeatability error of modern function generators is in the order of 0.1% of the maximum function value.

The discussion so far assumed ideal diodes, i.e. diodes the internal impedance of which jumps from infinity to a low finite and constant value at a defined

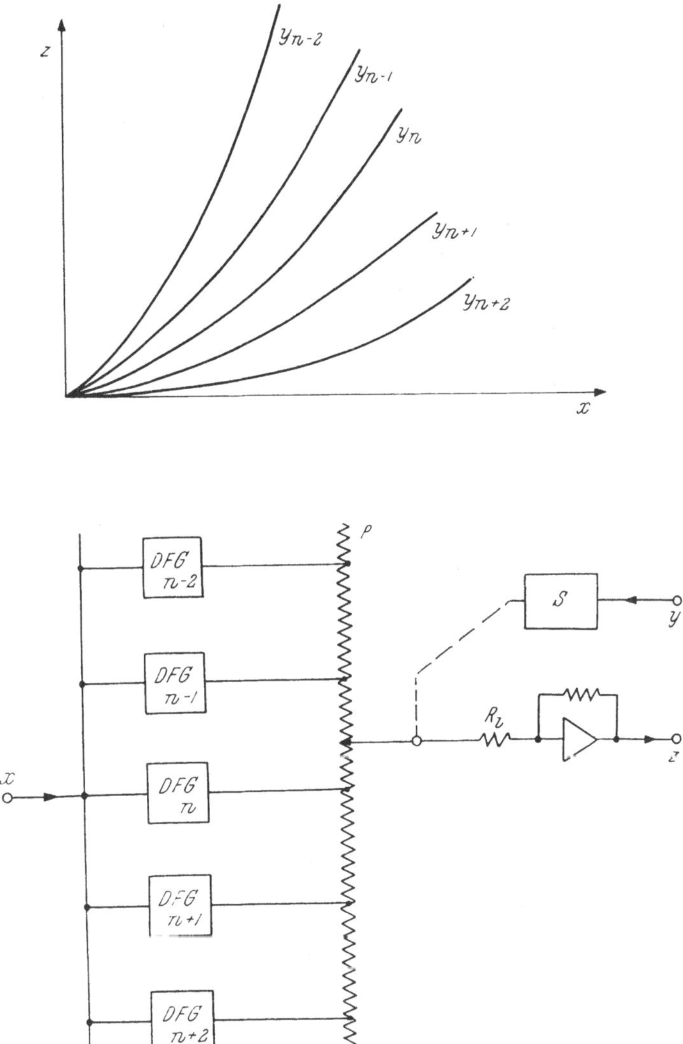

Fig. 21. Generator for Functions of Two Variables Using the Interpolation Method

voltage. The actual "rounding off" of the diode characteristic around the breakpoint is a phenomenon which is generally advantageous in the approximation of continuous functions. It leads to a function in which the transition from one segment to the next is continuous. Since it is difficult to predict this effect, the final polishing in the setting of a function is a trial and error procedure. The function actually obtained has to be compared to the desired one and breakpoints and slopes habe to be readjusted empirically in order to obtain an optimum approximation.

The described technique of function generation with diodes can be extended to cases where the output variable is a function of two input variables:

$$Z = f(X, Y) \tag{18}$$

Many approaches are possible. A straight-forward approach is an interpolation method. It has the advantage that it can be set up from existing one-variable function generators. But its accuracy is limited since a close match to the functional relationship in each of the variables requires a considerable amount of equipment and care in setting up the functions. Fig. 21 describes the principles of the interpolation method.

Each of the single-variable function generators DFG_n represents the functions $Z = f(X)|_y$ for a fixed Y-value. The staggering must be close enough to provide sufficient matching in the relationship $Z = f(Y)|_x$. The outputs of the individual function generators are connected to taps of the potentiometer, P. Its ends are open and its wiper is brought into a position which is proportional to the variable, Y, by the servo, S. Linear interpolation between taps is achieved if the output

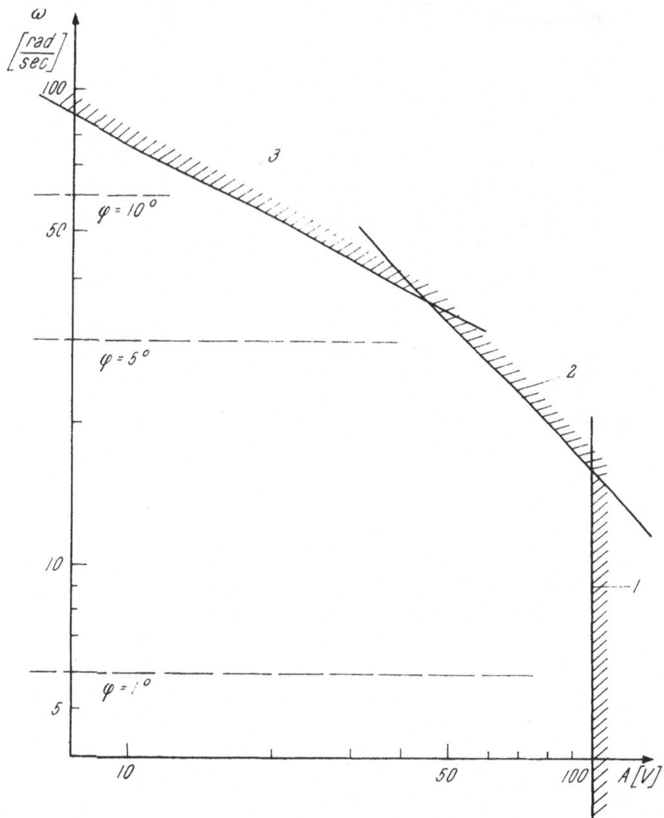

Fig. 22. Performance Limitation of a Servo by Saturation Effects

impedances of the individual function generators are small and the load impedance, R_l, is large with respect to the resistance of one segment of the potentiometer, P.

3.245. Electromechanical Devices. The common feature of these computer components is the fact that their input variable is a mechanical quantity, namely, an angular position, and their output variable an electrical quantity, a voltage. The components in question are linear potentiometers which are used for multiplication, tapped potentiometers used for the generation of arbitrary functions and potentiometers with special windings used as resolvers. Another important example are synchros. Their output is an *AC* voltage, related by a sine function to the shaft position. Since the general form of the variables in a *DC* analog computer are *DC* voltages, these synchros require an adequate demodulator.

These computing components, potentiometers and synchros, provide a static accuracy of better than 0.1% of the full signal value and are free from dynamic errors.

However, for all these components a servo system is needed to transform the input variable, originally given as a *DC* voltage, into an angular position. It consists of an electric motor, the servo amplifier and the follow-up potentiometer. The latter is driven by the same shaft as the computing components, it measures their angular position in form of a *DC* voltage which in turn is compared to the original input voltage. These servos are the limiting factor for the accuracy of the electro-mechanical devices. Static limitations are given by friction and by the addition of the tolerances of the computing and the follow-up potentiometers. A practical over-all figure for the static accuracy is about 0.1% of the full signal value. But the important limitation of servos are the dynamic errors. They are caused by the finite bandwidth and by saturation of the servo. The latter is a non-linear effect and makes the dynamic accuracy dependent on the magnitude and the structure of the signals to be handled. In Fig. 22 an attempt is made to describe approximatively the dynamic performance of a practical servo. It is assumed that the signals are of sinusoidal form of peak amplitude, A, measured in volts, and a frequency, ω, measured in $\frac{\text{rad}}{\text{sec}}$. The signal characteristics, A and ω, must be small with respect to the values designated by the limiting lines, 1, 2, and 3. These lines represent the saturation effects of the servo, 1, the maximum possible deflection, 2, the maximum possible velocity, and, 3, the maximum possible acceleration. If a signal which exceeds these limits is forced on the servo, severe errors will result. But even signals within these limits will be subjected to linear dynamic errors which result from the finite bandwidth of the servo. These linear errors are described in terms of phase shift, as indicated by the horizontal lines in Fig. 22.

3.3. The DC Analog Computer System

3.31. The Patchboard

This chapter will describe the steps and considerations which are necessary to combine computing components into a useful and effective computer system. As pointed out previously (see 3.232), this discussion of Analog Computers will concentrate on "general purpose" installations. In the "special purpose" case, the components required to perform the computation processes are selected and assembled in an optimal and fixed fashion. But in the general purpose case one must be prepared to deal with problems of different character, size, and complexity. Besides the necessity of providing components sufficient in number and diversity for all foreseeable problems, it is necessary to select and combine them properly for any given problem. It may seem to be superfluous to emphasize such a requirement, since the task to connect electrical components in a desired way quite certainly constitutes no major technical problem. But in order to work efficiently with the computer the problem deserves some consideration. The present solution is the patchboard. It is a plugboard on which all the leads to the computing components are terminated and can be connected by plug-in cables. Such a patchboard is the heart of general purpose analog computers. It is the manifestation of the basic principle, namely, that a selection of different process components is available and that they can be combined at will in such a way as to give a simulation of the actual problem under study. The following points of view have to be considered in the design and lay-out of a patchboard:

a) Electrical interactions between the great number of cables concentrated on the patchboard area have to be avoided. Since the circuits involved are mainly of high impedance this is achieved by electro-static shielding.

Fig. 23. Exchangeable Patchboard (Electronic Associates, Inc.)

b) Provisions have to be made to avoid involuntary short circuits if connections are changed when the computer is in operation.

c) The connections on the patchboard should define uniquely the computer set-up. This is not quite possible, since the adjustments of the various coefficient potentiometers and function generators, which are a part of the characteristics of the problem, are not represented on the patchboard. However, switching of any kind in the computer components themselves should be avoided.

d) The grouping of component terminals on the patchboard should be clear and systematic to avoid errors during the patching of a problem. Since present patchboards have about 3000 terminals this problem is obviously an acute one. A favored solution is the combination of terminals of equal meaning, e.g. input terminals of electronic multipliers, in areas of a certain color.

e) Routine connections, such as combining a high gain amplifier with resistors or capacitors for operation as an operational amplifier or as an integrator, should be as straight forward as possible.

f) Crowding of connecting cables should be avoided in order to facilitate the check-out of a problem set-up. This requires careful consideration of the size of the patchboard.

g) Sufficient terminals for connections to input-output equipment, to other computers or to external components which might be incorporated in the computing process must be provided.

One feature which is of high practical importance is incorporated in most present machines, namely, the exchangeability of patchboards. It permits to remove the complete patchboard carrying all plugged-in connections and thus to preserve the problem configuration for possible later use. Also, it makes it possible to prepare a set-up on such a removable patchboard while the computer is used for the solution of another problem. This feature increases the efficiency of computer operation significantly.

Fig. 23 shows a practical patchboard arrangement.

3.32. Reference Supply and Precision Divider

The components of the computer which represent the actual physical process operate on certain input signals and produce output signals. These signals are the representation of the behavior of the system under investigation. It was pointed out that in the *DC* analog computer these signals have the form of *DC* voltages, independent of the physical phenomenon they represent. So, an essential part of a computer system is a voltage source from which the actuating signals are derived. Actuating signals in this definition are the ones which represent the forcing functions and the initial conditions of the differential equations describing the problem under study. This voltage source is known as "reference supply". It produces a fixed positive and an equal negative voltage of an amount which can be handled by the computing components without overloading or overdriving them. In most present installations this voltage is ± 100 Volt. Actual signals are defined and measured as fractions of this reference voltage. Thus, the use of voltmeters with a high absolute accuracy can be avoided. The measurement of a signal voltage is performed by comparing it to another voltage which is derived from a precision divider. Such precision dividers are built with a better accuracy than voltmeters at a cheaper price. In present installations dividers with an accuracy of about 0.01% are customary.

However, the method of relative definition of the signal voltages implies the necessity of providing a constant reference voltage. This is because readings are taken at different times and fluctuations of the reference voltage would produce erroneous transient signals. In actual installations the reference source is a *DC* power supply with a fast acting regulation, maintaining a constant voltage within 0.01% of the nominal value.

3.33. Input and Output Equipment

The task of generating input signals of an arbitrary form and of reading out the results of the computation process, the output signals, requires special equipment. The simplest input components are coefficient potentiometers, which are used to define the initial conditions for the integrators and, in combination with relays or switching devices, such fundamental forcing functions as steps or approximated impulses. The "ramp function"

$$\begin{aligned} x(t) &= a \cdot t \quad \text{for } t > 0 \\ &= 0 \qquad \text{for } t < 0 \end{aligned} \tag{19}$$

can be generated by integrating a unit step. The means for producing another important class of functions, sinusoidal waves, are normally available in every laboratory. In addition, it is possible to generate precisely defined sine and cosine waves with computer components. Details of such a set-up will be explained later. Another important class of forcing functions which become increasingly of interest in system analytical studies are random signals. Their fundamental form is the "white noise" function. White noise generators are commercially available. In selecting them, care has to be taken that the produced noise band not only covers completely but exceeds significantly the frequency band of the system under study. With such white noise generators it is straight forward to produce random functions of any desired spectral composition by adequate filtering. It is frequently convenient to combine the necessary filter from computer components. Details of such a set up will be shown later. Certain difficulties can arise in defining quantitatively and measuring the properties of random signals. But again the computer itself provides the necessary tools. Its components can be used to establish precise squaring, integrating and averaging circuits.

The means described so far are adequate to generate certain fundamental forms of forcing functions. However, it is frequently necessary to make functions of arbitrary type available, which may be analytically defined or empirically given. For this purpose, function generators or curve followers as they were described before can be used. Since for most of these functions the independent variable is time, an input voltage to these input devices must be provided which is proportional to time. This again can be achieved by using an integrator. Its input must be a unit step which occurs at $t = 0$.

The task of output equipment is to present the result of the computing process, or, in other words, to read out the solution of the problem under study. In many cases it is sufficient to determine the value of certain problem variables at a predefined instant of time, or, if any other variable reaches a predefined value. To do this it is necessary to stop the computing process at the proper time and have all integrators hold the values of their output variable which they attained at this instant. The stopping of the computing process can be achieved by using diode elements of the kind as described in 3.244. A switching mechanism is activated if the preset breakpoint voltage of the diode is exceeded. This breakpoint voltage represents either the instant of time or the value of any variable at which termination of the computing process is desired. Special components for this purpose are available under different designations (Comparators, relay amplifiers). The circuitry required to hold the integrator outputs will be described later. The readout of the output signals under these circumstances is a simple task. The method described in 3.32 or a sufficiently accurate voltmeter can be used. A device which is used more and more for this purpose is the digital voltmeter. It presents the measured value in numerical form, usually in 4 decimal places, see Fig. 24. Its principle is to balance the voltage to be measured by a voltage derived by an automatic switching device from a group of precision decade dividers which are fed by the reference voltage. The positioning of the switching devices is displayed and can also be used for automatic readout, as will be explained later.

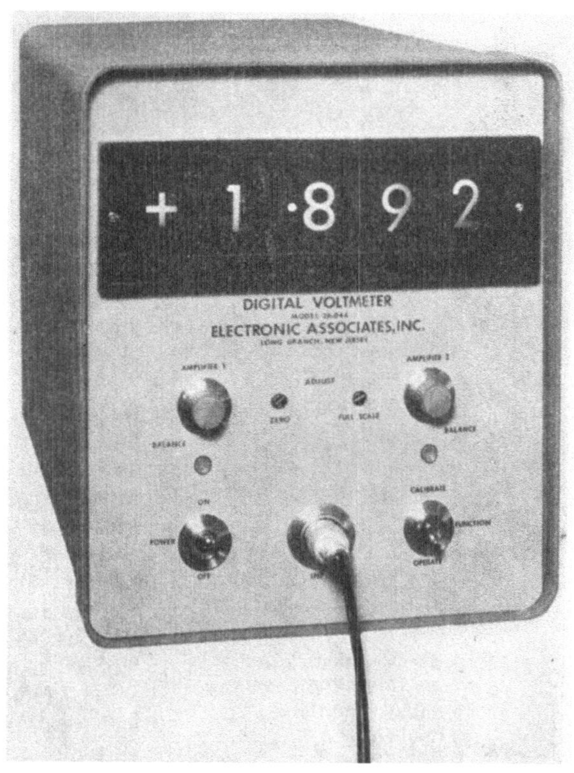

Fig. 24. Digital Voltmeter (Electronic Associates, Inc.)

But in the majority of cases the readout of terminal values is not sufficient. It is usually important to know the behavior of the system under study during the whole process in order to draw the necessary conclusions. One way to achieve this is to record the variables of interest as functions of time. Such recorders are well known devices. The paper is shifted continuously at a constant rate, proportional to time. A writing pen is deflected proportionally to the quantity to be recorded. A great variety of such recorders are commercially available. In most cases they are built as multi-channel recorders, permitting the observation of several quantities at the same time on the same paper. This is an important feature, since frequently the interrelations between several variables have to be studied. To facilitate such interrelation studies, special devices have been developed, which permit to plot one variable as a function of another one (see Fig. 10). The static accuracy of recorders and plotters does not quite match that of the computing components. It is in the order of 0.1% of full scale. In addition there are limitations due to the dynamic performance of the pen drives. But they are not too serious, since these dynamic errors do not affect the stability margin of the system under investigation. However, all these errors have to be considered carefully in the evaluation of a solution.

3.34. Operational Modes

The previous discussion indicated that it is necessary to provide certain special modes of operation, e.g. to stop the computing process and have the integrators hold the output values they attained at this instant. The major operational modes which have to be provided are the following:

a) Standby: Plate voltages are removed and the reference voltage is disconnected from the computing circuit. This mode is used during the warm-up period of the machine and to make changes in the computer set-up safely.

b) Initial Conditions (Reset): The reference voltage is connected and the components are operative with the exception of the integrators. Their circuit is changed in such a way that they do not react to input voltages but that the feedback capacitor can be charged to a voltage which represents the initial conditions of the integrator. The configuration is shown in Fig. 25a. The resistors, R_1 and R_2, are equal and so the output voltage, e_0, will be equal to $-e_{ic}$, the defined initial condition voltage.

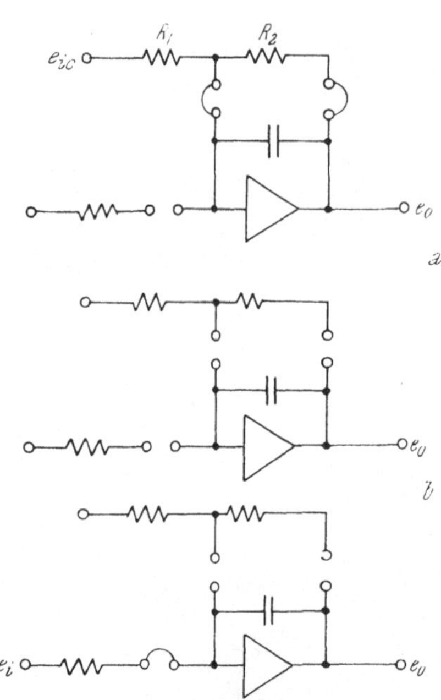

Fig. 25. Basic Operational Modes of an Integrator
a) Initial Conditions
b) Hold
c) Operate

c) Operate: The initial condition circuit, R_1 and R_2, is disconnected and the summing point of the amplifier is reconnected to its input e_i. The integrators react now to the input voltages and the given initial conditions, this is the mode of computation (see Fig. 25c).

d) Hold: To stop the computation process, the summing point of the integrator amplifier is disconnected from its input. Since no current flows into the summing point from the input, the current from the feedback path must be zero by necessity, i. e. the feedback capacitor cannot change its charge. However, changes in charge can be caused by the internal leakage of the capacitor, as described in 3.241.

The Hold-mode is not only important for terminal readout purposes, which were discussed before. Another important application is to stop the computing process at a predetermined time, to reset coefficients and then to continue the computation. The purpose of such a scheme will be better understood when problem scaling will be discussed. It is mainly used to provide optimum scale factors during the whole computation. Such a change in scale factor requires that the results of the first interval of computation be read out, and, after resetting coefficients, the machine be brought in the initial condition mode to insert new initial conditions which represent the previous results under the changed scale factors. This is quite a tedious procedure and can be facilitated by using storage integrators. The required mode interactions are elaborate and detailed description would exceed the framework of this presentation.

These fundamental operational modes are normally provided in every installation. The necessary circuit switching is performed by relays which in turn are controlled from an operation switch or push buttons located on the main control panel. In addition, it is possible to control these relays from other command sources. An example for this was discussed before, namely, to bring the machine into "Hold" if a predetermined level is reached by one of the variables. Another example is to stop the computing process at a predetermined time by a signal derived from a preset time counter. Or the machine can be made to go automatically through a complete mode cycle in a repetitive way. This is important if a large sample of measurements has to be made in a statistical investigation or to display the computer solution on an oscilloscope. All this requires additional relay circuitry which is available in most large scale computers. Quite frequently more operational modes are provided in addition to the fundamental ones discussed above. They are mostly concerned with special check-out procedures. The philosophy of problem check-out will be discussed in 3.4. If special check-out modes are provided, they constitute an automatization of the respective procedures. The necessary relay circuitry is involved and adapted to the specific system.

3.35. Auxiliary Equipment

In order to make a computer system operable and complete, certain additional components are indispensable. They are:

a) Power Supplies: They are of the conventional type, regulated to the extent required by the properties of the computing components. In large installations with high utilization factors, emergency supplies are quite frequently provided which automatically take over if power delivery fails. It is especially important not to interrupt the heating of the temperature ovens, since it takes a long time before they attain the prescribed temperature. Another supply feature is to provide means which allow to increase the filament voltage slowly from zero to its operating value when the computer is turned on. Thus, the life expectancy of vacuum tubes is considerably increased.

b) Temperature Ovens: They house the passive high precision computing components and normally maintain a constant temperature within better than $\pm 1^\circ$ F. They have to be in operation permanently to avoid temperature cycles which would deteriorate the computer components.

c) Air Cooling: As long as the active computer components are equipped with vacuum tubes a carefully planned cooling system is necessary. The planning considerations are the same as with all electronic equipment. A specific point of view which should be kept in mind is to reduce to a minimum the noise which unfortunately is a by-product of many cooling installations. A computer room is an area where highest mental concentration is required and air cooler noise is specifically annoying under these circumstances.

In addition to the essential auxiliary equipment discussed above there is a feature in most computers which is not directly necessary for its operation, but which increases the reliability of the operation considerably. This is the overload indicator. Its purpose is to give a warning indication, if the signal voltage on any of the active components exceeds a limit beyond which linear operation is not guaranteed any longer and errors will result. This limit is usually between 100 and 150 volts. Despite great care in scaling of a problem it frequently happens that such overloads occur. Without the warning system they probably would remain unnoticed and would cause errors in the computation. With the overload system, however, the operator can always be assured that the scaling of a problem does not lead to overdriving a component.

In one of the modern large scale installations an additional provision is made. It is the "Minimum Excursion Indicator", the purpose of which is to check all component outputs continuously and to warn automatically if any of the signals involved do not exceed a certain minimum value during a complete computer run. This assures the operator that the scaling provides an adequate signal to noise level. So these two devices, overload indicator and minimum excursion indicator, are valuable tools to correct a scaling scheme empirically and to obtain maximum computing accuracy.

3.36. Labor Saving Devices

The general trend to relieve human operators from routine functions by performing them automatically is also gaining momentum in the field of operating Analog Computers. Some of the features which were already discussed quite certainly are of such a nature, but the subsystems to be described in this paragraph are distinct and more comprehensive. They have two main tasks: To assist the operator in setting up the computer and in the readout of results. In addition they provide documents on each step which was performed. This latter feature certainly is important, particularly in installations with highly efficient operation. There a problem investigation is frequently interrupted for evaluation of the previous results and it is desired to use the computer in the meantime for the evaluation of another problem. The patchboards with the plugged in connection cables are removed and stored. The problem then can be reinserted into the machine for further investigation in a very short time, if complete and accurate documents on coefficient settings are available. The systems of different manufacturers to achieve this are different in their details and in their designations and an attempt will be made to describe their common basic features.

An automatic device for setting coefficient potentiometers consists of a servo system which is controlled by address commands to connect it mechanically to any coefficient potentiometer. This then is set to a desired value, which again is controlled by a proper value command. These commands, address and value, are generated either on a push button panel, an automatic typewriter or taken from a punched tape. Relays are used to translate the command codes into the desired actions of the servo. Since such a system can set a potentiometer decidedly faster (less than 1 sec) than a human operator with at least the same accuracy, the saving of computer time and the convenience to the operator are quite obvious. The documentation mentioned above is either given by the command tape, or, by the print-out on the automatic typewriter.

The basic element of the automatic readout system is an analog-to-digital converter, mostly a digital voltmeter as described in 3.33. It is connected by a proper address command to the output terminal of any desired computer component and its digital output in turn is printed out either on an automatic typewriter or punched on tape, together with the respective address command. Again relays are needed to perform the necessary coding and switching operation. This readout scheme assists in what was formerly called "terminal readout" for which the computer has to be in the "Hold" mode. Recorders or plotters are still needed if the complete solution function has to be known. Here also automatic devices for the operation and calibration of recorders are available.

The combined automatic setting and readout system can be extended to perform checkout operations such as gain measurements of individual amplifiers or of parts of the whole computer setup. Other features are advertised. The flexibility of these systems is high and normally a great number of labor saving functions can be programmed. Fig. 26 shows a practical installation of such automatic facilities.

Another automatic device which is discussed is a setting device for diode function generators. The techniques considered are different. One basic scheme is again the use of servos, coupled by appropriate commands to the potentiometers for setting the breakpoints and slopes of the characteristics of the diodes. Another approach uses punched cards which by direct contact control the arrangement of resistor matrices. These automatic setting devices for diode function generators promise to be an essential help in the operation of analog computers.

A much discussed problem area remains, namely, the "automation of the patchboard". It is tempting to build switching devices which connect automatically, controlled by proper commands, the necessary components to the desired computer setup. The technical means are available and well understood, but

Fig. 26. Automatic Input-Output System (Beckman/EASE Computers)

so far all attempts of mechanization resulted in much too expensive equipment. But it is questionable whether such a device is really necessary or desirable. After all, the patchboard is the most direct manifestation of the philosophy of analog computation. It represents the physical system which is available to the operator. Normally, the engineer wants to check into special problem characteristics or to modify the system configuration. All this can be done very easily by proper changes of the connections on the patchboard. But it is difficult or impossible to insert such changes into the total body of commands in an automatic device. To sacrifice the operational flexibility of the patchboard in favor of a gain in setup-speed would be justified only in a very few special cases.

3.37. Planning of Computer Systems

It certainly became evident, that a wide variety of computing components and auxiliary devices is available. In order to obtain an installation which optimally meets the individual requirements, a careful systems planning is essential. Despite the fact that manufacturers offer defined types of computers, there is still sufficient leeway to tailor an installation to specific needs. Commercial computers cover a wide range with respect to size, capabilities and accuracy, most of them adopt a "building-block" feature and most manufacturers are willing and capable of providing desired modifications. Here an attempt will be made to outline the considerations which are important for planning an Analog Computer system.

The main feature of course is the character of the problems to be solved. But another item has to be considered first and is frequently overlooked. If

Fig. 27. Small Computer, Table Model (Heathkit)

taken into account properly it may lead to entirely different basic concepts of Analog Computer installations. It is the philosophy of approach to solving scientific and engineering problems which prevail in the agency planning to use the computers. Two main trends are possible in this respect: Organizational units highly specialized in different techniques and organizational units grouped around projects (team work structure). In practical reality the organization will not be absolutely clear-cut, normally there will be some overlapping of the basic structural forms. So the answer to the questions raised in the following will be a

Fig. 28. Medium Computer, Console Model (Donner Scientific Company)

management decision. In the case of the primarily specialized organization it is logical to create a computation unit which with its special equipment and knowhow is available to solve the problems arising in any of the other units. In this case the computer installation will have to be centralized, large, flexible, highly automatized and manned with trained personnel in order to provide efficient operation. On the other hand, in an organization of prevalent team work structure, a decentralized arrangement of smaller computer units may be preferable which brings the computers as near as possible to the men who have to solve the problems. As was already pointed out, the successful operation of analog computers comes naturally to every engineer and physicist and it is always surprising what intimate understanding of a problem he can obtain if he does the computer work himself. This is significantly different from getting a formalistic answer to a specified question from people who quite naturally cannot have the profound understanding of the problem as the originating engineer himself. The decentralized approach is justified primarily in such cases where one team deals with one problem for a long time, proceeding from basic concepts to the detailed design. A computer assigned to such a team will be set up in a permanent fashion for the problem under study. It will be available to every team worker directly to answer his questions and so contribute immensely to the efficiency of the analytical work. The computer then can be considered as a special laboratory tool which is the basic philosophy of analog computation as was stated before. Of course, there are practical limitations. If the problems assigned to a team are very large and complex, the economic feasibility of the decentralized solution

Fig. 29. Medium Computer, Rack Model (Midcentury Instrumatic Corp.)

may become questionable. Another factor may be the necessity of maintaining a high degree of computer utilization. Again the decentralized installation lags in this respect. But its imponderable advantages should be weighed carefully against the possible economic disadvantages. Industry offers a wide selection of small and medium sized machines, which are very adequate for the decentral-

Fig. 30. Repetitive Computer (George A. Philbrick Researches, Inc.)

ized approach. Since most of them employ a building block principle, computer components which are not needed too frequently can be used by different teams on an exchange basis. This would permit the simulation of quite large problems in a flexible way at tolerable investment costs.

Centralized installations normally are large and comprehensive and have to be designed for maximum efficiency. This requires high flexibility in changing from the one problem to the next, avoiding idle computer time. The machine must work reliably to minimize trouble shooting time. It will be advantageous to use all available automatic features for setting, checking, programming and reading out. A strict routine maintenance scheme will have to be set up. Use should be made of test benches and other checkout facilities which permit to test and to repair computer components without interfering with the operation of the computer itself. In general, maintenance requirements are very similar to those encountered in the operation of communication equipment. This pertains to procedures, number and qualifications of personnel.

The planning of a centralized facility must be based on a sound estimate of the size and character of the problems to be solved immediately and in the future. The appraisal of the size of the expected problems is important to determine whether it will be feasible to sub-divide the installation into a number of "stations", which can be used together to solve a large problem, or, individ-

Fig. 31. Large Computer Installation (Beckman/EASE Computers)

ually to solve a number of smaller problems simultaneously. Such a station must then be capable of working as a complete, independent computer, and it must be possible to combine it with other stations for larger problems. This requires a sufficient number of connecting trunk lines and operational stability of computer components operating with such lines, which in turn implies a carefully planned grounding system. If the stations work together, it must be possible to exercise operational control over all stations from any of the other ones. In short, it will not be sufficient to merely install a conglomeration of computer components, but it is necessary to plan a system which meets the requirements optimally. Such a system quite certainly will have many features which were not mentioned but which are typical for the agency which is planning the installation and the problems which have to be solved. All of them have to be carefully considered. But the experience of computer manufacturers results in a wide variety of meticulously planned computer units which meet the requirements as building blocks for most practical computer systems.

In assessing the manpower requirements for a centralized computer installation it seems to be profitable to consider the establishment of an analytical section. It consists of engineers and scientists who are well familiar with the problems to be solved, with all details of the computers and with all pertinent analytical procedures. They are not computer operators and their task is to give advice to the users of the computers with respect to the best computational procedure and to discuss formulation and possible simplifications of the problems. They design special check procedures, analyze problem solutions and establish cross-check computations in order to clarify question areas. They have to be familiar with error-analytical methods and have to apply them as extensively as possible. This group maintains the intelligent human control over the mechanistic processes performed by a large computer installation.

Fig. 32. Large Computer Installation (Electronic Associates, Inc.)

Fig. 33. REAC Computer Installation (Reeves Instrument Corp.)

3.4. Operation of a DC Analog Computer

3.41. Introduction

The discussion so far was concerned with providing a basic understanding of analog computing techniques, of the equipment involved, and of its organization. The remaining important area to be covered now is the fruitful use of an analog computer. It is not enough to explain the operation of a computer by dicussing a few characteristic examples. This is essential and will be done. But the main intent of this discussion will be to demonstrate the fundamental simplicity of analog computation. Quite certainly, a large installation will be most efficiently operated by specialized, trained personnel, following fixed rules and procedures. However, as was emphasized already, the operation of an Analog Computer does not basically require this. Anyone with a scientific education, who is able and willing to think logically, can operate it after a surprisingly short period of familiarization. It is this ease of operation together with the contribution to a more profound understanding of the problem under study which makes the Analog Computer such an attractive tool for scientific work. This is documented by the following interesting trend: It becomes more and more common practice to describe a physical situation not by a mathematical relation but by a block diagram, specifically a block diagram of the respective analog computer setup. Despite the fact that this has only formalistic aspects, it is certainly interesting to note that the method to think in physical analoga is successfully competing with the classical method of mathematical description.

There is no absolutely optimal method of setting up a computer. Authors differ considerably in their concepts and every operator will tend to develop his personal method. What is important is strict consistency in following the rules once established. So, an attempt will be made to describe the process of handling problems on an analog computer in simple logical steps. It is not claimed that the methods presented are commonly used or that they are even valuable for efficient routine operation. But it is hoped that they will provide an understanding of Analog Computer philosophy.

3.42. Derivation of a Computer Diagram from Physical Concepts

It is possible to derive an analog computer setup directly from the physical interrelations of the problem without formulating it mathematically. This is normally not done, but since such a procedure demonstrates so clearly the principle of establishing an analogon to the real situation, the first simple example will be derived in this way.

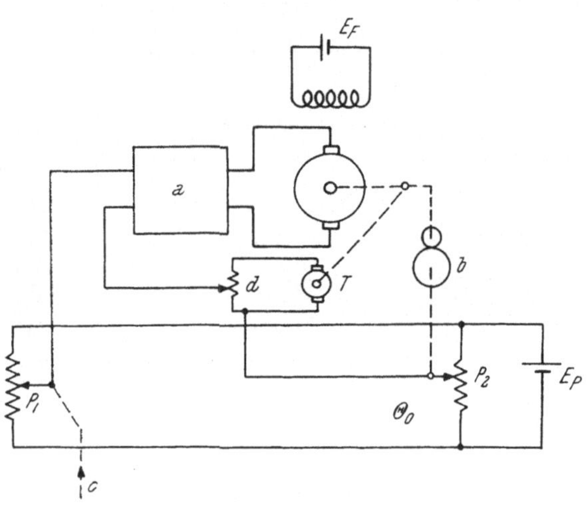

Fig. 34. Simplified Schematic Diagram of a DC Positioning Servo System

This first example is the problem of determining the optimum design of a position controlled servo system. "Optimum" may be understood as the shortest possible settling time. Any other criterion may be applied and investigated. The selection of the criterion does not reflect on the computer setup. Fig. 34 shows a general block diagram of the system to be simulated. The armature of a *DC* shunt motor is driven from a *DC*-amplifier with gain, *a*. It drives a potentiometer, P_2, over a gear train of gear ratio, *b*. The voltage derived from P_2 is deducted from the one derived from potentiometer, P_1. Its position, C, commands the position, Θ_0, of the output shaft. Both will be equal after all transients have died out. The output of a tachometer, T, is added to the difference voltage derived from C and Θ_0 and the resulting voltage is fed into the input terminals of the amplifier.

The first step is now to develop the basic computer block diagram, disregarding the quantitative values of the coefficients.

Let the computer voltage on point 1 in Fig. 35 represent the motor shaft position, Θ. Position is the integral of velocity, so we find on the input terminal

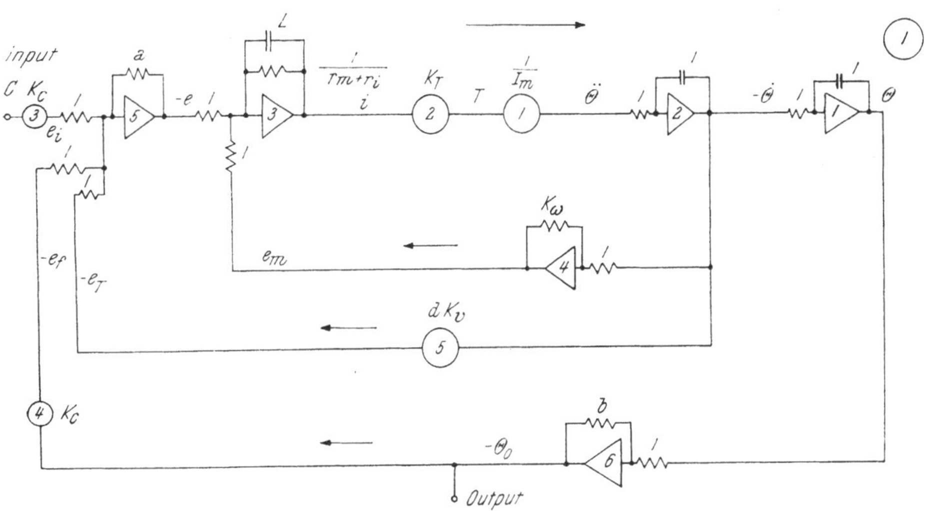

Fig. 35. Basic Computer Diagram

to integrator 1 a voltage representing $-\dot{\Theta}$. It is important to note the inverse sign relation characteristic to all circuits using high gain amplifiers. Feedback capacitor and input resistor have unity values (i.e. 1 microfarad and 1 megohm respectively). Since velocity is the integral of acceleration, the input voltage to integrator 2 represents angular acceleration, $\ddot{\Theta}$. Angular acceleration in turn is derived from the driving torque, T, by division by the moment of inertia, I_m. This is a fixed quantity, so either a coefficient potentiometer or an amplifier of fixed gain can be used to derive $\ddot{\Theta}$ from T. For the time being, coefficient potentiometer 1 is provided, it has to be adjusted to a value representing $\frac{1}{I_m}$.

The torque is produced by the current, i, through the winding of the armature. Assuming linearity of the magnetic circuit, a constant, K_T, must be given which relates current and torque: It is represented tentatively by coefficient potentiometer 2. The current is driven through the armature of the motor by a voltage e. If the armature winding were a pure inductance, L, the current-voltage relationship would be a pure integration with integration constant, $1/L$. So, integrator 3, which represents that relationship, must be set up in such a way that its integration constant, $\frac{1}{CR_i}$, must be equal to the actual constant $1/L$, or, if R_i is tentatively selected at unity, C in microfarads must be equal to the Henry value of L. But the inductance is not pure, there is a total resistance,

$r = r_m + r_i$, in the actual circuit, r_m being the resistance of the winding and r_i the output resistance of the amplifier. So, for a given fixed voltage, e, the current cannot integrate to infinity but reaches a maximum value, $i = \frac{e}{r_m + r_i}$. Therefore, integrator 3 must obtain an additional feedback element, a resistor of the value $\frac{1}{r_m + r_i}$. This last step is not immediately obvious, but the following check shows the validity of the concept: Let e_i and e_0 be the input and output voltages, respectively, of an integrator with C and R_f in parallel in the feedback path and R_i in the input path. Then the current j_i flowing from the input to the summing point is

$$j_i = \frac{e_i}{R_i} \tag{20}$$

and the feedback current will be

$$j_f = C\frac{de_0}{dt} + e_0 \cdot \frac{1}{R_f} \tag{21}$$

Since the sum of both currents must be zero it is found

$$e_i = -\left(e_0 \frac{R_f}{R_i} + C R_i \frac{de_0}{dt}\right) \tag{22}$$

This is equivalent to the relationship governing the current flow through a lossy inductance

$$e = i \cdot r + L\frac{di}{dt} \tag{23}$$

And to repeat: Output voltage e_0 of the computer integrator represents the current i of reality and input voltage e_i the voltage of reality. $\frac{R_i}{R_f}$ represents r and CR_i represents L. The quantitative details of the representation of the circuit constants will be discussed later. It is somewhat confusing if the computer has to simulate relations of an electrical circuit of the real problem but this is a difficulty which can be overcome easily.

Continuing the discussion of the computer setup, an interesting point is now met. The voltage driving the current through the armature of the motor is the amplifier output voltage reduced by a voltage proportional to angular velocity which is induced in the armature during rotation. So, the input to integrator 3 on the computer must consist of the e from the amplifier output and a voltage, e_m, proportional to $\dot{\Theta}$ and of opposite sign to e. This is achieved by inserting amplifier 4, adjusted to represent the coefficient, K_ω, which describes the relationship of the induced voltage, e_m, to the angular velocity of the armature. It has to be noted, that the one input, e, to integrator 3 and the output of integrator 2 are of the same sign, but the two inputs to 3 must be of different sign and so amplifier 4 is needed to invert the sign in this feedback path. Even if the required gain setting in this path would be smaller than 1, a coefficient potentiometer would not be sufficient since it does not have this sign inverting feature.

Continuing again with the discussion of the simulation of the system, it is easy to represent an actual amplifier which is assumed to be linear and unrestricted in frequency response by the operational amplifier, 5, set to gain, a. Its input again is composed of several components: a voltage, e_1, representing the command, C, and, opposite in sign to it, the position feedback voltage, e_f, representing the output shaft position, $-\Theta_0$, and the damping voltage, e_t, which is derived from the tachometer. The proportionality constant which connects e_i and e_f to the respective angular positions is K_c. It is tentatively represented by coefficient potentiometers 3 and 4. The constant describing the tachometer output is K_v. It is represented in combination with factor d (see Fig. 34) in coefficient potentiometer 5.

It certainly has been noted that the computer diagram was developed in a backward way, starting out from the output variable and partially working against the actual signal flow direction, which is indicated by arrows in Fig. 35. Experience indicates that such a procedure is advantageous for system involving feedback loops. And, as will be seen later, it is advantageous also if the diagram is developed from the mathematical formulation, since a differential equation describes the behavior of a system in terms of functions of the output variable.

A basic computer diagram is now established. It is not yet quantitative but it presents important information about the system in a similar way as a general mathematical formulation. It can be seen that it is a multiple-loop feedback system. It has three energy storages, the three integrators. They can lead to phase shifts of more than 180° within the loop and so instability is possible even if the feedbacks are degenerative. Consequently, an important purpose of the investigation on the computer will be to evaluate systems constants which avoid instability and, in addition, provide a desired transient character or frequency response. Furthermore, it can be seen that the two damping feedbacks, K_ω and $K_v d$, are essentially equivalent. It certainly would be possible to combine amplifier 5 with integrator 3 by proper consideration of gain a. The computer diagram could be simplified in this way, but then it would be difficult to investigate nonlinearities in the characteristic of the servo amplifier. This is usually necessary, because amplifier saturation is frequently encountered. The same holds for saturation of the magnetic circuit. However, these phenomena will not be considered in this basic example.

So, it was demonstrated, that a basic computer diagram can be developed from the physical understanding of the problem under study directly, without using the bridge of mathematical formulation. Actually, the effort and the requirements to do this are the same as in finding a mathematical description of a physically given system. As already indicated, analog computer diagram and mathematical formulation are two equivalent forms of system description, each of its own right.

However, in normal practice, problems to be solved are formulated mathematically. The procedures to find the basic computer diagram in these general cases will be discussed now.

3.43. Derivation of a Computer Diagram from Mathematical Formulation

The example used will be the same as in 3.42. The mathematical description can be of different forms. It can be one complex equation or it can be given as a set of simpler equations. Since the latter is usually the case, this form will be used.

The description is split arbitrarily into 3 equations:
Motor reaction to armature currents:

$$i \frac{K_{\mathrm{T}}}{I_{\mathrm{m}}} - \frac{d^2 \Theta}{dt^2} = 0 \tag{24}$$

Current-voltage relations in the armature:

$$i\,(r_{\mathrm{m}} + r_{\mathrm{i}}) + L\,\frac{di}{dt} - e + K_\omega \frac{d\Theta}{dt} = 0 \tag{25}$$

External circuitry:

$$C K_{\mathrm{c}} - \Theta\, b\, K_{\mathrm{c}} - \frac{d\Theta}{dt} K_{\mathrm{v}} d - e\,\frac{1}{a} = 0 \tag{26}$$

In order to translate these equations into a computer diagram, the following procedure is suggested:

The form of the equations, a sum of terms on the left hand side being equal to 0 on the right hand side, is identical to the equation defining the characteristics of an operational amplifier or integrator:

$$\Sigma j_{\mathrm{n}} = 0 \tag{27}$$

The symbol, j, is used to describe the computer currents flowing into a summing point from all input and feedback paths. An interpretation of the left hand terms of equation (24), (25) and (26) as currents flowing into a summing point should lead directly to a computer diagram. The only additional information needed is to know which variables are the inputs and which the outputs.

This procedure for the given equations is discussed following Fig. 36.

In equation (24), Θ is clearly the output and i the input variable. On the summing point in question, the second derivative of Θ is needed. This is established by the feedback path of integrator 2, the output of which represents $-\frac{d\Theta}{dt}$. Integrator 1 is then needed to derive Θ from $-\frac{d\Theta}{dt}$. Thus, the current, j_{f}, flowing into the summing point of integrator 2 through its feedback path is:

$$j_{\mathrm{f}} = C\,\frac{de_0}{dt} \equiv -\frac{d^2\Theta}{dt^2} \tag{28}$$

e_0 is the output voltage of the integrator, which represents $-\frac{d\Theta}{dt}$. C is assumed to be equal to unity. The other current component, j_{i}, must be equal to $i\,\frac{K_{\mathrm{t}}}{I_{\mathrm{m}}}$ according to the equation. The instrumentation is obvious.

In equation (25), i is clearly the output variable and e the main input. Four different paths must meet at the summing point in question since the left side of the equation has four terms. Two of them must be feedback paths, because they contain functions of the output variable, i, the other two must be input paths. The following relations for the feedback paths of amplifier 3 are easily established with e_0, its output voltage, representing the current i of the actual problem:

$$j_{\mathrm{f1}} = \frac{e_0}{R_{\mathrm{f}}} \equiv i\,(r_{\mathrm{m}} + r_{\mathrm{i}}); \qquad R_{\mathrm{f}} \equiv \frac{1}{r_{\mathrm{m}} + r_{\mathrm{i}}} \tag{29}$$

$$j_{f_2} = C\frac{de_0}{dt} \equiv L\frac{di}{dt}; \quad C \equiv L \tag{30}$$

The first input current term, depending on e, must be of negative sign according to the equation. This can either be achieved by using a sign inverter acting on e, or to require a negative e as an input to this part of the computer. The latter was preferred and properly noted on the diagram. So with input resistor of

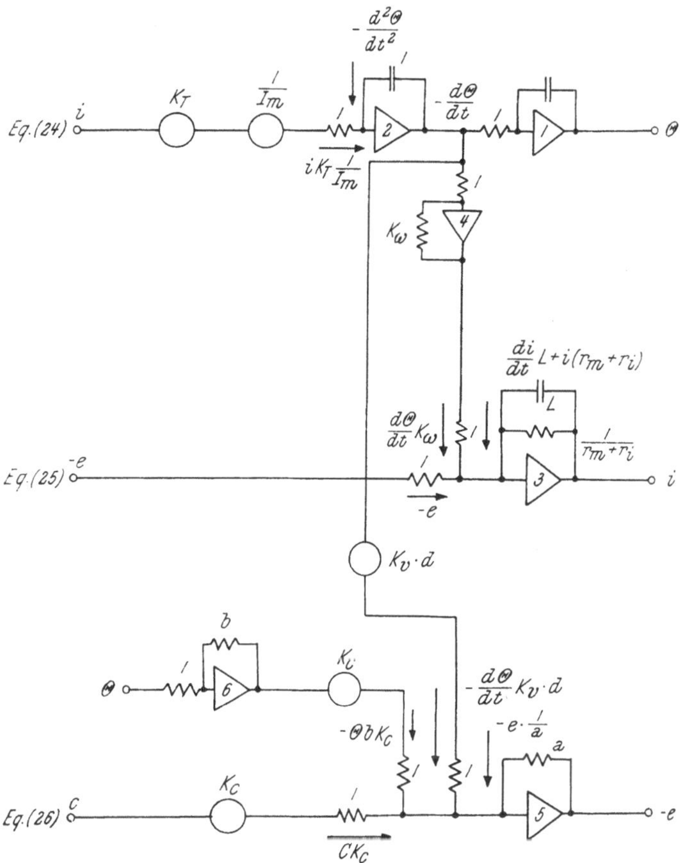

Fig. 36. Basic Computer Diagram. Derived from Equations (24)—(26)

unity the resulting computer current represents $-e$. The last input current is derived from $\frac{d\Theta}{dt}$. A voltage representing this quantity is already available at the output of integrator 2, but it carries a negative sign and a positive current is required here. So amplifier 4 is needed for sign inversion. It is used at the same time to represent the coefficient K_ω. With the respective input resistor to 3 being unity, the current to the summing point in this branch is then $K_\omega \frac{d\Theta}{dt}$.

The output variable in equation (26) is clearly e. Again, at the respective summing points there must be 4 currents, one of them flowing through a feedback path, because only one of the four terms of the equation is a function of e. Since in a former step, $-e$ was selected as a problem variable, the same is done here and is properly noted. The feedback current for amplifier 5 is then $-e \cdot \frac{1}{a}$, if the feedback resistor has the value a. The first input term, derived from C, is straight forward. The second term, derived from Θ, must have a negative sign. Since Θ is available already in the setup with positive sign, sign inverter 6 is required, which at the same time is used to provide the coefficient, b. The final input term is easily derived from $-\frac{d\Theta}{dt}$, no sign inversion is required.

To complete the basic computer diagram, all terminals carrying the same notation must be connected. In many practical diagrams this is not done, the notation of the terminals is considered to be sufficiently clear, but certainly these connections must not be forgotten if the setup is finally wired on the computer.

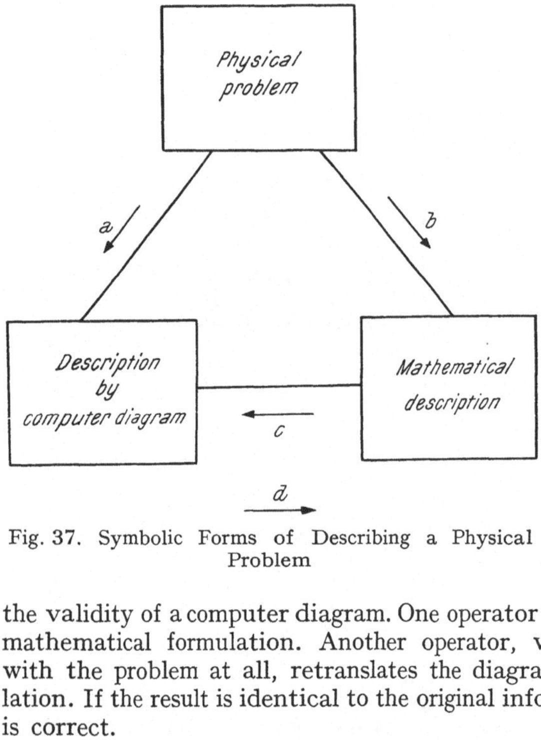

Fig. 37. Symbolic Forms of Describing a Physical Problem

An inspection of Fig. 36 reveals absolute identity with Fig. 35. The relation between the two methods used to describe a physical problem is established. This situation is explained in Fig. 37. Procedure (*a*), deriving a computer diagram directly from the physical problem, was performed in 3.42. Procedure (*b*) is assumed to be known and procedure (*c*) was just finished. It is important to note that procedure (*d*) namely, the derivation of a mathematical description from a given computer diagram, is useful also. It is frequently used to check the validity of a computer diagram. One operator designs a diagram from a given mathematical formulation. Another operator, who preferably is not familiar with the problem at all, retranslates the diagram into a mathematical formulation. If the result is identical to the original information, the computer diagram is correct.

3.44. The Final Computer Diagram, Scaling

The basic computer diagram which was derived so far is only programmatic. It was shown that it is of similar significance as a general mathematical formulation. It shows the interrelation between the variables and so gives important information about the character of the problem. But it is not yet sufficient to describe a computer setup quantitatively. For instance, a coefficient potentiometer may be designated to represent a coefficient K of a physical problem. Assume that K has a value of 345 $\left[\frac{lb\ sec}{ft}\right]$, what is the required setting of the potentiometer? The same question arises with the definition of the characteristics of each computing component. Obviously, the answer depends on how the relationship of the variables of the actual problem with the computer variables is defined. The process of fixing these relationships, of providing "scale factors" for the variables and for the "gains" of the computing components, is known as "scaling". Again no generally adopted optimal method exists, but any method employed, if used consistently, will provide an answer. However, there is little probability that any method will yield a fully satisfactory result after the first attempt. Corrections derived from an error study of the first computing results will usually be necessary. The scaling method to be demonstrated in this short discussion is based on a few simple rules, is fast and mechanistic in its application and leads theoretically to an optimum answer with respect to signal-to-noise-ratio of the computer variables and with respect to component requirements, but it sacrifices to a certain extent the intimacy of the relationship between the final computer setup and the original problem. Nevertheless, it is used because of its simplicity. Normally, any individual operator will develop his own method which is most adequate to his personal way of thinking.

To perform the quantitative process of scaling, all coefficient values, integrating constants and empirical functional relations of the given problem must be known quantitatively and must be of defined physical dimension. In addition, it is necessary to know what values all the problem variables will attain during a typical computer investigation. This information is not easily available since it requires a solution of the problem, but normally useable estimates can be made. And, if these estimates turn out to be not too successful, the scaling can be corrected using the first computer results. It is necessary to know these expected values of the variables in order to define scale factors which achieve the following:

a) Avoid, that the computer variables exceed the limiting values of $\pm$ 100 [V]. Otherwise, overloading would occur which leads to severe computing errors.

b) Avoid, that the computer variables remain too small. Otherwise, errors would be introduced from an insufficient signal-to-noise-ratio of the computer variables.

There is certainly a "squeeze" imposed on the designer of the computer setup, resulting from the limited allowable dynamic range of the computer variables. He can either decide to follow a general policy which keeps the signal level high and then to accept the risk of incurring overloads. Or he can proceed in the other way. The policy followed here is the first one. The reason is that one will get a clear warning of overloads from the overload indicator system. The other case, too small signals, is not immediately obvious and significant error contributions might remain undetected.

An estimate of the expected maximum amount of all computer variables can be derived from known magnitudes of the forcing functions which have to be applied and from given initial conditions. If saturating devices are included in the problem, additional valuable information is available. The main difficulty is to arrive at a sound estimate of the dynamics of the signals. To know them is important in order to scale the integrators properly. The best procedure for practical purposes is to estimate the maximum frequencies which can occur in the system under investigation. Some information on its frequency response will be available in many cases. If not, an approximative analysis can be made by simplifying the system to lower order and by fixing variable coefficients to representative values. Such a study leads to satisfactory results in most cases and helps tremendously in the understanding of the system.

The scaling procedure consists in establishing scale factors, i. e., factors relating the computer voltages to the actual physical variables. This can be done in the following steps:

Let x be an actual physical variable, measured in certain physical units, $[PU]$.

It is represented on the computer by a voltage X. Now in normal practice the computer voltage is not measured in volts but in "Machine Units" $[MU]$, following the definition:

$$1\ [MU] = 100\ [V] \tag{31}$$

This is convenient to do since most electronic multipliers provide an output voltage of 100 $[V]$ if both inputs are equal to 100 $[V]$.

Now a "scale factor" is defined by the relation:

$$X\ [MU] = x\ [PU] \cdot a_x \tag{32}$$

The scale factor, a_x, is consequently of the dimension $[MU/PU]$. It is important to label the scale factor, together with the physical variable, on each point of the computer diagram, in order to be able to interpret a voltage measured at this point with respect to its physical meaning.

Example: Assume that a certain point in the computer diagram is labelled $0.2\,\beta\ [PU]$ and a voltage, B, of 70 $[V]$, which is equivalent to 0.7 $[MU]$, is read out at this point. The physical meaning of this voltage is then:

$$\beta = \frac{B}{\alpha_\beta} = \frac{0.7}{0.2} = 3.5\ [PU] \tag{33}$$

One has to be aware that the omission of explicit dimensional information frequently leads to confusion in the interpretation of computer results.

The scale factors which were selected must be properly considered in the scaling of forcing functions and initial conditions.

Example: Let $a_x = 0.2\left[\frac{MU\ \text{sec}}{ft}\right]$ be the selected scale factor of an integrator output and assume that an initial condition of $x\,(O) = 1.5\left[\frac{ft}{\text{sec}}\right]$ is required. Then the initial voltage on the integrator must be

$$X\,(O) = x\,(O) \cdot a_x = 1.5 \cdot 0.2 = 0.3\ [MU] \tag{34}$$

The scale factors for each point in the computer diagram are selected by the following inequality:

$$X_{max} = a_x \cdot x_{max} \leqq 1\ [MU] \tag{35}$$

To follow this rule is the best guarantee to make the computer variables as large as possible with respect to the noise level of the components.

After the desired scale factors for the variables are fixed, the important step of scaling the coefficient and parameter settings has to be performed. Consider the physical problem:

$$y = A \cdot x \tag{36}$$

This is represented on the computer by:

$$y \cdot a_y = A \cdot a_A \cdot x \cdot a_x \tag{37}$$

a_y and a_x are already determined and in order to find a_A the required relation (36) is substituted in (37) and it is found:

$$a_A = \frac{a_y}{a_x} \tag{38}$$

If a_x and a_y are selected as described above, namely, to make the maximum value of each machine variable exactly equal to 1 $[MU]$, then Aa_A will be equal to 1. In other words, a coefficient potentiometer or amplifier can be omitted and the multiplication by a fixed coefficient is expressed in the scale factors of the variables. This is certainly advantageous because it saves computer components and leads to an optimum signal to noise ratio on all points of the computer. On the other hand, this procedures makes the task of interpreting the physical meaning of the computer variables more difficult. Great care must be taken to indicate the correct scale factor on each point of the computer diagram. And it will have to be noted that certain computer variables can have two physical meanings (e. g. force and acceleration), which will have to be indicated properly.

The approach used in (36) through (38) can be applied to find the "gain settings" of any operational process. The case of scaling around a summing point deserves special mention:

Let the physical problem be:

$$\Sigma A_i x_i = y \tag{39}$$

It can be assumed that the a_{x_i} and a_y have been pre-selected under optimum scaling considerations. Then the individual gain settings for each input lead of the summing amplifier have to be defined by:

$$a_{A_i} = \frac{a_y}{a_{x_i}} \tag{40}$$

This is normally accomplished on the computer by providing the proper input resistor in each lead. But since precision resistors are available only with certain fixed values, either additional coefficient potentiometers have to be inserted or the scale factors of the x_i's have to be changed in an adequate way.

So, the process of scaling in a simple straight forward way consists of two steps:

a) Estimation of the maximum expected value of all physical variables on all points of the system and selection of optimal desired scale factors for each point. An error of judgment in this estimation of maximum values and in the resulting selection of scale factors for the variables does not lead to an erroneous computer setup if the selected scale factors are consistently taken into consideration in the following step of the scaling process. Such an error in judgment will merely lead to either too small or too large computer variables. If necessary, the scaling of the variables has to be revised in accordance with the observations from the first computer runs.

b) Evaluation of the necessary coefficient and gain settings under consideration of the preselected scale factors of the variables.

As an example, this process will now be applied to the physical system discussed before.

The characteristic values of the physical system, referring to the notation used in (24) through (26) and Fig. 34 through 36 are the following:

Servo Motor Data: $K_T = 2.5 \left[\frac{in\ oz}{A}\right]$

$$K_\omega = 0.02 \left[\frac{V\ sec}{rad}\right]$$

$$I_m = 5 \cdot 10^{-4} \left[\frac{\text{in oz sec}^2}{\text{rad}}\right]$$

$$\begin{aligned} r_m &= 30\ [\Omega] \\ L &= 1\ [Hy] \end{aligned}$$

Amplifier Data: $a = 2$

$$r_i = 30\ [\Omega]$$

Circuit Data: $b = 0.01$

$$K_c = 10\left[\frac{V}{\text{rad}}\right]$$

$$K_v = 0.05\left[\frac{V\ \text{sec}}{\text{rad}}\right]$$

d is not known, in fact, it is one of the primary purposes of the supposed task to evaluate its optimum value. But in order to scale the computer, a sensible estimate is required. It will be discussed later how it is derived.

First, the expected maximum values of the problem variables have to be estimated. For reasons of clarity it is convenient to draw another basic computer diagram, which is used to note at each point the maximum expected values of the variables and the desired scale factors. This is done in Fig. 38. Referring

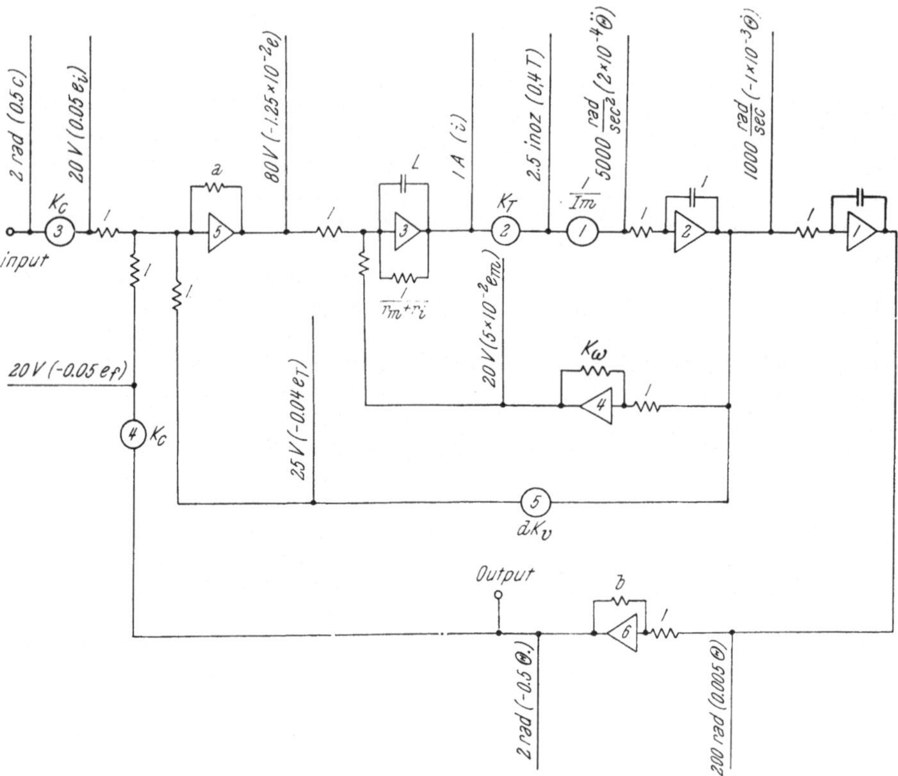

Fig. 38. Estimation of Maximum Values of the Variables and Selection of Scale Factors

to Fig. 34, it is assumed that the maximum possible deflection of the potentiometers P_1 and P_2 of the servo is restricted to about $\pm$ 100 [degrees], or, since it is preferred to define all angles in radians, to about $\pm$ 2 [rad]. So, 2 [rad] is the maximum output signal of the system. The input variable appears at the input of potentiometer 3 and the output at the output of amplifier 6. It is again convenient to work backward from the output point. So, clearly at the input of amplifier 6, a signal of 200 [rad] is needed, since the coefficient b is equal to 0.01. But in order to find the necessary input signal to integrator 1 dynamic information is needed.

An estimate of the frequency range of the servo under study was derived by neglecting the dynamic influence of the inductance of the motor winding. This reduces the complexity of the system and makes it representable by a second order differential equation, for which the natural frequency can be easily evaluated. An estimate for the necessary coefficient d was derived under the same assumptions. A value of $d = 0.5$ was selected in such a way as to obtain a relative damping coefficient of the second order system of approximately 0.7. The natural frequency of the simplified system was found to be 4.1 $\left[\frac{\text{rad}}{\text{sec}}\right]$. For the practical purpose of scaling it was assumed to be 5 $\left[\frac{\text{rad}}{\text{sec}}\right]$.

The estimation of maximum signals and the selection of optimum scale factor can now be resumed. The maximum output signal of integrator 1 has an amplitude of 200 [rad] and will be of a maximum frequency of 5 $\left[\frac{\text{rad}}{\text{sec}}\right]$. The maximum input signal to integrator 1, the derivative of its output, therefore has a value of 1000 $\left[\frac{\text{rad}}{\text{sec}}\right]$. A scale factor of 1×10^{-3} $\left[\frac{MU\,\text{sec}}{\text{rad}}\right]$ is consequently selected. The input situation to integrator 2 is found by the same consideration.

The torque T necessary to produce an acceleration of 5000 $\left[\frac{\text{rad}}{\text{sec}^2}\right]$ on a moment of inertia of 5×10^{-4} $\left[\frac{\text{in oz sec}^2}{\text{rad}}\right]$ is 2.5 [in oz]. An optimum scale factor is 0.4 $\left[\frac{MU}{\text{in oz}}\right]$. The torque of 2.5 [in oz] is produced by a current of 1 [A] considering the torque constant K_T of the motor of 2.5 $\left[\frac{\text{in oz}}{A}\right]$. So the output scale factor of amplifier 3 is defined. To find its input scale factors, the inductance L is temporarily neglected. A short check can be made whether this will lead to significant errors in judgment in determining the maximum values of the variables: The effective time constant of the motor winding, τ_m, is defined by

$$\tau_m = \frac{L}{r_m + r_i} = \frac{1}{60}\ [\text{sec}] \tag{41}$$

It represents a low pass filter with a bandwidth of 60 $\left[\frac{\text{rad}}{\text{sec}}\right]$ and its insertion loss at a frequency of 5 $\left[\frac{\text{rad}}{\text{sec}}\right]$ is very small. No objection is consequently seen against neglecting L.

Thus, the voltage required to drive a current of 1 [A] through a resistor, $(r_m + r_i)$, of 60 [Ω] is equal to 60 [V]. Since the input to amplifier 3 consists of

2 leads, an estimate of the voltages in these 2 circuits has to be made. One of them is the velocity voltage $e_m = K_\omega \cdot \dot{\Theta}$. Since $\dot{\Theta}_{max} = 1000 \left[\frac{\text{rad}}{\text{sec}}\right]$, as noted on the output of integrator 2, $e_{m\,max}$ is 20 $[V]$, considering the value of K_ω of $0.02 \left[\frac{V \text{ sec}}{\text{rad}}\right]$. Thus, the maximum voltage, e_{max}, in the other lead can be estimated to be 80 $[V]$ in order to meet the total voltage requirement of 60 $[V]$. Again a simplification was made, since the possible phase shift between e and e_m was not considered. But, again, the resulting deviation of the scale factor of e from its optimum value was tolerated.

The input to amplifier 5 is composed of 3 leads and the total input requirement is 40 $[V]$ with a prescribed gain of the servo amplifier of $a = 2$. Checking the situation in the 3 input circuits, it is found that the scale factors in all of them are already defined:

The input voltage e_i is equal to $C\,K_c$, C being the commanded position. Its maximum value was assumed to be 2 [rad]. This leads to $e_{i\,max} = 20$ $[V]$ with $K_c = 10 \left[\frac{V}{\text{rad}}\right]$. The same holds for the position feedback voltage, $e_f = \Theta_0\,K_c$. The tachometer feedback voltage e_f is equal to $d\,K_v$. Its maximum value is 25 $[V]$, with $\dot{\Theta} = 1000 \left[\frac{\text{rad}}{\text{sec}}\right]$, $K_v = 0.05$ and $d = 0.5$.

This procedure of estimating the maximum signal levels on each point is simple and maintains a close contact with the physics of the actual system. It could be criticized that the proposed scale factors are too close and can lead to overloads of the computer. But the assumption of signals with maximum amplitude

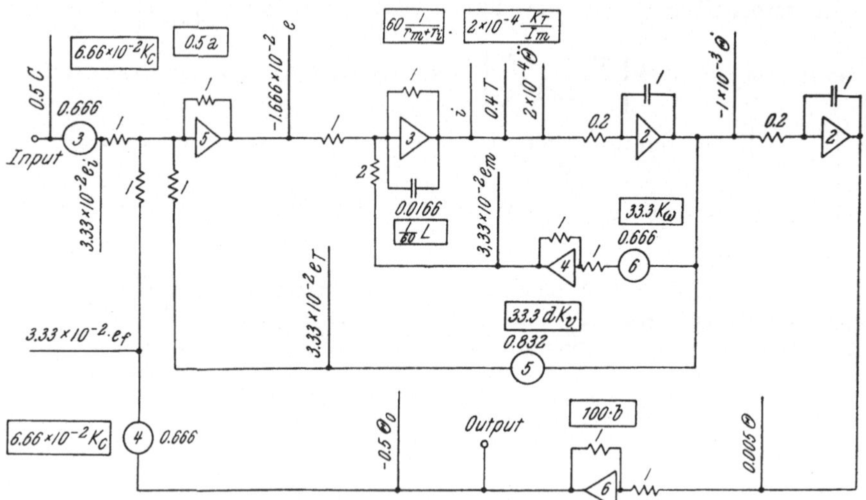

Fig. 39. Final Computer Diagram

at the natural frequency of the system is rigorous and normally provides sufficient leeway.

The next and final step after defining the desired scale factors of the variables is to evaluate the necessary component gain values. For the example under discussion this was done in Fig. 39, which is the final computer diagram. The process is simple and mechanistic after the scale factors for the variables have been selected. Following equations (38) and (40) the effective gain setting of any coefficient potentiometer, operational amplifier or integrator is simply the product of the physical factor the component is respresenting and the ratio of the selected scale factors of its output and input variables. If these scale factors were selected according to the procedure descriped above, this effective gain will be equal to unity. If they were selected according to other reasons, the values once selected have to be duly considered. It is very well feasible to change the previonsly selected scale factors of the variables during this process. However, such a change has to be clearly indicated in the computer diagram. Such changes were made in the example of Fig. 39 in the input leads of amplifiers 3 and 5 in order to obtain suitable values of the precision resistors. Furthermore, it is advisable to indicate in the diagram the relation of the actual component values to the physical coefficient they represent. If during the computation changes in the gain setting of any computer component are found to be desirable, such a notation allows an easy interpretation of the physical meaning of such a change.

The considerations so far were concerned with the scaling of the dependent variables. This process has to be performed in any case. But in addition it may turn out to be required to scale the independent variable, time. This can be necessary for two reasons:

If the problem under investigation occurs during a short time interval, or, if it contains high frequencies which certain computer components cannot handle without undesired phase shifts (see 3.231), significantly erroneous answers can be obtained. This can be avoided by making the time during which the process is performed on the computer larger than in physical reality. Using T for "computer time" it is defined:

$$T \equiv a_t \cdot t \tag{42}$$

a_t must be greater than one to represent fast processes.

On the other hand, the actual problem may be slow. Then unnecessary computing errors may be obtained by the accumulation of drift errors if the computation is performed in "real time". And it may be inconvenient to spend valuable time in waiting for solutions.

A time scale factor, a_t, which is smaller than unity then must be chosen to make the computer process faster than the actual one.

To mechanize time scale factors which are different from 1 on the computer, it has to be remembered that only integrators perform operations on the variables which depend on time. So, only the gain settings of integrators have to be considered in time scaling, all others remain unaffected. In particular it is found:

$$Y = C \int X \, dT; \; a_y \cdot y = a_x \cdot a_t \cdot a_c \cdot c \int x \, dt$$

$$C = a_c \cdot c = \frac{a_y}{a_x \cdot a_t} \tag{43}$$

C is the effective gain factor of the integrator. So, in practical work, it is advisable to scale the problem first for real time, as described before. Then, a final correction of all integrator settings according to (43) has to be performed, if the time scale factor has to be different from unity. The actual value of the time scale factor has to be properly considered in the interpretation of the computer results and in the mechanization of empirically given input functions. And, of course, real time presentation ($a_t = 1$) must be used, if actual physical hardware is to be incorporated in the computing process. As pointed out before, a significant advantage of the Analog Computer is its capability to simulate processes in real time, and deviations from real time scaling should be made only if absolutely necessary.

3.45. Computer Checkout

The more complex a problem is the more important it is to ascertain that the computer solutions are correct. Incorrect solutions can stem from three sources:

Mistakes in the design of the computer diagram.
Mistakes in setting up the computer from the diagram.
Component malfunctions.

To detect mistakes in the design of the computer diagram, it is helpful to formulate a "computer equation", a mathematical description of the system which is actually mechanized on the computer. The coefficients of this equation are the actual gain settings of the computer components. This computer equation then must be analyzed, as a whole or in parts, and its characteristics such as steady state gains, time constants, natural frequencies, and damping coefficients must be determined. If they are equal to the characteristics of the original equations, the validity of the computer diagram may be assumed.

A very helpful method to eliminate mistakes in the computer setup and in the computer diagram is to employ a person who is not familiar with the problem, or who is completely unbiased. He has to plot a diagram from the actual computer setup, which should turn out to be identical to the one which was originally used. And he again can interpret the computer diagram in terms of a mathematical formulation as mentioned above. If he does not detect any discrepancies the probability of setup mistakes is very small.

In order to find and eliminate component malfunctions, a wide variety of methods are in practical use:

a) Operational Checkout Mode. It is provided in most modern large scale computers, and essentially consists of the following functions:

Static Check: All integrator capacitors are replaced automatically by precision resistors of unit value. So the system on the computer is no longer dynamic and check solutions for defined, fixed input values can be found numerically without too many difficulties. This check takes care of all components involved in the specific setup except the integrating capacitors.

Dynamic Check: All integrators are disconnected automatically from the problem configuration and subjected to a defined fixed input voltage. The outputs are measured after a fixed time interval, which again is automatically defined. Thus, malfunctions of the integrating capacitors can be detected.

b) General Check Solution. A solution for one typical parameter configuration of the problem is worked out on a desk calculator or a digital computer. It is compared to the solution yielded by the analog computer. This method is expensive but comprehensive, since in addition it permits to perform a quantitative error analysis of the solution (see 3.47).

c) Sub-system Check. The overall complex system under investigation is split up in simple sub-systems, for which check solutions can be found comparatively easily. This essentially means to reduce the system to a set of first or second order differential equations, and to fix their coefficients to defined values if the system is time varying or non-linear. This method is flexible and helps considerably in the understanding of the physical problem. On the other hand it might be cumbersome.

d) Point-for-Point Check. A multichannel recorder is connected to as many as possible points in the computer setup and a computer run under a typical forcing function is recorded. The expected transfer characteristics between two points can be evaluated numerically without difficulties, if the points are properly selected. So, any discrepancies in the computer solution will be detected immediately. This method again is fruitful in contributing to the understanding of the system under investigation. It has the additional advantage of indicating deficiencies in scaling, since actual signal levels and possible computer noise are presented directly.

The selection of a checkout method or a combination of methods depends on available facilities, the type of the problem and the philosophy of approach of the operators. In any case, erroneous computer solutions can be avoided even for complex problems with reasonable efforts.

3.46. Problem Solution

After all preparatory steps are performed, the proper purpose of all efforts can now be accomplished. The variety of possible questions which may have to be answered is enormous. So, an attempt will be made to describe the more important types of investigation which are performed on dynamic systems such as normally mechanized on Analog Computers.

a) Time Domain Investigation. The characteristics of the system are described by the transient response to typical initial conditions and to basic types of forcing functions. One of these is the unit step function, verified by applying a fixed input voltage at the proper time. Another one is the ramp function, verified by the output voltage of an integrator, to the input terminals of which a unit step is applied. The most important of them is the impulse function. The transient response of the system to an impulse, frequently called the weighting function, is an important tool in analytical work. Unfortunately, an ideal impulse cannot be produced. It has to be approximated by a pulse of defined amplitude and duration. The duration must be short with respect to the period of the natural frequency of the system under investigation. Fig. 40 shows how such a pulse can be produced by using computer components. It is a good example for the versatility of an Analog Computer.

The most important element is a relay-amplifier combination, as shown in Fig. 40a. Diode D_1 is conductive at low output voltages, D_2 is nonconductive. So, at low output voltages, the combination has a gain $\frac{R_f}{R_i}$ (see Fig. 40b). At a certain output voltage, $e = \frac{E_{r_1}}{r_2}$, the effective voltage across D_1 approaches 0 and D_1 starts to cut off. In doing so, the feedback current is reduced, the effective amplifier gain increases and leads to higher output voltages, blocking the feedback path even more. So, the amplifier flips over sharply to the new state of open loop gain, the output voltage jumps as indicated in Fig. 40b. To avoid overloading of the amplifier, Diode D_2 opens at the output voltage $e' = E\,\frac{r_1'}{r_2'}$. This leads to saturation of the output voltage at this level, as was explained in 3.244. e′ must be selected such as to effect a safe and fast response of relay S. A possible arrangement to produce impulses of controlled character is now shown in Fig. 40c. Definitions are explained in Fig. 40d. The closing of switch S_0 at the reference moment applies voltage to the input of integrator 1 and Relay S_1

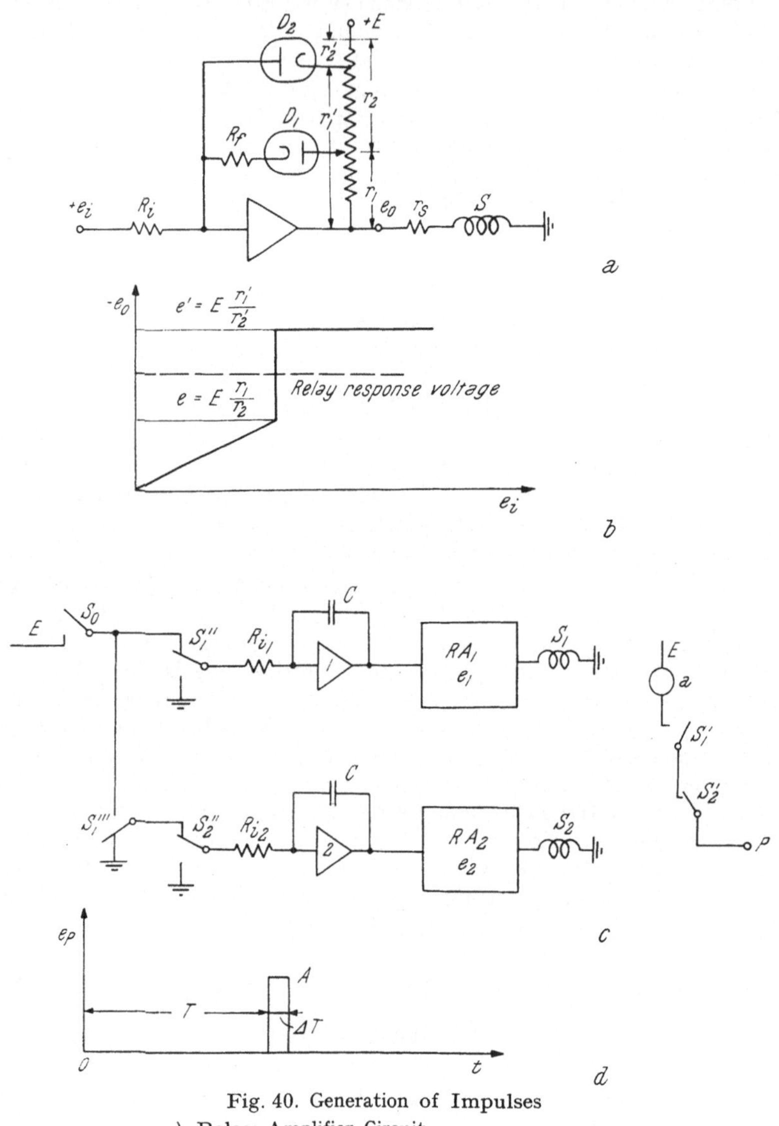

Fig. 40. Generation of Impulses
a) Relay Amplifier Circuit
b) Output-Input Relation in Relay Amplifier
c) Complete Impulse Circuit
d) Impulse Waveform

reacts at the instant when the output voltage of relay amplifier RA_1 reaches the preset value e_1. So, a voltage, aE, is now available at terminal P. At the same time the input to integrator 1 is grounded to keep it from integrating further and from final overloading. At the same time, input voltage is applied to integrator 2. Relay S_2 reacts when the output voltage of $RA2$ reaches the preset value e_2. The pulse voltage at terminal P becomes O and the integrator 2 is grounded to prevent it from overloading. The pulse is under full control, as is evident from the following equations:

$$A = a \cdot E; \; T = \frac{E}{e_1 C R_{i1}}; \; \Delta T = \frac{E}{e_2 C R_{i2}} \tag{44}$$

The possibility of controlling the time of occurrence, T, of the pulse was included because it is important for the investigation of systems with time-varying coefficients. Their reaction depends on the moment of time when the disturbing pulse is applied.

Pulses generated in this way are only approximations to the Delta-Dirac function, since they are of finite duration. But the Analog Computer provides the possibility of an exact simulation of this function also. It is based on the fact that the disturbance caused by an impulse is identical to one caused by a certain set of initial conditions which can be easily provided on the computer. The respective theory exceeds the framework of this discussion.

b) Frequency Domain Investigation. Another important method of describing the behavior of dynamic systems is its frequency response. The techniques required to evaluate the frequency response of a system simulated on an Analog Computer are simple and straight-forward. Basic tools are a sine wave generator and a multichannel recorder. Amplitude and phase relations between input and output for several test frequencies can be evaluated directly from the recordings. In addition, there are transfer function analyzers commercially available which permit to read directly either the real and imaginary component or the amplitude and phase of the output signal.

c) Statistical Investigation. The task of "optimizing" a system if the input signal is spoiled by random components, noise, becomes of more and more interest. A favorite criterion for such an optimization is to obtain a minimum of a mean squared error:

$$\overline{\varepsilon^2} = \frac{1}{T} \int_0^T \varepsilon^2 \, dt \rightarrow \min \tag{45}$$

The error, ε, is the difference between the response of the system under investigation to the input signal spoiled by noise and a desired response to the pure input signal:

$$\varepsilon = (e_S + e_N) \, \{S\} - e_S \, \{D\} \tag{46}$$

The symbolism $e \, \{S\}$ is used to describe the effect of an operation performed by a system S on an input voltage e. The ideal operator, $\{D\}$, is mostly assumed to be equal to 1, i. e. the ideal output of the process is identical to the input. The indices, S and N, represent the pure signal and the noise, respectively. Since a mean squared quantity is the object of the investigation, it is sufficient to describe the signals involved in mean square terms, specifically, by their power spectral density functions. Thus, the investigation is valid for the whole set of functions which have a common power spectrum. Such a power spectrum can easily be defined in the case of e_N, the voltage representing the physical random component, the noise. It is normally assumed to be "white", i. e., independent of frequency. Now a physical simulation of such a process can only be an approximation, since the frequency range over which a practical noise spectrum is constant is always finite. But it is sufficient to provide a noise spectrum which is wider by a factor 5 to 10 than the pass-band of the system under investigation,

S. Random noise generators which meet this practical requirement are commercially available. The voltage representing the pure signal, e_S, is normally defined by a power spectrum which is a given function of frequency. It can be verified for the investigation on the Analog Computer by applying a proper filtering process to the output of a random noise generator.

Fig. 41 shows a basic diagram of the computer setup which is needed in addition to the simulation of the system under investigation to perform such an

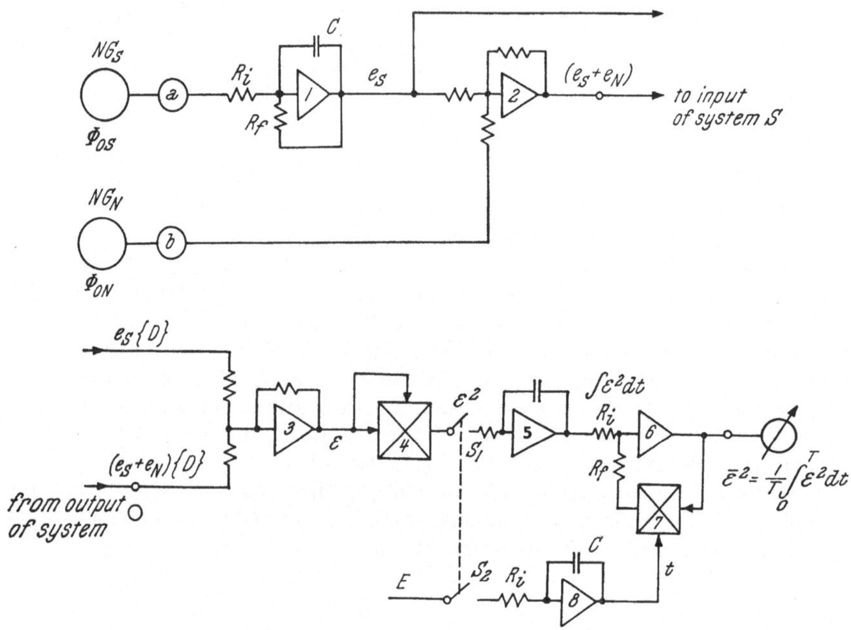

Fig. 41. Circuit for Statistical System Evaluation Using Mean Squared Error Criterion

optimization process. NG_S and NG_N are two separate random noise generators. Their output is described by a power spectrum with spectral densities, Φ_{OS} and Φ_{ON}, respectively, which are independent of frequency and extend over a sufficiently wide frequency band. Two separate generators are needed to provide statistical independence between signal and noise. The "filter" provided by the circuit of amplifier 1 serves to shape the signal spectrum in a desired way. In this example, the frequency response of the filter is:

$$\frac{e_0}{e_i} = -\frac{R_f}{R_i}\,\frac{1}{j\left(\frac{\omega}{\omega_0}\right)+1}; \quad \omega_0 = \frac{1}{C R_f} \tag{47}$$

The signal voltage, e_S, then has a power spectrum

$$\Phi_S = \Phi_{OS}\cdot a^2\cdot\left|\frac{e_0}{e_i}\right|^2 = \Phi_{OS}\cdot a^2\cdot\left(\frac{R_f}{R_i}\right)^2\cdot\frac{I}{\left(\frac{\omega_0}{\omega}\right)^2+1} \tag{48}$$

This relation occurs frequently in practical problems. It is interesting to note how the components of the computer can be used to synthezise an electrical filter. The signal voltage, e_S, is summed with the noise voltage in amplifier 2. Its output, $(e_S + e_N)$, serves then as an input function to the system under investigation, S. The output of S, $(e_S + e_N) \{S\}$, is fed into amplifier 3 and subtracted from the ideal response, $e_S \{D\}$. The ideal operation is assumed to be a multiplication by a factor of unity. If different requirements exist, it is necessary to synthesize the ideal system on the computer and let it operate on the input signal, e_S. The output of amplifier 3 represents the error, ε. It is squared in multiplier 4 and ε^2 is integrated in 5. Amplifier 6 has multiplier 7 in its feedback path, the second input of which is a voltage proportional to time. It performs the operation:

$$e_0 \cdot a \cdot t \cdot \frac{1}{R_f} = -e_i \cdot \frac{1}{R_i}; \quad \frac{e_0}{e_i} = -\frac{R_f}{R_i} \cdot \frac{1}{a \cdot t} \tag{49}$$

Finally, integrator 8 provides the voltage which is proportional to time:

$$e_0 = E \cdot t \cdot \frac{1}{R_i \cdot C} \tag{50}$$

The averaging process, performed by components 5 through 8 extends over a period of time defined by the closing of the pair of switches, S_1 and S_2. The mean squared error is represented by the output voltage of 6. The desired investigation can now be performed. Normally, $\overset{2}{\overline{\varepsilon}}$ will be evaluated as a function of different parameter configurations of the system under study and a decision on the optimum configuration can then be made. This process requires a certain series of measurements and basically is empirical. But it has to be noted that such an empirical approach is frequently the only possible one in the synthesis of nonlinear systems. The capability of an Analog Computer to handle such complex situations in a comparatively straight forward way is considered to be one of its most important merits.

d) Special Investigations. The investigations described above are useful for the analysis of dynamic systems because they provide response characteristics to general types of input functions. But it is frequently desired to evaluate how a system will behave in a specific situation. In such cases, an empirical input function will be given and certain initial conditions will be defined. It is then necessary to reproduce the physical function as a voltage function with an appropriate scale factor, to feed it into the system which is simulated on the computer and to record the system output. The equipment required to produce the input functions, curve followers and function generators, were discussed before.

3.47. Error Analysis

An important question to be answered in all computer work is the one for the accuracy of the solution. The problem of course is closely related to the checkout of the computer setup (see 3.45). But even if the computer was prepared correctly and the machine worked properly, the solution will be of finite accuracy. On the Analog Computer, this is caused by the finite accuracy of the computing components. Theoretically it is possible to evaluate the expected total error if the individual component errors are known. But the analytical processes involved in such a study are very complex. The practical approach is to analyze the solution itself and not to attempt to formulate an "a priori" error expectancy. Methods which can be applied are the following:

a) Repeatability Check. A computer run is repeated several times under identical conditions. A comparison of the different solutions yields an estimate of the statistics of the random component of the computer error.

However, an estimate of systematic error components is more difficult to obtain. The following procedures are feasible:

b) Digital Check Solution. Its merits and disadvantages were discussed in 3.45. During the analysis, it must be kept in mind that its accuracy is also finite. However, the comparison of two solutions derived from two fundamentally different computing processes normally yields a good estimate of the actual error.

c) Dynamic Check. It consists in repeating a typical computer run with all integrator capacitors replaced by greater ones, i.e., in using a time scale factor $a_t > 1$. In many modern installations, this replacement is performed by an automatic switching process. This check serves to evaluate systematic errors introduced by the limited dynamic capabilities of the computer components. If these errors are marginal, it is advisable to continue the investigation with an extended time scale.

d) Substitution Checks. The values of the variables obtained in the computer solution can be substituted in the original set of equations. If these equations are not met, an estimate of the error can be derived from the observed discrepancies. This method, though tedious, is very flexible and fruitful. One can concentrate on certain quantities of interest, and one can achieve a high precision solution by an iterative process.

3.48. Miscellaneous Examples

To deepen the understanding of the capabilities of Analog Computers, the basic computer diagrams for a few typical application problems will be derived in this chapter.

3.481. Dynamics of an Airframe. The designer of control and guidance equipment for missiles or aircraft is vitally interested in knowing the dynamic response characteristics of the airframes. They constitute an important "block" in his system and must be carefully considered. Dynamic response characteristics

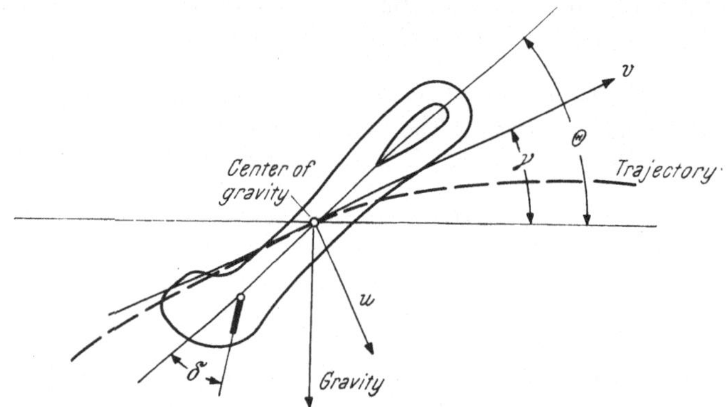

Fig. 42. Definition of Aircraft Motion

needed for this purpose are the angular motions of the airframe caused by changes in position of the control surfaces, rudders, elevators, or ailerons.

The complete mathematical description of the motions of an airframe is very complicated. It has six degrees of freedom, i. e., three of linear motion (forward and in the two directions perpendicular to it) and three of angular motion (roll, pitch, yaw). For many purposes an investigation restricted to certain modes of motion is practically sufficient. So, for this example, the following configuration will be evaluated (see Fig. 42):

The aircraft moves on a trajectory which is confined to the vertical plane. Only two linear motions have to be considered, the forward motion, described by the velocity, v, and the lateral motion, described by the velocity, u. The amount of the former is assumed to be known, the latter has to be computed. The orientation of these vectors is defined by the flight path angle, γ, the tangent to the trajectory, which has to be computed. The only angular motion to be considered here is the pitch motion, defined by the attitude angle, Θ, and its derivatives. It has to be computed. The quantity which influences all these variables, the input variable, is the deflection angle, δ, of the elevators. Since two forms of motion have to be computed, two equations of motion are needed. They are found by equating to zero the sum of all quantities which drive and retard the respective motions:

$$\Sigma F = 0 \tag{51}$$

F: Forces perpendicular to the flight path.

$$\Sigma M = 0 \tag{52}$$

M: Moments acting on the aircraft in the pitch plane.

The main forces are the following:

$m \cdot v \cdot \dot{\gamma}$	Centrifugal force, m is the mass of the aircraft.	
$m \cdot g \cdot \cos \gamma$	Component of gravity perpendicular to flight path	
$C_L \cdot \frac{v^2 \varrho}{2} \cdot A$	Aerodynamic lift force.	(53)
	C_L: Lift Coefficient.	
	A: Characteristic area of the air frame.	
	ϱ: Density of air. It is a function of altitude h, which, in turn, is supposed to be known.	

The main moments are:

$I \frac{d^2\Theta}{dt^2}$	I: Moment of Inertia.	
$C_M \cdot \frac{v^2 \varrho}{2} \cdot A \cdot d$	d: Distance between center of gravity and center of pressure.	
	C_M: Moment coefficient.	(54)

Now, the two characteristic aerodynamic coefficients, C_L and C_M, are not constants but complicated nonlinear functions of the flight conditions of the aircraft. But in the majority of practical cases it is sufficient to restrict the interest of the investigation to small deviations from given flight conditions. It is then sufficient to "linearize" the coefficient functions, i. e. to replace them by the first term of the respective Taylor series. One, then, has to define the partial derivatives of the coefficient functions with respect to important flight parameters. One of them is the angle of attack, α:

$$\alpha = \Theta - \gamma \tag{55}$$

The main derivatives, frequently called the stability derivatives, are:

$$C_{L_\alpha} = \frac{d C_L}{d \alpha}$$

$$C_{L_\delta} = \frac{d C_L}{d \delta}$$

$$C_{M_\alpha} = \frac{d C_M}{d \alpha}$$

$$C_{M_\delta} = \frac{d C_M}{d \delta}$$

$$C_{M_Q} = \frac{d C_M}{d Q}$$

Here, d is used to represent the partial differentiation operator to avoid confusion with the deflection angle of the control surfaces, δ. Q is the rate of change of the pitch attitude angle, Θ.

These stability derivatives have to be known from wind tunnel measurements or flight tests. They, again, are not constants, but depend on flight conditions, primarily on v. Actually they are functions of many more variables, and their complete functional description is a formidable task. For the purpose of this example it is assumed that they are only functions of v and that their functional relationship to v is empirically known from wind tunnel measurements and is documented in graphical form.

So, the set of equations to be represented on the Analog Computer is:

$$m \cdot \dot{\gamma} - A \frac{v \varrho}{2} (C_{L_\alpha} \cdot \alpha + C_{L_\delta} \cdot \delta) + \frac{g \cdot m \cdot \cos \gamma}{v} = 0 \tag{56}$$

$$I \ddot{\Theta} - A \cdot d \cdot \frac{v^2 \varrho}{2} (C_{M_\alpha} \cdot \alpha \dot{\Theta} C_{M_\delta} \cdot \delta - C_{M_Q} \cdot \dot{\Theta}) = 0 \tag{57}$$

$$\alpha = \Theta - \gamma \tag{58}$$

$$C_{L_\alpha}, C_{L_\delta}, C_{M_\alpha}, C_{M_\delta}, C_{M_Q} = f(v) \tag{59}$$

In setting up the problem on the computer it is recommendable to split the work in two phases (see Fig. 43). The first is the instrumentation of the basic equations and the second the instrumentation of the coefficient functions. Equation (56) is set up by equating to zero the currents on the summing point of amplifier 1. Multipliers 1 and 2 have to be provided, because the inputs δ and α have to be multiplied by the respective coefficient functions which will be provided later. Integrator 2 provides γ, which will be needed later to form α and the component of the gravity force, for which the resolver, *Res*, is required. Equation (57) is instrumented by working backwards from Θ and establishing $I \cdot \ddot{\Theta}$ by using integrators 3 and 4 and potentiometer 2. Then again the summation of terms is represented by the input currents to amplifier 5. All input terms have variable coefficients and so multipliers 3—5 are provided. Finally,

α is produced in amplifier 6. In doing all this, strict care has to be taken of all signs involved. Here it is assumed that multipliers and resolvers do not invert

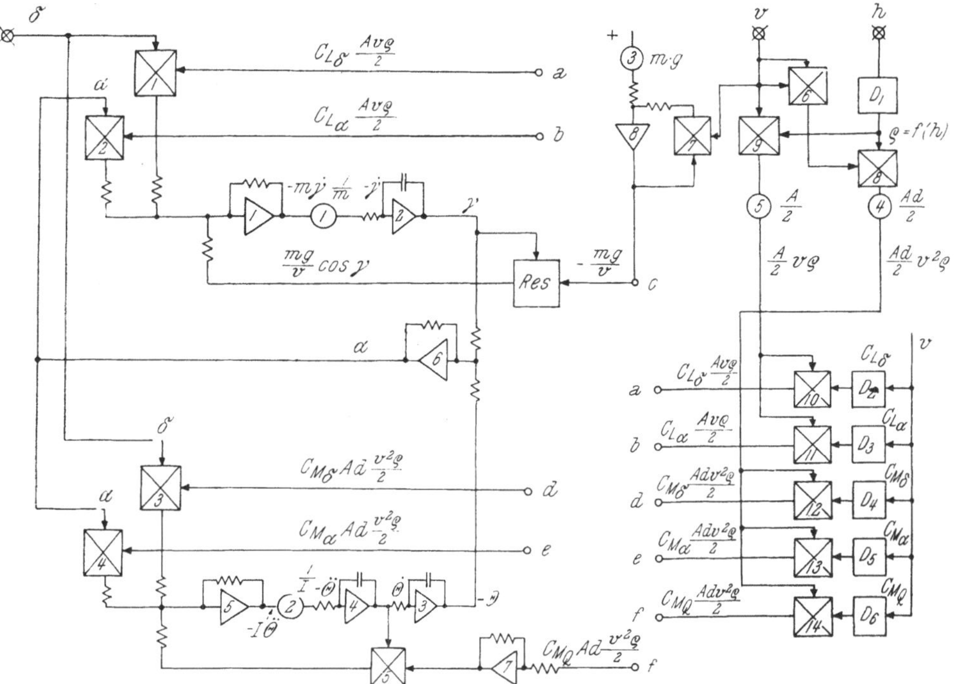

Fig. 43. Basic Computer Diagram for Aircraft Problem

signs, but this depends on the specific components which are used and may not be true in all cases.

It remains now to provide all the necessary coefficient control functions. The main controlling quantities are v and altitude, h, which are assumed to be available. They are fed into the computer at the respective terminals. Since h is not needed explicitly but only in form of the related air density, ϱ, diode function generator $D1$ is used to provide $\varrho = f(h)$. v is needed in various powers, so multiplier 6 is used to provide v^2 and the combination of amplifier 8 and multiplier 7 for $\frac{1}{v}$, multiplied by the constant, $m \cdot g$. The final coefficient functions contain the terms $\frac{A \cdot v \cdot \varrho}{2}$ and $\frac{A \cdot d \cdot v^2 \cdot \varrho}{2}$. Multipliers 8 and 9 and potentiometers 4 and 5, respectively, are used to produce them. The last step then is to produce the stability derivatives as individual functions of v. This is performed in Diode Function Generators $D\,2$ through $D\,6$. The complete coefficient functions are then produced by the respective multiplications in multipliers 10 through 14 and are available on terminals, a through f. They have to be considered to be connected to the respective terminals on the left side of Fig. 44. All function generators are set empirically, i. e., the slopes and breakpoints of all the segments are set in such a way as to match as closely as possible the empirically given functions.

Although the setup is quite formidable, it has to be noticed that it was derived by following the simple rules established before. The example again serves to demonstrate how analog computation does not require a specialized training but can be handled by the common sense of every scientist and engineer. It is certainly possible to reduce the number of required components, but for reasons of clarity it is always recommendable to start out with a broad outlay in the first approach to the basic diagram. Possible simplifications will become evident in the later process of scaling. But one important possibility of reducing component requirement has to be pointed out here: Several of the many multipliers have common input variables and so can be combined in "slaved" groups. They are the following:

No. of Multipliers	Common Variable
1, 3	δ
2, 4	α
6, 7, 9	v
10, 11	$A\,\frac{v\,\varrho}{2}$
12, 13, 14	$A \cdot d \cdot \frac{v^2\varrho}{2}$

The scaling and the establishment of the final computer diagram follows the same rules which were established before. To check out the computer setup it is recommendable to insert fixed defined values of v and h. All system coefficients are then fixed and known. If, in addition, the gravity input is disconnected, it is not too difficult to calculate or construct graphically a check solution. After the computer solution has been made to match the check solution, it remains to check separately the gravity and all coefficient circuits, which is easy to do. The probability then that the overall solution is correct for any arbitrary configuration is quite high. The actual investigation of the system can have any of the forms described in 3.46, the variable, δ, being the system input and any of the other variables the outputs of interest.

3.482. Automatic Control Problem. The task of automatically controlling an aircraft or missile consists in keeping it on a pre-defined course and to provide an adequate dynamic reaction to commands or disturbances.

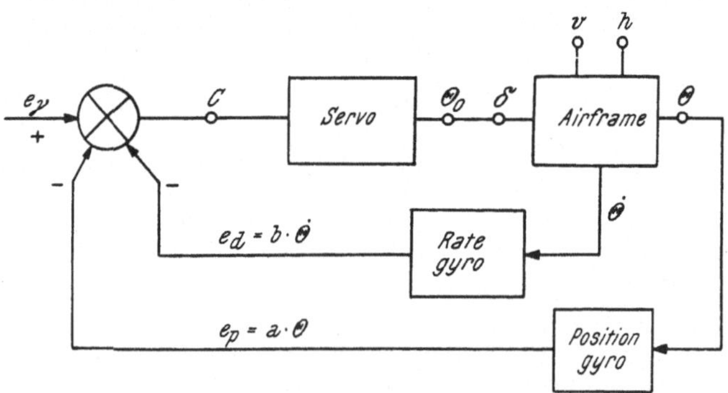

Fig. 44. Aircraft Control Configuration

The basic control mechanism is described in Fig. 44. An input voltage, e_γ, represents the desired flight path angle, γ. It is compared to a voltage, e_P, which is derived from a position gyro and which represents the actual attitude of the airframe. If the two are not equal, a finite command voltage, C, will be fed into the servo, the output of which is a finite deflection, δ, of the control surface of the airframe. It is seen that such a system does not control the actual flight path angle but the attitude of the airframe, due to the properties of the position gyro. Since the angle of attack is normally small, the resulting deviations are accepted. If they are not acceptable, additional procedures have to be inserted which exceed the scope of this discussion. The dynamic performance of the loop system is under control by feeding back a damping voltage, e_d, the output of a rate gyro measuring the rate of change of the attitude angle of the airframe.

The Analog Computer representation of the two main blocks of the control loop has been discussed before. Comparatively little has to be added to perform the complete study. Fig. 45 shows the complete setup. Amplifier 1 adds the

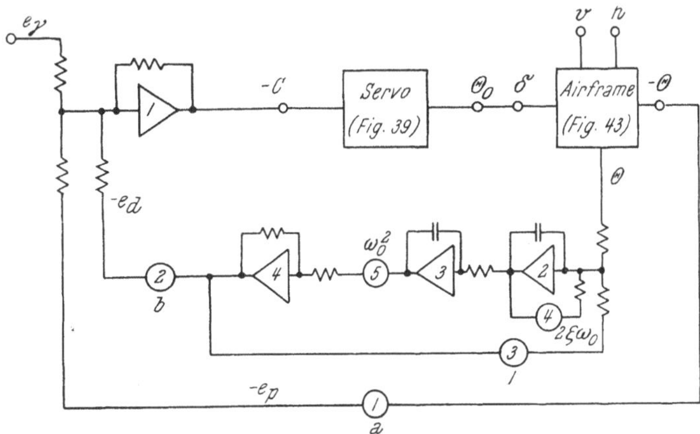

Fig. 45. Basic Computer Diagram for Aircraft Control Prob

input and feedback terms and coefficient potentiometer 1 represents the position gyro. An adequate simulation of the rate gyro must take into consideration its limited dynamic response. It is described by the second order differential equation:

$$\dot{\Theta} = \frac{1}{b}\left(e_d + \frac{2\zeta}{\omega_0} \cdot \dot{e}_d + \frac{1}{\omega_0^2} \cdot \ddot{e}_d\right) \tag{60}$$

ω_0 represents the natural frequency and ζ the relative damping coefficient. The equation is instrumented in the now well known way, using integrators 2 and 3, amplifier 4 and coefficient potentiometers 2 through 5.

The investigation of the complete automatic control loop can now be performed by inserting typical commands into $e\gamma$ and studying its response in Θ. If this response is not satisfactory, it can be improved by evaluating optimum settings of the servo system (potentiometers 4, 5 in Fig. 39) and an optimum rate gyro coefficient. These are the parameters which can be changed in the actual technical system. The others, particularly those of the airframe must be considered as being fixed. However, the dynamic response of the airframe depends on its "environment", velocity, v, and altitude, h. So, either compromises in the optimization of the free parameters have to be made or methods of adapting them to the flight conditions have to be designed.

Such an investigation is an extensive one and only its main features are demonstrated. On the other hand, the example indicates what an extraordinary help an Analog Computer can be. The mathematics even of the simplified example are so complex that it is impossible to find an analytical solution. The pure experimental way, i. e., to find the desired answers from flight tests, is enormously expensive and may even be dangerous.

3.483. Partial Differential Equations. The previous discussions demonstrated the excellent suitability of Analog Computers for the solution of problems which are described mathematically by ordinary differential equations of any form. In physical reality, however, there are many problems described by partial differential equations. One important class is concerned with the propagation of waves through continuous media. This statement already points to the fact that Analog Computers cannot provide exact solutions to such problems since they consist of lumped and not of continuously distributed operational elements. But solutions of any desired accuracy can be obtained by substituting the continuous medium by a sequence of finite intervals, the characteristics of which can be represented by lumped operational elements. In doing this, a compromise must be made between achievable accuracy and required number of components. The basic principles of the procedures will be explained using the example of the propagation of a plane sound wave along an axis x. The partial differential equation describing the phenomenon is:

$$\frac{\partial^2 p}{\partial x^2} = \frac{1}{c^2} \cdot \frac{\partial^2 p}{\partial t^2} \tag{61}$$

p is the instantaneous pressure increment around the local pressure and c is the velocity of sound propagation, the coefficient describing the medium. The second space derivative of p is now replaced by the second order differences of p over pre-selected, finite intervals Δ_x. Let x_n be one point along x and x_{n-1} and x_{n+1} the next points to the left and the right, respectively, spaced by the amount Δ_x, then (61) can be rewritten:

$$\frac{p_{n-1} - 2p_n + p_{n+1}}{(\Delta_x)^2} = \frac{1}{c^2} \frac{d^2 p_n}{d t^2} \tag{62}$$

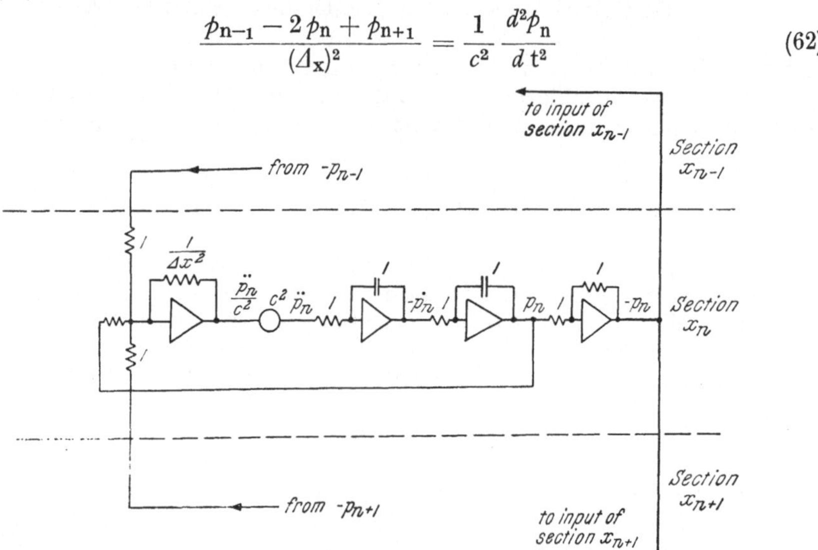

Fig. 46. Section of Computer Diagram for Partial Differential Equation

This equation can now be "literally" translated into a basic computer diagram. It is shown in a non-optimized form in Fig. 46. In practical scaling of the problem,

Δ_x must be selected to be small with respect to the shortest acoustical wavelength of interest. Time scaling should be selected in such a way that the actual computer frequencies do not exceed 100 cps. Changes in the propagation medium can be simulated by proper adjustment of the coefficients c^2.

3.484. The Time Delay Problem. The problem to shift a given function of time by a defined increment of time without distorting the function becomes increasingly of interest. It is encountered, among others, as "transportation lag" in industrial process investigations, in the evaluation of dynamic systems which contain digital computing processes and in the analysis of stochastic functions.

If the function which is to be shifted is empirically given, a curve follower as described in 3.244 can be used with an appropriately shifted reading head. Specifically magnetic tape devices with a movable reading head are well suited for this purpose. If properly designed, they can even be used to shift a function which is generated during an Analog Computer process and can be used immediately in the computer after the time shifting.

But there are different possibilities to synthesize a time shift process using standard computer components. The requirement to be met consists in providing a certain time delay, τ, for all frequencies up to a desired value, ω_0. The most straight forward approach is to synthesize the desired arrangement by a sequence of N second order systems. This is equivalent to building an electrical delay line which is loss-free and consists of lumped elements.

An estimate of the necessary amount of components can be made by using the following relation:

$$\tau = \frac{d\varphi}{d\omega} \sim \frac{\pi}{2} \cdot \frac{1}{\omega_0} \cdot N \tag{63}$$

The N second order systems, consisting of $2N$ integrators, must have the natural frequency ω_0 and a relative damping coefficient of 0.5 in order to provide adequate phase linearity up to ω_0. However, such an arrangement can have considerable distortions of its amplitude gain factor within the passband, if N becomes large. This can be avoided, if adequate compensating or equalizing terms are inserted into the second order system. One frequently used compensated second order system is described by the following equation in operational notation, where p denotes the complex frequency variable:

$$\frac{e_0(p)}{e_i(p)} = \frac{1 - \frac{1}{2}(p\tau) + \frac{1}{12}(p\tau)^2}{1 + \frac{1}{2}(p\tau) + \frac{1}{12}(p\tau)^2} \tag{64}$$

The natural frequency of such a system, ω_0, is equal to $\frac{3.46}{\tau}$, its relative damping coefficient, ζ, is equal to 0.865. Its phase angle is π at the natural frequency and it provides an amplitude response which is equal to 1 and independent of frequency within the operating range of the computer components. So it is definitely advantageous over a simple second order system, it needs only half as many components for a given delay requirement and has constant amplitude response.

There is a frequently used method of computer instrumentation for equations of this type, which contain derivatives of the output function, or p-terms in the denominator (lag terms), and derivatives of the input function, or p-terms in the numerator (lead terms). To explain it, (64) is split into two equations:

$$e'(p) = e_i(p) \frac{1}{1 + \frac{1}{2}(p\tau) + \frac{1}{12}(p\tau)^2} \tag{65}$$

$$e_0(p) = e'(p)\left[1 - \frac{1}{2}(p\tau) + \frac{1}{12}(p\tau)^2\right] \tag{66}$$

The first of them is a normal second order equation, instrumented in Fig. 47 by integrators and amplifiers 1—4.

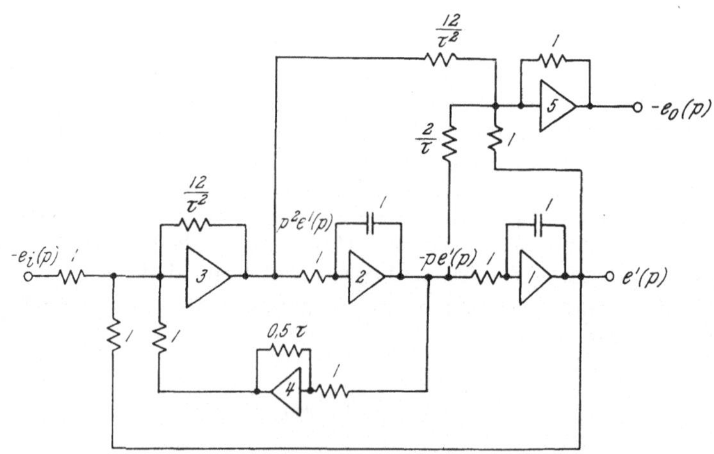

Fig. 47. Compensated Second Order System

To obtain $e_0(p)$ it is necessary only to collect the terms on the right hand side of equation (66) which are already available on the computer. This is done by amplifier 5 with the proper input resistors.

So, in order to design a time delay arrangement of this kind with a desired time delay, τ_{tot}, the phase response of which is approximately linear up to a desired frequency, ω_0, it is necessary to evaluate N, the total number of circuits to be connected in series:

$$N = \tau_{tot} \cdot \omega_0 \cdot \frac{1}{\pi} \tag{67}$$

Each of those circuits has to provide a time delay

$$\tau = \tau_{tot} \cdot \frac{1}{N} \tag{68}$$

Now the individual circuits can be designed using the scheme of Fig. 48.

All the methods discussed so far are approximations, since the frequency range is limited within which the phase response is linear. So the function which is processed is not only shifted but distorted to a certain extent.

An ideal arrangement has the transfer function:

$$\frac{e_0(p)}{e_i(p)} = exp\,(-p\tau) \tag{69}$$

This can be rewritten in the form:

$$\frac{e_0(p)}{e_i(p)} = \frac{1}{1 + (p\tau) + \frac{1}{2!}(p\tau)^2 + \frac{1}{3!}(p\tau)^3 + \ldots} \tag{70}$$

Since this series converges slowly, it is not profitable in terms of required computer components to use it. A better and more profitable approximation to (69) is the Padé approximation, of which (64) is a special case.

In synthesizing delay networks, combinations of passive components can be used to save amplifiers. Such details exceed the scope of this discussion. Commercial delay components are available.

3.485. Spectrum Evaluation. The following Analog Computer processes are described as examples of pure mathematical operations performed on the computer. They stand against the simulation of physical processes which is the natural application of the Analog Computer. The examples of evaluating frequency spectra of given functions of time were selected, because they are important for many types of analytical work.

3.4851. Fourier Transform. An approximation to the true transform

$$F(j\omega) = 2\int_0^T f(t)\; exp\;(-j\omega t)\; dt \tag{71}$$

is instrumented as shown in Fig. 48. The given function of time, $f(t)$, defined over an interval, T, is derived from the curve follower. It is multiplied by sin ωt

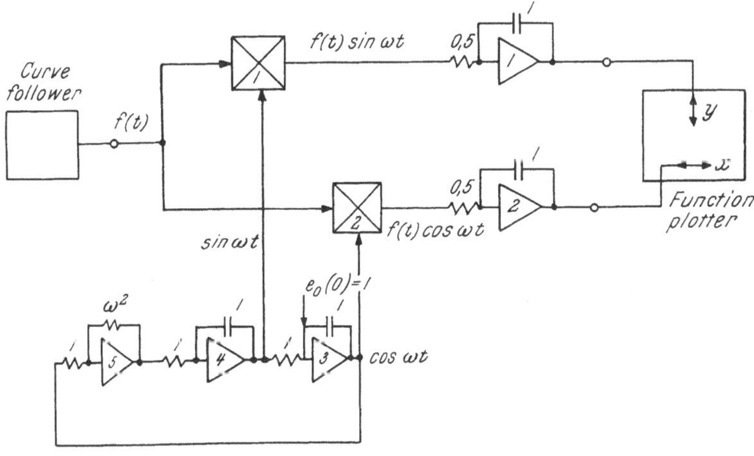

Fig. 48. Basic Computer Diagram for Fourier Transformation

and cos ωt, the two products are integrated and the results fed into the x and y servos of a plotting table. The pen of the plotter is lifted during the computation process and lowered to print out one point after the process is finished. The computation has to be repeated successively for different values of ω. The sequence of plotted points yields a representation of the Fourier spectrum in polar coordinates. To perform such a repetitive routine process the automatic features of a modern computer which were described in 3.36 are extremely helpful.

An interesting detail in Fig. 48 is the combination of integrators and amplifiers 3 to 5. It serves to solve the equation:

$$\frac{1}{\omega^2}\frac{d^2 e_0}{d t^2} + e_0 = 0; \; e_0 (0) = 1 \tag{72}$$

Its solution is $e_0 = \cos \omega t$. Then the function $\sin \omega t$, the negative derivative of the output, can be taken from amplifier 4. This circuit is frequently used to produce pure sine and cosine functions of exactly defined frequency. It is a second order system with no damping and actually maintains its oscillation amplitude over a long period of time with most modern computer components.

3.4852. Auto-correlation Functions and Power Spectra. In many types of analytical work concerned with stochastic processes it is important to know the correlation functions and the power spectra of empirically given functions of time. Estimates of both are derived from the equations:

Auto correlation function:

$$R(\tau) = \frac{1}{T}\int_0^T f(t)\, f(t-\tau)\, dt \tag{73}$$

Power Spectrum:

$$W(\omega) = 2\int_0^{\tau_{\max}} R(\tau) \cos \omega\tau \, d\tau \tag{74}$$

The instrumentation for (73) is shown in Fig. 49. The delay unit has been discussed in 3.484. The process has to be repeated for a sufficient number of values of τ.

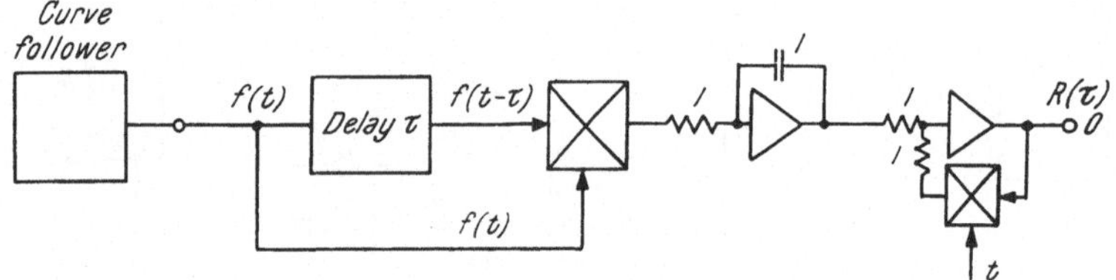

Fig. 49. Basic Computer Diagram for Autocorrelation Function

If the evaluation of the power spectrum is desired, the autocorrelation has to be plotted as a continuous function, inserted into a curve follower and processed in the setup of Fig. 48, omitting the sine term.

3.486. Difficulties in Analog Operation. Difficulties arise if the problem setup requires that a number of operational amplifiers form a closed loop system which does not contain any integrators. If this number is even, and the required loop gain is larger than 1, then the feedback is regenerative and the loop is unstable. Such a configuration is often encountered in the solution of sets of algebraic equations. The only possibility of solving the problem in such a case is by a proper reformulation of the equations in order to make the required loop gain smaller than 1. But even such loops consisting of an odd number of amplifiers can become unstable. This is due to the finite bandwidth of the amplifiers and occurs if the effective loop gain is equal or larger than 1 at the frequency for which the total phase shift in the loop is 180°. Since this frequency is normally very high with respect to the frequencies of interest in the problem, an additional filter inserted in the loop may suppress these oscillations without interfering significantly with the dynamics of the problem.

Fortunately, difficulties of this kind arise very seldom in the proper application area of Analog Computers, namely, the representation of physical systems.

3.5. Conclusions and Outlook

The best way to conclude this attempt to provide an understanding of the philosophy, the techniques, the advantages and limitations of analog computation is to quote an authority and pioneer of the art. Dr. G. A. Philbrick concluded an address given at the General Electric Computer Seminar in September 1955 by the following advice:

"You will certainly continue to succeed in engineering ventures even if you follow doctrines exactly opposite to mine, but I shall try your patience a little farther with some suggestions which I believe are sound, and which are sincerely distilled from a fairly broad experience with computers under many different conditions.

When and if you make computing facilities available to your engineering staff, set up the lines of origination and action so that your creative engineers may have direct access to the computing machinery itself. In this I am speaking of analog computation; to set up rules for the other types would be presumptuous of me. The best usuage is to avoid turning a problem into a numerically specified equation, and then seeking a single numerical solution. For one thing, the machine can better deal with the primary equations themselves, before mathematical consolidation. But more important, for the greatest benefits in typical cases, a whole spectrum of questions will require answers, and one of the vital questions may be 'What question should be asked next?' The exploratory procedure is thus generally sequential, or experimental, meaning that there are logical loops which the machine can help to unravel if given a part in the deliberations. The thread of the tale can easily be lost if an organization intervenes between the engineer and his crystal ball.

If you want results, promote a free interchange of ideas with the analog machine. Odd as it may sound, the computer will frequently make suggestions at an engineering level, when an understanding develops. Take it from me, it can even invent. But not by itself.

Above all, be assured that you cannot replace brain power with a computer. No substitute for creative thinking has yet been reported. Nor can the machine convert mediocre technical men into prodigies. The proper application of analog instrumentation is to extend, to augment, and to liberate the developmental and creative engineering brain power which is already available in your departments."

The main property of the Analog Computer, namely to be the direct and natural working tool of the creative engineer and scientist, quite certainly outweighs its limitations with respect to static accuracy. But development and progress continue. An important attempt is to combine the high accuracy of digital methods with the philosophy of approach of analog computation. It consists in providing computing components using the working principles of a high speed Digital Differential Analyzer, which can be combined to a required computation setup on a patch board. So the evolution process toward an ideal computer is still underway.

Bibliography

Because of the very general character of the survey presented in this chapter, it is impossible to indicate the individual sources where all the ideas and procedures were first described.

The reader who is interested to learn more about Analog Computers is referred to the following books which contain comprehensive bibliographies:

Korn, G. A., and Korn T. M.: "Electronic Analog Computers (D-C Analog Computers)". McGraw-Hill Book Company, New York, 1956.

Johnson, Clarence L., "Analog Computer Techniques". McGraw-Hill Book Company, New York, 1956.

Chapter 4

Digital Differential Analyzers

By

Hans W. Gschwind (Dr.-Ing.)

(Chief, Modification and Development Branch, Analysis and Computation Division, Air Force Missile Development Center, Holloman AFB, New Mexico, USA.)

With 86 Figures

4. Digital Differential Analyzers

Digital differential analyzers are a class of electronic computers which have not yet had the general recognition they undoubtedly deserve. The probable reason for this fact is that there is only a narrow field of application in which digital differential analyzers offer more advantages than either analog or digital computers.

The digital differential analyzer, similar to an analog computer, is a machine whose main function is to integrate and which, therefore, can handle only problems whose solutions are reducible to integration processes. Similar to a digital computer, it performs this integration by a digital approximation. It may seem paradoxical that this approximation yields more accurate results than the theoretically exact model in an analog computer. In reality, solutions by a digital differential analyzer are never exact, but — different from an analog computer — any desired degree of accuracy can be obtained. As we shall see later, the accuracy is not limited by the principle used but rather imposed by practical considerations such as the amount of hardware incorporated into a certain computer design or the time available to find the solution to a given problem on a given machine.

The digital differential analyzer, therefore, is a special purpose computer for high accuracy integration. In this application, it is superior to any analog computer. Unfortunately we cannot, without restrictions, say that it is in this respect also superior to a digital computer. A digital computer can do everything a digital differential analyzer can and much more. All that we may say here in favor of the digital differential analyzer is that it can perform high accuracy integration faster and more economically than a digital computer, simply for the reason that it is a special purpose machine built specifically to perform this task.

Up to the present time, computer designers, and especially manufacturers, have somewhat neglected the digital differential analyzer, although not completely without reason. A great many customers are interested in high accuracy integration but are not able to utilize a digital differential analyzer to the extent that it becomes economical to operate. Instead of a digital differential analyzer, they use a general purpose digital computer which they can apply to almost any problem, including their business administration, and with which they get high accuracy integration as a by-product. For other customers, interested in integration requiring not too high an accuracy, the analog computer is the appropriate machine. A small analog computer can be bought for a price which is much less than that of a digital differential analyzer and, when the need arises, the system can be easily enlarged simply by the addition of more units of the desired type. In addition, the analog computer is well known, simple in design, and somewhat easier to program. A third group of customers wants to perform many types of integration. For this group, a combination of analog and digital computers is a good choice. The fourth group, then, able to justify a digital differential analyzer on a strictly economical basis, is only a small fraction of all computer users.

With the increasing number of computers, this situation will probably change in the future. First of all, a larger number of customers will have enough specialized problems to warrant an economical full-time use of a digital differential analyzer. Secondly, a sufficient number of customers will have need for both high speed and high accuracy integration, especially for real-time applications, where a physical process and the related computation proceed simultaneously.

High speed and high accuracy integration, these are the characteristics which in some fields of application can make the digital differential analyzer definitely superior to both the analog and the general purpose digital computer, especially if proper effort is put into its design. There is no doubt that its speed for integration can be higher than that of a digital computer. The reason is fairly clear. The digital differential analyzer has a "built-in" program for integration whereas time-consuming non-integration type operation are required to make a digital computer integrate. In addition, the digital differential analyzer can be designed so that all its integrators work truly in parallel, a feature which cannot be equalled by a general purpose digital computer.

So, even if the digital differential analyzer is probably not regarded as a very important type of machine at present, it certainly has its merits and most likely will play an important rôle among modern electronic computers in the future.

4.1. Description

4.11. Components

4.111. Integrators. The basic component of a digital differential analyzer is the integrator. Integration is performed as a digital process by built-in electronic circuitry. Digital integrators may differ with respect to the digital approximation they use and with respect to the electronic circuitry (which we shall disregard here).

4.1111. Integration in a Digital Differential Analyzer. The basic function of any integrator is the evaluation of:

$$z = \int_{x_0}^{x_1} Y(x)\, dx \tag{1}$$

The integrators in a digital differential analyzer perform the evaluation of (1) continuously. The lower limit of integration x_0 is the initial value of the variable x, i. e., the value of x at the time when the computation is started. The upper limit of integration is in any instant the current value of the variable x. Therefore, we may write:

$$z(x) = \int_{x_0}^{x} Y(x)\, dx \tag{2}$$

Under the given circumstances we may consider the integrator as a mechanism which approximates a function $z(x)$ according to equation (2) from a variable x and a given function $Y(x)$.

For the following considerations it is advantageous to show the previous relation also in differential form:[1]

$$dz = Y\,dx \tag{3}$$

and the variable z as:

$$z = z_0 + \int_{z_0}^{z} dz \tag{4}$$

So far, we have shown only exact relations. Approximations used by digital integrators are in effect those commonly used for the numerical and graphical evaluation of an integral. The differentials dx, dy, dz are replaced by finite increments Δx, Δy, Δz and the integration is replaced by a summation over a finite number of terms. The justification for doing so is given by the very definition of the integral:

$$\int_{x_0}^{x_1} Y\,dx = \lim_{\|\Delta x_\nu\| \to 0} \sum_{\nu=1}^{n} Y_\nu\,\Delta x_\nu, \tag{5}$$

where $\|\Delta x_\nu\|$ denotes the maximum value of Δx. The sum in (5) will be the closer to the value of the integral, the finer the resolution in Δx_ν is. From equations (3) and (4) we may now write the following approximations:

$$\Delta z_\nu = Y_\nu\,\Delta x_\nu \tag{6}$$

$$z_n = z_0 + \sum_{\nu=1}^{n} \Delta z_\nu \tag{7}$$

Combining (6) and (7), we obtain:

$$z_n = z_0 + \sum_{\nu=1}^{n} Y_\nu\,\Delta x_\nu \tag{8}$$

Finally, if all increments Δx_ν are equal to Δx, then equations (6) and (8) simplify to:

$$\Delta z_\nu = Y_\nu\,\Delta x \tag{9}$$

$$z_n = z_0 + \Delta x \sum_{\nu=1}^{n} Y_\nu \tag{10}$$

Interpreting the latter two equations geometrically, we perform a simple, graphic integration. The area between the curve $Y(x)$ and the x-axis from $x = x_0$ to $x - x_n$ is approximated by the sum of the areas of all the rectangles of width Δx and length Y_ν (see Fig. 1).

Digital differential analyzers use simple schemes for integration, such as the one indicated above. However, before we consider the details of digital integrators, we should turn our attention to two peculiarities of digital differential

[1] A reader not interested in the mechanics of digital integration may want to skip to 4.1115.

analyzers. The first is a feature of any numerical operation by nature. Values are represented by numbers, and since it is impossible to have an unlimited number of digital positions in a machine, a truncation at some digital position is always necessary. The (continuous) variable Y in Fig. 1 can therefore assume only a finite number of values within the computer and is, in an exact sense, represented by a step curve. Stated a little differently, changes in Y can take place only in discrete steps. These changes can be very small and perhaps seem of no great importance in a particular problem. However, changes in x may be of the same order of magnitude, so, if we pay attention to this fact at all, we should do so in both instances.

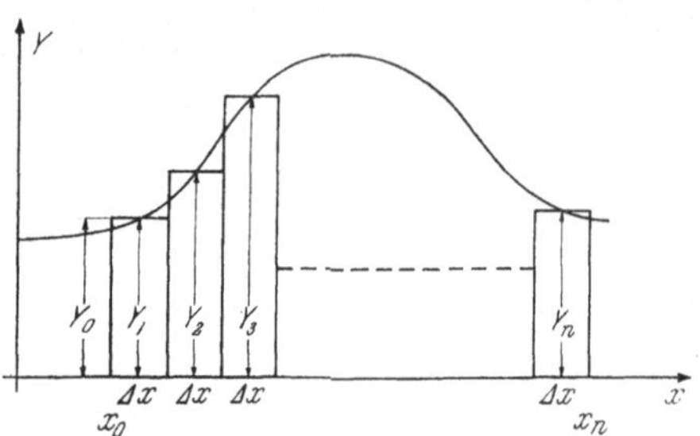

Fig. 1. Simple, Graphic Integration

The second property may be considered a consequence of the first. Digital differential analyzers are invariably incremental machines. This means increments or changes in variables are transmitted throughout the system rather than the total values of the functions. Electronically, this is much easier to accomplish, and since increments have to be in discrete steps, as we have seen, this is the simplest way of doing it.

In order to find the current value of a variable, say Y, during a computation, the computer has to sum over all increments Δy so far received. Then we obtain:

$$Y_{\text{current}} = Y_0 + \Sigma \Delta y \tag{11}$$

Y_0 is the value of Y at the beginning of the computation and $\Sigma\Delta y$ is the sum of all increments Δy (which may be positive or negative), so far received. In order to keep equation (11) as general as possible, no exact limits are shown over which this summation is to be performed. The difficulty is that there might be more than one increment Δy during one interval of integration. In this case, the computer has to find an "average" Y_ν for every interval. This Y_ν will be different for integrators using different approximations and we will have to consider these different cases one at a time.

4.1112. Rectangular Integration. Rectangular integration is, for digital differential analyzers, the least difficult type of integration to perform. The "average" Y_ν used during an interval of integration is simply the current value of Y at the time the machine takes a step in the x direction. Electronically, the step in x direction is caused by a pulse. If such Δx pulses signify the end of an intervall, we have an integration as shown in Fig. 2.

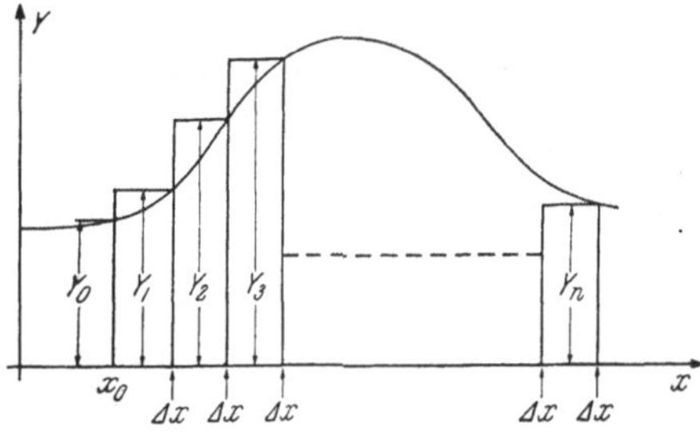

Fig. 2. Rectangular Integration

This, certainly is not the best method of integration. There is, however, an excuse: the computer compensates for the relatively rough integration method by using extremely small increments.[1] This way, the error is kept small and well below that of any electrical or mechanical analog.

[1] The number of steps covering the full range of integration in an actual problem may well be in the order of 100,000 or more.

Referring to Fig. 2, we find for Y_1:

$$Y_1 = Y_0 + \sum_1 \Delta y \tag{12}$$

Y_0 is the initial value of the integrand and $\sum_1 \Delta y$ is the summation over all increments, Δy, ariving during the first interval of integration.
Correspondingly, we have:

$$Y_2 = Y_0 + \sum_1 \Delta y + \sum_2 \Delta y \tag{13}$$

And in general:

$$Y_\nu = Y_0 + \sum_{\mu=1}^{\nu} \sum_\mu \Delta y \tag{14}$$

The double summation is simply the accumulation of all increments received up to the time when the computer makes its ν-th step in x direction. Equation (14) together with equation (10) is sufficient to describe the process of rectangular integration.[1] Obviously, there are only two arithmetic operations involved, i. e. addition and multiplication. A further simplification is given by the fact that the multiplication is by constant Δx, which, once chosen stays the same during the computation. Considering only increments of "unit" size and, therefore, of the arithmetic value one,[2] integration reduces to only one arithmetic operation: that of addition.[3] An integrator has to perform now two tasks: it has to accumulate the current value of Y from increments Δy according to equation (14) and it has to accumulate the current value of z from the current values of Y_ν for every step in x direction according to equation (10).

Having stated the requirements, let us now find the mechanics to perform this integration. Since the integrator works digitally, it has to have a device which keeps the numerical value of the integrand. As in a simple desk calculator, this storage device is called a register. In order to keep the value of the integrand current, the Y-register must have facilities for the input and addition of increments Δy. In other words, it must have the properties of an accumulator. For the evaluation of z, we need a second register also with accumulative properties. Later on, we will have need to modify this register, but let us be satisfied for the moment and call it the Z-register. We can now draw the block diagram of our digital integrator.

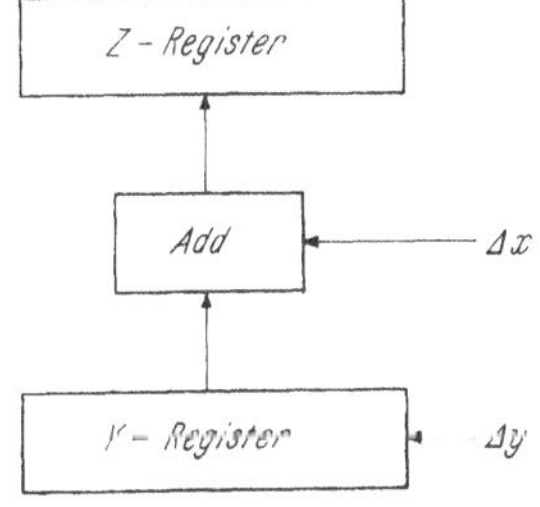

Fig. 3. Block Diagram of a Digital Integrator

The Y-register contains the value of the integrand. Inputs of Δy increments take care of always keeping the value current. For every step in x-direction, the integrator receives a Δx increment and adds the current contents of the Y-register to the contents of the Z-register.[4] In this way, the contents of the Z-register are an accumulation of the partial areas $Y_\nu \, \Delta x$ with $\Delta x = 1$ according to Fig. 2. If a problem requires an initial value of Y or z which is different from

[1] Equation (14) replaces the more general equation (11) for rectangular integration.

[2] It is arbitrary what we call a unit. The actual problem has to be "scaled" so that a unit is a sufficiently small value. See 4.22.

[3] The term addition as used here is meant to include the addition of negative values required for negative functions or negative increments.

[4] If, for some reason the variable x should decrease in a problem, i. e. a negative increment Δx arrives, we have to subtract the current value of Y from Z, i. e., to add the negative value of Y.

zero, we simply enter these initial conditions into the Y- or Z-registers before starting the integration.

Our integrator so far works correctly, but it has one disadvantage. We really should have an output in incremental form, in other words a Δz in order to have compatible inputs and outputs. There is a very simple way of accomplishing this, even though it may not be obvious.

Suppose we split the Z-register in Fig. 3 in a left and a right half. We provide for the right half only as many digital positions as the Y-register has. Then, during the process of integration when the integrator keeps adding the contents of Y into Z, the right half will overflow into the left half as soon as the capacity of the right half is exceeded. More exactly, if Y contains a very large number, say 9999, we will get an overflow practically every time a Δx increment is received.[1] If Y is equal to zero, no overflow occurs and if Y happens to be 5000... there will be one overflow for every two increments in x. We notice that the frequency of overflows is proportional to the contents of the Y-register.[2] On the other hand, the frequency of overflows is also proportional to the frequency of Δx arrivals. If we have frequent Δx increments, we will get relatively frequent overflows. If increments Δx occur rarely, we rarely have an overflow.

A rate of overflows proportional to the value of Y and the rate of Δx is exactly what we would expect of the Δz output (equation 6). There is nothing then keeping us from calling this overflow the Δz increment.[3] Instead of regarding the contents of the complete Z-register as the value of the integral, we now will say the total value of the integral is represented by the number of overflows occured so far plus the number contained in the right half of the register. Since the right half of Z contains only the remainder of the integral, we will call it from now on the R-register.

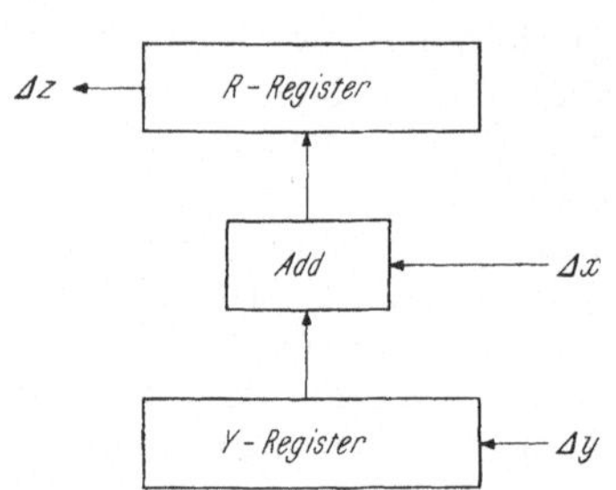

Fig. 4. Digital Integrator with Incremental Output

The block diagram of the digital integrator with incremental output is given in Fig. 4.

This arrangement has the advantage over that of Fig. 3 that outputs are compatible with inputs. The disadvantage of not having the complete value of the integral in numerical form can be easily remedied by simply feeding the Δz output into a second integrator as Δy input and so accumulating the total value of z in this second integrator.[4]

Expressing the contents of the R-register mathematically, we obtain:

$$R_n = R_0 + \Delta x \sum_{\nu=1}^{n} Y_\nu - \sum_{\nu=1}^{n} \Delta z_\nu \tag{15}$$

[1] Digital integrators usually have a special code for a number which is one larger than 9999.... the largest number which normally could be contained in Y. This special code will produce an overflow *every* time when an increment Δx is received.

[2] For negative values of Y we obtain negative contributions towards the total value of the integral. In this case the right half of the Z-register has to "borrow" from the left half. This borrow is considered a negative overflow. The frequency of borrows is again proportional to the value of Y.

[3] Positive overflows correspond to $+\Delta z$ increments. Negative overflows or borrows correspond to $-\Delta z$ increments.

[4] See e. g. Fig. 78.

and the outputs Δz become:

$$\Delta z = R_{\nu-1} + Y_\nu \Delta x - R_\nu \tag{16}$$

Note: Using an integrator identical to the one discussed so far, we may have an integration procedure according to Fig. 5 instead of Fig. 2.

The only difference here is that the increments Δx arrive at the beginning of an interval instead of the end. This way, the integrator uses the value of Y at the beginning of an interval as Y_ν. Equations (12, 13 and 14) are then slightly modified:

$$Y_1 = Y_0 \tag{17}$$

$$Y_2 = Y_1 + \sum_1 \Delta y \tag{18}$$

$$Y_\nu = Y_0 + \sum_{\mu=1}^{\nu-1}{}' \sum_\mu \Delta y \tag{19}$$

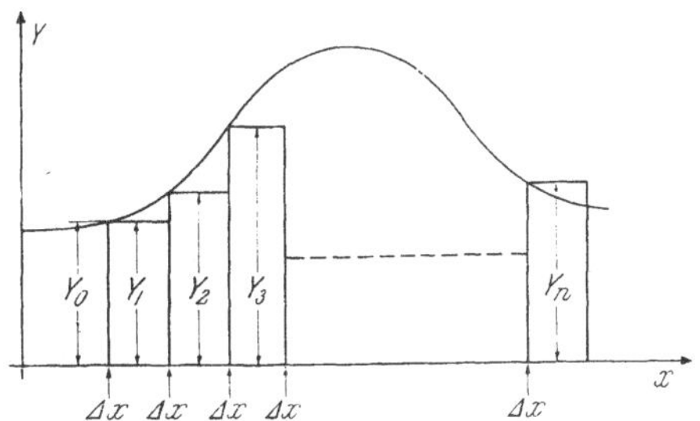

Fig. 5. Rectangular Integration with Δx Arriving at the Beginning of an Interval

4.1113. Interpolative Integration. As we can see from Fig. 2, rectangular integration yields only a rough approximation to the true integral. Some digital differential analyzers, however, use this scheme. True, by taking extremely small increments, we can reach any accuracy we desire, but we have to pay for this accuracy by a relatively high number of integration steps and — more important — by the time to execute them in the computer. A much better approximation should be obtained by a first order interpolation (according to the trapezoidal rule). Instead of taking the current Y either at the end or at the beginning of an integration interval, we now take the arithmetic mean of the two as Y_ν. Graphically interpreted, we have the straight line approximation given in Fig. 6.

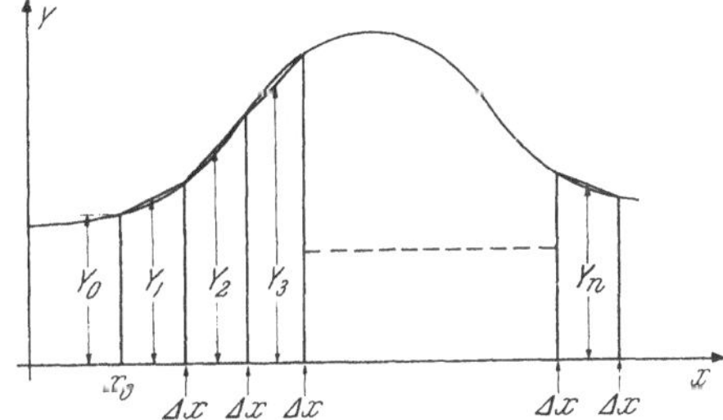

Fig. 6. Trapezoidal Integration

Of course, this type of integration is too complicated to be performed in the digital integrator described previously. If the Y-register is used to keep the value of the integrand current, then we must have an additional storage device for the following reason: At the end of an integration interval we need not only the current value of Y but also the value of Y in the middle of the interval. One register is not sufficient to hold both values. Suppose $Y_{i\nu}$ is the value of Y at the beginning of the ν-th interval, then we can use the second register to accumulate $Y_{i\nu}$ according to:

$$Y_\nu = Y_{i\nu} + \frac{1}{2} \sum_\nu \Delta y \tag{20}$$

Equation (20) gives the same mean value of Y as customarily obtained by taking one half of the sum of Y at the beginning and Y at the end of an interval, but the division of the input rate is electronically simpler to accomplish than a division of the numbers representing Y.[1] The block diagram for trapezoidal integration is shown in Fig. 7.

The Y-register keeps the current value of the integrand at all times. At the beginning of the computation and every time an increment Δx arrives, the contents of the Y-register are copied into the Y_ν-register. The contents of this register are then increased by $^1/_2\, \Sigma \Delta y$ during every interval. At the end of the interval, the Y_ν register contains the Y_ν according to the trapezoidal rule (20) and this is added to the contents of the R-register in the usual manner, generating or not generating an output Δz. The integrator for trapezoidal integration is not much more complicated than the integrator for rectangular integration. Naturally, we have to pay for the additional circuitry, but let us see what we get in return. As we shall see in 4.32, a general error analysis is not feasible. The actual accuracy of both methods will depend upon the type of function to be integrated, the size of increments Δx, the frequency of increments Δy and similar factors. It is, however, possible to construct examples where the error of the trapezoidal integrator may well be one or more orders of magnitude smaller than that of the rectangular integrator, assuming equal steps Δx in both integrators. More important — allowing the same error for both types of integrators' the trapezoidal integrator may work one or more orders of magnitude faster than the rectangular integrator in such an example. Since the expense for both types of integrators is still in the same order of magnitude, the additional investment seems to yield a good return.

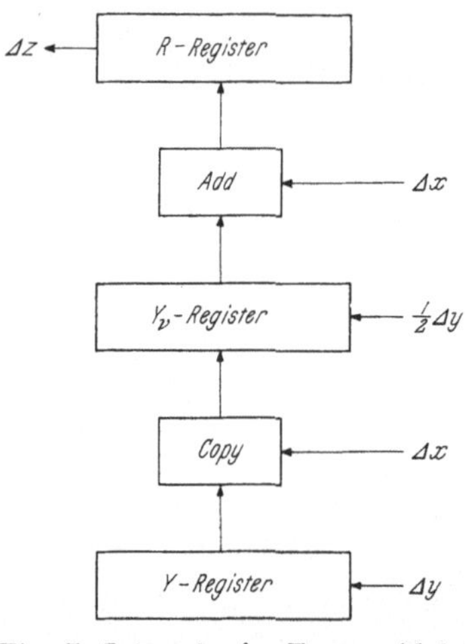

Fig. 7. Integrator for Trapezoidal Integration

It is entirely conceivable to use a higher order interpolation method in a digital integrator. However, there is so far no digital differential analyzer in existence using such a method, and, in addition, the trapezoidal integrator seems to be very close to the optimum of accuracy and speed versus cost. We have seen that rectangular integration requires one Y-register and trapezoidal integration requires two Y-registers in a digital integrator. Using quadratic interpolation, a digital integrator has to have three storage devices for Y values and for cubic interpolation, four. In addition, the hardware to perform the arithmetic gets so much more complicated whereas the gain in accuracy is much less than in the step from rectangular to trapezoidal integration. There are two more defects which make the value of higher order interpolation at least doubtful. There are seldom sufficient increments in Y to allow a high order interpolation within one interval of integration. If the interpolation is extended over more intervals, then there will be a serious time delay between inputs and outputs of the integrator; besides, no matter whether we consider interpolation within one interval or over more intervals, higher order interpolations require a rather exact knowledge of x values corresponding to increments in Y, so that the integrator would have to interpolate between increments in x in order to find these.

[1] In a binary computer, this division is performed by adding the increments Δy into an additional digital position to the right of the normally least significant digit. The Y_ν and the R-registers have then one more digital position than the Y-register.

4.1114. Extrapolative Integration. All digital integrators discussed so far have a built-in delay between inputs and outputs. By the very nature of the digital approximation, the integrator has to receive input pulses before it can generate the corresponding output. This delay between input and output may be of no importance for some problems; for other types, it may be a serious drawback which in effect lowers the accuracy by a systematic error.

The simplest example to show this difficulty is a case where the Δz output of an integrator is fed back into the Δy input of the same integrator.[1] This way the Δz output of a certain interval can be used as Δy input only during the next interval of integration.

In order to correct this situation, the increment in Y would have to arrive before the evaluation of Δz in an interval. On the other hand, Δz has to be first in order to obtain the correct increment in Y. The only way out of this dilemma is to estimate the new integrand previous to the evaluation of Δz, in other words, to perform an extrapolation of the integrand.

Perhaps one could call an integration according to Fig. 5 an extrapolation. However, in this simple scheme we assume that the integrand will not change from its value at the beginning of an interval throughout the interval. So this type of integration will not help in the situation we are in. The simplest extrapolation method which can take care of future changes of variables is a linear extrapolation, somewhat analogous to the linear interpolation described in 4.1113. In a linear extrapolation, we assume that the slope of the (variable) integrand in the new interval will be the same as in the previous interval. The graphical representation of this type of integration is given in Fig. 8.

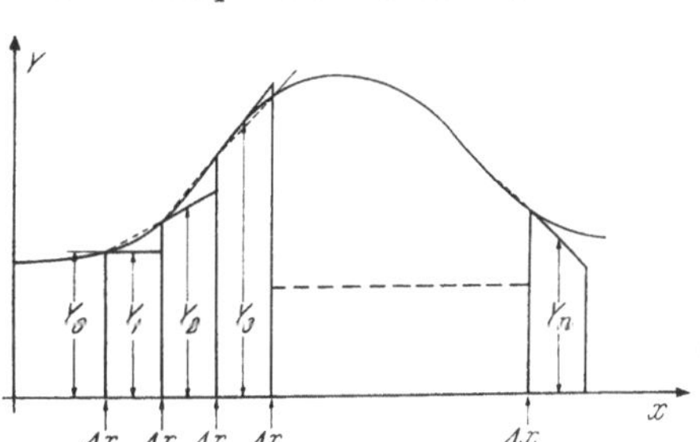

Fig. 8. Linear Extrapolation

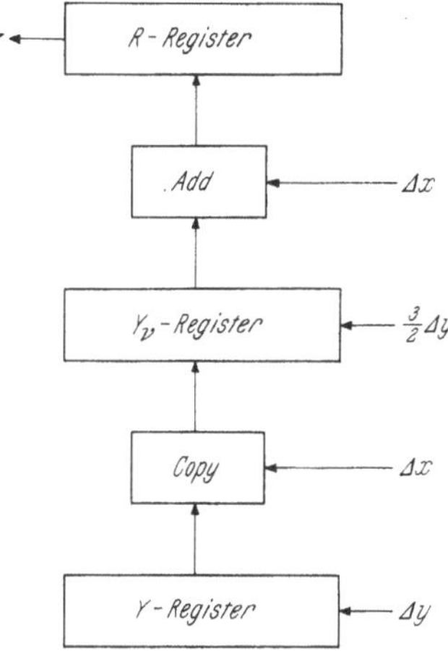

Fig. 9. Integrator with Linear Extrapolation

The new Y_ν is found by linearily extending the slope of the integrand in the $(\nu - 1)$-th interval into the ν-th interval. In mathematical form, it is:

$$Y_\nu = Y_{i\nu-1} + \frac{1}{2}\sum_{\nu-1}\Delta y + \sum_{\nu-1}\Delta y \tag{21}$$

$Y_{i\nu-1}$ is the value of the integrand at the beginning of interval $\nu - 1$; $\sum_{\nu-1}'\Delta y$ is the summation of all increments received during this interval.[2] The corresponding integrator block diagram is given in Fig. 9.

[1] See e. g. Fig. 23 .

[2] Note that this formula for the evaluation of Y in the ν-th interval does not require any knowledge of inputs during this interval.

Again, it would be entirely possible to use higher order extrapolation. The arguments for and against this are similar to those for higher order interpolation.

4.1115. Schematic Representation of Integrators. Let us forget the details of digital integrators for the moment and pay more attention to practical aspects. We have seen that a digital integrator is a unit which produces an output Δz from inputs Δx and Δy according to equations (6) and (11). From a practical standpoint, however, we would prefer a unit which produces the differential dz from differentials dx and dy, since practical problems are more likely than not stated in differential form. It is customary to call the output of even a digital integrator dz and the inputs dx and dy respectively. This is perfectly all right as long as we keep in mind that a digital integrator produces only an approximation to the relation (3) between these differentials.

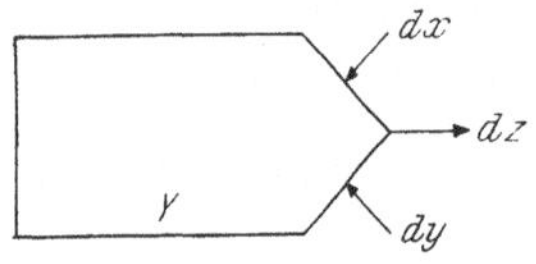

Fig. 10. Block Diagram Representation of an Integrator

It is also customary to use a symbol for integrators which is given in Fig. 10. This symbol greatly facilitates the representation of integrator interconnections for all types of problems.

The labelling of inputs, outputs, and the integrand corresponds to the actual problem values like $d\,(\sin \alpha)$, $d\,(x^2)$, or $d\,(e^{-t})$, etc.

4.112. Units with Special Features. So far we have discussed only integrators and their use for integration. During the setup of a problem for a digital differential analyzer, situations will be encountered where it is necessary to have units for other tasks, like adders, multipliers, servos, etc. Most of these units consist of circuits which are basically those of an integrator which, however, are sometimes operated in a fashion completely different from an integration process. Even then, the name integrator is retained as a general term, probably because integrators usually can be "programmed" to perform these special functions. This programming can be done by switches which introduce a slightly modified circuitry into an integrator or by pulses introduced into the system which perform the switching electronically. However, certain computers use to some extent special units with slightly simpler or more efficient circuits than those of an integrator. Here we shall consider only the features of these units. Their application will be seen in 4.21.

4.1121. Output Sign-Reversal. A simple but very useful feature is that of output sign-reversal. It, in effect, changes the sign of increments Δz. In cases where the output would be conventionally in the form of positive increments, we now obtain the same number of negative increments and vice versa. Electronically, it is only required to reverse the polarity of positive and negative pulses.[1] The selection of this feature is indicated by a minus sign inside the symbol representing an integrator.[2]

4.1122. Signum Function. This feature is similar to an output sign-reversal; however, the selection is automatic. The sign of the output of a certain integrator is reversed if the integrand in a certain other integrator becomes negative. This feature — if incorporated at all — is usually restricted to physically or logically neighboring pairs of integrators. It is useful e. g. when generating absolute values of a variable or for an electronic switch.[3]

[1] On computers having a patchboard and carrying positive and negative increments on two separate lines, an output reversal can be conveniently accomplished by reversing the output terminals.

[2] See e. g. Fig. 11.

[3] See 4.21117 and 4.21143.

The integrator which changes its sign and the one on which the change depends are usually interconnected by an S-shaped symbol in the block diagram.

4.1123. Accomodation of Several dy Inputs. Most digital integrators have the ability to accept the increments of more than one variable on the dy input.[1] The use of this feature is indicated in the block diagram by more than one arrow feeding into the integrator symbol.

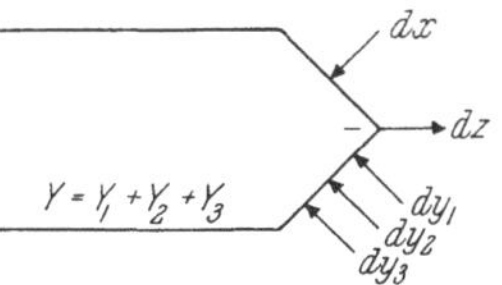

Fig. 11. Integrator with Sign Reversal and Three dy Inputs

The circuitry of an integrator of this kind is slightly more complicated than that of an integrator with one input, because several increments may arrive simultaneously and may be of arbitrary sign. The adding circuits connected to the Y-register must therefore have the capability of adding increments which have an arithmetic value different from one. Integrators may have the capability of accepting up to eight different dy inputs.

4.1124. Adders. If an addition of variables is required, a servo adder is used as described in 4.21115. Some computers, however, have the equivalent circuitry contained in a special unit called an adder.

4.1125. Constant Multipliers. In many instances, it may be desired to multiply the output of an integrator by a constant. A second integrator can be used for this purpose.[2] However, the integrators of some digital differential analyzers have a built-in constant multiplier.

One approach to the problem requires a slight modification of the R-register. Instead of generating an output Δz only when the most significant digit in R changes from 9 to 0, an output is also generated when there is a change from 4 to 5. This produces twice as many increments z as usual, or in effect, the output is multiplied by a factor of two.[3] By generating an output for every change from an odd to an even number in the most significant digit, the output is multiplied by five. This method of multiplication is restricted to a choice of only a few constant factors. It has, however, some advantages for the scaling of a problem.

The second method has complete freedom in the selection of constant factors. It uses the principle explained in 4.21111. An integrator of this type may be considered as a combination of two integrators. It has one additional Y_2-register and one additional R_2-register. The integrand of the Y_2-register is filled once and cannot be changed by increments during computation.

4.1126. Multipliers. Two variables can be multiplied by two integrators and a servo adder.[4] Some digital differential analyzers provide essentially the same circuits as two integrators and a servo adder in a special unit called a multiplier. However, the multiplier, by a slight modification, avoids a systematic error which will be introduced by using two regular integrators with rectangular integration. It evaluates the product of two variables correctly according to (22) whereas using two integrators, we obtain (23).[5]

$$\Delta\,(u\,v) = u\,\Delta\,v + v\,\Delta\,u + \Delta\,u\,\Delta\,v \tag{22}$$

$$\begin{aligned}\Delta\,(u\,v) &= (u + \Delta\,u)\Delta\,v + (v + \Delta\,v)\,\Delta\,u \\ &= u\Delta\,v + v\Delta\,u + 2\,\Delta\,u\,\Delta\,v\end{aligned} \tag{23}$$

[1] This feature, in many cases, eliminates the necessity for a separate adder. It is provided only for dy inputs. If more than one input is required for dx, a servo adder is used to generate the sum of several inputs. (See 4.21115.)

[2] See 4.21111.

[3] For a change from 0 to 9 and from 5 to 4, a negative increment Δz is produced.

[4] See 4.21112.

[5] Compare also Fig. 14.

In this latter case, the small area $\Delta u\, \Delta v$ in Fig. 12 is incorrectly counted twice.[1]

4.1127. Operational Integrators. Operational integrators considerabley increase the number of types of problems which can be solved on a digital differential analyzer. They can be used as servos, automatic switches, limiters, clippers, etc.[2] Unfortunately, no uniform nomenclature exists. Operational integrators are usually designated by their use rather than by differences in design. Their operation is only remotely similar to that of a digital integrator. The output Δz still depends upon the variable Y and the input $d\,x$, but Y is no longer the integrand, only a number which, according to a set of rules, determines the output. A commonly employed set of rules is given in (24)

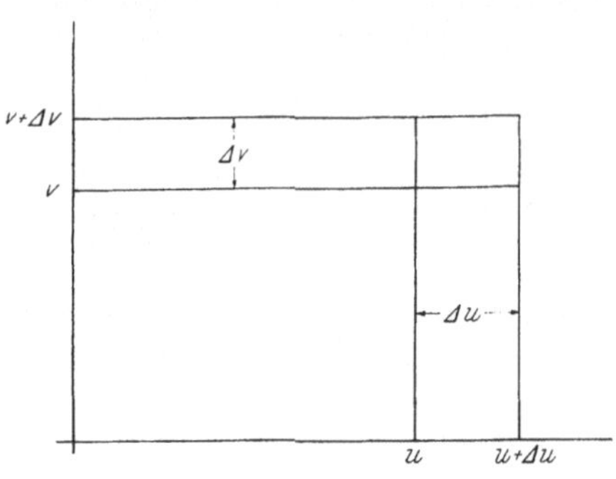

Fig. 12. Increments of a Product

$$\begin{aligned} &\text{If } Y \text{ is positive, then } \Delta z = \Delta x \\ &\text{If } Y \text{ is zero, then } \quad \Delta z = 0 \\ &\text{If } Y \text{ is negative, then } \Delta z = -\Delta x \end{aligned} \tag{24}$$

Using the output sign-reversal we can change the polarity of the outputs to the opposite of the one given above, leaving a zero output for $Y = 0$.

The most common use for this type of operational integrator is in servos.[3] In this application, the operational integrator receives a continuous string of positive increments on its dx input. The Y-register contains an error term.[4] If there is no error, then the contents of the Y-register are equal to zero and no output is generated. If the error has a finite positive value, the servo will produce a string of positive increments on its output which are used to correct the error until it is reduced to zero. If the error is negative, a string of negative increments is produced which has the tendency to drive in the opposite direction until the error is again zero.[5] Since the servo performs a simpler function than a regular integrator, its circuitry may also be simpler. For instance, an R-register is no longer required. Some computers, therefore, provide special units for servos with a less complex circuitry than that of an integrator.

It is interesting to note that a regular integrator[6] can be used as a servo. Normally the Y-register is designed so that it will change to the largest negative number after it had contained a positive number and is augmented in positive direction beyond the capacity of the register. Alternately, it will contain the largest positive number when it is augmented in negative direction beyond capacity. Usually this feature is of no consequence, but suppose the Y-register is operated in the neighborhood of this overflow condition for an error practically equal to zero and receives increments of the error as dy input. If, in a certain moment, the Y-register contains the largest possible positive number, the inte-

[1] In other schemes, this area is omitted.

[2] For applications, see 4.2113 and 4.2114.

[3] A servo is usually marked in block diagrams by the letter S.

[4] e. g. the difference between two variables which are supposed to be equal (see 4.2113).

[5] A detailed example of a servo operation is given in 4.2113.

[6] See e. g. Fig. 4.

grator produces a positive output. This output tends to correct the error (which we assume is practically zero). The correction overshoots and we get a positive increment for the error. This increment makes the Y-register overflow to the largest possible negative number. Then the next time, the integrator puts out a negative increment which tends to correct back to the old position. For no error, therefore, the Y-register oscillates between the largest possible positive and negative numbers, producing alternately positive and negative outputs. These alternating increments cancel in effect so that we obtain a zero output for no error. As soon as the error becomes appreciable, the integrator will put out a string of only positive or only negative increments until the error is reduced to practically zero again.

More elaborate types of operational integrators may have the same basic operation, but a more complicated set of rules. An example is the following:

$$\begin{array}{ll} \text{If} & \text{Then} \\ Y > H & \Delta z = 0 \\ 0 < Y \leqslant H & \Delta z = \Delta x \\ Y = 0 & \Delta z = 0 \\ -H \leqslant Y < 0 & \Delta z = -\Delta x \\ Y < -H & \Delta z = 0 \end{array} \tag{25}$$

This set of rules is similar to the one discussed so far except there are more intervals in which we get a different action. H is usually a fixed value which cannot be changed for a given machine. An operational integrator liks this can be used for switches, limiters, and clippers in addition to its use as a servo.[1]

There are also operational integrators with a flexible set of rules like the one below:

$$\begin{array}{ll} \text{If} & \text{Then} \\ Y \geqslant K & \Delta z = 0 \\ Y < K & \Delta z = \Delta x \end{array} \tag{26}$$

K is the limiting value which can be entered into a special register of this particular integrator. Since the limiting value can be changed easily, this scheme is especially valuable for limiters and clippers when K is a parameter and has to be changed repeatedly.

4.12. The System

4.121. The Computer. Simply a large number of integrators or special units is not sufficient to make up a computer or a computer system. There are many more things necessary to make a computer operation possible, efficient and convenient.

4.1211. Machine Rate. Previously we have not paid too much attention to where the inputs to an integrator come from. True, they may come from other integrators, but something must originally drive the first integrator in a problem setup. We must have a source for an independent variable. For this purpose the machine generates a continuous sequence of equally spaced pulses, which each are equivalent to Δx. The frequency of these pulses is called the machine rate. The pulses may be generated by an oscillator, or they may be taken from a magnetic drum, where they have been permanently recorded. The machine rate (the number of increments per second) is the highest frequency

[1] For detailed applications, see 4.2113 and 4.2114.

at which an integrator can accept incremental rates. Since all electronic operations in a digital differential analyzer are synchronized with it, the machine rate determines the speed of the computer.[1]

4.1212. Interconnection of Integrators. In order to be able to interconnect a number of integrators or special units so that they represent a specific problem, we must have a suitable device. In the simplest case, this will be a plugboard with jacks for the machine rate and all integrator inputs and outputs. Jumpers between these jacks connect any desired input to any desired output. If the computer system has any external equipment attached to it, the connections for inputs and outputs are also made through the plugboard.

A more convenient system will use an automatic interconnection, somewhat similar to an automatic telephone exchange where telephone sets can be connected by dialing. In a system like this, every integrator input has a register containing the "dialed" number of another integrator's output. Connections are made electronically and require no human interference. The main advantage of this system is that it is possible to "fill" the integrator interconnections together with functional values and other codes, e. g. the mode of integration of a certain integrator automatically from a previously prepared program tape.

4.1213. Filling of the Computer. Before a computation can be started, the initial conditions of all integrators used in the problem must be entered into the registers. In addition, codes for the interconnection of integrators and the selection of their modes have to be filled if the computer is capable of electronic integrator interconnection and mode selection. Computers with *manual fill* have a keyboard for numbers and special codes. By pressing the desired keys, numbers and codes are entered into the machine as on a desk calculator. Integrators and registers to be filled are selected by one or more switches.

For computers with an *automatic fill* feature, all initial conditions and codes together with integrator numbers and register identification are punched into a paper tape[2] prior to the filling of the computer. In order to fill the computer, this paper tape is run through a reading mechanism. Integrators are automatically selected and the information entered.

An automatic fill feature perhaps seems to be a luxury. However, it is very likely that the operator will make one or more mistakes in manually filling the several hundred numbers required for an average problem. It is practically impossible to find an error without double checking every digit filled into the machine. Even then the procedure is not foolproof and problems have to be filled and run repeatedly in order to be sure that even the least significant digit filled corresponds to the actual codes. Therefore, the manual fill wastes a considerable part of relatively valuable computer time and the automatic fill is a feature which well pays for itself. An additional advantage is the fact that preparing the paper tape produces a typewritten copy of the filling which can be referred to in a case of doubt. Here we have mentioned only paper tape as initial storage of the program. However, it would be entirely possible to use other means such as punched cards or magnetic tape.

4.1214. Monitoring Read-Out. For the detection of errors, it is practically a necessity to have a visual indication of the contents of registers. Such a monitoring read-out facilitates not only a check on the filling of a program, but also allows the monitoring of a problem while it is running on the computer and permits the visual read-out of the results. There is usually only one read-out

[1] For actual problems, it is convenient but not necessary to have the negative machine rate (a continuous string of negative increments) available.

[2] In a form very similar to the one used on teletypewriters.

circuit provided with sufficient indicators for all digits contained in a register. The register itself and the integrator which is to be read out are selected by switches similar to or the same as those used for the filling.

A simple but very convenient and efficient feature is an additional read-out for the integrator output Δz during the last cycle. This indication is a great help in debugging a program (and also helps to determine malfunctions of the equipment).

4.1215. Fault Indicators. There are some program errors which the computer by itself is able to detect. All of these errors are so serious that corrections in the program are necessary before further attempts to run the program can be made. The computer should, therefore, stop and give an indication specifying the type of fault.

The most common fault of this type is an *overflow* in the Y-register of an integrator. This overflow occurs when during the run of a problem the integrand becomes larger than anticipated and exceeds the capacity of the register.

In order to determine the cause of the error quickly, there should not only be an indication of the type of fault, but also an indication of the integrator which overflowed. If an overflow in a certain integrator is allowed or desired, as in certain types of operational integrators,[1] then there should be means in the form of switches or special codes to suppress the overflow fault for this integrator.

Servos might be the cause of another type of error. Suppose a servo puts out corrective increments but is simply not fast enough to compensate for changes in a variable. In this case, the error in the servo becomes larger and larger and the servo is overdriven. The machine should stop on an *overdrive fault* and indicate the overdriven servo.

External equipment might cause a third type, an *input or output fault.* This fault occurs either when the computer puts out increments faster than they can be accepted by the external equipment or when the external equipment generates increments faster than they can be accepted by the computer. A fault of this type can be practically eliminated by proper electronic interlocks.

4.1216. Printer. The printer connected to a digital differential analyzer is usually an electric typewriter.[1] It facilitates a computer output in tabulated form. A typical example of a printed output is a list of y, $\dot{y}$, $\ddot{y}$, versus time in the solution of a differential equation or a table of trigonometric functions versus the argument. Advantages of a printer are: permanent record of results, no reading error, and the possibility of unattended computer runs. For a distribution of results, the typewriter can print several copies or can type on masters for reproduction. The typewriter prints only the integrands of those integrators which are selected by switches or special codes. Printouts are usually in the sequence of integrator numbers.

4.1217. Automatic Timing. An automatic print timing allows predetermination of intervals at which the typewriter automatically prints out partial results. These intervals usually comprise a large number of integration intervals, since the computer takes extremely small steps compared to conventional numerical integration methods. It is not at all out of the ordinary to perform 1000 or 10,000 integration cycles (1000 or 10,000 increments of the machine rate) between consecutive printouts. The timing is usually performed in an integrator entirely devoted to this job. The dx input is fed by the machine rate. The integrand is a relatively small number so that the time between consecutive increments on

---

[1] See 4.1127.

[1] The typewriter frequently has a paper tape punch and reader attached which can be used for automatic fill or dump (see 4.1213 and 4.1219).

the output is large. As soon as an output occurs, the computer is stopped and a print cycle is initiated. After all integrands marked for printing are printed, the machine resumes the computation. The time (the number of increments in machine rate) between consecutive prints can be varied by varying the number in the print timing integrator.

In special cases like the trouble-shooting of the machine or of a program and for spot checks at the start or in the middle of a problem, it may be desired to have a print-out after every integration cycle. This can be facilitated by a switch overriding the control for the initiation of a print cycle by the timing integrator. This switch may be turned on or off at any time the operator desires. It may also be used for the print of the initial conditions prevailing in the machine before a computation is started.

An additional integrator can be used for an automatic halt in a fashion similar to the one used for print timing. The increment on the output of this integrator stops computation. A manual restart is necessary if it is required to start again. This feature can be used, for example, for stopping the computer automatically at the end of a lengthy computation otherwise requiring no attendance. The main advantage, however, is in stopping at an exact point during computation where some conditions have to be changed. It may happen that integration steps or parts of the integrator hook-up have to be changed in order to take care of new conditions. A typical example of this latter condition may be the calculation of a rocket trajectory where at certain times, the booster is turned on or off.

Usually a "stop every cycle" switch is provided which overrides the stop timing integrator. This switch is mainly used for debugging problem setups.

4.1218. Initial Conditions Storage. This feature is a great convenience for consecutive re-runs of the same or of a slightly modified problem. Such re-runs are frequently required during the search for an error, after an error is found, or for solutions with variations in parameters. The initial conditions in the computer are modified, and therefore lost, as soon as the computation starts. A consecutive re-run, therefore, requires a renewed filling. For computers with the automatic fill feature, this disadvantage is not too severe because the renewed filling can be easily accomplished. However, for machines with only a manual fill, the time which is lost may be considerable.

A solution to this problem is provided in the form of a separate initial condition storage, containing nothing but the initial conditions. A simple transfer which can be performed repeatedly restores the working registers to initial conditions. Changes in parameters can be accomplished by manually filling new values into the few affected integrators after the transfer of initial conditions. Initial condition registers are, in most cases, provided only for integrands, since codes for integrator hook-up, print markers, etc., usually stay the same for repeated runs. Provisions may be made for an *automatic initial condition variation*. This feature makes consecutive re-runs with changes in parameters still more convenient. The initial conditions of one or more integrands are automatically modified for re-runs by preselected values or by values which are the result of previous runs.

4.1219. Problem Dump. There are several possible reasons why it is sometimes required to interrupt the computer operation in the middle of a problem. In these cases, it is desirable to be able to perform a problem dump, i. e. to store the entire current contents of the machine on some storage device.[1] In order to resume operation at a later time, it is only necessary to reload and start again. The

[1] Usually the problem dump uses the same storage device as the automatic fill, i. e. paper tape. Again, it is entirely possible to use other kinds of storage devices.

computer will then resume operation at exactly the point where it left off. The problem dump can be used when the amount of available computer time is less than the time required to finish a problem. It can also be used with advantage by minimizing lost time due to unexpected interruptions, like power failures, cooling trouble, or machine failures. If the operator is requested to perform a routine problem dump every half hour, then the machine time lost in case of an unexpected interruption is, at the most, half an hour, since operation can be resumed at the point where the last problem dump was made. For problems taking several hours, or perhaps days, to finish, the routine problem dump is a worthwhile precaution.

4.122. External Equipment. External equipment comprises the class of auxiliary or peripheral devices which are not part of the basic computer. However, these devices can be connected directly to the computer and are therefore considered part of the computer system. The typewriter, the paper tape reader, and the paper tape punch correctly belong in this category. Since these devices have been discussed previously, we will regard here only the remainder.

4.1221. Curve Plotters. Curve plotters facilitate a continuous graphical output of results and therefore, allow a convenient monitoring of the computation. Digital differential analyzers usually have provisions for the connection of several plotters. Plotters have a stylus containing a pen or a ballpoint pen which is electro-mechanically driven in two coordinates with respect to the paper on which it is writing. Normally, the plotters connected to digital differential analyzers are of the incremental type. Increments which are the output of integrators move the stylus of the plotter in discrete steps in x and y direction during the computation. The steps have a small size, say one hundreth of an inch, so that the resulting curve can be considered continuous for all practical purposes. Since plotters of this type are electro-mechanical devices, their maximum acceptable input rate is relatively slow. Therefore, precautions must be taken in scaling a problem not to overdrive the plotter, i. e. exceed the maximum acceptable rate. The scale (the size) of the plot is easily adjusted to the requirements by scaling the two input variables.

Plotters need no attendance during operation. At the beginning of a plot, however, the stylus has to be moved manually to a point in the coordinate system which corresponds to those values of the two variables which are filled as initial conditions into the computer. This drawback could be avoided to a certain extent by using plotters which are able to accept total numbers (e. g. values of integrands) rather than incremental values. Plotters of this type are more complicated and the transfer of total values is more difficult; the additional cost is not justified by the slight advantage.

Analog plotters which are commonly used in analog computer systems can be connected to a digital differential analyzer via a digital-to-analog converter.[1]

4.1222. Curve Followers. The curve follower is a device which permits using functions for computations which are either given graphically or which are impossible or highly inconvenient for the computer to generate. A more or less typical example would be the drag coefficient of an airplane versus velocity. The curve follower will read the graph of such a function and makes the reading automatically available to the computer. A digital differential analyzer usually has provisions for inputs from several curve followers.

The mechanics of a follower are very similar to those of a curve plotter. Instead of the stylus, the curve follower carries a photocell. The movement of

[1] See 4.1223.

the photocell in the direction of one axis is controlled by computer outputs (independent variable). The movement along the second axis is controlled automatically so that the photocell always follows the given curve. The photocell will move in both directions in discrete steps of approximately $^1/_{100}$ inch. The movements along the second axis are translated into increments, so that for every step of the photocell, one increment is sent to the computer. The resulting string of increments can be used as an integrator input. Again, proper scaling in the computer is necessary to interpret the magnitude of steps correctly. Curve followers connected to digital differential analyzers are again most conveniently incremental devices. Strictly analog curve followers can be connected via an analog-to-digital converter.

In some instances, it may be desired to have a curve follower with capabilities in more than two dimensions. Suppose a function is not only dependent upon the variable x but also upon a second variable p. The ideal solution to this problem would be a three-dimensional curve follower driven by x and p, generating the function $f(x, p)$. The ideal solution cannot be realized with any known device, but a regular curve follower with some modifications can be used as an approximation to a three dimensional follower. If we assume that $f(x, p)$ can be drawn as a family of curves $f(x)$ with p as parameter, then we can make the curve follower jump from one curve to the other (from one parameter to the other) if it receives increments in p. For a positive increment in p, the photocell is guided to the neighboring curve with a larger value of p and for a negative increment in p to the curve with the next lower value of p. The difference in values of p for neighboring curves have to be sufficiently large so that the curves do not merge and the photocell can distinguish between specific curves. For this reason, the resolution in values of p is perhaps an order of magnitude lower than in x and $f(x)$ but adequate for a great many practical problems.

4.1223. Digital-to-Analog and Analog-to-Digital Converters. Digital-to-analog converters permit the digital differential analyzer to transmit information to any type of analog device, whereas the analog-to-digital converter allows the acceptance of information from any analog device. We have already mentioned analog plotters and curve followers as possible analog devices. Other examples would be an analog computer, perhaps working simultaneously on parts of the same problem requiring not too high an accuracy or analog actuators like servo mechanisms and analog measuring devices like pressure or strain gauges. The ability to communicate with analog devices is especially valuable in instances where the digital differential analyzer acts as a control device in physical processes.

Again, best suited for the connection to digital differential analyzers are incremental type converters, which are of simpler construction than converters for total values. Converters usually have several channels, i. e. capabilities to handle several inputs and outputs simultaneously or on a time sharing basis. They are usually designed for voltages representing analog variables in the range between zero and five or zero and one hundred volts.

4.2. Operation

The term "operation" in its broadest sense includes everything which has to be done from the time a problem arises until the solution is found. More specifically, we will find it necessary to perform tasks in the following categories:

1. Setting up of mathematical equations for the physical problem.

2. Rearrangement of equations into a form suitable for the digital differential analyzer.
3. Designing a schematic diagram of integrator interconnections.
4. Deriving initial and maximum values for every variable in the problem.
5. Scaling every variable to suit the actual problem and the machine requirements.
6. Coding, i. e., translating scaled values, integrator interconnections, print selections and timing for print and halt into the machine language.
7. Filling the programm, i. e., filling the code and setting special selections switches or jumpers.
8. Running the computer.
9. Checking the results.

The above tasks are listed in the sequence in which they ordinarily are performed. In some instances, it will be possible to omit certain steps (e. g. step 1 is obviously not required if the problem is presented in mathematical form). In other instances it may be necessary to go back a few steps if a selected approach does not work out as anticipated. Any one of the above listed categories may be the one which consumes most of the time or effort in a particular case.

The following two chapters will deal with only a part of the overall operation. Category 1 is clearly beyond the present scope. Categories 6 and 7 require relatively simple manipulations according to a set of rules which differ from machine to machine and which are the proper subject for computer operation manuals. Categories 8 and 9 will be treated to some extent in 4.32. In the remaining categories, we find two closely related pairs. Categories 2 and 3 will be treated in one chapter (4.21). In order to know which equations are suitable for a digital differential analyzer, one must know which integrator hookups are possible. Categories 4 and 5 will be treated in 4.22. The derivation of maximum values will be illustrated in a few sample problems.

4.21. Design of Integrator Interconnections

4.211. Standard Integrator Configurations. Before we attack more complicated problems, let us consider some commonly used integrator configurations which perform relatively simple operations. In many cases, the complete integrator hookup for a problem consists of a number of such standard integrator configurations.

4.2111. Arithmetic Operations.

4.21111. Multiplication by a Constant. The multiplication of a variable by a constant is one of the simplest operations to be performed, requiring only one integrator.[1] The differential of the variable is used as primary input to the integrator. The Y-register of the integrator contains the constant factor K. No secondary inputs are required. According to equation (4.1—3), the output is the differential of the desired product. For negative values of K, we simply enter the negative number, represented by K, as integrand or we can use the sign reversal feature if provided. This scheme works only for machine-values of $|K| \leqslant 1$.[2] However, in most cases the scaling of a problem may be used to reduce the actual value of K to a machine value smaller than one.

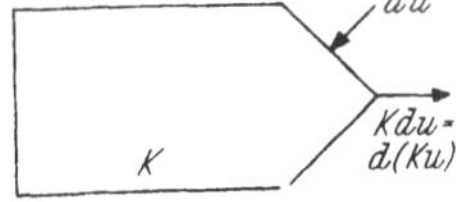

Fig. 13. Constant Multiplier

[1] See also 4.1125.

[2] We notice that due to the design of digital integrators, we never can obtain more increments on the output than there are on the dx input.

If for some reason a variable has to be multiplied by a machine value larger than one, a servo can be used as a multiplier (see 4.21116).

4.21112. Multiplication of two Variables. The multiplication of two variables requires in general two integrators.[1] The mechanization is according to the rule for the differentiation of a product:

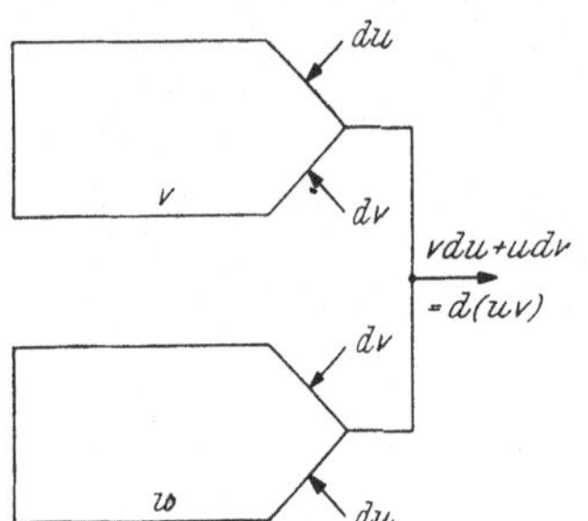

Fig. 14. Multiplication of Two Variables

$$d\,(u\,v) = v\,du + u\,dv \tag{1}$$

One integrator generates the product $v\,du$, the other $u\,dv$. The sum of both outputs is the differential of the desired product.

The block diagram in figure 14 contains a simplification which is commonly used, but perhaps not quite correct. The output of the two integrators is shown as one line. In reality, the outputs cannot be simply connected. If they have to be used as the dy inputs to a third integrator, the two lines have to be connected to two separate dy inputs of this integrator. If the third integrator has only one dy input, or if the lines have to feed the dx input of an integrator, a servo adder has to be used (See 4.21115).

4.21113. Square of a Variable. A special case of multiplication is the squaring of a variable. One integrator is generally sufficient for this operation. The mechanization is according to:

$$d\,(v^2) = 2\,v\,dv \tag{2}$$

The inconvenience of having only half of the desired output (Fig. 15a) can be eliminated in many cases by scaling. In other instances, we can use a servo multiplier to multiply the output by a factor of two or use the scheme given in Figure 14 with u identical to v.

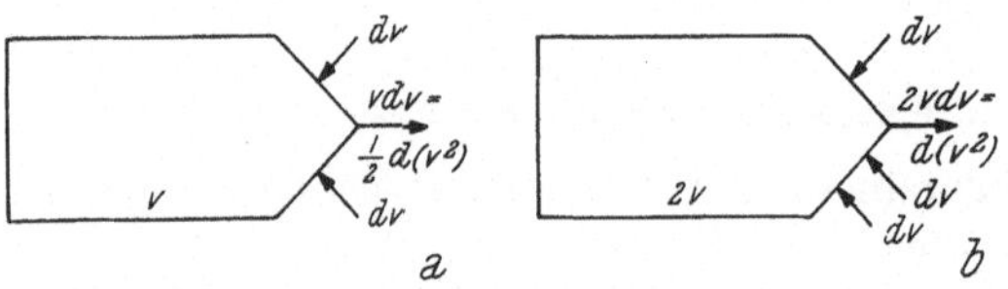

Fig. 15. Square of a Variable

For integrators able to accomodate several dependent variables, there is a solution according to Fig. 15b possible.

4.21114. Reciprocal of a Variable. The evaluation of the reciprocal of a variable is based on relation (3).[2]

$$d\left(\frac{1}{u}\right) = -\frac{1}{u^2}\,du \tag{3}$$

Consider now the following: Suppose we had all the terms on the right hand side of the equation (3) available; then we have also the left hand side, i. e., we have generated the required reciprocal. Conversely, if we have generated the required reciprocal, we can generate all terms required on the right hand side. Translating this into an integrator schematic diagram, we proceed in two steps. First we set up an integrator to generate $d\,(1/u)$ according to equation (3), not caring where eventual necessary inputs come from (top half of Figure 16). Then we generate the required input $d\,(1/u^2)$ from the available output $d\,(1/u)$. We note that the required variable $1/u^2$ is the square of the available $1/u$, so we can use an inte-

[1] See also 4.1126.

[2] For another method of generating the reciprocal, see 4.21123.

grator hookup equivalent to the one in Fig. 15b for its generation (lower half of Fig. 16).[1]

This procedure may look like putting the cart before the horse, so let us consider this integrator hookup again from a different point of view. If the initial condition of u in a problem is known, then we can calculate and fill the initial values for $1/u^2$ and $2/u$ into the two integrators generating the reciprocal. As soon as the computer starts and increments du arrive, the top integrator will generate increments $d\,(1/u)$. These increments are used by way of the second integrator to properly increment the integrand $(1/u^2)$. In this way the top integrator generates the correct reciprocal not only initially, but throughout the computation.

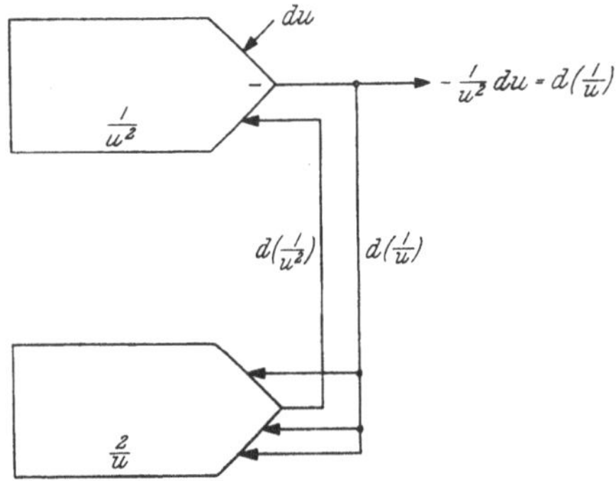

Fig. 16. Reciprocal of a Variable

4.21115. Addition of Variables. The addition of variables requires no special setup if the sum is only to be used as the dependent variable for integrators with several dy inputs. In all other cases, a servo is required. Fig. 17 shows as an example the addition of three variables.

We remember that a servo produces no output for an integrand equal to zero. For a positive integrand, the output rate is equal to the rate of the independent input. For a negative integrand, the output rate is equal to the negative rate of the independent input. Since the machine rate is used as independent input in Fig. 17, the servo will produce increments at the fastest possible rate if the integrand is not equal to zero. Since the output sign-reversal feature is used, the servo will generate negative increments for a positive integrand and positive increments for a negative integrand. If the integrand is zero, no output is produced. Suppose now a positive increment arrives on one of the inputs du dv, or dw. The integrand becomes positive and the servo starts putting out negative increments. Since the output of the integrator is fed back as input, the integrand becomes again equal to zero after the first increment on the output and no further outputs are produced. In a similar way, the servo produces a positive increment on the output for a negative increment on the input. If instead of one increment on one line we would have simultaneous increments of the same polarity on all three inputs, the servo would put out three increments before the integrand becomes zero again. The number of increments on the output is apparently equal to the sum of increments on all inputs. However, the polarity is, reversed. In most cases, this reversed output is equally convenient to use as an output with the correct sign. If for some reason it should be inconvenient, we can use opposite polarities on the input (e. g. by using the sign-reversal feature in those integrators generating the variables to be added) or we can use a constant multiplier with a constant equal to -1 to change the polarity of the output.

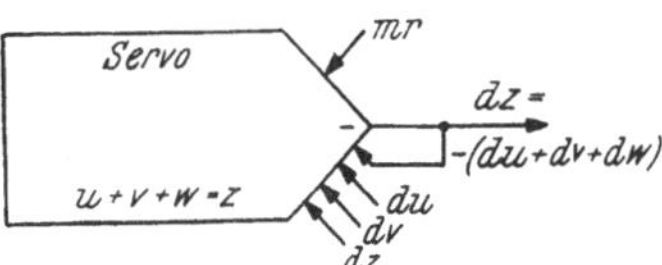

Fig. 17. Servo Adder

Subtraction is a special case of addition. In order to generate the difference

[1] Note that this scheme produces also the square of the reciprocal. A division of two variables can be performed by a multiplication of one by the reciprocal of the other.

of two variables, we feed the two variables into the servo with opposite sign. The integrator hookup is given in Fig. 18. When a servo is used, we have to be careful not to overdrive it. If the sum of all input rates exceeds the machine rate, the servo cannot put out sufficient increments for a correct result.

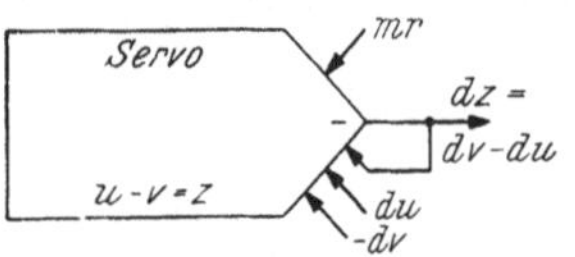

Fig. 18. Servo Adder as Subtractor

If a regular integrator operating near the overflow condition is used as a servo,[1] the diagrams remain the same. The only exception is that the sign-reversal in the integrator is omitted. (Positive increments on the input make the integrand overflow to a negative number, so that the integrator all by itself will put out a negative increment.)

4.21116. Servo Multipliers. The servo multiplier is based on a similar principle as the adder. The exception is that the integrator output is multiplied by a constant before it is fed back as integrator input. The integrator configuration is given in Fig. 19.

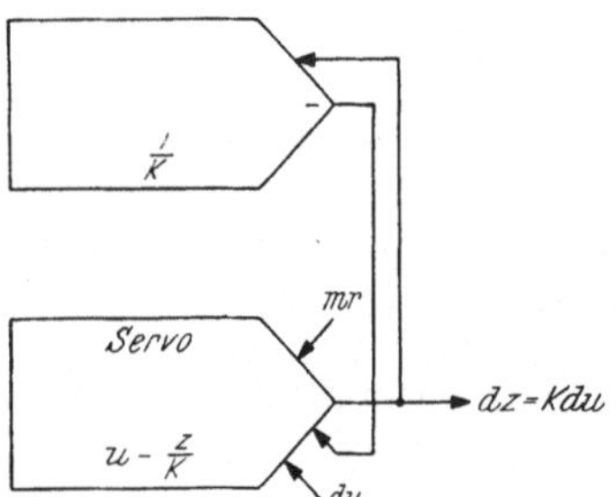

Fig. 19. Servo Multiplier

K is the value by which we want to multiply the variable u. Suppose K has the machine-value 10, then $1/K$ is one tenth. For every increment du, the servo has to put out ten increments dz before the integrand in the servo is zero again. In general, the servo will put out K increments for one increment du.

In this way it is possible to multiply a variable by a machine value larger than 1 (or to divide by a machine value smaller than one). Again we have to be careful not to overdrive the servo.

4.21117. Absolute Value. We have at least two relatively simple approaches to generate the absolute value of a variable. The first one uses the signum function (see 4.1122). The integrator configuration is given in Fig. 20.

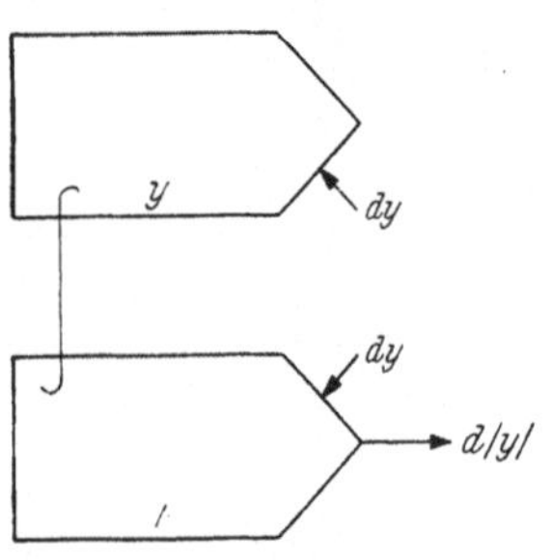

Fig. 20. Generation of the Absolute Value by the Signum Function

The top integrator is used to detect the sign of y. If y is positive, then the bottom integrator works in the usual manner putting out the rate dy. However, if y in the first integrator becomes negative, the second integrator will reverse its output and, in effect, put out $-dy$. The output rate is therefore equal to $d|y|$.

The second approach uses an operational integrator, designated in Fig. 21 as decision integrator. As long as the integrand is positive, the output is equal to the independent input du. If the integrand is negative, the output is the reverse of the independent input du. In this way, the output is equal to $d|u|$.

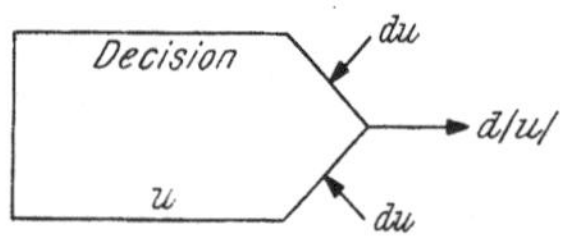

Fig. 21. Generation of the Absolute Value by a Decision Integrator

4.2112. Direct Generation of Functions. Any function which is a solution of a differential equation can be generated by setting up an integrator hookup representing this differential equation and driving it with the independent variable. Even though we may not

[1] See 4.1127.

have thought of it this way, the integrator hookups in Fig. 15 and 16 are examples of a function generation of this type. The following three paragraphs will give a few additional examples. Due to their frequent application we still may consider the circuits standard integrator configurations.[1]

4.21121. Exponential Function. The generation of the exponential function is the classical example for the direct generation of a function in a digital differential analyzer. The differential equation producing e^x as solution is:

$$f'(x) = f(x) \quad (4)$$
$$\text{or } d f'(x) = d f(x) \quad (5)$$

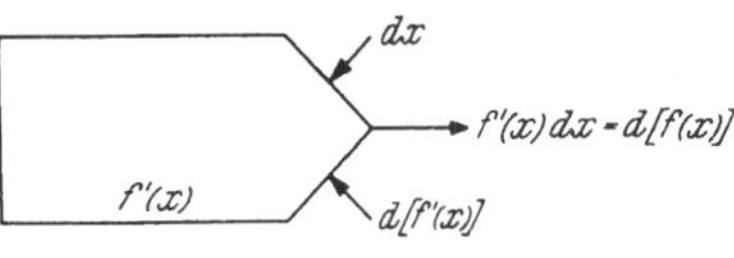

Fig. 22. Generation of $df(x)$ from $df'(x)$

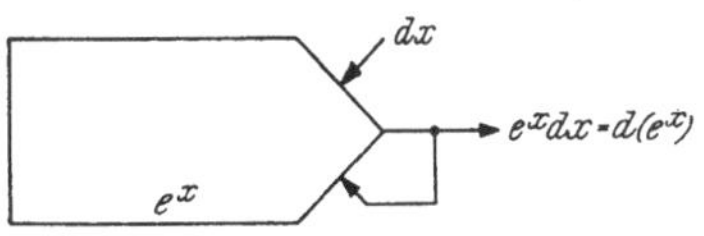

Fig. 23. Generation of e^x.

The right hand side of equation (4) is the integral of the left hand side. So, having one side, we can generate the other by an integrator (Fig. 22). Since the integrator output according to equation (5) is equal to the integrator input, we simply have to connect both and label the variables according to our problem (Fig. 23).

4.21122. Generation of sin α and cos α. The differential equation which has $\sin \alpha$ or $\cos \alpha$ as solution is:

$$f''(\alpha) = -f(\alpha) \quad (6)$$
$$\text{or } d[f''(\alpha)] = -d[f(\alpha)] \quad (7)$$

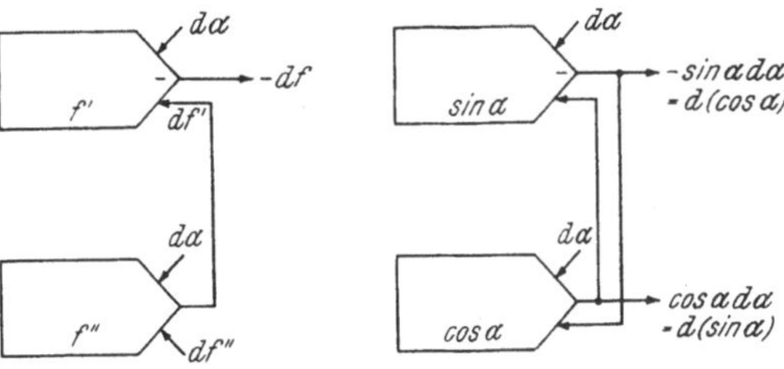

Fig. 24. Generation of $\sin \alpha$ and $\cos \alpha$

Two integrations must be performed to derive the right hand side from the left hand side, therefore, the corresponding integrator hookup will make use of two integrators (Fig. 24).

4.21123. Generation of ln u. The differential equation which has $\ln u$ as a solution is:

$$f'(u) = 1/u \quad (8)$$
$$\text{or } d[f(u)] = 1/u\, du \quad (9)$$

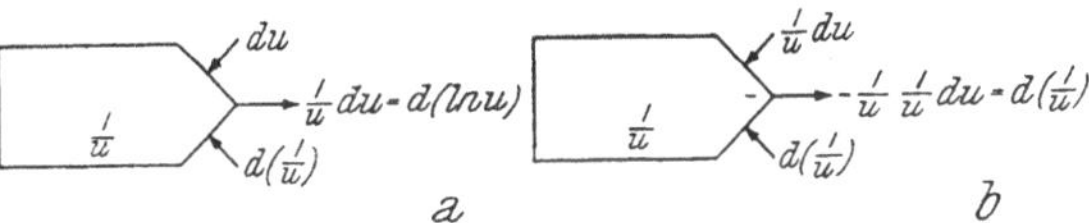

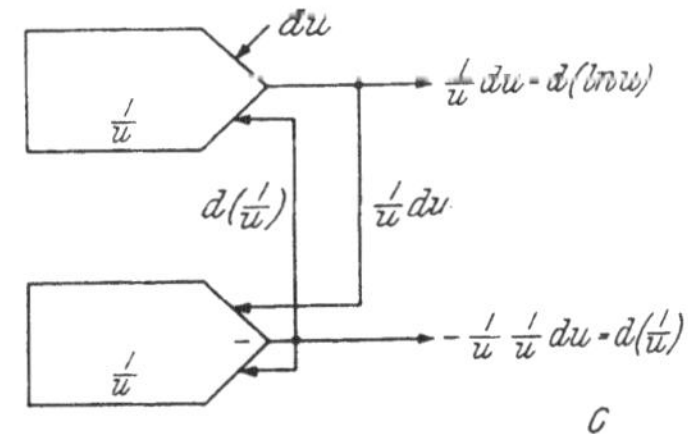

Fig. 25. Generation of $\ln u$

If we had the variable $1/u$ available, we could generate the left hand side of equation (9) in one integrator according to Fig. 25a. Since, in 4.21114, we have already seen a method to obtain the variable $1/u$ from $d\,u$, the problem is principally solved. In this example, however, a further simplification is possible. We note that:

$$d(1/u) = -1/u^2\, du = -1/u\,(1/u\, du) \quad (10)$$

[1] For the solution of more complicated differential equations, see 4.2121.

In a second integrator, according to Fig. 25b, we can generate this required variable $d\,(1/u)$. Both integrators now have the integrand $1/u$ which can be derived from the output of the second integrator. Connecting input and outputs properly, we obtain the total integrator hookup given in Fig. 25c.

4.2113. Function Generation by Servos. Until now we have seen how we can generate functions which are either stated explicitly or are solutions of differential equations. In other words, we have been seeking the value of $f\,(x)$ for a given x. In many instances, we will find it necessary to perform the opposite procedure. Given the value of $f\,(x)$, we have to find the corresponding value of x, i.e. we have to deal with functions which are given implicitly. A typical example for this case is the generation of $\sin^{-1} x$. The problem is to find the angle x which corresponds to a given $\sin x$.

In all cases where we have an integrator configuration to generate $f\,(x)$ from a given x we can also find x from a given $f\,(x)$. In order to accomplish this inverse generation, we have to drive the given configuration with an auxiliary variable until the produced $f\,(x)$ corresponds with the given one. The value of the auxiliary variable at this time is the wanted x. The servo is a convenient source of such an auxiliary variable. It produces increments until its integrand (the error between the given $f\,(x)$ and the one produced in the integrator configuration) is reduced to zero. Let us agree to call the given variable $f\,(x)$ and the one which is generated $f\,(y)$. We have then a setup according to Fig. 26:

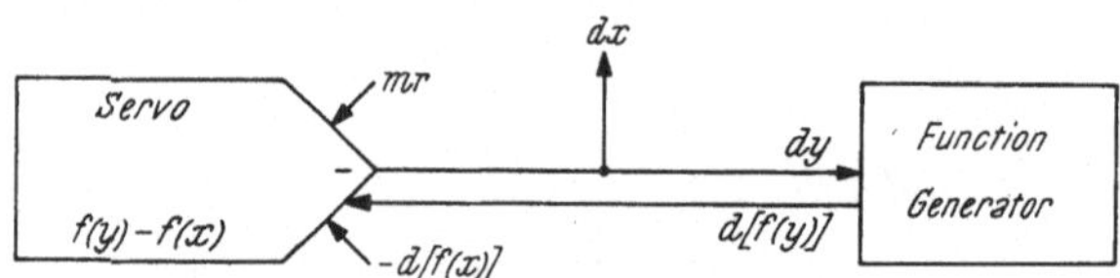

Fig. 26. Function Generation by Servo

As long as the generated function $f\,(y)$ is equal to the given function $f\,(x)$, the servo produces no output and the function generator will remain in the given state. As soon as increments $d\,[f\,(x)]$ arrive, there is a discrepancy between $f\,(x)$ and $f\,(y)$, and the servo will put out a string of dy increments driving the generator to a state where $f\,(x)$ and $f\,(y)$ agree again. The increments dy are equal to the increments dx which we wanted to generate.

The following few paragraphs give examples for this type of function generation. We shall restrict ourselves to relatively simple cases, which are frequently used and can be regarded as standard integrator configurations.

4.21131. Generation of ln u by Servo. In 4.21123, we found a method for the direct generation of $\ln u$. Sometimes an indirect method is used. There is no general advantage of either method. However, by selecting the proper method, we may have advantages in scaling a problem. The method in 4.21123 is suited for machine-values $u \geqslant 1$, whereas the indirect generation of $\ln u$ works for machine-values of $u \leqslant 1$. For the indirect generation of $\ln u$ we use the definition of the natural logarithm:

$$e^{x} = u \qquad x = \ln u \tag{11}$$

We will use the integrator configuration for the generation of e^{y} (see 4.21121) and drive it by a servo until e^{y} corresponds to the given $u = e^{x}$. The value of y at this time is the wanted value of $\ln u$. The schematic diagram is given in Fig. 27.

Using relation (11), we may label the functions of x in terms of u so that the generation of $\ln u$ becomes more apparent (Fig. 28).

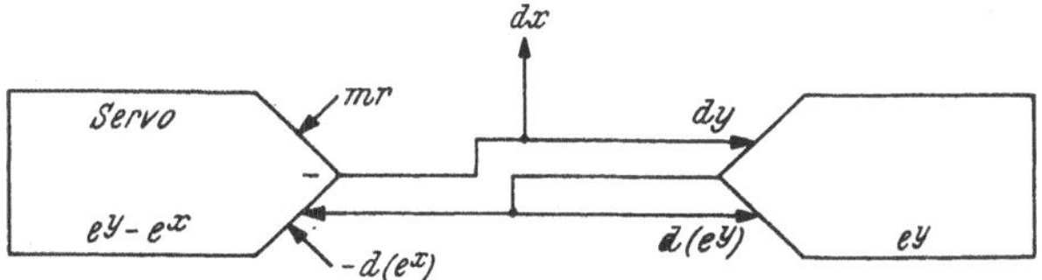

Fig. 27. e^y-Generator Driven by a Servo

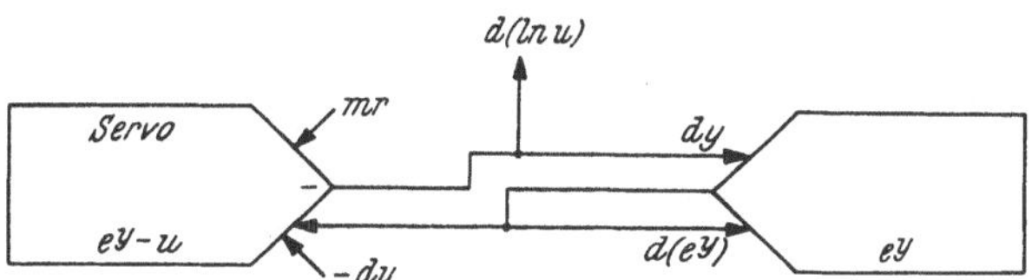

Fig. 28. Generation of ln u

4.21132. Generation of $sin^{-1} u$. Since the configuration for the generation of the sine is known (4.21122), we can immediately find the hookup for the inverse function $\sin^{-1}$ (Fig. 29). The principle used is the same as in the previous paragraph. The relation between u and x is:

$$\sin x = u \qquad x = \sin^{-1} u \quad (12)$$

4.21133. Generation of the Square Root. The function generating part of the integrator diagram is the same as the one generating the square (4.21113). It is used to generate a y^2 which corresponds to a given u. The square root of u is then equal to y (Fig. 30).

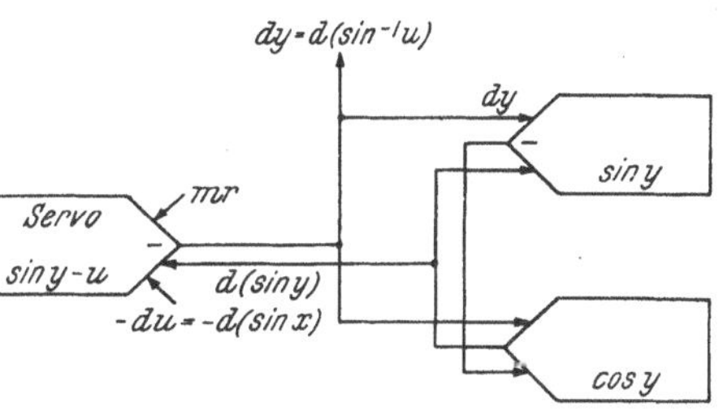

Fig. 29. Generation of $\sin^{-1} u$

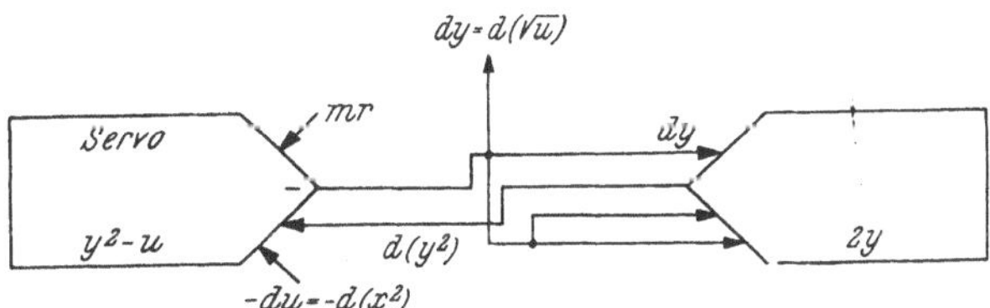

Fig. 30. Generation of the Square Root

4.21134. Differentiation of a Variable. A digital differential analyzer normally performs integration, and has no direct ability to differentiate. Fortunately, most of the problems which can be solved on a digital differential analyzer can be reduced to integration. However, in some cases ist may be necessary or convenient to derive the differential quotient of a variable.

In order to make the computer differentiate, we use the same general approach as in previous chapters. We note that differentiation is the inverse operation to integration. We then use an integrator hookup to integrate an auxiliary variable y.

We further use a servo to make the integral over the auxiliary variable equal to the given variable u. The auxiliary variable y is then the wanted differential quotient (Fig. 31).

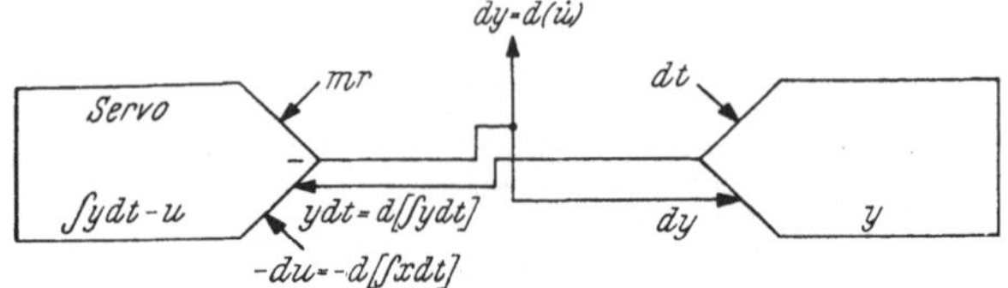

Fig. 31. Differentiation of a Variable

The relations thereby used are the following:

$$du = \dot{u}\, dt \tag{13}$$

and

$$d\left[\int y\, dt\right] = y\, dt \tag{14}$$

Inputs to the circuit are du and dt. The output is the required $d(\dot{u})$.

The circuit according to Fig. 31 has to be used with caution. If increments dt are arriving at a slow rate, then the servo will produce entirely too many increments dy before the function generator has a chance to produce an output $y\,dt$, which stops the servo action. One way to avoid this situation is to use dt instead of the machine rate on the servo input and scale the problem so that there will never be more than one increment in u for one increment dt.

4.2114. Mechanization of Logical Operations. In addition to their use as servos, operational integrators can be applied to logical operations. Such operations are required, for instance, where problems require abrupt changes in variables, or where different equations are used to describe a problem within different regions. The following paragraphs are examples for frequently used applications of operational integrators to logical operations.

4.21141. Limiters. As the name implies, limiters are used for the limitation of functional values. An example for a physical quantity which requires such a limitation would be the magnetic flux in an iron core excited beyond saturation.

Suppose the problem is to generate the (limited) function $g(t)$ from a given function $f(t)$ according to Fig. 32.

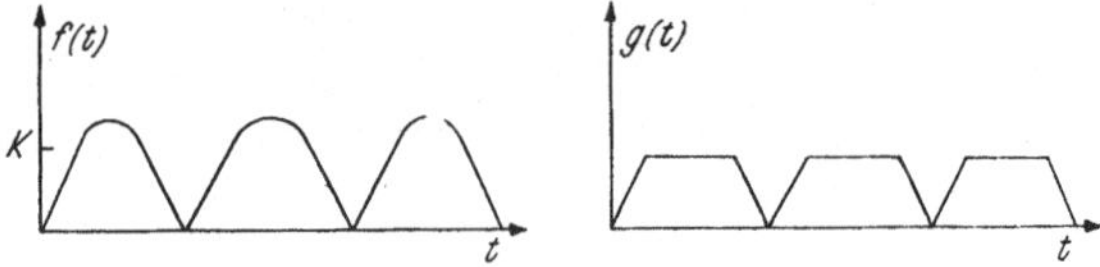

Fig. 32. Example for a Limited Function

In mathematical form, the relation is as follows:

$$g(t) = f(t) \text{ for } f(t) \leqslant K \tag{15}$$

$$g(t) = K \quad \text{for } f(t) > K \tag{16}$$

Depending upon the types of operational integrators available, a great variety of circuits can perform the limitation. $g(t)$ is most conveniently obtained in a limiter, i.e., an operational integrator with flexible rules into which the limiting value K can be entered.[1] The integrator arrangement is given in Fig. 33.

The value of K is entered into a special register. As long as the value of $f(t)$ is smaller than the value of K, the output of the limiter is equal to $d[f(t)]$. If the value of $f(t)$ exceeds the value of K, the limiter produces no output.

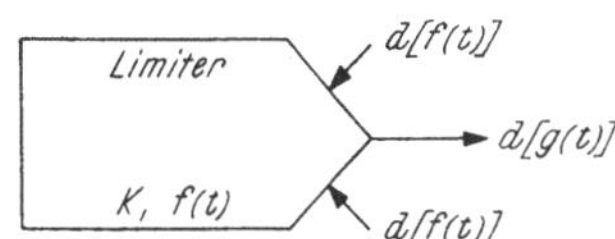

Fig. 33. Limiter with Flexible Rules

If a limiter is not available, an operational integrator with a fixed set of rules (according to 4.1—25) can be used instead. The corresponding integrator hookup is given in Fig. 34.

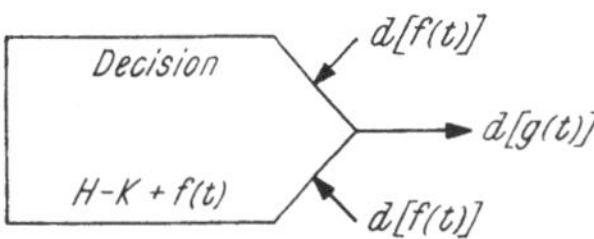

Fig. 34. Limitation by Decision Integrator

If $f(t)$ is smaller than K, then the Y-register of the decision integrator contains a number smaller than H and the output is equal to $d[f(t)]$. If $f(t)$ is larger than K, then the Y-register contains a value larger than H and the integrator produces no output.

Even the simplest type of operational integrator (according to 4.1—24) may be used as a limiter in connection with a servo adder. The circuit is given in Fig. 35: If $f(t)$ is smaller than K, the integrand in the decision integrator is negative and the output is $-d[f(t)]$. This rate is added in the servo adder with another $-d[f(t)]$ so that the output is $2d[f(t)]$. If, however, $f(t)$ is larger than K, the decision integrator produces $+d[f(t)]$ so that the total output is equal to zero. By multiplying either the output or the input rates with a factor of .5 we obtain the desired output $d[g(t)]$.

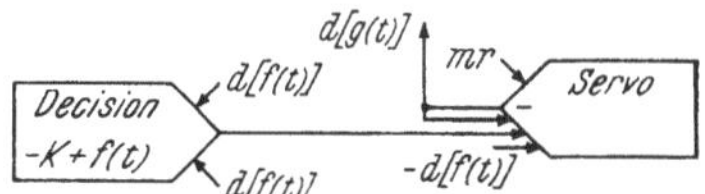

Fig. 35. Limitation by Simplest Type of Operational Integrator

4.21142. Clippers. Limiters can be used to disregard parts of a variable which exceed a predetermined limit. Clippers perform the opposite operation. They regard only those parts of a variable which exceed a certain limit. As an example, let us suppose we want to derive the curve $h(t)$ in Fig. 36b from the curve $f(t)$ in Fig. 36a. In mathematical form we would state:

$$h(t) = 0 \quad \text{for } f(t) \leq K \qquad (17)$$
$$h(t) = f(t) - K \quad \text{for } f(t) > K \qquad (18)$$

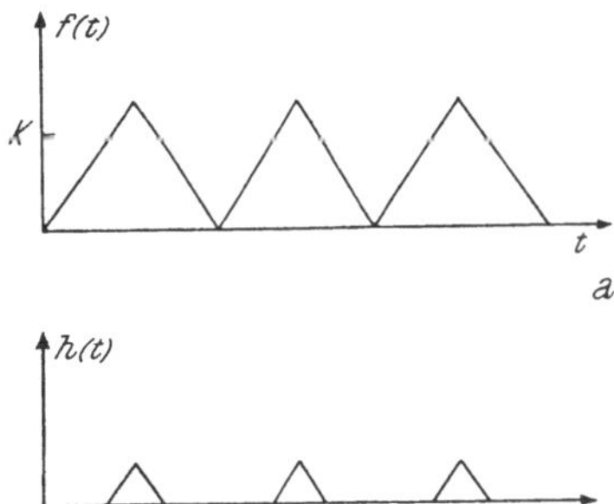

Fig. 36. Example for a Clipped Function

There are again many different ways to perform this operation, depending on the types of operational integrators available. Basically, all approaches use a limiter as described so far in the arrangement given in Fig. 37. The limiter is shown as a box which may contain any one of the circuits described in the last paragraph.

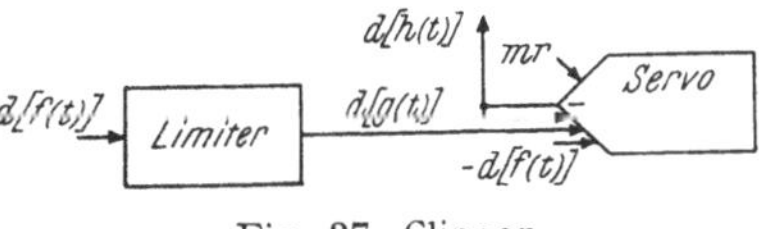

Fig. 37. Clipper

The rate $g(t)$ is equal to the rate of $f(t)$, if $f(t)$ is smaller than K. The servo adder, fed by two opposite but otherwise equal rates, will produce no output. If, however, $f(t)$ is larger than the limiting

[1] See equation 4.1-26.

value K, the limiter produces no output, whereas the servo adder produces the desired rate $d[h(t)]$.

4.21143. Switches. Switches are used to decide between alternate courses of action. Examples are: the selection of integrator circuits which represent the equation which is valid in a certain region of the problem and the handling of discontinuous variables. The switching operation is performed automatically, i.e. after a certain elapsed time or during the run of a problem when certain conditions are met. Closely considered, the limiters and clippers described in the last two paragraphs also perform a switching operation. Depending upon a criterion, they produce outputs according to different mathematical rules. However, in accordance with common usage, only those circuits, which, depending upon a criterion, produce either the full machine rate or zero output are here called switches.[1] One of several possible circuits for a switch is given in Fig. 38. Depending upon the value of x (which may represent time or any other variable in the problem), the decision integrator produces either the full positive or the full negative machine rate. This output rate is multiplied by .5 and added to another rate effectively equal to one half of the machine rate. Therefore, the total output is either the full machine rate, if x is positive and the decision integrator puts out the positive machine rate, or zero if x is negative and the decision integrator produces the negative machine rate.[2] Actual problems usually require switches which are more elaborate than the basic circuit if Fig. 38. Suppose a problem is represented by an integrator configuration A for times $t \leqslant a$ and by an integrator configuration B for times $t > a$. A switch is to be used to drive either one of the integrator hookups depending upon the value of t. A circuit according to Fig. 39 will do this very nicely. If $t < a$, the decision integrator will produce a negative rate and integrator configuration A receives the full positive rate, whereas integrator configuration B receives no increments at all. If $t > a$, the decision integrator produces a positive rate and integrator configuration B is driven by the full positive rate: Principally, the hookup of Fig. 39 acts like the electrical switch pictured in Fig. 40.

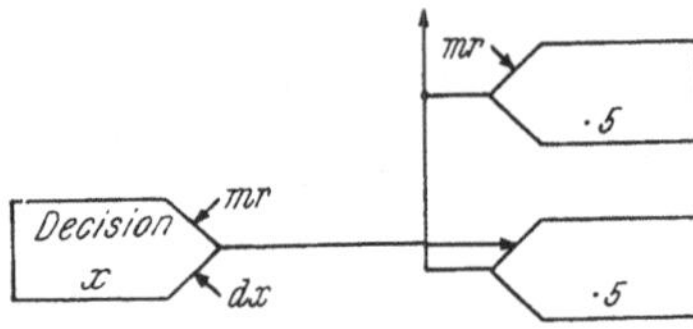

Fig. 38. Basic Integrator Hookup of a Switch

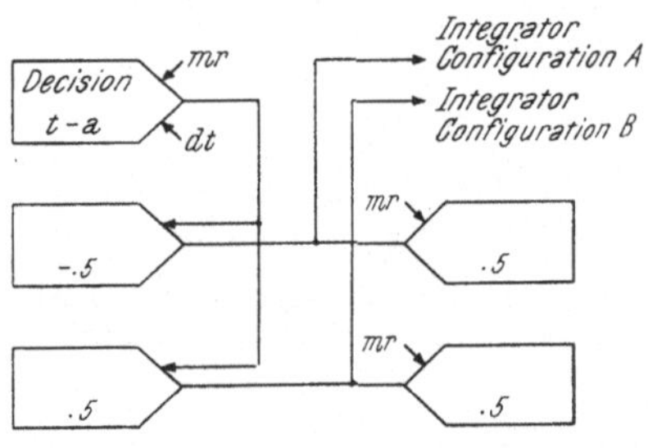

Fig. 39. Switch for the Selection of Two Integrator Configurations

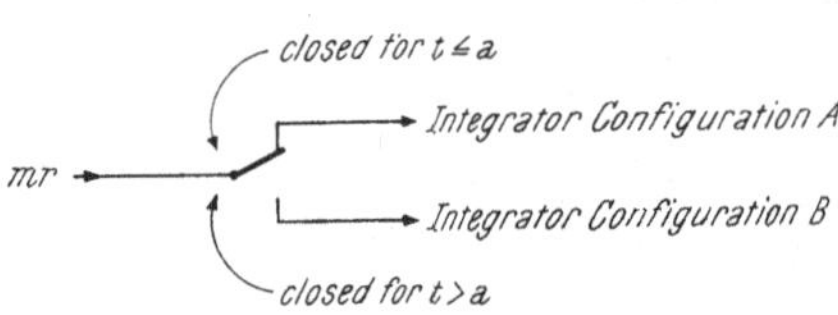

Fig. 40. Electrical Switch

These circuits, like electrical switches, can be combined to mechanize more complicated switching functions. Fig. 41 is an

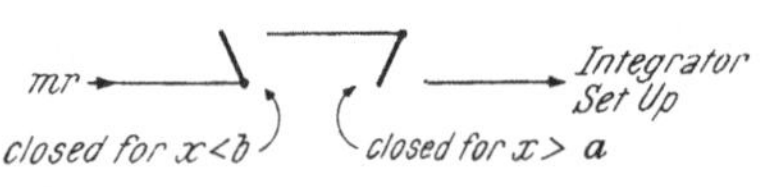

Fig. 41. Switch for the Condition $a < x < b$

[1] Actual problems require mostly a switching of the machine rate. The given principles might, however, be applied to any other rate.

[2] In most instances, a servo adder is required for the addition of the two half machine rates.

example where an integrator setup is driven only for conditions $a < x < b$.

If a computer has built-in signum logic,[1] the basic switch may be mechanized according to Fig. 42. Depending upon the sign of x, the output is either zero or the full machine rate.

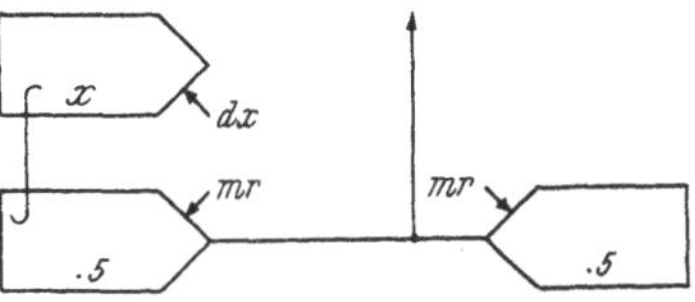

Fig. 42. Basic Switch with Signum Logic

4.21144. Handling of Step Functions. Step functions require an instantaneous change of functional values which normally cannot be realized in incremental machines of fixed step size. Therefore, it may seem that the handling of step functions is beyond the capabilities of a digital differential analyzer. Nevertheless, this may be accomplished by the proper use of a switch to interrupt the actual computation while the value of a variable is being increased or decreased. Fig. 43b is an example of a switching network which, in effect, produces a step curve according to Fig. 43a.

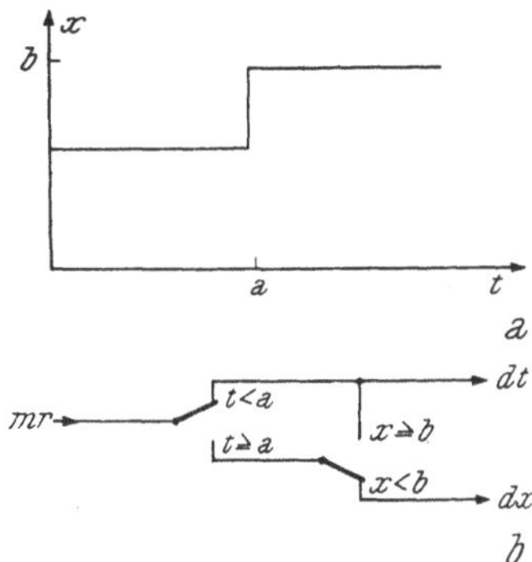

Fig. 43. Switching Network to Produce a Step Curve

Suppose dt is the independent variable for the problem. Basically it is identical to the machine rate mr. However, at the time $t = a$, the increments dt and the computation are interrupted. Now x is increased by the rate dx until $x = b$. Then new increments dt are produced and the computation is resumed.

More complicated step functions, of course, require a more complicated switching network, but cause no principal difficulty.

4.21145. Decision Integrators as Saw-Tooth Generators. An unusual application of decision integrators is the generation of a saw-tooth curve according to Fig. 44b. The integrator diagram is given in Fig. 44a.

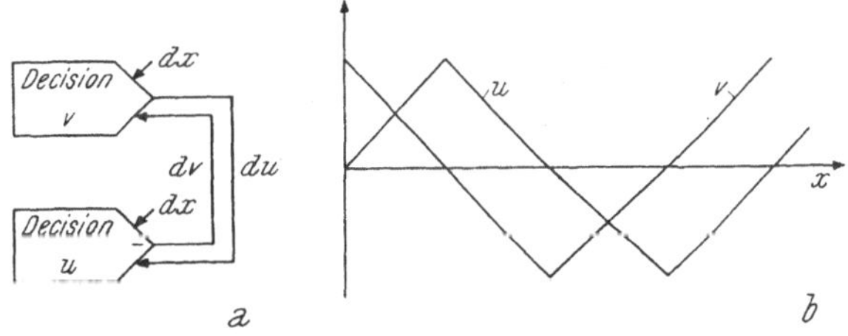

Fig. 44. Saw-Tooth Generator

The decision integrators will produce a rate equal to either a positive or negative rate dx. Suppose at a certain moment, u is equal to zero and v is positive. Increments du are positive. Therefore, u becomes positive and the rate dv becomes negative. The value of u is increasing and the value of v is decreasing. As soon as v is decreased to zero, the top integrator will reverse its sign and produce a negative rate du. Now, both u and v are decreasing. As soon as u is decreased to zero, the bottom integrator changes its output: v is increasing whereas u is still decreasing. As soon as v is increased to zero, the top integrator changes its sign and a new cycle begins.

[1] See 4.1122.

By means of switches, the play of the two decision integrators could be interrupted at proper intervals and, in effect, trapezoidal or even more complicated curves would result.

4.212. Interconnections for Specified Types of Problems. Until now we have concentrated on details of certain basic operations rather than on solving general problems. Nevertheless, we should have acquired some feeling for the capabilities of a digital differential analyzer and the methods employed in breaking down a problem into more elementary parts. The intent of the following paragraphs cannot be to show the exact solution for every problem which may be encountered. Rather, we will try to show the typical reasoning which is followed in preparing different types of problems for the solution on the computer.

4.2121. Ordinary Differential Equations. Most physical processes can be described in terms of differential equations; and, undoubtedly, problems involving the solutions of differential equations are the ones most frequently solved on digital differential analyzers. Let us begin with the simplest type, i.e. a single homogeneous linear differential equation and proceed through various degrees of complexity to systems of non-linear differential equations.

4.21211. Homogeneous Linear Differential Equations with Constant Coefficients. Normally, an equation of this type is given in the form:

$$a_n y^{(n)} + a_{n-1} y^{(n-1)} + \ldots + a_1 y' + a_0 y = 0 \tag{1}$$

$$\text{where: } y^{(\nu)} = \frac{d^\nu y}{d x^\nu}. \tag{2}$$

a_ν is the (constant) coefficient of $y^{(\nu)}$. Dividing equation (1) by a_n and transposing, we obtain an equation of the form:

$$y^{(n)} = b_{n-1} y^{(n-1)} + b_{n-2} y^{(n-2)} + + \ldots + b_1 y' + b_0 y \tag{3}$$

Fig. 45. Generation of $d\,(y^{(n-1)})$ from $d\,(y^{(n)})$

Differentiating with respect to x and multiplying by dx we obtain the form most suitable for the digital differential analyzer:

$$d\,(y^{(n)}) = b_{n-1}\, d\,(y^{(n-1)}) + b_{n-2}\, d\,(y^{(n-2)}) + \ldots + b_1\, dy' + b_0\, dy. \tag{4}$$

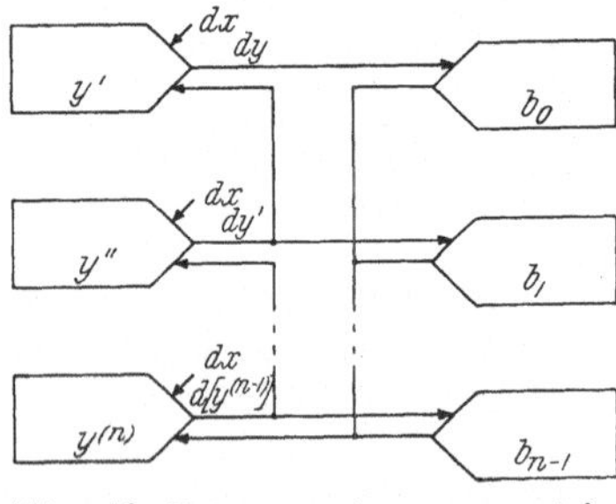

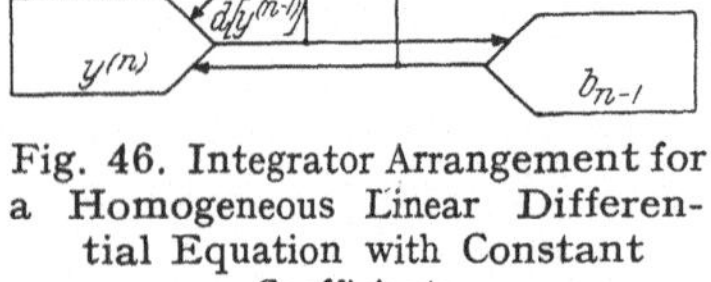

Fig. 46. Integrator Arrangement for a Homogeneous Linear Differential Equation with Constant Coefficients

We now have to determine an integrator schematic diagram which corresponds to equation (4). Suppose we had the rate of the highest derivative $d\,(y^{(n)})$ available, then we could generate the rate of the next lower derivative $d\,(y^{(n-1)})$ in one integrator according to Fig. 45. With $d\,(y^{(n-1)})$ available, we can generate $d\,(y^{(n-2)})$ and so forth until we finally have the differential of the dependent variable dy. This total integrator hookup is given in the left half of Fig. 46.

Having all derivatives of y available, we have to multiply them by the constants b_ν (right hand side of Fig. 46). The sum of all terms on the right hand side of equation (4) is then fed back as the rate of $d\,(y^{(n)})$ which we assumed available at the beginning of this discussion.

The only input which is required for the hookup is the independent variable dx, which is supplied by the machine rate. Fig. 46 shows the solution in principle. However, problems usually involve some elaborations. Therefore, let us consider a specific example of the discussed general type in more detail.

The damped oscillation of a mass around the point $y = 0$ and along the y-axis is described by the differential equation (5).

$$m\frac{d^2y}{dt^2} + k\frac{dy}{dt} + cy = 0. \tag{5}$$

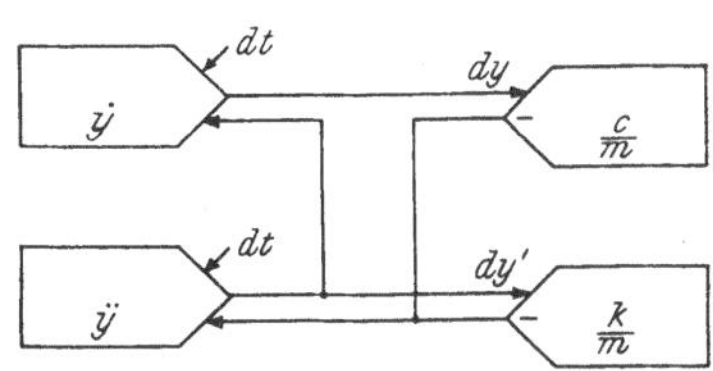

Fig. 47. Basic Integrator Arrangement for Second Order Differential Equation (Damped Oscillation)

The three terms in this equation represent physical forces. The first term is the force due to the acceleration d^2y/dt^2 acting upon the mass m, the second term is the force due to viscous damping which is proportional to the velocity dy/dt and the third term is the attractive (or repulsive) force of an elastic spring proportional to the displacement y of the mass. Following the outlined procedure we obtain in consecutive steps equation (6), (7) and the basic integrator arrangement in Figure 47.

$$\frac{d^2y}{dt^2} = -\frac{k}{m}\frac{dy}{dt} - \frac{c}{m}y \tag{6}$$

$$d(\ddot{y}) = -\frac{k}{m}d(\dot{y}) - \frac{c}{m}dy. \tag{7}$$

If we want to print and plot y, $\dot{y}$, and $\ddot{y}$ versus time, we have to enlarge the basic diagram to that of Fig. 48.[1] Integrators are numbered for reference. Integrators 2, 3, 4, 5 correspond to those of Fig. 47. Integrator 1 accumulates the value of y for printing. Integrator 6 accumulates the elapsed time and integrators 7 to 10 match the computer output of variables to plotter inputs. By programming an automatic print for integrators 1, 2, 3, and 6, we obtain a tabulation of y, $\dot{y}$, $\ddot{y}$ and t in intervals of T_1 determined by the print timing integrator 11. The last integrator in the diagram stops the problem automatically when t exceeds a predetermined time T_2. All plotters are driven by the variable dt in one direction. In the direction perpendicular to it, they are driven by the variables dy, $d\dot{y}$, and $d\ddot{y}$, respectively.

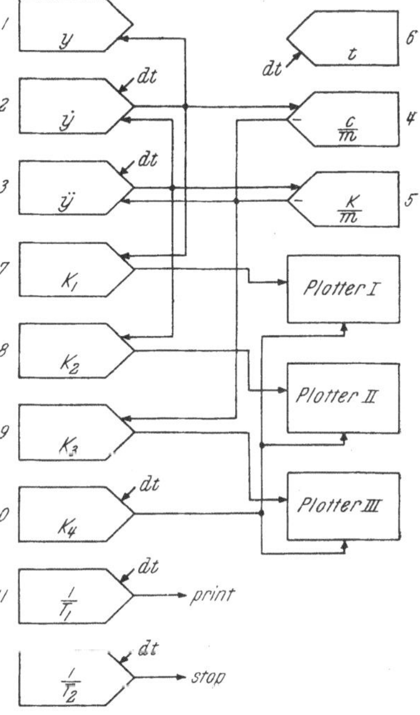

Fig. 48. Complete Diagram for Equation (7)

4.21212. Nonhomogeneous Linear Differential Equations with Constant Coefficients. A differential equation of this type is usually given in the form:

$$a_n y^{(n)} + a^{n-1} y^{(n-1)} + \ldots + a_1 y' + a_0 y = f(x). \tag{8}$$

[1] For the details of scaling this problem, see 4.222.

By the procedure explained in the last paragraph, we can transform this equation into a form suitable for the computer:

$$d\,(y^{(n)}) = b_{n-1}\,d\,(y^{(n-1)}) + b_{n-2}\,d\,(y^{(n-2)}) + \ldots b_1\,dy' + b_0\,dy + d\,[g\,(x)]. \quad (9)$$

This equation is very similar to equation (4) so that the corresponding integrator hookup will also be very similar to the one given in Fig. 46. The only essential difference is the provision for the term $d\,[g\,(x)]$ which we have to feed back as part of $d\,(y^{(n)})$. Since the nature of $g\,(x)$ is known for a specific problem, the additional difficulty encountered in a nonhomogeneous differential equation is reduced to the generation of the differential $d\,[g\,(x)]$ from an input dx. For the moment we will assume we have such a function generator available. The total integrator arrangement is then given in Figure 49. The design of the function generator depends upon the form of $g\,(x)$. For simple functions like $1/x$, x^2, $\sin x$, $\ln x$ etc., we can make use of one of the standard integrator configurations discussed in 4.211. For more complicated cases, the function generator will be an integrator arrangement which corresponds to a differential equation which has $g\,(x)$ as solution. If $g\,(x)$ is given empirically, we can use a curve follower. A fourth approach might use an approximation or regional approximation to $g\,(x)$.

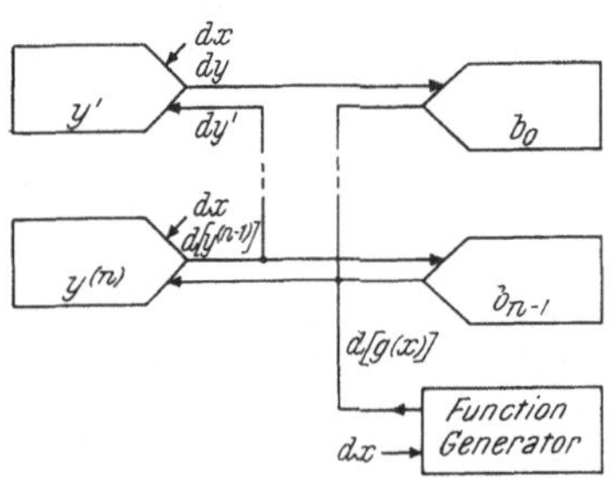

Fig. 49. Integrator Arrangement Representing a Linear Differential Equation with Constant Coefficients

4.21213. Linear Differential Equations in General. A linear differential equation which is neither homogeneous nor has constant coefficients is given by:

$$a_n\,(x)\,y^{(n)} + a_{n-1}\,(x)\,y^{(n-1)} + \ldots + a_1\,(x)\,y' + a_0\,(x)\,y = f\,(x) \quad (10)$$

The coefficients $a_\nu\,(x)$ are arbitrary functions of x.

Let us first assume the coefficient $a_n\,(x)$ of the highest order derivative is identically equal to one. We can then separate the highest derivative and, writing differentials rather than derivatives, we obtain:

$$d\,(y^{(n)}) = d\,[b_{n-1}\,(x)\,y^{(n-1)}] + \ldots + d\,[b_1\,(x)\,y'] + d\,[b_0\,(x)\,y] + d\,[f\,(x)] \quad (11)$$

Although equation (11) is more complex than equation (4) or (9), the considerations involved in finding the corresponding integrator hookup are still analogous to the ones outlined in 4.21211: If the rate of the highest derivative is available, then we can generate all lower order derivatives and the right hand side of equation (11), since, in a specific case, all $b_\nu\,(x)$ and $f\,(x)$ are known functions of x. The lower order derivatives have to be multiplied by functions $b_\nu\,(x)$ before they can be fed back as part of the highest order derivative. The function generators for the generation of $b_\nu\,(x)$ and $f\,(x)$ may be of the type described in the last paragraph for the generation of $g\,(x)$. The multiplication of the rates $d\,(y^{(\nu)})$ and $d\,[b_\nu\,(x)]$ is performed in a standard multiplier.[1]

The essential difference between the integrator hookup given in Fig. 49 and the one required here is within a "stage" of the overall diagram. Let us,

[1] See 4.21112.

therefore, show in Fig. 50 only the details of the stage for the ν-th derivative with the understanding that a total of n stages are required. Until now we

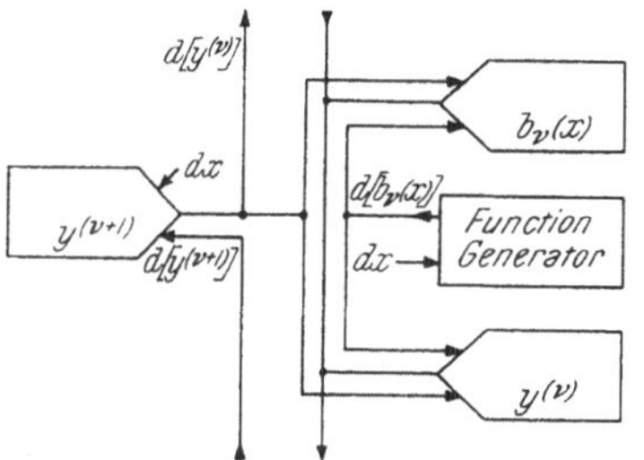

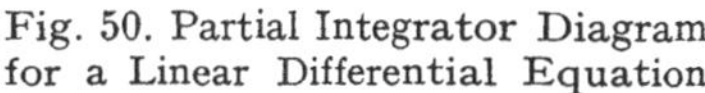
Fig. 50. Partial Integrator Diagram for a Linear Differential Equation

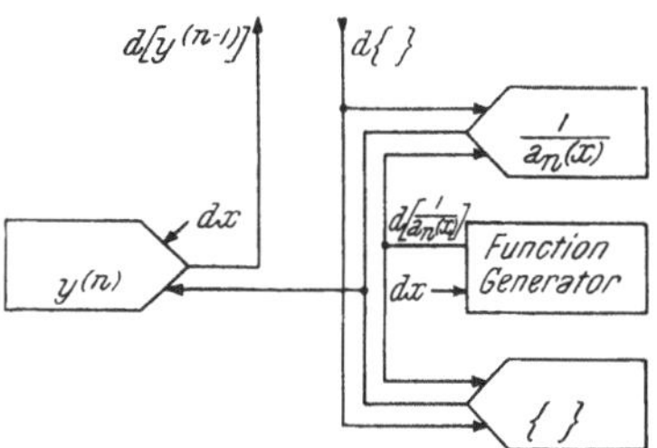

Fig. 51. Partial Integrator Diagram for a Linear Differential Equation of the Most General Type

have assumed that the coefficient $a_0\,(x)$ is identically equal to one. If this is not true, then we have to make a slight modification in our integrator hookup. Equation (10) is transformed into:

$$y^{(n)} = \frac{1}{a_n\,(x)}\left\{b_{n-1}\,(x)\,y^{(n-1)} + \ldots + b_1\,(x)\,y' + b_0\,(x)\,y + f\,(x)\right\} \tag{12}$$

Differentiating, we obtain on the right hand side the differential of a product which can be easily mechanized using the basic integrator configuration for multiplication of two variables shown in Fig. 51. (Note that the differential of the expression in braces is already derived in Fig. 50.)

4.21214. Systems of Linear Differential Equations of the First Order. The simplest system of linear differential equations would be the one of first order and with constant coefficients given by:

$$\left\{\begin{aligned} \frac{dy_1}{dx} &= a_{11}\,y_1 + a_{12}\,y_2 + \ldots + a_{1n}\,y_n \\ \frac{dy_2}{dx} &= a_{21}\,y_1 + a_{22}\,y_2 \ldots + a_{2n}\,y_n \\ &\vdots \\ \frac{dy_n}{dx} &= a_{n1}\,y_1 + a_{n2}\,y_2 + \ldots a_{nn}\,y_n \end{aligned}\right\} \tag{13}$$

The n functions y_1 to y_n are solutions to the system if they simultaneously satisfy (13).

The procedure which yields the integrator hookup is essentially the same as we have followed until now. We assume the highest derivatives of all variables to be available. Then we can generate the functions by integration. Thus, having the right hand sides of equations (13), we feed back the proper terms as part of the derivatives.

Rather than showing integrator interconnections for the general case, let us go through this procedure for an example with $n = 2$ (equation 14). The general case will yield a correspondingly more complicated network, but it presents no additional problems.

$$\left\{\begin{aligned} \frac{dy_1}{dx} &= a_{11}\,y_1 + a_{12}\,y_2 \\ \frac{dy_2}{dx} &= a_{12}\,y_1 + a_{22}\,y_2 \end{aligned}\right\} \tag{14}$$

Differentiating with respect to x and multiplying with dx, we obtain:

$$\left\{ \begin{array}{l} dy_1' = a_{11}\, dy_1 + a_{12}\, dy_2 \\ dy_2' = a_{21}\, dy_1 + a_{22}\, dy_2 \end{array} \right\} \tag{15}$$

The mechanization of these equations is given in Fig. 52.

If the four coefficients a_{11} to a_{22} are not constants but functions of x, we obtain (16) instead of (15).

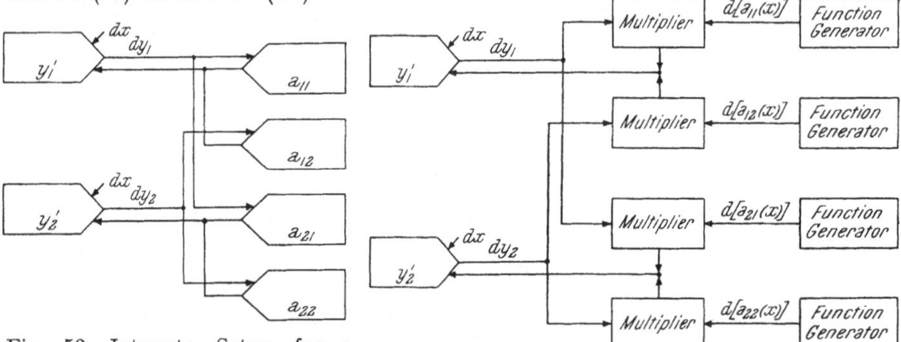

Fig. 52. Integrator Setup for a System of Two Linear Differential Equations with Constant Coefficients

Fig. 53. Integrator Schematic for System of Two Linear Differential Equations

$$\left\{ \begin{array}{l} dy_1' = d\,[a_{11}(x)\, y_1] + d\,[a_{12}(x)\, y_2] \\ dy_2' = d\,[a_{21}(x)\, y_1] + d\,[a_{22}(x)\, y_2] \end{array} \right\}. \tag{16}$$

The integrator network becomes slightly more complicated. Four function generators and four multipliers are required. Showing function generators and multipliers in simplified form, we obtain the schematic diagram given in Fig. 53.

4.21215. Systems of Linear Differential Equations of Higher Order. Systems of higher order present no principal difficulties over those of first order. Let us assume a system of second order according to (17):

$$\left\{ \begin{array}{l} y_1'' = a_{11}\, y_1' + a_{12}\, y_2' + a_{13}\, y_1 + a_{14}\, y_2 \\ y_2'' = a_{21}\, y_1' + a_{22}\, y_2' + a_{23}\, y_1 + a_{24}\, y_2 \end{array} \right\} \tag{17}$$

Differentiating, we obtain:

$$\left\{ \begin{array}{l} dy_1'' = a_{11}\, dy_1' + a_{12}\, dy_2' + a_{13}\, dy_1 + a_{14}\, dy_2 \\ dy_2'' = a_{21}\, dy_1' + a_{22}\, dy_2' + a_{23}\, dy_1 + a_{24}\, dy_2 \end{array} \right\} \tag{18}$$

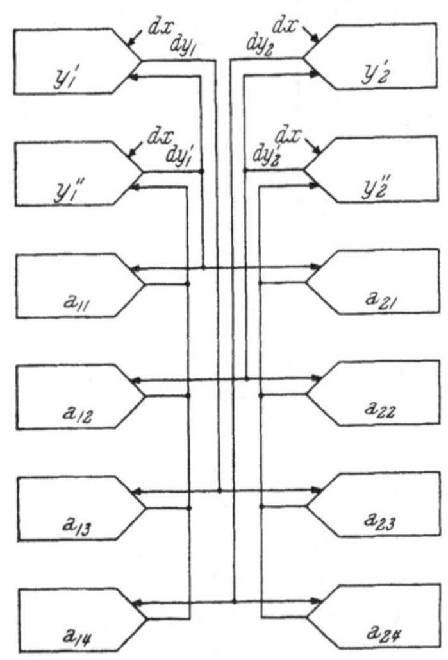

Fig. 54. Integrator Diagram for a System of Two Linear Differential Equations of Second Order

The corresponding integrator diagram is given in Fig. 54. We observe that the highest derivative of every variable is used to generate the lower order derivatives and the functions themselves. Appropriate terms are then fed back as part of the highest derivative. This method can be applied to a system of any order, whether or not the coefficients are constant.

4.21216. Nonlinear Differential Equations. The previous discussion of integrator networks for the handling of linear differential equations has been purposely detailed. We shall see that the indicated principles apply to all types of differential equations. In many cases, even the integrator hookups with very slight modifications can be used for nonlinear differential equations. For example, the integrator hookup given in Fig. 49 is for a linear differential equation with constant coefficients. Practically the same integrator hookup can be used for the nonlinear differential equation given by (19):

$$a_n y^{(n)} + a_{n-1} y^{(n-1)} + \ldots + a_1 y' + a_0 y = f(y). \tag{19}$$

The change in the integrator diagram of Fig. 49 to that of Fig. 55 is a very simple one: the function generator is now driven by dy and produces $d[f(y)]$ instead of $d[g(x)]$. In a similar way, simply by changing the function generators, the integrator diagram given in Figure 50 or 51 may be adapted to a differential equation which has functions of y as coefficients.

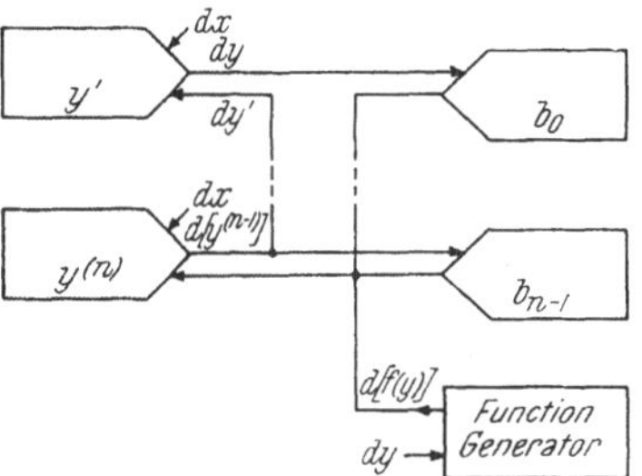

Fig. 55. Integrator Diagram for Equation (19)

In the most general case of an ordinary differential equation, the coefficients of derivatives are functions of both x and y. Even this presents no problem as it is relatively simple to generate functions of two or more variables. The basic principle still applies. We always generate lower order derivatives from the highest order derivative and feed back appropriate terms as part of the highest derivative. These parts are generated by cross connecting integrators according to the given equation. Let us illustrate this by considering a nonlinear differential equation of the first order.

An ordinary differential equation of first order is given by:

$$F(x, y, y') = 0 \tag{20}$$

F is a simultaneous function of x, y, and y'.

Separating the highest derivative, we find:

$$y' = f(x, y) \tag{21}$$

or:

$$dy' = d[f(x, y)] \tag{22}$$

Assuming dy' to be available, we can generate the right hand side of equation (22) and then feed back the appropriate terms as dy'. Let us take (23) as an example of a general non-linear differential equation of the first order.[1]

$$2xy' - x^2 - y^2 = 0 \tag{23}$$

Following our standard procedure, we separate the highest derivative:

$$y' = \frac{x}{2} + \frac{y^2}{2x} \tag{24}$$

Differentiating, we obtain:

$$dy' = \tfrac{1}{2}\,dx - \frac{y^2}{2x^2}\,dx + \frac{y}{x}\,dy \tag{25}$$

[1] This equation is not separable and has a family of hyperbolae as solution.

A general block diagram of the corresponding problem setup is given in Fig. 56. Here we have "a" solution to the problem. However, in this example, as for most problems, it may be rewarding to seek a simpler solution. Let us suppose we rewrite equation (25) as:

$$dy' = dx - \left(\tfrac{1}{2} + \frac{y^2}{2x^2}\right) dx + \frac{y}{x}\, dy = dx - 1/x \left(\frac{x}{2} + \frac{y^2}{2x}\right) dx + \frac{y}{x}\, dy. \tag{26}$$

According to (24) the term in parenthesis is equal to y', so we can write:

$$dy' = dx - \frac{1}{x}\frac{dy}{dx}\, dx + \frac{y}{x}\, dy, \quad (27) \qquad \text{or:} \qquad dy' = dx + \frac{y-1}{x}\, dy. \quad (28)$$

The corresponding block diagram is given in Fig. 57. This solution is less complex than the one given in Fig. 56. The simplification is due to the fact

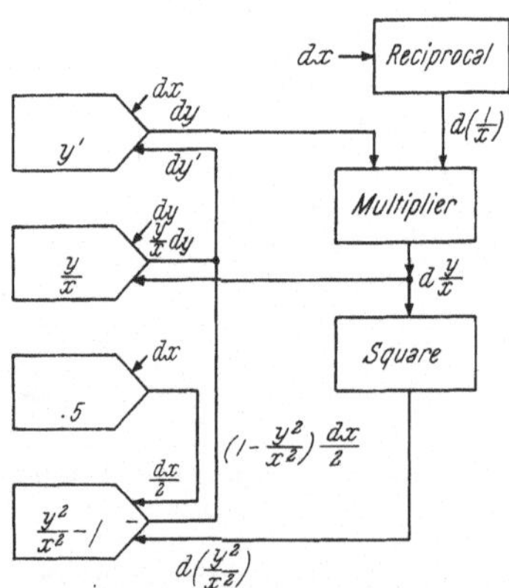

Fig. 56. Block Diagram of the Problem Setup for Equation (25)

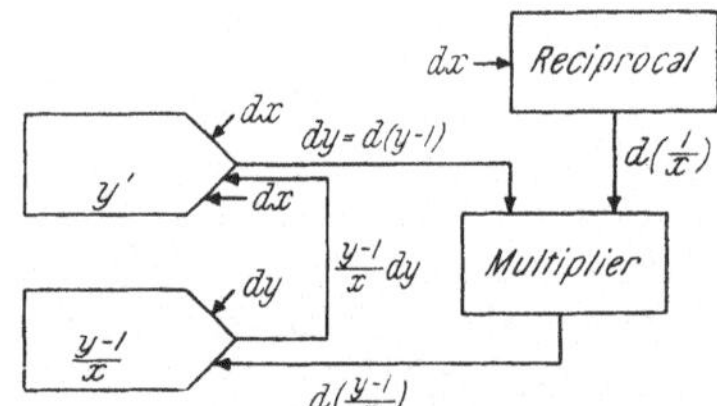

Fig. 57. Block Diagram for Equation (28)

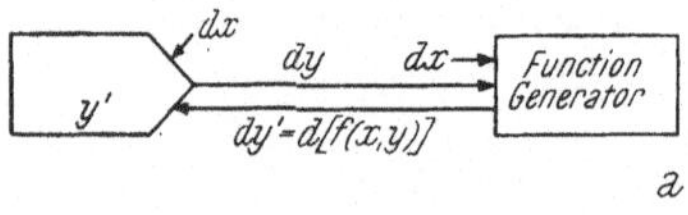

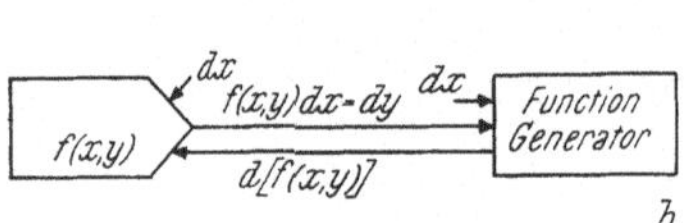

Fig. 58. Block Diagram for Equations (22) and (29)

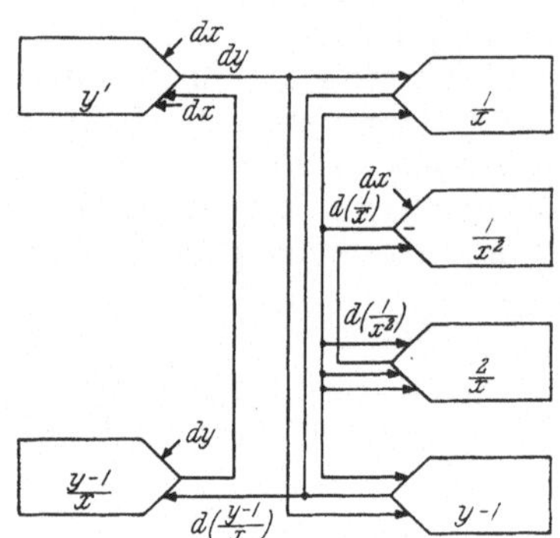

Fig. 59. Integrator Network for Equation (28)

that a digital differential analyzer can simultaneously integrate with respect to several variables. Counting integrators in the block diagrams,[1] we find nine integrators for Fig. 56 and six integrators for Fig. 57.

One might try to seek the solution of the same differential equation in a third way. So far, we have proceeded according to equations (21) and (22). However, we can rewrite equation (21) as

$$dy = f(x, y)\, dx \tag{29}$$

The integrator hookup for equations (22) versus (29) is given in general terms in Fig. 58, (a) and (b) respectively. For diagram (a), we assume dy' to be available and generate the correct feedback. In the diagram (b) we assume $d\,[f\,(x, y)]$ to be available. However, the resulting block diagram is the same. The only dif-

[1] A multiplier is equivalent to two integrators. The reciprocal can be derived by two integrators, and the square by one.

ference is in labelling. Therefore we should not expect any simplifications from this scheme.

The simplest problem representation is then according to Fig. 57 and is given in detail in Fig. 59.

4.21217. Systems of Simultaneous Nonlinear Differential Equations. Here, the procedure given for systems of linear differential equations has to be slightly modified. The feedback may be in form of functions of variables instead of the plain variables. Let us explain this in an example. Equations (30) and (31) are a set of two simultaneous equations describing the trajectory of a body in a uniform gravitational field without air resistance:

$$m \frac{dv}{dt} = - m g \sin \gamma \qquad (30)$$

$$mv \frac{d\gamma}{dt} = - m g \cos \gamma \qquad (31)$$

γ is the angle between the trajectory and the horizon. Equation (30) describes the forces acting on the body in direction of the trajectory and equation (31) describes those acting perpendicular to it. Separating the derivatives and differentiating, we obtain:

$$d\dot{v} = - g\, d\,(\sin \gamma) \qquad (32)$$

$$d\dot{\gamma} = - g\, d\left(\frac{1}{v} \cos \gamma\right) \qquad (33)$$

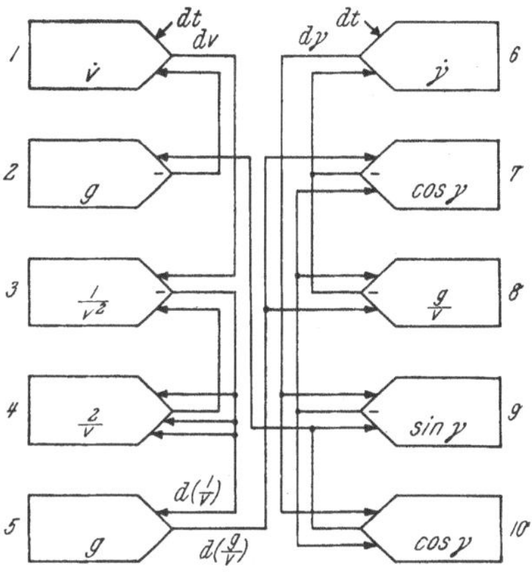

Fig. 60. Integrator Setup for Equations (32) and (33)

From equations (32) and (33), we derive the integrator setup given in Fig. 60:

The feedbacks are in form of functions of v and γ. The height y of the trajectory can be found by setting up a third differential equation:

$\dot{y} = v \sin \gamma$, (34) or $d\dot{y} = d\,(v \sin \gamma)$. (35)

The corresponding diagram is given in Fig. 61 and requires as inputs only functions which are available from the main integrator hookup.[1]

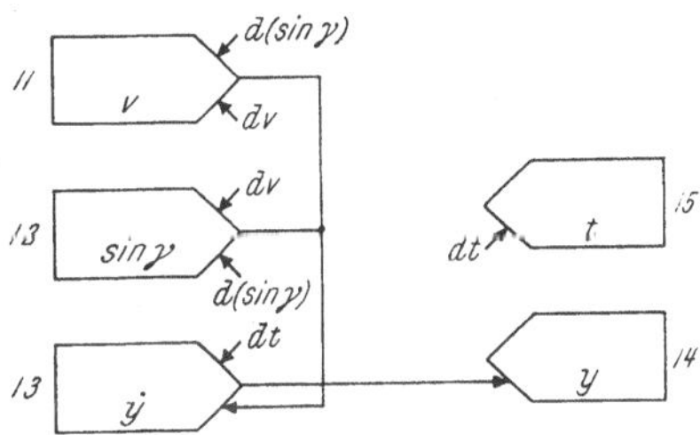

Fig. 61. Integrator Setup for Equation (35)

4.2122. Algebraic Equations. Let us consider the principle which enables us to solve algebraic equations on a digital differential analyzer by taking an example:

$$ax^2 + bx + c = 0 \qquad (36)$$

Probably nobody would try to solve this equation on a digital differential analyzer, but the principle applies just as well to higher order equations. If we consider x as a variable in this problem, we have:

$$ax^2 + bx + c = f\,(x) \qquad (37)$$

We are looking for a value of x for which $f\,(x) = 0$. Suppose we have a servo (the integrator on the left in Fig. 62) which has $f\,(x)$ as integrand and is fed by the machine rate. This integrator will put out increments as long as equation (36) is not satisfied. These increments are used to correct the current value of x;

[1] For the scaling of this problem, see 4.222.

in other words, these increments are used as dx. In order to keep the value of the integrand $f(x)$ current, we have to feed the servo with the differential:

$$d[f(x)] = d(ax^2 + bx + c) = 2\,ax\,dx + b\,dx \tag{38}$$

The total problem setup is given in Fig. 62:

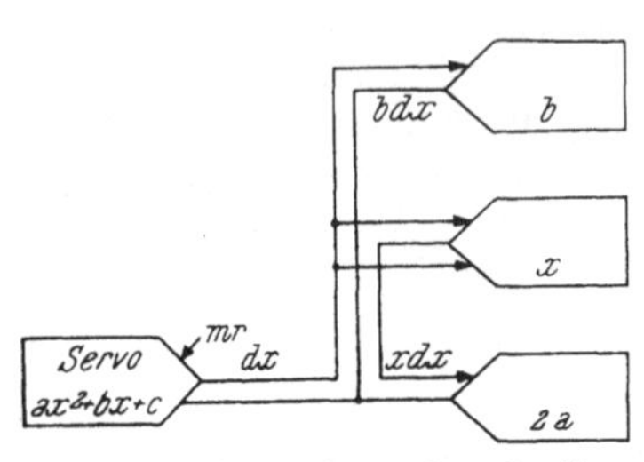

Fig. 62. Setup for a Quadratic Equation

The computation is started at some random point x_0 by filling the corresponding initial values into the computer. The servo will then drive the integrator hookup into a state where equation (36) is satisfied. The value of x will then represent the solution of this equation. If the approximate solution is known beforehand, it is preferable to use this value as starting point, in order to shorten the required computing time.

The second root of equation (36) (or the remaining roots of higher order equations) can be found by starting with different initial values so that the integrator hookup will "slide" into the corresponding state.[1] A knowledge of the approximate roots is here especially valuable. If no estimates of the roots are available, then the given method is essentially a trial and error method. One difficulty which may be encountered under these circumstances is, for instance, that the integrator hookup causes taking off in the wrong direction, i.e. in the direction in which $f(x)$ is steadily increasing. One remedy is to try another starting point or reverse the output sign of the servo.[2]

If necessary, an estimate of existing roots can be found by plotting $f(x)$ versus x in rough scale by the computer.

The outlined method is not limited to finding roots of polynominals but may just as well be applied to exponential equations or equations containing trigonometric functions and the like.

4.2123. Simultaneous Equations. Let us again take a more or less typical example. Suppose we have the following set of simultaneous equations:

$$\left\{\begin{array}{l} a_1x + b_1y + c_1z + d_1 = 0 \\ a_2x + b_2y + c_2z + d_2 = 0 \\ a_3x + b_3y + c_3z + d_3 = 0 \end{array}\right\} \tag{39}$$

As in the previous paragraph we assume x, y and z to be variables and we are looking for a value of x, y and z where the three equations given in (39) are simultaneously satisfied. Since three equations are to be satisfied, we will employ three servos. Each one of them will decide whether the corresponding equation is satisfied. If the equations are not satisfied, the three servos will put out increments dx, dy and dz, which tend to correct the error. The integrands of the three servos are the three left-hand members of equation (39). The feedback is in the form of the three differentials:

$$\left\{\begin{array}{l} d(a_1x + b_1y + c_1z + d_1) = a_1\,dx + b_1\,dy + c_1\,dz \\ d(a_2x + b_2y + c_2z + d_2) = a_2\,dx + b_2\,dy + c_2\,dz \\ d(a_3x + b_3y + c_3z + d_3) = a_3\,dx + b_3\,dy + c_3\,dz \end{array}\right\} \tag{40}$$

[1] In some instances, it may pay to reduce the degree of the original equation, if a solution is found.

[2] This has the same effect as using $-f(x)$ in equation (37) as criterion.

The complete problem setup is given in Fig. 63.

If no estimate of the solution is known, then some random values of x, y and z are filled initially. After the computation is started, the servos will "hunt" for a solution in a fashion which could be described only in terms of a relatively complicated mathematical expression but which is of no consequence for the present purpose.

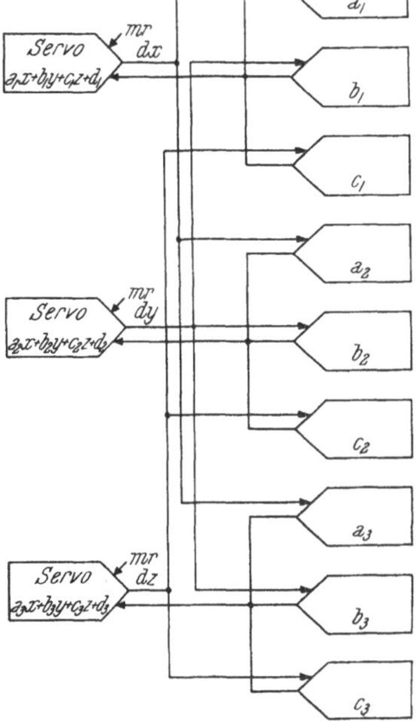

Fig. 63. Problem Setup for Equation (40)

If a solution is found, the integrands in all three servos are reduced to zero. The system is stationary and the solution can be read out of some integrators which are not shown in Fig. 63 but which simply accumulate increments dx, dy, dz.

In order to speed up the solution process, it is advantageous to take the output of that servo for a correction in a certain variable, whose integrand is affected most by a change in this variable. The given procedure might again be applied to more complicated simultaneous equations containing e. g. transcendental functions.

4.2124. Coordinate Transformation. A coordinate transformation is a process which is frequently required for normal calculations and for real time control applications. Let us again indicate the principle of the solution by an example. Suppose the problem is the conversion from cylindrical to cartesian coordinates. Inputs are in terms of the cylindrical coordinates $d\varrho$, $d\varphi$ and dz. Outputs shall be in terms of the cartesian coordinates dx, dy and dz. The equations which govern the conversion are:

$$x = \varrho \cos \varphi$$
$$y = \varrho \sin \varphi \qquad (41)$$
$$z = z$$

In order to make these equations solvable by the computer, we have to transpose them into differential form as:

$$dx = \varrho d(\cos \varphi) + \cos \varphi \, d\varrho$$
$$dx = \varrho d(\sin \varphi) + \sin \varphi \, d\varrho \qquad (42)$$
$$dz = dz$$

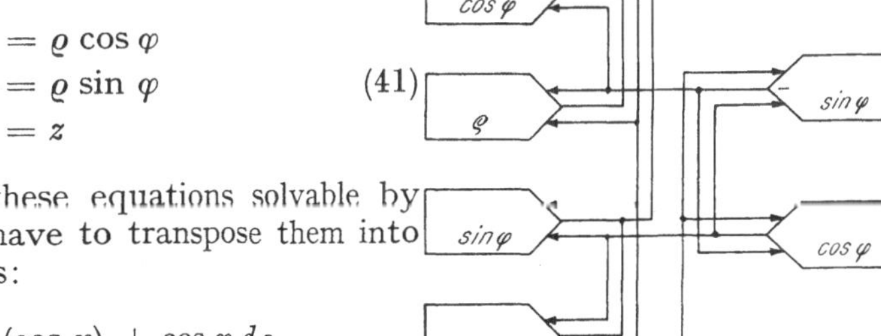

Fig. 64. Integrator Diagram for Conversion from Cylindrical to Cartesian Coordinates

Using the sine and cosine generator of 4.21122 we find the integrator diagram of Fig. 64.

In much the same way, the integrator diagram for the conversion from any coordinate system to any other can be found, including rotation and translation. In a similar manner, also the conversion of vector components from one coordinate system to another can be performed.

4.2125. Generation of Functions of Several Variables. The generation of functions of several variables is frequently required. The last paragraph has already involved a problem of this type. Let us discuss here a slightly different problem. Suppose we have the set of equations:

$$\begin{aligned} E_x &= \cos x \cos z \\ E_z &= \sin x \sin z \end{aligned} \tag{43}$$

These equations describe the electric field of an unattenuated transverse magnetic wave, travelling in the z direction, at a fixed time. Regarding x and z as independent variables, we find the schematic diagram of Fig. 65 to represent the given equations.

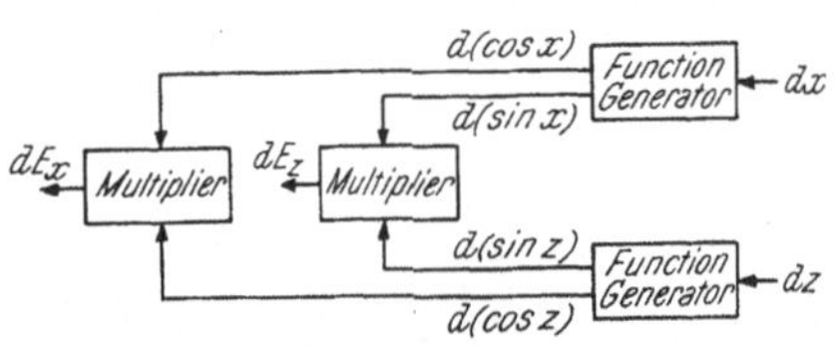

Fig. 65. Schematic Diagram Representing Equations (43)

Driving the integrators with input rates dx and dz we can find the components of the electric intensity at any point (x, z). Let us suppose now that we have to draw a diagram of the electric field, i. e. to plot the direction of the electric field vector E composed of the two mutually perpendicular components E_x and E_z in a family of curves as shown in Fig. 66. We can make the computer draw this diagram on a plotter by the following procedure: The function generator has, so far, complete freedom in input dx and dz or, in other words, the two variables are truly independent. If we can find a relation between x and z which is valid along the field line, then we may use the two now dependent variables x and z to drive a plotter along this line. Such a relationship is not hard to find. Suppose we start at point P in Fig. 66. If E_x is strong in this point (as it is in reality), the movement we want is mainly in the x direction. If, during our travel we encounter an E_z component, then we want a component of travel in the z direction proportional to E_z. If we find a point at which we have only an E_z component, then the travel is only in the z direction, i.e. dx is proportional to E_x and dz is proportional to E_z.

Fig. 66. Field Distribution According to Equation (43)

If we use two integrators, according to Fig. 67, to represent this relation, then the plotter driven by dx and dz, once started at a random point, will draw the complete corresponding field line.

Since we have not introduced any mathematical limits, the plotter will plot field lines in accordance with (43) beyond the boundaries assumed in Fig. 66.

Fig. 67. Driving Mechanism

If the additional problem of drawing orthogonal trajectories to these field lines exists, this can be easily accomplished by interchanging the outputs of the driving mechanism in Fig. 67.

The principle is not only applicable to the given relatively simple case but can be applied to cases where the vector components are functions of four variables (three coordinates and time), including complicated fields in cylindrical or elliptical wave guides. In a similar way vector fields representing forces, stresses, aerodynamic pressures and the like can be plotted, provided existing boundaries can be introduced or can be neglected.

4.2126. Some Suggestions for Complicated Cases. It is to be expected that the generalized procedures for the design of integrator hookups given in 4.21 do not fit all problems which may be encountered.

In cases like this it may pay to investigate one or more of the following approaches:

If the mathematical representation of a problem is apparently not suited for the computer, one may try a different mathematical approach (e.g. a problem stated in form of integral equations may perhaps be restated in form of differential equations).

If the mathematics of a solution to a problem are principally suited for the computer, but difficulties in the representation are encountered, one may try to neglect some terms. (An exact mathematical description of a problem frequently has terms which may influence the result less than the inherent error of the method of solution or which can be considered as second or third order corrections to a simpler description which may be sufficient for a given purpose.)

If a term has to be considered in a problem correctly as a variable, but taking care of this additional variable complicates the representation unreasonably, then one may use this term as a parameter and make several runs with different values assigned to it (e.g. one may describe a whole family of curves in order to determine one optimum point).

If the difficulty lies in the generation of variables, one may try consecutively to generate the variables as solutions of differential equations or as approximations (e.g. in terms of a polynomial), or obtain them from a graph of the function by a curve follower.

4.22. Scaling

The scaling of a problem means the matching of problem values with corresponding machine values. The most obvious reason why scaling is required is that the computer can handle only integrands with values $|Y| \leqslant 1$, as the following considerations will show:

Let us suppose we have an integrator according to Fig. 68 with:

$$\Delta z = Y \Delta x \tag{1}$$

The output rate Δz is proportional to the input rate Δx and the integrand Y. However the highest output rate we can obtain under any circumstances is equal to the input rate Δx. This is then the case, when the integrand Y is equal to the largest number which the Y-register can contain.[1] According to equation (1), the integrand is then equal to ± 1. For smaller integrands, the output rate is smaller than the input rate, and according to (1) the integrand has a value smaller than one as far as the machine is concerned. In other words, the machine value of Y is always less than, or at most equal to one.

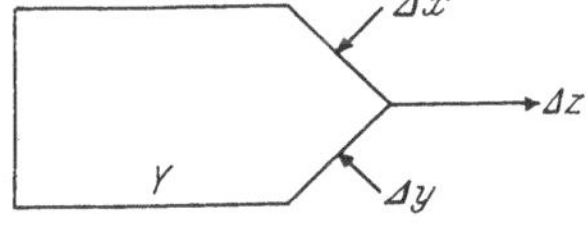

Fig. 68. Digital Integrator

$$|Y_{\mathrm{m}}| \leqslant 1 \tag{2}$$

Another reason for scaling is the fact that the machine considers only unit increments.

[1] See 4.1112.

This property may be inconvenient for an actual problem but it is no restriction in a real sense, since we still have the complete freedom of selecting an appropriate unit to measure the physical quantity represented. Suppose a problem deals with velocity and the highest velocity is 1000 feet per second. The velocity represented in feet per second is much larger than one, but represented in miles per second its value is well below one. In a similar manner, we may express weight in ounces, pounds, or tons to suit the machine. The restriction of equation (2) is even less critical as it may seem now because we can select almost any measure which is convenient in a particular case as machine "unit" e.g. 2×10^3 feet or 10^{-4} amperes, etc. Unfortunately, even though there exists no principal difficulty in "scaling" a problem, there are certain rules and relations of scale factors which have to be observed in order to obtain a true representation of the overall problem with sufficient accuracy.

4.221. Basic Scaling Relations for One Integrator. Considering only one integrator, we have the four quantities Y, dx, dy, dz for which the machine values in general differ from the problem values. The relation between machine and problem values can be expressed in the following manner:

$$Y_m = K_Y Y_p \tag{3a}$$
$$dx_m = K_x dx_p \tag{3b}$$
$$dy_m = K_y dy_p \tag{3c}$$
$$dz_m = K_z dz_p \tag{3d}$$

(All K's are positive.) The subscript m denotes machine values, the subscript p denotes problem values and K is the "scalefactor" of a certain variable.

Let us illustrate the meaning of the scalefactor K_Y by a simple example. Suppose in a particular case Y_p is 376 ft/sec and K_Y is equal to 10^{-3}, then Y_m becomes .376 disregarding the dimension. The unit which is used in the problem to measure the velocity is ft/sec and the unit in which the machine calculates is 10^3 ft/sec. In general the machine unit is always $1/K$ problem units. We note that a scalefactor smaller than one gives a machine value smaller than the problem value and a scalefactor larger than one gives a machine value larger than the problem value.

The scalefactor for differentials (3b, c, d) can be illustrated in a very similar way. We have just seen that one machine unit is equal to $1/K$ problem units. In other words, an increment of one machine unit is equal to an increment of $1/K$ problem units, or it takes an increment of K machine units for an increment of one problem unit. Now, suppose the variable x in an actual problem is time measured in seconds. K shall be 10^2. One machine increment (one Δx_m) corresponds then to an increment of 10^{-2} sec. in the actual problem or 10^2 machine increments ($10^2 \Delta x$'s) represent a change of 1 second in the actual problem.

Let us now begin to express some of the relations we found previously in terms of problem values. Equation (1) written in terms of differentials is:

$$dz_m = Y_m\, dx_m \tag{4}$$

Using equation (3) we can express this in problem values:

$$K_z\, dz_p = K_Y Y_p K_x\, dx_p \tag{5}$$

In order to perform a true integration in the problem we have to postulate:

$$dz_p = Y_p\, dx_p \tag{6}$$

From (5) and (6) follows:

$$K_z = K_Y\, K_x \tag{7}$$

This latter equation is the first basic scaling relation for one integrator. We note that if two of the three scalefactors are given, there is no freedom of choice for the third one.

The second basic scaling relation stems from equation (2). If $Y_{\mathrm{p\ max}}$ is the maximum problem value of an integrand in a certain problem, then the maximum machine value is:

$$Y_{\mathrm{m\ max}} = K_{\mathrm{Y}} Y_{\mathrm{p\ max}} \tag{8}$$

Since, according to equation (2), $|Y_{\mathrm{m}}|$ cannot be larger than one, we obtain:

$$K_{\mathrm{Y}} |Y_{\mathrm{p\ max}}| \leqslant 1 \tag{9}$$

or

$$K_{\mathrm{Y}} \leqslant \frac{1}{|Y_{\mathrm{p\ max}}|} \tag{10}$$

The third scaling relation expresses the connection of K_{Y}, the scalefactor of the integrand (3a) and K_{y}, the scalefactor of the increment Δy (3c). Suppose n is the number of positions in the Y-register (the number of significant digits which the machine uses in its calculation).

In the given example (Fig. 69), n is equal to 8, since the input Δy is added to the integrand in the eighth place after the machine decimal point. In this example then, it takes a total of 10^8 inputs Δy to make up one machine unit of Y_{m}. In general it takes 10^{n} increments Δy to make up one unit of Y_{m}. Consequently, it would take $10^{\mathrm{n}} K_{\mathrm{Y}}$ increments Δy to make up one problem unit Y_{p}, or K_{y} the scalefactor of these increments is:[1]

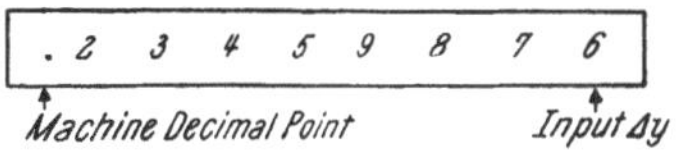

. 2	3	4	5	9	8	7	6

Machine Decimal Point — Input Δy

Fig. 69. Scaling of the Y-Register

$$K_{\mathrm{y}} = 10^{\mathrm{n}} K_{\mathrm{Y}} \tag{11}$$

The "length" n of the Y-register can usually be varied between limits by programming (e.g. from 1 to 7 for a decimal machine).

The three equations (7, 10, 11) give the basic relations (and restrictions) of scalefactors. They are necessary conditions, which have to be satisfied for a correct machine representation of a problem. These conditions are necessary and also sufficient as far as the machine is concerned. There is, however, one more restriction which deals with the accuracy of a problem representation and which has to be satisfied as far as the actual problem is concerned.

Suppose the variable s in a problem represents distance and is measured in feet. The variable shall be represented accurately within $\pm .5 \times 10^{-3}$ feet. Apparently then a machine increment Δs must be smaller or at most equal to 10^{-3} feet in the actual problem. The scalefactor of this variable, therefore, must be equal to 10^3 or larger. In general we have:

$$K \geqslant K_{\mathrm{min}} \tag{12}$$

K_{min} is the minimum number of increments which has to be used to represent one problem unit in order to obtain sufficient accuracy.[2]

Equations (7, 10, 11, 12) are now the complete set of conditions for a correct machine representation of a problem. For practical purposes, it is convenient to show them in a slightly different form.

---

[1] Equation (11) is valid only for decimal machines. For binary machines (machines which use the binary or base 2 number system for their calculations) we would have $K_{\mathrm{y}} = 2^{\mathrm{n}} K_{\mathrm{Y}}$.

[2] A sufficiently large scale factor is a necessary but not sufficient condition for the accuracy of a solution. See 4.32.

Inserting (11) into (7) we obtain:

$$10^n K_z = K_y K_x \tag{13}$$

This is the basic relation of the scalefactor of all integrator inputs, the integrator output and the number of digits in the integrand. Together with equation (11) it is a complete description of the operation of an integrator, as far as the relation of scalefactors is concerned.

The following equations give the limitations on the five values n, K_y, K_Y, K_x and K_z, which might be varied in a setup.

The limitation on n is obtained from equations (7, 10, 11 and 12), together with the consideration that n must be smaller than or equal to N, the maximum number of positions available in a computer.

$$\log (K_{y\,min} |Y_{p\,max}|) \leqslant \log (K_y |Y_{p\,max}|) \leqslant \log \frac{K_y K_x}{K_z} = n \leqslant N \tag{14}$$

The limitation on K_y, the scalefactor of the input Δy is obtained from (7, 10, 11, and 12).

$$K_{y\,min} \leqslant K_y = \frac{10^n K_z}{K_x} \leqslant \frac{10^n}{|Y_{p\,max}|} \leqslant \frac{10^N}{|Y_{p\,max}|} \tag{15}$$

The limitation on K_Y, the scalefactor of the integrand Y is obtained from (10, 11 and 12).

$$\frac{K_{y\,min}}{10^N} \leqslant \frac{K_y}{10^n} = K_Y \leqslant \frac{1}{|Y_{p\,max}|} \tag{16}$$

Interpreting the results found so far, we find that the lower limits of the three values n, K_y, K_Y, stem from accuracy requirements of the problem (12) whereas the upper limits stem from machine limitations, i.e., the restricted number of digital positions (N) to represent the integrand in a specific machine.

For the remaining two scalefactors, i.e., K_x and K_z we may well have a lower limit, given by accuracy considerations, however, no upper limitations imposed by properties of the computer. What we say here is, that we can make the scalefactors of K_x and K_z as high as we please or we may use as many increments Δx and Δz as we want, to represent one unit of the actual problem. Going back to Figure 4, we see that a large number of Δx inputs simply means a large number of Δz outputs and vice versa. The two rates are proportional. We, therefore, have no real upper limitation on the corresponding scalefactors. One of them can be as large as desired provided the other one is sufficiently large. Using equations (7, 10, and 13) we find:

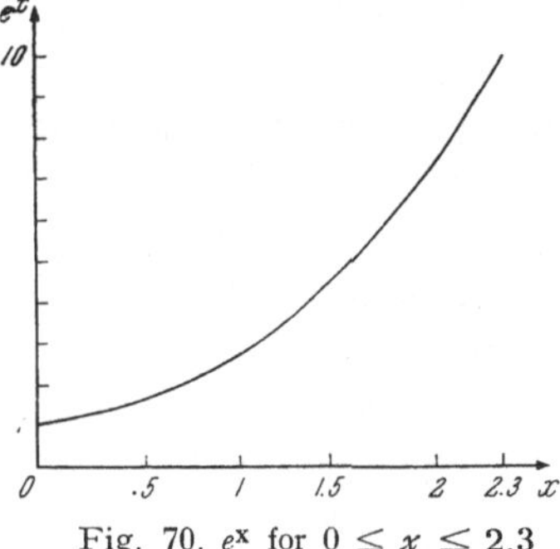

Fig. 70. e^x for $0 \leqq x \leqq 2{,}3$

$$K_z |Y_{p\,max}| \leqslant K_x = \frac{10^n}{K_y} K_z \leqslant \frac{10^N}{K_{y\,min}} K_z \tag{17}$$

$$K_x \frac{K_{y\,min}}{10^N} \leqslant K_x \frac{K_y}{10^n} = K_z \leqslant \frac{K_x}{|Y_{p\,max}|} \tag{18}$$

Let us now scale a sample problem which involves only one integrator: the generation of e^x.[1] Suppose, the problem is to generate e^x between the limits,

[1] For the basic integrator configuration refer to 4.21121.

$x = 0$ and $x = 2.3$. Increments in e^x shall be 10^{-3} or smaller ($K_{y\,min} = 10^3$). A rough graph of the solution is given in Fig. 70 for reference.

The integrand is e^x, so that $Y_{p\,max} = 10$ (see Fig. 70). Let us suppose that we have a machine with $N = 7$. The ranges of n and of the scalefactors are then:

$$\text{From equation (14)}:\ 4 \leqslant \log(K_y |Y_{p\,max}|) \leqslant \log \frac{K_y K_x}{K_z} = n \leqslant 7 \tag{19}$$

$$\text{From equation (15)}:\ 10^3 \leqslant K_y = \frac{10^n K_z}{K_x} \leqslant 10^{n-1} \leqslant 10^6 \tag{20}$$

$$\text{From equation (16)}:\ 10^{-4} \leqslant K_y\, 10^{-n} = K_Y \leqslant 10^{-1} \tag{21}$$

$$\text{From equation (17)}:\ 10\, K_z \leqslant K_x = \frac{10^n}{K_y} K_z \leqslant 10^4\, K_z \tag{22}$$

$$\text{From equation (18)}:\ 10^{-4}\, K_x \leqslant K_x \frac{K_y}{10^n} = K_z \leqslant 10^{-1}\, K_x \tag{23}$$

In this example, however, we have $K_z = K_y$;[1] therefore, and because of (20):

$$10^3 \leqslant K_z \leqslant 10^6 \tag{24}$$

and from (22):

$$10^4 \leqslant K_x \leqslant 10^{10} \tag{25}$$

We can give one of the five scalefactors any desired value within the given limits. However, since we have also to satisfy equation (13), we cannot select arbitrary values for the other four, even if they lie within the given limits. In other words: fixing one of the scalefactors to a value narrows the limits for the other four.

The natural place to start with the scaling in this problem is the scalefactor K_x. We have to use the machine rate to produce the input dx and the fewer increments we use to represent one unit of x, the faster the problem will run on the machine. So, strictly for economy in computer time, we will select the lowest possible value for K_x, i.e., 10^4.

According to (23), the limits on K_z are now:

$$1 \leqslant K_z \leqslant 10^3 \tag{26}$$

but (26) and (24) give: $K_z = 10^3$. Since we have $K_z = K_y$, K_y must have also the value 10^3.

From (19) follows:

$$n = 4 \tag{27}$$

and from (21) follows:

$$K_Y = 10^{-1} \tag{28}$$

Here, then, by selecting the lowest value for K_x, we left no choice at all for the other 4 scalefactors.

Having assigned the scalefactors, the next step in preparing the problem is to determine the initial conditions.

The starting value for x is zero; therefore, the initial value of e^x is 1. The initial value of Y_p is equal to 1 and $Y_m = .1$. A sketch of the Y-register as filled initially is given in Fig. 71.

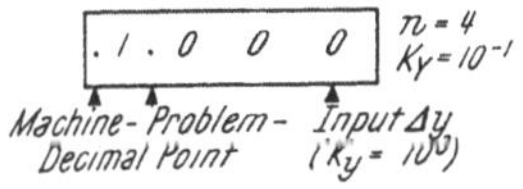

Fig. 71. Initial Contents of the Y-Register

With the given scalefactors, we have to consider the problem decimal point

[1] See integrator diagram in 4.21121.

to the right of the most significant digit. One increment Δy means an increment of 10^{-3} in e^x.

Let us suppose now we want a printout of the value e^x for $x_p = 0, 0.1, 0.2, 0.3$, etc. Since the scalefactor of x is 10^4, one machine increment means an increase of 10^{-4} in x_p. We therefore have to print every 10^3 increments Δx. By inserting 10^{-3} into the print timing integrator (integrator 2 in Fig. 72) and driving it with dx, we generate an output after every 10^3 increments Δx. This output is used to initiate the print cycle. The final stop should occur at $x = 2.3$ or after 2.3×10^4 increments Δx. Inserting $1/2.3 \times 10^4$ into the stop timing integrator (integrator 1 in Fig. 72) we generate an output at $x = 2.3$ which is used to stop the computer.

In order to be able to print both, e^x and the corresponding x, we have to use an additional integrator to accumulate the value of x (integrator 6 in Fig. 72). The maximum value of x is 2.3, so that for integrator 6: $Y_{p\,max} = 2.3$. According to (14) we obtain:

$$n \geqslant \log (K_y | Y_{p\,max}|) \geqslant \log (10^3 \times 2.3) \geqslant 3.3617 \tag{29}$$

Since n has to be an integer, we select $n = 4$. Both, integrator 3 and integrator 6 are programmed to be printed.

Suppose that a further requirement is to plot e^x as function of x. Available is a usable plotting surface of 10 by 25 inches on a plotter which makes 100 steps per inch. Selecting a scale of 1 inch per unit of e^x and 10 inches per unit of x, we make a rather efficient use of this surface. In order to achieve this scale, we have to use a scalefactor of 10^2 for e^x (100 machine increments = 1 unit of $e^x{}_p$ = 1 inch) and a scalefactor of 10^3 for x (100 machine increments = 1/10 unit of x_p = 1 inch). Using two constant multipliers (integrator 4 and 5 in Fig. 72), this reduction in scalefactor is easily obtained. The complete integrator diagram is then given in Fig. 72.

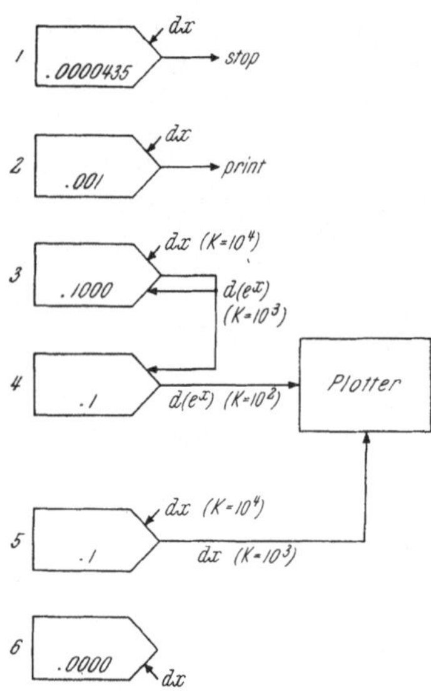

Fig. 72. Complete Integrator Diagram for the Generation of e^x $(0 \leqq x \leqq 2.3)$

We should bear in mind that the scaling of the sample problem as it stands now is only one out of the many possible solutions. In this problem, a full variation of scalefactors in the range given by equations (19 to 23) yields ten possible combinations of scalefactors for integrator 3. In a more general case— where the restriction $K_z = K_y$ is not valid — it is not unreasonable to expect a much larger number of possible scalings. It will not always be possible to find the "best" solution in a straight forward way, as in this sample problem. We will have to say more about this later.

Quite frequently it will be necessary to change the scalefactors of the whole problem or at least in a certain part of a total integrator hookup. This is true when an already designed integrator hookup is adopted as part of a new problem set-up or even if difficulties in the scaling of some part of the present integrator hookup are encountered.[1] In such instances it is often possible to save most

[1] A rescaling is also required for some accuracy checks. See 4.322.

of the work done by the following considerations: Suppose for some reason it would be required to run our sample problem with higher accuracy, let us say, with a maximum step width of 10^{-4} instead of 10^{-3} for e^x ($K_{y\,min} = 10^4$ instead of 10^3). This is accomplished without any further calculation simply by increasing n by one and increasing the scalefactors K_x, K_y, K_z by a factor of ten. By inspection, we see that, if equation (13) was satisfied before the change, it will also be satisfied after the change, so we obtain again a true representation of the problem with the new scalefactors. Of course, we have to be careful not to exceed the given limits for any one value (19 to 23). In the given example this is not the case; we may even increase the accuracy of the sample another two times by a factor of ten before we exceed the limits. Without any additional calculation, we obtain immediately a set of four scalings with a ratio of scalefactors 1 to 10 to 100 to 1000:

K_x	K_y	K_z	n
10^4	10^3	10^3	4
10^5	10^4	10^4	5
10^6	10^5	10^5	6
10^7	10^6	10^6	7

If the problem is the opposite one, i.e., we want to decrease the accuracy, then also we have immediately the following scaling:

K_x	K_y	K_z	n
10^3	10^2	10^2	3
10^2	10^1	10^1	2
10^1	10^0	10^0	1

Inspecting equation (11) we see that the given changes do not affect the scalefactor K_Y so that the filling of the Y-register stays the same for all of the above given scalings.

The given scheme is especially valuable if we have to rescale a complicated integrator hookup. By changing the scale factors and the n's of all integrators according to the outlined prodecure, we immediately have a new scaling of the total problem.

Since, according to this scheme, we change all scalefactors of a problem, we change also the scalefactor of the independent variable, the machine rate. A change of a factor ten in the scalefactor of this rate changes also the computing time of a problem by a factor of ten, since it now takes ten times more (or ten times less) machine increments until the same problem value is reached. An increase in accuracy requires an increase in computing time and a decrease in computing time requires a decrease in accuracy.

Although all of the general formulae (1 to 18) principally allow us to select any scalefactor desired, we have so far used only powers of ten. The reason for doing so is a matter of convenience. It is simply more convenient to interpret machine values which are ten or a hundred times the problem value than to interpret a machine value which is e.g. 7.363 the problem value.

If we want to make it a general rule to use only powers of ten as scalefactors, then we can somewhat simplify the already derived scaling relations.

To suit our purpose we will now write the relations of machine and problem values (3) in the following form:

$$Y_m = 10^{S_Y} Y_p \tag{30a}$$

$$dx_m = 10^{S_x} dx_p \tag{30b}$$

$$dy_m = 10^{S_y} dy_p \tag{30c}$$

$$dz_m = 10^{S_z} dz_p \tag{30d}$$

(All S's are positive or negative integers.) The first basic scaling relation (7) then becomes:

$$10^{S_z} = 10^{S_Y} 10^{S_x} \tag{31}$$

Or, taking the logarithm:

$$S_z = S_Y + S_x \tag{32}$$

The second basic scaling relation (10) becomes in the same manner:

$$S_Y \leqslant -\log|Y_{p\,max}| \tag{33}$$

Or, with the definition:

$$|Y_{p\,max}| \leqslant 10^m \tag{34}$$

We obtain:

$$S_Y \leqslant -m \tag{35}$$

Equation (11) converts to:

$$S_y = n + S_Y \tag{36}$$

and equation (12) to:

$$S \geqslant S_{min} \tag{37}$$

For equations (13 to 18) we obtain correspondingly:

$$n + S_z = S_y + S_x \tag{38}$$

$$S_{y\,min} + m \leqslant S_y + m \leqslant S_y + S_x - S_z = n \leqslant N \tag{39}$$

$$S_{y\,min} \leqslant S_y = n + S_z - S_x \leqslant n - m \leqslant N - m \tag{40}$$

$$S_{y\,min} - N \leqslant S_y - n = S_Y \leqslant -m \tag{41}$$

$$S_z + m \leqslant S_x = n - S_y + S_z \leqslant N + S_z - S_{y\,min} \tag{42}$$

$$S_{y\,min} + S_x - N \leqslant S_y + S_x - n = S_z \leqslant S_x - m \tag{43}$$

Since all S's and m's are integers, ranging between approximately -5 and $+10$ for most practical problems, the given relations require only a very simple arithmetic.

Tacitly, we have here assumed a decimal machine. For a binary machine, the change in the given formulae is very simple. All powers of ten become powers of two (e.g. scalefactors and m) and all logarithms to the base 10 become logarithms to the base 2.

4.222. Scaling of Problems Involving more than one Integrator. While the scaling of one integrator has in general a fair number of possible solutions, the variety of possible scalings for a more elaborate integrator network becomes very large. However, following a few simple rules one can strive from the very beginning to come close to the "best", i.e., the most efficient, scaling.

Apparently, the most efficient scaling is the one which produces a solution with a given accuracy in the shortest (computer-) time or which yields the highest accuracy within a given time. Accepting this as a general criterion, we are almost immediately able to establish a more specific criterion which applies to the scaling of any individual integrator. No matter where the inputs to an integrator come from, it takes a certain time to generate them. The time thereby is directly proportional to the accuracy, since it takes e.g. ten times as long to produce a rate with ten times the accuracy as we have seen in the last paragraph. The most efficient scaling for an integrator is the one which makes the most efficient use of the given time, i.e., which produces an output with the highest number of increments Δz under otherwise equal conditions or the one which produces the highest accuracy at the output for a given accuracy at the input.

In terms of scalefactors we can state: The most efficient scaling for an integrator is the one which produces the largest scalefactor at the output for a given scalefactor at the input or the one which requires the smallest scalefactor at the input for a given scalefactor at the output. Both statements are identical. Both call for a scaling which gives the maximum ratio of the two scalefactors.

Inspecting equation (7) or (31) we find that the scalefactor of the output dz depends directly only upon the scalefactors of the input dx and of the integrand Y. Let us write equations (7) and (31) in the following form:

$$\frac{K_Z}{K_X} = K_Y \tag{44}$$

$$\frac{10^{S_Z}}{10^{S_X}} = 10^{S_Y} \tag{45}$$

We see that is necessary to make the scalefactor of the integrand as large as possible in order to find the most efficient scaling, as far as the output dz and the input dx are concerned. The limit of K_Y or S_Y is given by (10) or (35).

Even though the scalefactor of dz is not directly dependent upon the scalefactor of dy, one could possibly try to improve the ratio:

$$\frac{K_Z}{K_y} = \frac{K_X}{10^n} \tag{46}$$

or

$$\frac{10^{S_Z}}{10^{S_y}} = \frac{10^{S_X}}{10^n} \tag{47}$$

Increasing the scalefactor of dx is undesirable since it will make the ratio of K_Z/K_X or $10^{S_Z}/10^{S_X}$ worse and decreasing the number n will decrease the accuracy of the output even if the scalefactor of the output becomes large, as we shall see in 4.32.

Let us now apply these considerations to a sample problem, the damped oscillation of a mass in one direction, discussed in 4.21211. The first step after finding the integrator network is to derive the maximum values of all integrands in this problem. Suppose the mass is 8 lb sec²/in. The initial displacement is 7 inches, the constant of the spring c is 0.5 lb/in and the coefficient of damping k is 2 lb sec/in. Since we have a damped oscillation, the initial deflection will be also the maximum deflection. y_{max} is therefore equal to 7 inches. The maximum velocity $\dot{y}$ can be found by the following consideration. The maximum kinetic energy must be less than the maximum initial potential energy which can be calculated as force times distance:

$$\frac{m v^2}{2} < \frac{c\, y_{max}}{2}\, y_{max} \tag{48}$$

Since $v = \dot{y}$, we obtain a maximum value

$$\dot{y}_{max} < \sqrt{\frac{2}{m} \frac{c \cdot y_{max}^2}{2}} < 1.75 \text{ in/sec}$$

The maximum value of $\ddot{y}$ is equal to the initial $\ddot{y}$

$$\ddot{y}_{max} = -\frac{c}{m}\, y_{max} = -\frac{.5}{8} \times 7 = -\ .4375 \text{ in/sec}^2$$

Using powers of ten as scalefactors we obtain from (34 und 35):

Integrator No.[1]	Maximum Value	m	$S_{Y\,max}$
1	$y_{max} = 7$ in	1	-1
2	$\dot{y}_{max} = 1.75$ in/sec	1	-1
3	$\ddot{y}_{max} = .4375$ in/sec²	0	0
4	$c/m = .0625$ 1/sec²	-1	$+1$
5	$k/m = .25$ 1/sec	0	0

Having derived all maximum values of interest we calculate the initial conditions. Using the highest possible scalefactors S_Y we also find the initial machine values according to (30a):

Integrator No.	Initial Problem Value	S_Y	Initial Machine Value
1	7 in	-1	.7
2	zero	-1	zero
3	.4375 in/sec	0	.4375
4	.0625 1/sec²	$+1$	.625
5	.25 1/sec	0	.25

Although we have already selected the scalefactors S_Y, the other scalefactors have still to be found. Suppose it is required to represent the solution of y with a scalefactor $S \geqq 10^3$ (i.e. at least 1000 increments per inch deflection) then we can immediately determine S_y for integrator 1 equal to 3 (by selecting the smallest allowable scalefactor we use the most efficient scaling). Proceeding to integrator 2 (compare Fig. 73) we consequently assign the scalefactors $S_Z = 3$ and because of (32) $S_X = 4$. For integrator 4 we have an input with $S_X = 3$ available, so $S_Z = 4$ according to (32), which gives $S_Y = 4$ for integrator 3. Available to integrator 3 is a scalefactor $S_X = 4$ so that $S_Z = 4$. Now all scalefactors are assigned. From (36) we can also calculate the number of digital positions n as they are given in Fig. 73. A double check using equation (38) proves the validity of the solution.

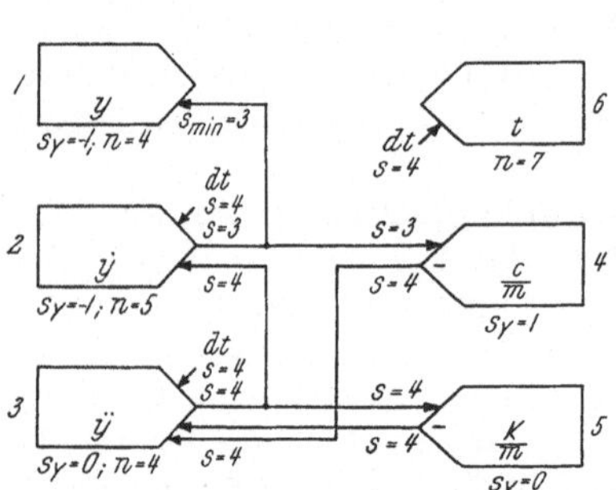

Fig. 73. Scaling of the Sample Problem

Integrator 6 has the maximum length $n = 7$ to accommodate the largest possible problem time. For $n = 7$ and $S_Y = 4$ we obtain (36) $S_Y = -3$ i.e. we could accommodate a maximum time of 10^3 seconds for the real problem.

The scaling of the remaining integrators 7 to 12 in Fig. 48 should present no difficulties beyond those discussed in the previous example.

Let us conclude the scaling of this sample problem with some general remarks. In order to arrive at the final scaling we went from a given restriction ($S_{Y\,min} = 3$, for integrator 1) through the integrator network (through integrator 2) to determine the minimum scalefactor for the independent variable (the machine rate) and then filled in all remaining scalefactors, according to the criterion outlined in the last paragraph. This, however, is not the only possible method. As a matter

[1] Refer to Fig. 48 and 73.

of fact many people prefer to start the scaling with the independent variable assigning an arbitrary scalefactor to it. Then they scale the problem in the sense of our criterion. If the resulting scalefactor in some parts of the problem is unsatisfactory, (e.g. if $K_{y\,min}$ in the previous sample problem is not reached or exceeded) the total problem is rescaled by one or more powers of 10 until all conditions are satisfied.

Usually it is not necessary to use a special block diagram for scaling as we have done here. Instead one can use a scaling sheet similar to the one given in Fig. 74. Let us illustrate this procedure with another example, the trajectory of a mass in an uniform gravitational field disregarding air resistance. The applicable equations and the integrator network are given in 4.21217.

Suppose it is required to find the trajectory of a projectile with an initial velocity of 5000 feet per second. The scaling shall be so that it is possible to allow for an initial angle between the direction of trajectory and the horizon in the range between 0° and 86° without changes in scaling. The representation of the projectile altitude in the solution shall be in steps equal to or less than one foot.

For the maximum values of integrands in this problem we find:

$$v_{\max} = v_{\text{initial}} = .5 \times 10^4 \text{ ft/sec}$$

$$\dot{v}_{\max} \approx g \approx .32 \times 10^2 \text{ ft/sec}^2$$

$$v_{\min} = v_{\text{initial}} \times \cos(86°) \approx .35 \times 10^3 \text{ ft/sec}$$

$$\left(\frac{2}{v}\right)_{\max} = \frac{2}{v_{\min}} \approx .58 \times 10^{-2} \text{ sec/ft}$$

$$\left(\frac{1}{v}\right)^2_{\max} = \left(\frac{1}{v_{\min}}\right)^2 \approx .84 \times 10^{-5} \text{ sec}^2/\text{ft}^2$$

$$\left(\frac{g}{v}\right)_{\max} = \frac{g}{v_{\min}} \approx .92 \times 10^{-1} \text{ 1/sec}$$

$$\dot{\gamma}_{\max} \approx \frac{g}{v_{\min}} \approx .92 \times 10^{-1} \text{ 1/sec}$$

$$t_{\max} \approx 2 \times \frac{v_{\max}}{g} \approx .31 \times 10^3 \text{ sec}$$

$$\dot{y}_{\max} \approx v_{\max} \approx .5 \times 10^4 \text{ ft/sec}^2$$

$$y_{\max} \approx v_{\max}^2/2\,g \approx .4 \times 10^6 \text{ ft}$$

$$(\sin\gamma)_{\max} \approx 1$$

$$(\cos\gamma)_{\max} = 1$$

As integrands of constant multipliers we have:

$$g = .32 \times 10^2 \text{ ft/sec}^2$$

Using these maximum values and referring to figures 60 and 61 we can fill the column m of the scaling sheet (Fig. 14). Using the maximum scalefactor for S_Y according to (41) we can also fill the column S_Y.

Int. No.	m	S_Y	S_x	S_y	S_z	n	Remarks
1	2	-2	4 **4**	3 **22**	2 **5**	5	
2	2	-2	5 **20**		3 **21**		
3	-5	5	2 **6**	9 **10**	7 **7**	4	
4	-2	2	7 **8**	7 **8**	9 **9**	5	
5	2	-2	7 **8**		5 **11**		
6	-1	1	4 **4**	5 **14**	5 **15**	4	
7	0	0	5 **12**	5 **18**	5 **13**	5	
8	-1	(1) 0	5 **18**	5 **12**	(6) 5	(4) 5	
9	0	0	5 **16**	5 **20**	5 **17**	5	
10	0	0	5 **16**	5 **18**	5 **19**	5	
11	4	-4	5 **20**	2 **6**	1 **23**	6	
12	0	(0) -1	2 **6**	5 **20**	(2) 1	(5) 6	
13	4	-4	4 **3**	1 **24**	0 **2**	5	
14	6	-6		0 **1**		6	$S_{y\,min} = 0$
15	3	-3		4 **4**		7	

Fig. 74. Scaling Sheet for Sample Problem

Assigning the minimum scalefactor $S_y = 0$ for integrator 14, we find $S_z = 0$ for integrator 13 and, with $S_Y = -4$, also $S_x = 4$ (32) for integrator 13. The independent variable dt, therefore, has the scalefactor $S = 4$. Inserting this as S_x for integrator 1, 6 and 15, we can find the rest of the scalefactors according to equation (32). The sequence of steps to be taken is indicated by bold numbers in Fig. 74. The corresponding integrator length is found by equation (38).

For integrators 8 and 12, the resulting values are shown in parentheses. Referring to the integrator diagram, we see that there exists a discrepancy between S_z of integrators 7 and 8 which feed both into Y of integrator 6 and therefore have to have the same scalefactor. Since it is impossible to increase the S_z of integrator 7 to the value 6 (we remember that we have scaled for the maximum possible values) we have to reduce the scalefactor S_z of integrator 8 to a value of 5, and in order to satisfy equation (38), to select a value $n = 5$. The same discrepancy exists between S_z of integrator 12 and 11. We therefore have to select for integrator 12: $S_z = 1$ and $n = 6$. In order to satisfy equation (36) we have to select a value of $S_Y = 0$ for integrator 8, and $S_Y = -1$ for integrator 12.[1]

[1] For some accuracy considerations of this problem, see 4.321.

4.3. Capabilities and Limitations

4.31. Applications

Since integration is the only basic function of a digital differential analyzer, it can essentially solve problems whose solutions are reducible to integration. On the other hand, the types of problems whose solutions can be reduced to integration are surprisingly numerous. As we have seen in the last chapter, they comprise essentially all classes of problems which require or can be reduced to the handling of variables. As far as variables are concerned, the digital differential analyzer can not only perform the four basic arithmetic operations of addition, subtraction, multiplication, and division, but it also can calculate functions of these variables like the absolute values, square roots, logarithms, transcendental functions, and the like, in addition to performing integration and differentiation. Since the computer can be considered as consisting of a number of truly independent units (the integrators) there is complete freedom on the number and type of independent variables.

If we were to describe the capabilities of the digital differential analyzer in one short statement, we could say that it is well suited for almost any calculation associated with physical processes. For this type of problems it combines the advantages of the analog computer (where the problem is represented in the form of a model with a recognizable relationship to the physical process rather than in terms of a mathematical expression) with the advantages of a digital computer (i.e., high accuracy and capability of handling several independent variables).

Typical fields of applications might be the following:

simulation of linear and non-linear dynamical systems
stability problems
trajectories
heat transfer problems
frequency analysis
parameter studies
aid in curve fitting
plotting of vector fields

In addition, the digital differential analyzer is perfectly suited for the vast field of real time computations as soon as it has attained sufficient speed.[1] Typical examples of real time applications might be: airborne guidance, flight control, master control for oil refineries or power generation plants.

The mathematical problems which can be attacked by a digital differential analyzer involve primarily:

evaluation of definite integrals,
generation of functions, explicit and inverse algebraic, trigonometric and other transcendental functions of real or complex variables (in component form),
plotting of functions of one or more variables,
solution of ordinary differential equations (linear and non-linear),
systems of simultaneous ordinary differential equations,
coordinate and vector transformations.

In addition, the digital differential analyzer has capabilities for the solution of algebraic equations (single equations or sets of simultaneous equations) and for solutions of partial differential equations.

This latter type of problem requires some comments: The basic restriction of being able to handle only one independent variable (which is usually claimed to

[1] See 4.33

be the main obstacle for handling partial differential equations on an analog computer) is no longer true for the digital differential analyzer. One should expect, then, the field of partial differential equations to be open for the digital differential analyzer. Surprisingly, the progress in this area is very slight. Partial differential equations are still handled with the same tools with which they can be handled on an analog computer and on a mechanical differential analyzer[1] i.e., by using equations of differences and network methods. The only exception are perhaps partial differential equations which can be represented as a set of related ordinary differential equations and can be solved without difficulty on a digital differential analyzer.[2]

4.32. Accuracy

Like any other numerical method, the digital process performed in a digital differential analyzer is only an approximation to the true problem to be represented. Naturally, then, one would like to know how good this approximation is. The accuracy of the principle upon which the digital differential analyzer is based is theoretically unlimited. By providing more and more digital positions for every register in the machine and by representing a certain change in a variable by more and more refined increments, any accuracy can be obtained. No technical difficulty is involved. Higher accuracy is a simple matter of cost. This is reassuring, but really it is not the point in question.

Perhaps one should ask then, for some general figure of accuracy for a given computer, as it is in common use for analog computers. Well, in the same sense as the integrator in an analog computer has the accuracy of one or one tenth percent i.e., one part in a hundred or a thousand, the integrator in a digital differential analyzer may have an accuracy of one part in ten million or one part in a hundred million. The limitation is given by the number of digital positions provided per register. Existing computers do not provide more than 7 or 8 positions for decimal machines and 27 or 30 positions for binary machines for the simple reason that practical calculations rarely require any higher accuracy. Unfortunately this relatively simple measure of accuracy is of doubtful value. It represents an upper limit of accuracy which can be obtained only under the most favorable conditions. Essentially there are two reasons why this accuracy is practically never reached for any real problem. The first one is a simple time consideration. As we have seen, accuracy and computing time are directly proportional (e.g. it takes ten times as long to run a problem with ten times smaller increments under otherwise equal conditions). So, in order to run a problem with extreme accuracy, it may take hours or days until the solution is found. It then simply becomes impractical to require such high accuracy.[3] The second reason is given by the propagation of errors. A solution calculated by a method of limited accuracy and calculated from values with limited accuracy will in general always have a higher error than either the original values or the method. The resulting error is not only dependent upon properties of the computer like the mode of integration and time lags between inputs and outputs of an integrator, but is also dependent upon the type or problem under consideration and the corresponding integrator interconnections.

---

[1] See Chapter 3.483 and Appendix II.

[2] The field lines in 4.2125 are, for instance, the solution of a partial differential equation with the two independent variables x and z.

[3] The accuracy of functions introduced by curve followers is approximately 1 part in 1000.

To tell exactly how good a computer approximation is, requires then, a detailed error analysis of not only the computer, but also of the problem. Unfortunately this error analysis has to be repeated for every new problem or even for a modification in an existing integrator configuration. Furthermore, a rigorous analysis is extremely cumbersome and has so far been attempted only for a very limited number of problems.

Even though this situation seems hopeless, it is not quite as bad as it looks. In spite of the fact that no exact error analysis is readily available, there are several ways to check the accuracy of a computed result, as we shall see later. There is also a possibility of predicting the magnitude of the error in some instances before the computation is attempted. Since the latter method gives also an idea of what would be involved in an exact analysis, let us discuss it here in some detail.

4.321. Prediction of the Accuracy of a Solution. Keeping in mind that we want to predict only the magnitude of an error, which we can expect for a problem set up, let us be satisfied with formulae giving an approximate error rather than the exact one. In doing so, we can, under certain conditions, disregard the type of problem under consideration and are able to find a generally applicable result.

The error in the output of a single integrator is apparently due to three sources: the error in the Δx input, the error in the Δy input, and the error of the integration process itself. Let us now investigate the influence of these three sources separately and one at a time. Even though it is not true in general, for the time being let us assume that the error in any one input is not more than the value of one machine increment. As a first step let us investigate the error due to the inaccuracy of the input Δx. Let us consequently assume that the input Δy is so accurate (i.e. the steps in Y are so small) and the process of integration is so exact (i.e. the average Y for one step of integration is so well determined) that only the error due to Δx is present in the output of the integrator.

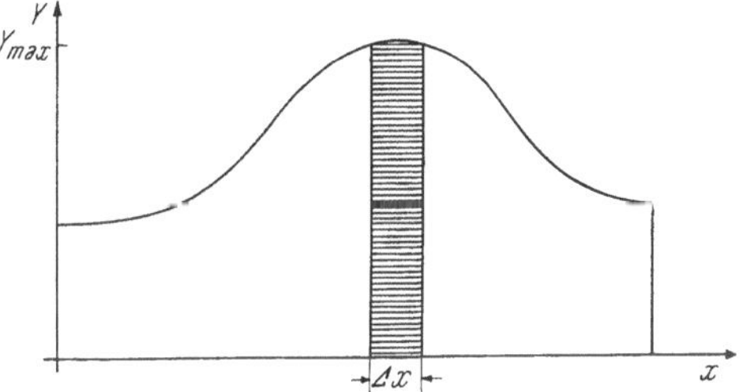

Fig. 75. Error due to Δx

Since we agreed previously that the input dx is off by not more than one increment Δx, we obtain the maximum possible error of the integral: $Y_{\max} \Delta x$ (see figure 75).

However, since the input Δx is at most off by one increment, it will in the average be off by one half increment and the average will be only one half of the above given value. Furthermore, the error in Δx will be sometimes positive, sometimes negative, and Y will be in general smaller than the maximum value (see Fig. 75) so we are justified in even taking a smaller value[2] for the expected error, let us say one third.[3]

$$\text{Expected error due to the inaccuracy in } \Delta x\text{:} \approx \frac{Y_{\max} \Delta x}{3} \tag{1}$$

As a next step let us investigate the error due to the inaccuracy of Δy. We assume again that the process of integration is exact and also that the representation of

[1] See 4.33.

[2] For the "expected" or probable error we should take a value neither too large nor too small.

[3] This value corresponds to the standard deviation or the RMS value of an uniformly distributed error in the range ± one increment.

x is so accurate and fine that only an error due to Δy results. Since the input Δy is presumably not off more than one increment, the maximum error is equal to $x_{\max}\,\Delta y$ (see Fig. 76). For the same reasons as previously, we are justified in taking approximately one third of the maximum error as expected error.

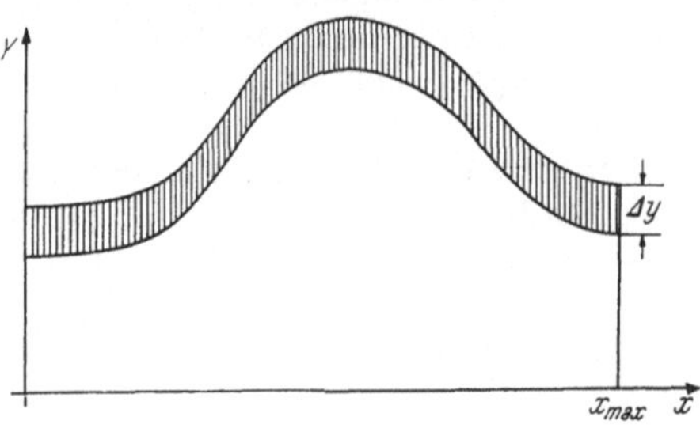

Fig. 76. Error due to Δy

Expected error due to the inaccuracy of Δy: $\approx \frac{x_{\max}\,\Delta y}{3}$ (2)

Now as a final step we investigate the error due to the integration process itself. Assuming that the values of x and Y are accurately represented we obtain a maximum error of $\Delta x\,\Delta y$ for one step of integration (see Fig. 77).

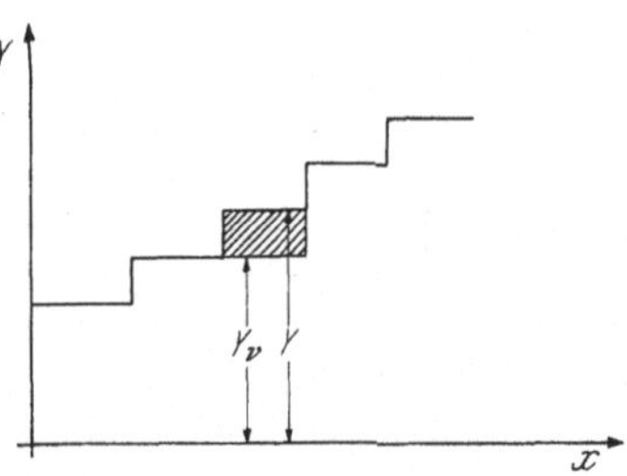

Fig. 77. Error due to the Process of Integration

This maximum error is obtained only if the function to be integrated is a step function and the "average" Y is evaluated immediately previous to a step increase. For the total range of integration we obtain the maximum error $x_{\max}\,\Delta y$. However, since in general the function to be integrated is not a step curve of this particular type, we are entitled to assume approximately one half of the above given value as the probable error. Furthermore, since errors for partly increasing and partly decreasing functions compensate and x will not be equal to $x_{\max}$ at some arbitrary time during a calculation, we are again well justified in expecting an error which is smaller than one half of the maximum.

Expected error due to the integration process: $\approx \frac{x_{\max}\,\Delta y}{3}$ (3)

The total error which we have reason to expect at the output of an integrator will be approximately equal to the sum of the three errors (1, 2, and 3).

Total expected error: $\approx 1/3\,(Y_{\max}\,\Delta x + 2 x_{\max}\,\Delta y)$ (4)

Since the computer output is in form of Δz increments, it would be convenient to have the error in terms of Δz. Let us suppose that we are able to select the four scalefactors for Y, Δx, Δy, and Δz in such a way that:

$$\Delta z_{\mathrm{p}} \approx Y_{\mathrm{pmax}}\,\Delta x_{\mathrm{p}} \approx x_{\mathrm{pmax}}\,\Delta y_{\mathrm{p}} \tag{5}$$

Then we can rewrite equation (4) as follows:

$$\text{Total error} \approx 1/3\,(\Delta z_{\mathrm{p}} + 2\,\Delta z_{\mathrm{p}}) = \Delta z_{\mathrm{p}} \tag{6}$$

We see that the error is approximately one increment Δz. This result is very interesting. First of all, if we feed an integrator with inputs which are in error by

[1] The maximum error could be $Y_{\max}\,x_{\max}$ if Δx is selected equal to $x_{\max}$. Fig. 77 tacitly assumes that the steps in x and Y are approximately equal, a condition which will be introduced later.

one increment we expect an error of one increment at the output. This is of course true only if equation (5) is satisfied. If, however, (5) is satisfied for all integrators in a problem network, then feeding the output of this integrator into another one we expect an error in the output of this second integrator which is again approximately one increment. This consideration can be repeated for the total integrator hookup with the result that we can expect an error in any of the variables which is in the same order of magnitude as one increment of this variable. Since the size of an increment is determined by the scalefactor, the scalefactor of a variable (which has to be known anyhow) is a direct indication of the magnitude of the error.

Another interpretation we may give to this result is that the step size Δ of a variable is only then a measure of accuracy when the condition (5) is satisfied. Let us now see what condition (5) means. Rewriting (5) in a slightly different manner, we obtain:

$$\frac{\Delta x_p}{x_{p\,max}} \approx \frac{\Delta y_p}{Y_{p\,max}} \tag{7}$$

This means that the maximum values of both variables should be divided into an approximately equal number of increments or that the step size of each variable should be about the same fraction of its maximum value. If condition (5) is to apply to every integrator of a network, then the step size of every variable should be about the same fraction of its maximum value. From equation (5) we also see that the problem value of $Y_{p\,max}$ has to be represented in the computer with a value rather close to unity in order to generate an increment Δz for every increment Δx. This agrees with the requirements already found in 4.222 to make the scalefactor K_Y or S_Y as large as possible. A requirement which an integrator scaling has to satisfy if it is to satisfy condition (5) is then:

$$S_Y = -m \tag{8}$$

The other requirement can be deducted fairly easily from equation (7). Using the definition of the scalefactors (4.22—30), we obtain:

$$\frac{\Delta y_p}{Y_{p\,max}} = \frac{\Delta y_m \; 10^{-S_y}}{Y_{m\,max} \; 10^{-S_Y}} \tag{9}$$

But since Δy_m has a machine value of unity and $Y_{m\,max}$ shall, according to the just previously found criterion, be as close as possible to unity, we can write:

$$\frac{\Delta y_p}{Y_{p\,max}} \approx \frac{10^{S_Y}}{10^{S_y}} \tag{10}$$

And with equation (4.22—36) we get:

$$\frac{\Delta y_p}{Y_{p\,max}} \approx \frac{1}{10^n} \tag{11}$$

Since the quotient of one increment in a variable and the maximum value of this variable shall be approximately equal for all variables in a problem, we have the result that the value of $1/10^n$ shall be approximately equal for all integrators in a network, or, in other words, the length n of all Y-registers has to be equal.

Here we have two simple criteria for scalings which satisfy equation (5). The scalefactor S_Y has to be equal to $-m$ and the n's for all integrators have to have the same value. The test to see whether or not equation (5) is satisfied is reduced in this manner to a simple inspection of the scaling sheet. If both of these conditions are satisfied we have reason to expect an error for every variable in the problem of the magnitude of one increment. The problem value of this error can easily be derived from the scalefactor of this variable.

Perhaps a word of caution is appropriate. For an "average" problem, the given rule of thumb will yield a fairly good prediction. There are, however, instances where the propagation of the errors throughout the problem representation may not follow the law of averages but consistently lean toward the worst possibility. Even in these cases, one can obtain at least some idea about the error. Furthermore, the validity of a solution has to be established before it is accepted, even if it is only for the reason of proving that no errors in the coding or filling have been made.

Let us now see what errors we can expect if condition (5) is not satisfied for the scaling of all integrators in a problem.

Again we consider an integrator with inputs which are not off more than one increment. Equation (4) still holds. The expected error is in the order of $Y_{p\,max}\,\Delta x_p$ or $x_{p\,max}\,\Delta y_p$ whichever is larger. Knowing the scalefactors of x, y, and Y we are able to express this error in terms of problem values. Knowing the scalefactor of Δz we can express it also in terms of increments Δz.[1]

Let us elaborate a bit on the meaning of this result. Suppose we first have an integrator satisfying equation (5). Now we make the following experiment in our mind. We change the scalefactor of the input Δx to one which is ten times as large. Consequently we get 10 times as many Δx increments as before and obtain 10 times as many increments Δz on the output. The scalefactor of the new output is therefore ten times as large as before. The error in the output, however, still is about as large as before since we did not change the term $x_{max}\,\Delta y$ in equation (4). The error is still about one original increment Δz even though ten new increments Δz are used to represent this value. Practically we did decrease the error according to figure 1, whereas the error according to figure 2 remained the same. If, on the other hand, we would try to increase the scalefactor of Δy, the error according to figure 2 decreases, whereas the error according to figure 1 stays the same, so that we have not essentially increased the accuracy of the output. If we decrease the scalefactor of either Δx or Δy or both by a factor of ten, the error becomes ten times as large, as we can see from equation (4) or Fig. 75 and 76.

Let us see now how the error propagates. Suppose we have a variable as in the experiment above, which has an error of approximately 10 increments. If this variable is used as input to a second integrator which satisfies (5), then the error in the integration becomes just as large as if we used the same variable with a scalefactor ten times smaller. In other words it is ten times as large as we would expect according to the scalefactor. If this second integrator again does not satisfy (5) then the error becomes perhaps 100 or 1000 times as large as we would expect according to the scalefactor. But in such a case a much more detailed analysis is required which really tracks errors through the problem for every step of integration.

Without a detailed analysis we are able to make only a very general statement. As we have seen previously, we can expect an error of one increment or an error

[1] Let us suppose the inputs to integrator 13 in Fig. 61 are not more off than one increment. According to the scalefactor of the output (Fig. 74), one increment Δz has the value of one foot in the actual problem. According to (2) we may, however, expect an error of approximately $^1/_3\, t_{p\,max}\, \Delta \dot{y}_p \approx {}^1/_3 \times 310 \times 10^{-1} \approx 10$ feet or of approximately ten increments Δz.

which is equal to the fraction $\Delta v/v_{max}$ of the maximum value of every variable if an integrator network satisfies condition (5) throughout. (The ratio $\Delta v/v_{max}$ is assumed to be approximately the same for every variable under consideration.)

Let us suppose now that we have a few variables in the problem for which we have a lower value of the above ratio i.e., we have smaller increments in these variables than required by condition (5). This network will perform at least as good as the one with the high ratio throughout. The error which we have reason to expect, therefore, is given by the high ratio $\Delta v/v_{max}$ in the problem (and we may have hope that some parts of the network perform better due to occasional lower ratios). Inspecting the ratio for every variable in a problem, we can find the highest value and calculate from this the expected errors for all variables. Let us again take an example.

From the scaling sheet Fig. 74 and from the given list of maximum values we can derive the following ratios:

$$\Delta y/y_{max} \approx 2 \times 10^{-6}$$
$$\Delta t/t_{max} \approx 3 \times 10^{-7}$$
$$\Delta v/v_{max} \approx 2 \times 10^{-6}$$
$$\Delta \sin \gamma/\sin \gamma_{max} \approx 10^{-5}$$
$$\Delta \cos \gamma/\cos \gamma_{max} \approx 10^{-5}$$
$$\Delta (2/v)/(2/v)_{max} \approx 2 \times 10^{-5}$$
$$\Delta (1/v^2)/(1/v^2)_{max} \approx 10^{-4}$$
$$\Delta (g/v)/(g/v)_{max} \approx 10^{-4}$$
$$\Delta\dot{\gamma}/\dot{\gamma}_{max} \approx 10^{-4}$$
$$\Delta\dot{y}/\dot{y}_{max} \approx 2 \times 10^{-5}$$

The highest ratio has the value 10^{-4}. Without a detailed error analysis, we would, therefore, expect an error in the order of 10^{-4} for this problem. This means all variables will probably be accurate within approximately .01% of their maximum values.

4.322. Verification of Solutions. In the previous chapter we have seen that a rigorous error analysis is at least extremely inconvenient. Even though predictions of errors in a problem might be possible in certain cases, they will yield at best the order of magnitude of the errors. For this reason and also in order to prove the validity of integrator representation, in practically all cases, a check on the accuracy of a solution is highly desirable. There are several of these checks in use, and fortunately none of them is very complicated.[1]

4.3221. Rerun of the Problem with Different Scalefactors. From the discussion in the last paragraph, it should be obvious that it is hard to determine the error in an arbitrary problem. However, it should be also clear that no matter what the error is, we can expect less error, if we run the same problem with, let us say, ten times the original scalefactor for all variables. If it were not for computing time and the limitation in digital positions, we could go to extremely large scalefactors and, in this way, we could be sure that the solution has the required accuracy. For practical purposes we cannot go this far but we can do the following: We can first run the problem with a relatively small scalefactor and get, in this

[1] No single check will give complete assurance of the accuracy of a solution. Preferably, several checks are employed for the same problem.

way, an idea of what the solution looks like. Then we increase the scalefactor by a factor of, let us say, 10 throughout the problem and run it again (the change of scalefactors is fairly easy accomplished according to the method given in 4.221). The solution is now more accurate than the first one. Now we rerun the problem several more times, changing each time the scalefactors by a factor of ten. Watching the consecutive solutions, we will see that the change from one solution to the next will become smaller and smaller, until finally no appreciable change is experienced. We then can assume with very good reason that any further reruns would not improve the solution, i.e., we can be confident of those digits which remained unchanged in consecutive solutions.

The method as it stands now has two disadvantages. First of all it requires a large amount of computer time. Even if only one rerun is required beyond the one which gave the required accuracy, the computing time necessary to check the accuracy is already ten times as long as the computing time to find the solution with the required accuracy. Another disadvantage is the fact that this "upscaling" of a problem soon reaches the limit of computer capabilities. Let us take the example discussed in 4.222. Examining the scaling sheet (Fig. 74) we see that the largest integrator length is $n = 6$.[1] So if we assume a machine with a total of seven digital positions, the upscaling of the problem by a factor of ten can be done only one more time.

A variation of the original method will avoid both of these difficulties, perhaps at the price of a lower confidence. Let us suppose we have scaled a problem and run it on the computer as it is. The appropriate solution, say S_1, certainly has an error, say Δ. If S is the exact solution we have:

$$S_1 = S + \Delta \tag{12}$$

Neither S nor Δ is known at this time, only S_1. Let us now rerun the problem with a set of scalefactors which is decreased by a factor of ten. It is not unreasonable to expect the new solution S_2 to have an error which is ten times as large, i.e., 10Δ.[2]

$$S_2 = S + 10\Delta \tag{13}$$

Equation (12) and (13) together are two equations in the two unknowns Δ and S. If we solve for Δ, the error of the original solution, we obtain:

$$\Delta \approx \frac{S_2 - S_1}{9} \tag{14}$$

The evaluation of (14) preferably is done at several points of the functions S_1 and S_2 since a set of two corresponding points on S_1 and S_2 might accidentally be close together although the error is large. Here, the rerun requires only one tenth of the computer time for the actual solution.

If the error Δ is too large for our anticipated purpose, then a consecutive rerun can be made with ten times the original scalefactor and the solution S_3 and S_2 can be used in the same manner to evaluate the error of the new solution S_3.

Another advantage of this method, in addition to economy in computer time,

[1] Integrator 15 is a purely auxiliary device in this setup and we may disregard $n=7$. The number of digital positions may be decreased by decreasing the scale factor S_y, e.g. by a constant multiplier.

[2] Compare also Fig. 75 and 76.

is the fact that an estimate of the true solution can be made from two inaccurate solutions. If we solve the two equations (12) and (13) for S, we obtain:

$$S \approx \frac{10\,S_1 - S_2}{9} \tag{15}$$

The evaluation of (15) can again be made at points of interest along the solution. An extrapolation of this type probably will not be as good as a rerun with a set of higher scalefactors, but it can be used to advantage where, e.g., this rerun is not possible due to the limited length of registers or is not feasible due to the increased computing time.

4.3222. Spot Checks. Spot checks have the advantage that they do not consume any computing time if performed after a solution is found by the computer, and they cost only very little or no computing time (in form of interruptions) if they are done while the computation is in progress. The latter method has the additional advantage that errors in the integrator hookup or in the scaling of a problem can be detected before any appreciable computing time is wasted. For this reason one will practically always resort to spot checks either to determine the accuracy of a solution or to prove the correctness of a problem representation.

Essentially we can distinguish two kinds of spot checks. The first type takes advantage of some previous knowledge of the solution and compares computed results with known points. In the already discussed problem of the trajectory in vacuum, e.g., we know that the projectile must hit the ground with a velocity which is equal to the initial velocity, or that the velocity at the top of the trajectory is equal to the initial velocity times the cosine of the initial angle, whereas $\dot{\gamma}$ at this point is equal to the constant of gravity divided by the just derived velocity.

In a similar way, we are able to apply a check to the generation of a function, let us say, $e^x \sin x$. The zeros of the resulting function should occur at the same values of x at which the function $\sin x$ has zeros, whereas at points x which correspond to a maximum of $\sin x$ (or zeros of $\cos x$), the generated function should assume the value $\pm e^x$.

The deviations of computed solutions from exact values is a very good indication of the overall accuracy of the solution.

In some instances (especially at the start of a newly programmed problem) even some approximate information about the behavior of the solution can be helpful to detect errors in the problem representation, e.g., the velocity should decrease or a certain differential quotient should tend to become positive.

The second type of spot checks may be called substitution checks. They can be applied to advantage if no reliable previous information about the solution is available. The principle is simple enough. The computed values of a solution are inserted into the original equation and a check for equality is made. Let us again take an example. Suppose we know nothing about the solution of the equation (4.212—7). However, the values y, $\dot{y}$, and $\ddot{y}$ (which are functions of time) are supposed to satisfy this equation not only initially, but throughout the computation. By reading out the values of these three variables (e.g., when printouts occur or by stopping the computation in random intervals) and inserting them into the original equation we can see how well it is satisfied. The resulting discrepancy is again an indication for the prevailing accuracy not only at the points checked but throughout.[1]

[1] In some cases, e. g., where approximations or servos are used (which may be overdriven) it may be well to use a special integrator to accumulate and display the discrepancy in the original equation. In this way the error can be evaluated continuously and the computation interrupted when it becomes too large.

4.3223. Running a Problem in Reverse. There is one more check possible, which is worth mentioning. It is especially valuable for long running problems where the error in integration according to Fig. 76 may become relatively large even though the deviation of the integrand at all check points may be found to be small by other methods. In addition, the method is well suited to detect errors caused by time lags between inputs and outputs of integrators.

The idea of the test is again a very simple one. If there would be no error in the problem representation, then one could exactly reconstruct the initial conditions from the results. However, if we make the same experiment with errors present, there will be a deviation between the original initial condition and the conditions derived by back-tracking the calculated solution. This deviation is an indication of errors made during the computation. Let us again take the example of a trajectory as illustration. Having calculated the trajectory we know the computed results for the velocity, the acceleration, the angle of trajectory, its derivative, and so on at the point where our calculations ended. Knowing all these values we can reverse the procedure and calculate where a projectile had to come from in order to achieve all these values at the given point. Fortunately, we need no new integrator network, nor do we have to have some special filling of initial conditions to do this calculation on the machine. We simply have to reverse the independent variable of the problem (which is dt in this case) and to start the computer again in order to make the projectile fly backwards in its path.[1]

Due to the errors in the calculation, the projectile will not end up at the starting points of its path with exactly the same velocity and angle of trajectory, etc.; and as a matter of fact, it will not end up at exactly the point in space where it started. All these deviations are, as we have said before, an indication of the accuracy of the calculation.

A word of caution is again appropriate. The method will not work for highly damped functions. For instance, if the damped oscillation of a mass described in 4.222 has died out to a point where practically no amplitude is left, the best calculations can no longer reconstruct the initial conditions.

4.3224. A Measure to Reduce Initial Errors. An initial difficulty may exist in some problems when the R-registers of all integrators contain zeroes at the start of a computation. In this way negative increments (borrows) have a tendency to occur earlier than positive increments (overflows).[2] Considering a chain of integrators, it may take a relative long time (a few integration cycles) before positive increments are produced. The slight error of perhaps a few increments generated this way might be serious in a type of problem where small changes in initial conditions cause large changes in the final result. In order to overcome this difficulty one should fill the R-registers initially.

The easiest but not the best way is to fill some "average value", let us say .5 for decimal machines. In this way positive and negative increments have the same chance of being generated. A better approach would be to fill the exact value of R. We remember that the R-register contains the remainder of the integral, i.e., the least significant digits or the part of the integral which has been accumulated but is still smaller than one increment Δz.[3] Considering now the part of a typical integrator hookup given in figure 78, we see that the most significant part of the

[1] This may look somewhat unconventional since we are used to thinking always of an increasing time, however for the computer, dt is a variable which might just as well be negative as positive.

[2] See 4.112.

See 4.112.

integral is accumulated in the Y-register of integrator 2, whereas the least significant digits are contained in the R-register of integrator 1. Knowing the initial conditions of the integrand of integrator 2, we should fill then the most significant digits into the Y-register of integrator 2, whereas those digits which are not represented in the (limited) digital positions of this register, should be filled into the R-register of integrator 1.

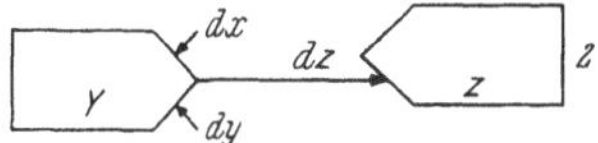

Fig. 78. Typical Part of an Integrator Hookup

There is still a third approach possible. It consists of starting a problem a few cycles early, let us say at $t = -\delta$ for a computation which would normally start at $t = 0$. By experimenting with values inserted into the R-registers and perhaps making small changes in the values of Y-registers we can reach the required initial conditions for all functional values at the time $t = 0$ with the advantage that the computation has "taken off" already and no initial difficulties are encountered at $t = 0$.

4.33. Speed

Slow digital differential analyzers have a speed of approximately 60 integration cycles per second (for every integrator in the computer). The fastest digital differential analyzers of today have a speed of up to 100,000 integration cycles per second. Considering present day electronics, if one is not frightened by the cost, one could even achieve speeds more than ten times as high.

Being so much faster than a human calculator, the speed of the computer seems to be of secondary importance for all ordinary problems. For a slow computer and stringent accuracy requirements one may, however, have to deal with hours or even days of computing time (which besides being annoying increases the chance for a machine error). The real requirement for high speeds, however, comes from real time applications where the computer is performing control or analysis functions concurrently with a physical process. Here the speed of the computer is of utmost importance since the calculation cannot be allowed to lag behind the actual physical process. For this application, the highest frequency which can be handled is a more important measure than speed. Frequencies of the actual process which are higher than this limit cannot successfully be analyzed or controlled. The value of this limit depends to a certain extent upon the type of calculation to be performed. We may, however, obtain a fairly good indication of the highest frequency which a computer can accept by investigating what the highest frequency is, which a computer can generate.[1]

Let us suppose a digital differential analyzer has to generate a triangular curve according to Fig. 79. The required accuracy be one part in 1000. We then need 1000 increments in order to bring the variable from zero to full amplitude. For one cycle of the triangular wave we need therefore 2000 increments.

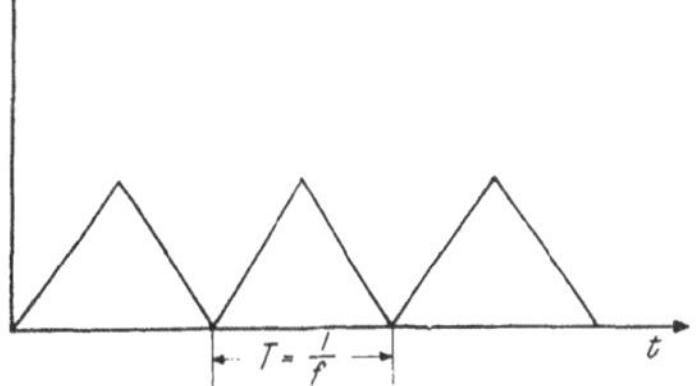

Fig. 79. Frequency of a Triangular Curve

Let us now suppose the computer is slow and can only produce 60 increments per second, i.e. its machine rate is 60 pps. It then takes approximately 33 seconds to generate one cycle of the triangular wave, or, its frequency is 1/33 cycles per second. Such a computer, apparently, cannot handle rapidly changing variables. If the computer is fast and produces, let us say, 100,000 increments per second, the frequency of

[1] This is approximately equal to the highest frequency a computer can follow.

the triangular wave would be 50 cycles per second. If we reduce the accuracy requirement to one part in hundred, the frequency would go up to 500 cycles per second, which represents a rather good real time capability.

This value is, of course, only approximate. The frequency of a generated sine wave would be e.g., less than the frequency of a triangular wave. On the other hand, there exist capabilities with lower accuracy beyond the derived frequencies. The accuracy for handling a problem is also affected by the mode of integration used by the computer.

Let us now compare our results to other types of computers. The capability of handling a few hundred cycles per second with an accuracy of one part in a hundred is approximately equivalent to the capability of an analog computer. For real time applications we could therefore say that the speeds of an analog computer and a digital differential analyzer of today are about equivalent. The digital differential analyzer has the advantage of complete freedom in variables, the justified hope for higher speed and accuracies for lower frequency components which are much higher than those of an analog computer.

Compared with a general purpose digital computer, the advantage of the digital differential analyzer is fairly obvious. For the most elementary operation the speed of both devices is approximately the same since both use equivalent electronic techniques. For more complicated operations, the digital differential analyzer is definitely superior. The digital computer can perform only one operation at a time and, therefore, has to share its capabilities for the various operations required in a problem. Practically, the frequency limit of a fast digital computer is more in the order of a few cycles than in the order of a few hundred cycles per second. The advantage of the digital computer is that it can handle problems which cannot be reduced to integration.

4.34. Design

It is not the purpose of this book to discuss the design of computers, but it may be appropriate to mention those design features which essentially determine the characteristics of a digital differential analyzer.

Digital Process of Integration: The design philosophy of the digital differential analyzer is very similar to that of an analog computer in that both computers are constructed of integrators which may be considered separate and independent units. Because of the digital nature of integration in a digital differential analyzer solutions are reproducible, an important distinction and a great advantage. In this way it is possible to examine the effect of very small changes in parameters, whereas otherwise the drift of the computer might have caused observed deviations.[1] An additional advantage of the digital process is that there is no undesired interaction between units and no feedback or loading effects are experienced. No minute calibration is required to obtain high accuracy.

Clock Rate: This is the speed at which internal switching functions are performed. It gives no direct indication of the speed of a computer.

Machine Rate: It determines the maximum number of integration cycles performed per second for all integrators in a machine. It is a true indication of the speed of a computer. The machine rate is, in most instances, used as the independent variable in a problem.

[1] An integrator setup employing curve followers will not deliver reproducible solutions due to the analog nature of the input.

Mode of Integration: The simplest mode uses a step curve. Better modes are trapezoidal interpolation together with linear extrapolation. In some applications, these modes effectively may be equivalent to another order of magnitude in accuracy or speed under otherwise equal conditions.

Representation of Variables: The representation of variables is in incremental form. Simpler designs provide for only positive or negative increments (binary rates). Preferable is a ternary rate which consists of positive, negative, and zero increments. This latter rate may effectively double the speed or accuracy of a computer under otherwise equal conditions.

Number System: There are only two different number systems in practical use: the decimal (base 10) and the binary (base 2). The decimal system requires a slightly more complicated computer hardware but has the advantage of convenient interpretation of machine values. The binary system requires a conversion of numbers from the binary to the decimal system and vice versa, but has advantages both in simpler computer design and in scaling.

Representation of Negative Numbers: Negative numbers are generally represented by their complement for reasons of simpler computer design. Decimal machines should have a built-in conversion for printouts. Otherwise they lose part of their advantage of simple interpretation of machine values.

Number Range: The number range of most digital differential analyzers is between -1 and $+1$. For special purpose integrators, like limiters, a larger number range, e.g., from -2 to $+2$ may be occasionally employed.

Mode of Operation: A serial operation requires less hardware, but results in slower speed. A parallel operation is faster but more expensive. In the simplest (but slowest) mode the addition of, e.g., the Y- and the R-register is performed digit by digit in a serial fashion and one integrator after the other is operated on in sequential fashion. We might call this a serial-serial mode of operation. The fastest possible mode is a parallel-parallel mode, where integrators operate simultaneously and the addition in every integrator is simultaneous in all digits. In any case, the machine rate is a true measure for the speed of the computer.

Number of Integrators: The complexity of problems which can be solved on a computer is limited by the available number of integrators. In some designs it is possible to add more integrators if desired. Other designs allow a parallel operation of more than one computer.

Appendix I. Existing Digital Differential Analyzers

Name	MADDIDA	CRC 105	DA 1	Litton 20, 40	NATDAN	TRICE	SPEC
Manufacturer	Northrop Aircraft, Inc. Hawthorne, California	The National Cash Register Company, Electronics Division Hawthorne, Cal.	Bendix Computer, Division of Bendix Aviation Corporation, Los Angeles 45, California	Litton Industries, Beverley Hills, California	Autonetics, Division of North American Aviation, Inc., Downey, Cal.	Packard Bell Computer Corporation, Los Angeles 69, California	Computer Control Comp., Inc., Los Angeles 64, California
Number of Integrators	22 in prototype 44 in commercial version	60 (plus 60 built in constant multipliers)	108 (plus 108 built in constant multipliers)	20 for Litton 20 40 for Litton 40	93	Expandable	20
Number System	Binary	Decimal	Decimal	Binary	Binary	Binary	Binary
Significant Digits	29 incl. sign	6 excl. sign	7 excl. sign	18 incl. sign	27 incl. sign	30 incl. sign	20 incl. sign
Arithmetic	Serial	Serial	Serial	Serial	Serial	Serial	Serial
Integrators working	Sequential	Sequential	Sequential	Sequential	Sequential	Simultaneous	Sequential
Integration cycles per second per integrator	60	64	34	62 for Litton 20 31 for Litton 40	17.2 for NATDAN A 34.4 for NATDAN B	100,000	2380
Increments	Binary	Binary	Ternary	Binary	Ternary	Ternary	Ternary
Remarks	This computer can be considered as prototype of all digital differential analyzers. Its manufacture is discontinued.	The production of this computer is discontinued. The developmental model of the CRC 105 was CRC 101.	The DA 1 is a digital differential analyzer attachement to be used only in conjunction with the G 15 D general purpose digital computer. Its features are similar to the discontinued D 12 digital differential analyzer.		A prototype of this computer is the NADAN The following digital differential analyzers are classified: D-10 VERDAN D-7 MIDGE	TRICE stands for: Transistorized Real-Time Incremental Computer Expandable	SPEC stands for Stored Program Educational Computer. SPEC is an educational device which can be operated as digital differential analyzer or as digital computer or as logic circuitry for other purposes.

Fig. 80. MADDIDA, Model 44 A, The First Commercial Digital Differential Analyzer (Northrop Corp.)

Fig. 81. G-15 General Purpose Computer with DA-1 Digital Differential Analyzer Accessory. (Bendix Computer)

Fig. 82. CRC 105, With Cover Removed (The National Cash Register Company, formerly Computer Research Corp. of California)

Fig. 83. Control Console for CRC 105 (The National Cash Register Company, formerly Computer Research Corp. of California)

Fig. 84. NATDAN, An Inertial Navigation System Computer for Submarines. (Autonetics)

Fig. 85. LITTON 20, With Digital Plotter-Follower (Litton Industries)

Fig. 86. TRICE, With One Integrator Partially Removed. (Packard-Bell Computer Corp.)

Appendix II.

Bibliography

Sprague, R. E., "Fundamental Concepts of the Digital Differential Analyzer". Mathematical Tables and Other Aids to Computation, January, 1952, Vol. **6**, No. 37, pp 41—49.

Donan, J. F., "The Serial-Memory Digital Differential Analyzer". Mathematical Tables and Other Aids to Computation, April, 1952, Vol. **6**, No. 38, pp 102—112.

Weiss, E., "Applications of the CRC 105 Digital Differential Analyzer". Transactions of the IRE (Professional Group on Electronic Computers) December, 1952, pp 19—24.

Palevsky, M., "The Design of the Bendix Digital Differential Analyzer". Proc. IRE, Vol. **41**, No. 10, pp 1352—1356, October, 1953.

Mendlesohn, M. J., "The Decimal Digital Differential Analyzer" Aeronaut. Engng Rev., Vol. **13**, No. 2, pp 42—54, February, 1954.

Braun, E. L., "Design Features of Current Digital Differential Analyzers". Convention Record of the IRE., pp 87—97, March, 1954.

Richards, R. K., "Arithmetic Operations in Digital Computers". D. Van Nostrand Company, Inc., New York, 1955, pp 303—311.

Johnson, C. L., "Analog Computer Techniques", McGraw Hill, New York, 1956, pp 233—246.

Palevsky, M., "An Approach to Digital Simulation". Proc. National Simulation Conference, January, 1956.

Klein, Williams, Morgan, Ochi, "Digital Differential Analyzers". Instrument Automation, Vol. **30**, pp 1103—1110, June, 1957.

Forbes, George F., "Digital Differential Analyzers". Private Print, 1957 (134745 Eldridge Ave, Sylmar, California).

Braun, E. L., "Digital Computers in Continuous Control Systems". IRE Transactions on Computers, Vol. *EC-7*, June 1958, pp 123—128.

Gill, Arthur, "Systematic Scaling for Digital Differential Analyzers". IRE Transactions, Vol. *EC-8*, No. 4, pp 486—489, December 1959.

Silber, Walter B., "Function Generation with a DDA". Instruments & Control Systems, November 1960, pp 1895—1899.

The following literature on the Mechanical Differential Analyzer might be helpful in finding integrator interconnections for special problems.

Amble, O., "On a Principle of Connection for Bush Integrators". J. Sc. Instrum. December, 1946, p 284.

Bush, Vannevar, "Differential Analyzer". J. Franklin Inst. October, 1931, Vol. **212**, No. 4, pp 447—488.

Bush, Vannevar, "Differential Analyzer". Mech. Eng., January, 1932, Vol. **54**, No. 1, pp 56—57.

Crank, J. J., "The Differential Analyzer", Longman, Green, London, 1947.

Hartree, Douglas R., "Calculating Instruments and Machines". University of Illinois Press, Urbana, Illinois, 1949.

Michel, J.G.L., "Extensions in Differential Analyzer Techniques". J. Sci. Instrum. October, 1948, pp 357—361.

Chapter 5

Computing Control Systems

By

Martin G. Jaenke (Dr.-Ing.)
(Chief, Simulation and Computation Division, Air Force Missile Development Center, Holloman Air Force Base, New Mexico, USA

With 4 Figures

5. Computing Control Systems

5.1. Introduction

Each of the words of the title of this chapter is of considerable weight in the language of modern technology, each encircles a separate field of modern engineering endeavor. Though old in their roots, these fields experienced a rapid growth only during the last decade and even in this short time had a noticeable impact on society. These fields are:

Computers. Nothing has to be added here about their capabilities and importance.

Control Engineering. Also known as the field of feedback control or of servomechanisms, it deals with the techniques which are required to keep an effect under automatic control of a given cause within specified tolerances, statically and dynamically. The fundamental and comprehensive importance of such feedback control mechanisms, in man-made and in living systems, has been pointed out prominently in [1].

Systems Engineering. Though still fluent in its exact definitions, this endeavor became a necessity with the increasing human capability to master complex processes. It deals with the analytical understanding of the processes, their optimization in a technical and economical sense, their interactions with other processes and their environments, their reliability, and their logistics. [2]

In Computing Control Systems, elements of all three fields will be found. To describe such systems shortly: They consist of a number of feedback loops exercising automatic control over certain functions of a process and a computer controlling these controllers with respect to what to do and how to do it. The systems engineer designs the computer program, i.e. he decides what information will be made available to the computer and what solutions have to be found.

In order to make this chapter readable for those not experienced in this area, a short introduction to the concepts of control engineering will be given, and, after a description of the role of computers in such systems, the problems the system designer is confronted with will be indicated. The available space is not sufficient to describe practical systems in detail. But frequent reference will be made to the monthly publication "Control Engineering", [3], which is considered to be the main source of information from the young but steadily growing field of Computing Control Systems.

5.2. Basic Principles of Control Engineering

The fundamental principle to achieve automatic control is the application of feedback. It consists of measuring the actual value of the controlled effect, the "output" in the language of the control engineer, of comparing it to the controlling quantity, the "input", and of using the difference between input and output, the "error", to act on the output in such a way as to keep the error at a minimum. The term "output" stands for a wide variety of physical variables. Positions, velocities, temperatures, electrical power, voltages or currents, frequencies, chemical compositions of mixtures are a few examples of quantities which might be desired to be kept under control. The term "input" stands for similar quantities but not necessarily the same as the outputs. For example, in a temperature controller, the output (temperature) may be measured by an instrument which presents the temperature as an electrical voltage. It would then be recommendable to define the desired temperature, the input, by an electrical voltage also. In the following discussions, output variables will be generally designated by the symbol, e_o, and input variables by e_i.

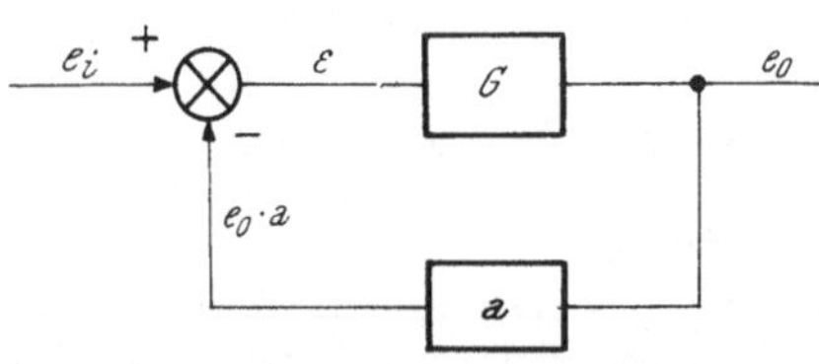

Fig. 1. Principle of Closed Loop System

A simple, basic example of a feedback control system is described in the block diagram of Fig. 1. The actual output, e_o, is measured by an instrument with a scale factor, a, the measured quantity, $e_o a$, is subtracted from the input, e_i, to form the error, ε, which in turn, after amplification with gain, G, produces the output. This interaction of the quantities involved is known as a "closed loop" situation. It can be described mathematically in the following way:

$$e_i = e_o \cdot a + e_o \cdot \frac{1}{G} \tag{1}$$

In order to define an effective gain, G^x, this can be reformulated:

$$G^x = \frac{e_o}{e_i} = \frac{1}{a + \frac{1}{G}} \tag{2}$$

This shows, that, if G is numerically large, the effective gain of this closed loop system is practically equal to $\frac{1}{a}$. Thus, an accurate control of e_i over e_o depends primarily on the accuracy of the measuring scale factor, a, provided G can be made large enough.

Unfortunately, practical situations are not quite as simple. If the operation represented by G is considered to be a physical "process", it will be noticed that it contains one or more energy storages, such as heat capacity in a thermal process, inductances and capacitances in electrical processes, masses and elastic members in mechanical systems. The presence of such a storage prevents instantaneous reaction of the output to the error signal and this effect can be described mathematically by an integrator. In the simplest case it is found:

$$e_o(t) = G \int \varepsilon(t)\, dt \tag{3}$$

The equation for the closed loop in such a simple case is found by modification of (1).

$$e_i(t) = e_o(t) \cdot a + \dot{e}_o(t) \cdot \frac{1}{G} \tag{4}$$

with $\dot{e}_o(t)$ representing the first derivative of $e_o(t)$ with respect to time, t.

In the general case, with the process containing N energy storages, the mathematical formulation has the form:

$$e_i(t) = e_o(t) \cdot a + \dot{e}_o(t) \cdot b + \ddot{e}_o(t) \cdot c + \ldots \overset{(N)}{e_o}(t) \cdot n \tag{5}$$

This is a differential equation in $e_o(t)$ of order N with the forcing function $e_i(t)$. The analytical treatment of such equations is well known if they are linear and with constant coefficients. But the majority of practical equations are non-linear and have varying coefficients. In order to be able to use the tools of linear analysis one will try to linearize them and to investigate within limited time intervals, during which the coefficients are approximately constant. But for all correct evaluations, a computer will be needed.

Every linear analysis has to determine first, whether the system is stable or not, i.e., whether the transient resulting from any disturbance approaches a finite steady state value and does not build up to infinite values. The Routh-Hurwitz criterion is used to find this answer. Then the systems reaction to standardized types of forcing functions is investigated. The most important of them is the Delta-Dirac impulse function. The respective systems reaction is called the weighting function, $W(t)$, it can be used to find the system response (output) to any arbitrary forcing function (input) by evaluating the convolution integral:

$$e_o(t) = \int_0^t e_i(t-\tau)\, W(\tau)\, d\tau \tag{6}$$

Quantities such as the natural frequency of an oscillatory transient, its damping coefficient and time constant and the steady state gain can be derived from the response to an impulse function. They are normally sufficient to describe the properties of the system to the experienced analyst and quite commonly systems properties are specified in such terms.

An alternative analytical approach of considerable practical importance is the use of Laplace transform methods. The differential equation in t (time domain) thereby becomes an algebraic equation of a complex variable, the frequency $s = \sigma + j\omega$ (frequency domain). System stability and characteristics then are determined by investigating the location of the singularities (poles) in the complex plane (root locus method of system synthesis). The input-output relation for arbitrary input functions is given by the "transfer function" $Y(s)$:

$$e_o(s) = e_i(s) \cdot Y(s) \tag{7}$$

$Y(s)$ is the Laplace transform of the weighting function $W(t)$. Extensive tables are commonly available to find the frequency functions, $e(s)$, for given $e(t)$ and vice versa. The simplicity of the relation (7) which is equivalent to the operation described in (6) is one of the principal attractions of Laplace transform methods.

Working in the frequency domain, it is of interest to know the response of a closed loop system to "real frequencies", sinusoidal functions of amplitude, E, and period, $\frac{2\pi}{\omega}$. It is easy to produce them technically and to actually measure the response of a system to such functions. Analytically, the situation is described by replacing the variable s by $j\omega$ in the Laplace transform expressions. It will be found that $e_0 (j\omega)$ is related to $e_1 (j\omega)$ by the gain or magnitude relation and that the two sinusoids are shifted in phase one against the other. Gain and phase shift are defined by the "frequency response function" of the system $Y (j\omega)$. They are graphically represented either in polarcoordinate form or as individual functions of frequency. For each method of representation, suitable procedures of analysis are available, including stability criteria. The first was developed by Nyquist, the second by H. W. Bode. Thus, the analyst of linear control system has a wide selection of analytical tools which are essentially equivalent.

The problem one is normally concerned with is to design a control system according to certain specifications in the presence of "constraints". In the terminology used here this means that a part of the functions performed in the complex operation, G, (Fig. 1) are given and cannot be changed, they are the "processes", over which control must be exercised. Examples for such processes are the dynamics of the airframe of an airplane or missile, which is to be held on a desired course, the behavior of a gun turret, which is to be directed in such a way that the fired projectiles hit a moving target, or a chemical reaction, which is expected to yield products of prescribed characteristics. Usually, such a process is very complex and mostly will require the application of a number of basically independent control loops to exercise proper control. But the constraints do not comprise only the process functions but the "transducer" and "actuator" elements. "Transducers" are the instruments which measure the output variable of the process and represent it as a signal of a form which is adequate for the control procedures, either as a electrical, mechanical, hydraulic, or pneumatic signal. Examples are gyros, complete tracking radar systems, transducers for measuring temperature, pressure, flow, position, velocity or acceleration. "Actuators" are components which perform command functions on the process in order to achieve the desired outputs. Examples are servo motors, hydraulic valves or switches. All these elements can have quite complex individual transfer functions. Though the designer has a certain freedom to select these components, he will have to regard their properties as a part of the total constraints. The task is then to synthesize a control loop around these constraints which meets given specifications. This is achieved by inserting additional components, known as "loop compensation "or "controller" elements. A typical block diagram of such a basic process control system is shown in Fig. 2. If the input to such a system is of fixed value, it is frequently designated as the "set-point" and the whole control loop as a "regulator". Its purpose is then to hold the output constant in the presence of internal disturbances.

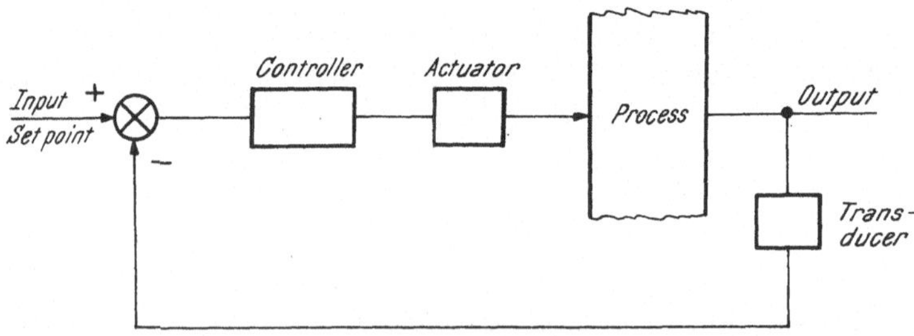

Fig. 2. General Process Control Loop

This short introduction to basic control systems was necessary to make the role of computers in more complex systems understandable. For more detailed information an extensive literature is avaible. One of the most recent sources is in the form of a handbook and contains a comprehensive listing of references. [5]

5.3. Computers in Control Systems

The role of computers in control systems is highly diversified, frequently several functions are assigned to such an expensive component. In many cases an available computer is time-shared between several control systems, particularly if the process under control is of slowly changing character. It is also possible to separate the computer from the controlled process with respect to its location and provide adequate information channels to integrate the complete system. In the following, an attempt will be made to classify the functions a computer can be expected to perform in a control set-up to provide an understanding of how significantly control techniques can be improved by the application of computers.

5.31. Specific Computer Functions

5.311. Compensation or Controller Function. As mentioned in 5.2, a control loop containing given fixed elements (constraints) must be completed by inserting proper compensation functions to achieve the specified characteristics. They consist mostly of a combination of proportional, differentiating and integrating operations performed either on the error signal, as indicated in Fig. 2, or on the feedback signal. Other important examples are non-linear operations such as saturation processes, which can serve to achieve minimum transient times. Normally, all these functions are performed by electrical networks, if the loop works with electrical signals, or by their equivalents with other signal forms. All these functions can be taken over by analog computer components, either in a "special purpose" configuration if the specifications of the control loop are not expected to change, or in a "general purpose" configuration if a flexible adaptation to changing specifications is required. But the use of analog computers in this case does not constitute a basic advantage over the use of a normal compensation network, which, in a wider interpretation, is also an analog computing device. This is different, if the use of a digital computer is feasible. While all functions to be executed on analog computer components are subject to the same requirements of physical realizability as compensation networks, this is different with digital computer processes. In addition to their higher accuracy, they allow to synthesize compensation functions which are difficult to obtain with "physical" (analog) components. Thus, a wider area of possible compensation functions is opened for the systems designer. Details of this approach will be discussed in 6.34.

5.312. Computation of Optimum Set-Point. The set-point of a control loop, or its input, is clearly defined in many cases. For instance, in a room temperature control system, it is selected by the individuals living in the room. In a tool positioning system of an automatic lathe the set-point is derived from the drawing of the part to be machined. In an autopilot system of an aircraft, the desired course is set under consideration of the expected wind conditions. But in many cases the set-point is a complicated function of many factors, specifically if an optimum result of the process under control is desired. The task to evaluate continually or within discreet time intervals the most desirable set-point under such circumstances is perfectly suited to be performed by a computer. Again, the selection of an adequate computer type depends on the required accuracy and speed of the computation and on considerations of possible time-sharing of the machine among many computation tasks. In order to perform the task properly, the necessary information has to be fed into the computer. It consists of measurements of the physical quantities which are needed to compute the set-point, and in industrial processes it may contain policy factors which are dictated by economical and competition considerations. The requirements of an optimized chemical process, for instance, may depend on the market price of raw materials and of the end-and by-products. This may reflect significantly on the set-points of the various control loops involved.

A classical example for a system with computed set-points is a fire control system. It consists of servo systems which position the gun in azimuth and elevation. The set-points for these servos are complicated functions of relative target position and velocity and solutions must be computed in "real-time", i. e. without any significant computation lag. In fact, there is a prediction problem involved to take care of the finite flying time of the projectiles. For a fast moving target, it is impossible to perform all the necessary evaluations of the observations and all the calculations "by-hand" and the use of a computer is unavoidable.

Considering the real-time requirement, the natural choice will be an analog computer. But with high speed digital computers becoming available, their high accuracy will be a strong argument for their use. The transducer which measures the relative motion of the target is a radar set, preferably an automatic tracking radar, which in itself is a quite complicated control system. Its dynamic properties and those of the gun positioning servos have to be properly considered in the program for the computation of the set points.

An example from the field of industrial processes control is "Computing control applied to a sintering process" [6]. The purpose of the process is to sinter fine iron ore into usable large particles which in the subsequent smelting process will not be blown through the blast furnace. The sintering is achieved by mixing the iron ore with coke and other materials in a predetermined ratio, feed the mixture at an automatically controlled rate to a moving grate and ignite the mixture shortly after entering the grate. The burning process penetrates through the layer of the material as it moves along with the grate and is desired to be completed, to "burn through", shortly before the material reaches the end of the grate in order to obtain maximum yield at optimum quality. So the task of the computer is to determine the set point for the feed rate control loop in such a way as to achieve location of the burn-through point on the grate at a predetermined spot. This requires a measurement of its actual location, which is performed by a number of equally spaced thermo couples from which the exact location is interpolated. The necessary computations are performed by special purpose analog computer components.

5.313. Computation of Optimum System Characteristics (Adaptive Control). Most processes to which control functions are applied change their characteristics with changing environments. For example, an airplane or missile in flight will show different natural frequencies and damping coefficients in the dynamic reaction of its turning rate to the positioning of its control surfaces with different altitudes or velocities. If such an airframe is stabilized by an autopilot, this autopilot must be adapted to the characteristics of the airframe in order to obtain desired over-all dynamic characteristics of the complete control loop which contains the air-frame and the autopilot. The necessary calculations to evaluate the instantaneous optimum settings of the autopilot coefficients can be performed by a computer. To make such a self adaptive computing control system fully automatic it is necessary to provide actuators which perform the act of resetting the coefficients in accordance with the information given by the computer. These may have the form of mechanical servos positioning potentiometers which define the gain of an amplifier, or variable-μ tubes, the gain of which is defined by its grid bias.

So far it was assumed that the characteristics of the process under control (in the example above: the flying airframe) could not be manipulated and adaptive steps had to be taken in the compensation part of the loop. But there is a wide class of processes, in which the coefficients can be manipulated. An important example are chemical reactor processes, the characteristic coefficients of which are functions of primarily temperature and pressure. The purpose of adaptive computing control is then to calculate optimum values of these coefficients and realize them by proper actuator systems, e.g. temperature or pressure control loops. An adequate optimizing criterion in such a case might be a requirement to perform the process in minimum time with a specified quality of the end-product. Similar to 6.312, management considerations will enter the definition of the optimizing criterion and will be reflected in the program of the computer in such an adaptive computing control system.

5.314. Information Computers. The computing control systems as described in the previous chapters are highly automatic. However, it became obvious that the human element cannot be fully eliminated. At least it will be involved in making policy decision as described above. Other human activities which not only cannot be eliminated but to the contrary will become more important with the increasing complexity of the systems, are the maintenance and repair functions. And then there is the wide range of possibilities, in which the system is not completely automatic and depends on human operators to perform functions which cannot be performed automatically in a reasonably economical way (man-machine systems).

In all cases where humans are involved it is necessary to make information data available in an adequate form for the respective purpose and this will normally require to perform computation processes on the original raw data. The form of the data must be such that human decisions based on them are as simple as possible and can be made as fast as possible. In the case of management policy decisions, the information must account for quantity and quality of the end products, by-product and raw materials, actual time and energy requirements, breakdown times and malfunction periods. In short, it must provide the possibility to check the economy and effectiveness of the controlled process against expectations. Analog computers applied for this purpose will normally lead to graphical representation of the information and digital computers to tabulated forms. Maintenance guides may consist in a simple accounting of operation hours of the installation or may present the results of a periodic evaluation of the actual performance characteristics of critical components or subsystems. Such an evaluation may involve quite complex computations.

In man-machine systems, computational aides have to be provided in order to simplify the task to be performed by the operator as a component of the control system as much as possible. [9]. Again the computations which are involved may be quite complex.

5.315. Conclusions. The foregoing must be considered as an attempt to classify the functions of computers in complex control systems. This attempt seems to be justified in view of the wide variety of computer applications in such systems, which leaves the reader of current literature with the desire to discover common trends in this practically unlimited field. In most actual cases, a large computer unit will perform a combination of these tasks and it may be not easy to isolate analytically the individual functions. Other classification guide lines may be thought of. However, the basic approach used here, namely to discriminate between operations on the systems signals (or variables) and operations on the systems coefficients seems to be fruitful from the standpoints of systems analysis and of the systems designer.

5.4. Design Considerations

This chapter will be devoted to the necessary steps which have to be taken in the design of a complex automatic control system and an attempt will be made to indicate the points of view which have to be considered in the selection of control computers.

5.41. Systems Engineering

The fundamental step must be made by the systems engineer. He, in cooperation with management, must clearly define the ultimate purpose of the installation. He will have to investigate very critically the economic situation: Will the investment, which can be quite considerable, be justified in the light of expected results? If this is questionable, an adequate compromise has to be sought, possibly achieved by sacrificing automatic features in favor of human control. How does the planned installation fit into the picture of over-all operations? Will it cause problems in logistics? What must be considered to make a later extension of the facility possible?

Many questions of this type have to be answered in all cases, be the planned installation a part of a "Weapons System" of the military area, or, be it a part of a production plant of the industrial area. As a final result of his investigation, the systems engineer has to establish over-all systems performance specifications, he has to define the permissible investment and operational costs and he has to establish guide lines with respect to centralized use of expensive equipment, such as control computers.

5.42. Mathematical Models

The first step the control engineer has to take in the design of the system is to formulate a mathematical model of the process he has to deal with. It is the basis of all the analytical work he will have to perform. He will derive this model from theoretical considerations and experimental observations or a combination of both and he will first be concerned with defining the coefficients of the differential equations or transfer functions which describe the process. If these coefficients in turn are functions of the systems variables (non-linear systems) or of other environmental factors (variable coefficient systems) a thorough and complete analysis can only be performed on a computer. It seems to be proper to emphasize here the enormous importance of computers in the design phase of control systems. Without them it would have been impossible to design automatic control systems of such a complexity as it is frequently observed in modern applications.

After defining the systems coefficients and their functional character, mathematical models of the expected systems variables (input and output signals and disturbances) and their functional behavior will have to be found. In many cases, it will be impossible to predict exactly the sequence of events, specifically with respect to disturbance functions. Then an attempt can be made to gather at least sufficient information to define the average signal power (mean square values). Mathematical tools to do this are second statistical moments such as auto-correlation functions and power density spectra. Such "statistical design" methods become more and more important.

Formulating a mathematical model of the process to be controlled is not yet sufficient to describe all the "constraints" one will encounter in the design of the control loops. As was mentioned already, one has to consider the transducers, actuators, and, if necessary, information transmission channels. All of them have to be described in form of differential equations or transfer functions. However, these constraints are normally not absolutely fixed, there will be a certain selection of available elements. In this first design stage, a survey of available components and their characteristics has to be made and the ones optimally suited for the purpose will be selected at a later stage. If information transmission channels are involved, it may frequently be necessary to use pulse modulation systems or similar digital channels. The consequences of using such devices within a physical closed loop system are related to those resulting from the use of digital computers as control elements and will be discussed later in more detail.

5.43. Specifications for the Control Loop

The requirements which the individual feedback loops have to meet in controlling the process are of course a part of the over-all systems specifications. Based on these, the control engineer then has to formulate detailed requirements for each of them covering the following areas:

a) Stability. This is of particular interest if the part of the process to be controlled by the loop is by itself unstable. The possibility to operate processes which are normally unstable by applying automatic control is of considerable importance.

b) A steady state gain constant meeting certain tolerances.

c) Satisfactory dynamic performance in following a changing input or in settling after an internal process disturbance. It can be defined in terms of natural frequency and damping coefficients and related properties.

d) If the definition of signals and disturbances is possible only statistically, an attempt has to be made to define the permissible error (deviation of output signals from their desired relation the input signals) on a mean square basis. If a meaningful definition in this sense can be found, then the mathematical tools for the design of the system are available. [4]. Otherwise, the difficulties of an analytical approach are considerable.

5.44. Design of the Control Loop

After having defined the properties of the constraints, the task is to complete the loops in such a way as to meet specifications, i. e. to design the proper compensation or controller elements. The classical approach to do this is essentially empirical. Based on his experience, the designer will start out with a simple configuration and improve it stepwise until a satisfactory solution is found. To do this, he either has to experiment with the process hardware, but, since this in many cases will not be possible or advisable, he will experiment with a simulated configuration. Analog computers are the instruments most naturally suited for such a purpose, they represent the actual situation by physical analoga and provide the possibility of inserting actual hardware components into the simulation process. The empirical approach may turn out to be insufficient to determine whether a given specification can be met at all. In this case the statistical design approach is a valuable supplemental analytical tool. It provides the means to define the optimum system with the minimum error which is theoretically possible in a given situation.

Whatever design approach is used, the findings will lead to compensation elements defined by certain differential equations or transfer functions. The normal way to proceed is then to reformulate these functions in such a way as to obtain "physically realizable" elements. In the language of the time domain analysis this means to define dynamic subsystems which do not react before they are excited and in frequency domain terminology this means to define networks or "filters" which meet the "minimum phase" condition. The advantage of defining physically realizable compensation elements is obvious. The classical methods of network synthesis then can be used to determine a compensation network consisting of resistors, capacitors, inductors and amplifiers in an electrical system and of their equivalents in other cases. It seems to be very well justified to verify such a configuration of components by a "special purpose" analog computer. And, of course, it is possible to realize the required compensation network by using "general purpose" commercial analog computer components. The decision is with the designer and involves practical considerations such as flexibility and cost.

But there is another possibility to realize compensation or controller functions in a closed loop system, namely, to use digital processes, including digital computers. The justification for such an approach may be derived from practical considerations such as: digital form of information on process variables, produced by transducers with digital outputs; available information transmission channels which make it necessary to digitize the signals; accuracy requirements for the compensation processes which exceed the capabilities of physical and analog computer components; desirability to "time-share" the computation facilities with other control loops or even other systems, which preferably calls for digital computers, considering their flexibility with respect to automatic program changes.

However, there are certain analytical aspects in the use of digital processes in physical control loops which deserve a short discussion. An excellent comprehensive investigation of all the problems involved can be found in [7].

Generally speaking, the insertion of digital techniques requires to digitize, or "sample", the continuous analog information on process variables, to perform the necessary computation, and finally to reconvert the digital results into continuous analog form. The first step, the sampling process, consists of taking numerical samples of the respective variable periodically, with a defined sampling frequency. This is a non-linear process and can be understood as amplitude-modulating a pulse carrier with the time function of the variable. It can be seen instantly that the carrier frequency, which is the sampling frequency, must be sufficiently high with respect to the highest significant frequencies of the modulating signal spectrum in order to avoid overlapping of the original spectrum and the modulation spectrum, which would lead to "fold-back" or "aliasing" errors. The theoretical minimum requirement is that the sampling frequency be twice as high as the highest signal frequency (sampling theorem). A reasonable first estimate of the highest signal frequency involved is given by the natural frequency or bandwidth of the control loop under design, which should be specified. If the requirements of the sampling theorem can be met, then the original function of the variable can be recovered. Otherwise, such a recovery is not possible and considerable analytical difficulties arise. In view of this, all following discussions will be restricted to an assumption of sufficient sampling rate.

Investigating the next step, the digital computation, two factors have to be considered: First, the computer is expected to perform an operation on the data characterized by a certain specified transfer function. It will do this, provided, of course, that the programming is correct.

The second factor to be considered in digital computation qualifies the statements made above to a certain extent. It is the computation delay. Every practical digital computer requires a finite time to perform a specified operation, i. e., results are available only at a time which is delayed with respect to the sampling moment of the input signal. This time delay, T, imposes on the desired frequency response function of the computer process, $Y_c(j\omega)$, an additional phase shift and the effective function is found to be:

$$Y_c^*(j\omega) = Y_c(j\omega)\, e^{-j\omega T} \tag{8}$$

The additional phase shift is linearily proportional to frequency and increases with increasing delay time. It reflects on the stability and the dynamic properties of the over-all control loop and has to be taken into account properly.

The third step in digital information processing within a physical control loop consists in reconverting the digital data to analog, continuous data after the computation process. Actually, any physical dynamic component in the loop will perform this function to a certain extent, but in a way which may practically not be very effective and analytically difficult to describe. In practice, special circuits are used for this purpose, e. g., holding or "box car" circuits, which preserve the information given by the computer at one sampling moment over the whole interval until the next moment. The frequency response function of such a device is:

$$Y_{\mathrm{h}}(j\omega) = \frac{1}{j\omega}\left(1 - e^{-\frac{j\omega}{f_s}}\right) \tag{9}$$

with f_s being the sampling frequency measured in *cps*.

So, then, if a desired compensation function, $Y_{\mathrm{c}}(j\omega)$, is programmed on the computer, an effective function consisting of the product of (8) and (9) will result and has to be taken into consideration in the determination of loop characteristics, or, by an adequate change in the computer program.

The consequences of applying digital operations to the information in a physical closed loop system as discussed above are generally undesirable. They essentially consist in reducing the stability margin of the loop and force the designer to take adequate steps, i. e. to define a new appropriate compensation function. But, on the other hand, digital techniques open possibilities of system synthesis which are not obtainable with conventional networks and analog techniques. Their basic features will be discussed shortly in the following. Digital computers allow to perform operations, which are equivalent to physically non-realizable processes. This, of course, is possible only with historical data. Otherwise, it would be impossible to obtain "reaction before excitation", the important characteristic of physically non-realizable systems. For instance, it is possible to perform a digital computer operation on historical data which is equivalent to low-pass filtering with zero phase shift over the whole frequency range. This can be done by using an equal number of past and future samples with respect to the instantaneous reference moment to perform a properly weighted moving-arc smoothing process. It is rather difficult to determine the number of samples to be used and the proper distribution of weight factors in order to obtain a specified frequency response of the magnitude function. However, it is possible to establish frequency response functions with comparatively simple digital programs which would require very complicated physical networks for their realization. Details about these techniques can be found in [8]. Now, such a "physically unrealizable" filter can be used in a physical control loop, if an additional delay time is inserted. The information sample presented to the computer as the instantaneous one then actually is old, old enough that the interval between the "real-time" instantaneous moment, t_0, and the moment which is considered by the computer as instantaneous, t', is sufficiently large to provide to the computer the necessary "future" data to perform the specified smoothing operation. Fig. 3 explains this situation in detail. T' is the one-sided interval needed for the smoothing operation, T is the inherent computation delay of the

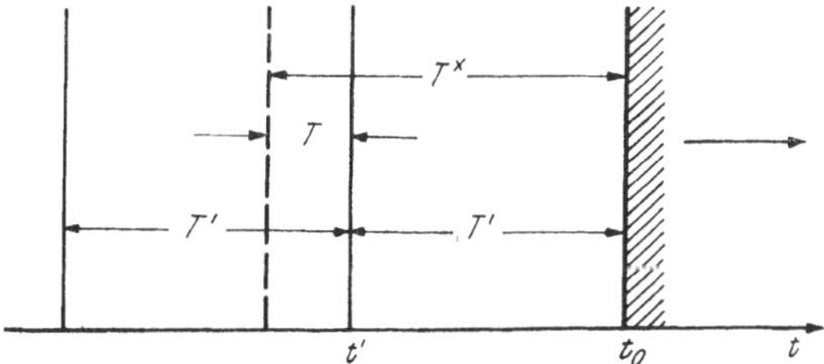

Fig. 3. Time Delays in Digital Computation with Smoothing Process

machine and T^x then is the total delay to be sacrificed for the filtering process. As can be seen from (8), the whole process then is not any longer free of phase-shift, but the relationship between the frequency response of the magnitude and phase functions is entirely different from that of "physically realizable" filters and opens a challenging new area for the systems designer.

5.45. Optimizing of Set-Point and System Adaptation

After the design of the basic control loop or loops is fixed, the system as a whole must be integrated and optimized. As pointed out before, one of the major steps in this direction is the determination of set-point functions for the basic loops which lead to desired over-all performance characteristics of the system. Environmental, economic, and policy factors may have to be considered and a general discussion of these problems is difficult in such a short space. Again, the whole system may be of closed loop form, i.e. the actual end result is continually compared with the desired one and corrective commands will be given as setpoint information to the basic control loops. Or, this feedback feature may be omitted and the system as a whole operates in "open loop" fashion. In any case, setpoint information can be pre-determined, if the whole sequence of events is deterministic and not subject to random disturbances. This leads to "programming control", using well known techniques of information storage. But in many other cases, the optimum set-point information may have to be continually computed, based on actual data observed during the process. This leads back to "computing control", and the points of view to be considered for the selection and the design of the computing processes are similar to the ones discussed in 5.44.

The other important area of computer application is adaptive control, i.e. the task to adapt the coefficients describing the performance of the process or of the various basic control loops to changing conditions in such a way as to achieve optimum over-all dynamic performance continually. Again, this can be achieved by programming control, if the situation is sufficently deterministic. But, in general actual coefficient values have to be continually evaluated and optimum settings of non-constrained coefficients have to be computed. This is a wide application area for computing control which is presently under intensive study. The designer is confronted with the following fundamental problem, the solution to which determines to quite an extent the computational methods to be employed. The evaluation of actual coefficients of a system or subsystems necessarily involves calculations based on its observed input and output signals. In order to be meaningful, the answer has to be the result of a calculation process extending over sufficiently wide intervals of both time and frequency. The question is then whether the signals encountered during a normal course of events possess a sufficient information content to permit a successful calculation. Basic signal structures are shown in the time-frequency plane of Fig. 4. Line A represents a sinusoidal wave, which spreads over time but not over frequency. Its opposite is line B, representing an impulse function. The ideal wave form in this respect is "white noise", represented by the homogeneously grey area C. Actual signals are complex

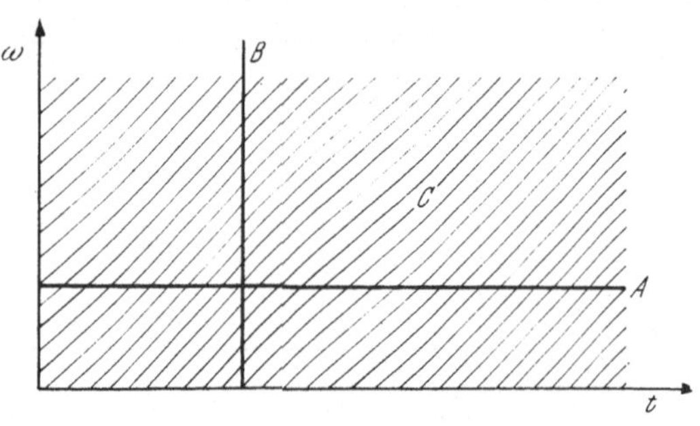

Fig. 4. Description of Wave Forms

conglomerations of these basic types and the designer has to decide whether or not they will be sufficient for the purpose of coefficient evaluation. If not, he has to super-impose an artificial test signal to the actual process signals, of small enough amplitude to avoid significant reactions on the process, but large enough to perform a sufficiently accurate coefficient evaluation. It is evident that white noise will be preferably selected in such a case. It provides the possibility to employ statistical crosscorrelation methods for coefficient evaluation in a simple straight forward manner. The exact mathematics of all this are quite involved and thus "adaptive control" is a challenging and comparatively new field for the application of computers in complex control systems.

5.46. Man-Machine Control Systems

If the active participation of a human operator in the control mechanism is necessary or not avoidable, the system designer again is confronted with problems which call for the incorporation of computing processes into the system. He has two choices. He can either determine the "human transfer function" as closely as possible, consider it as a given constraint in addition to the others and design the free parts of the system such as to achieve satisfactory over-all performance. But the human transfer function is extremely complex and variable in an unpredictable manner and severe set-backs with man-machine systems designed in this way are common. The other possible approach is to assume a human transfer function of a very simple nature and to design the system in such a way that the dynamic performance expected of the operator never exceeds that of a physical device having such a simple transfer function [9]. This relieves the operator of strenuous routine tasks and reserves his energy for his main task, namely, to make decisions in emergency situations during which automatic devices would fail to operate adequately. This design approach calls for the insertion of additional compensation functions, in this case called "aiding functions" which preferably are performed by proper computer components.

5.5. Conclusions

The intent of this short survey was to make understandable to the non-expert reader the immensely fruitful role which computers play in the field of control engineering. They make it possible to expand from the concept of the classical servo-mechanism to the highly automatized control systems with self-optimizing and selfadapting features, which are of continually growing importance in the fields of defense weapons systems and industrial process control systems.

Bibliography

[1] Wiener, N., "Cybernetics", John Wiley and Sons, Inc., New York, 1948.

[2] Goode, H. and R. Machol, "System Engineering", McGraw-Hill Book Company, Inc., New York, 1957.

[3] Control Engineering, published monthly by McGraw-Hill Publishing Company, Inc., New York.

[4] Wiener, N., "Extrapolation, Interpolation, and Smoothing of Stationary Time Series", John Wiley and Sons, Inc., New York, 1950.

[5] "Handbook of Automation, Computation and Control, Volume 1", edited by E. Grabbe, S. Ramo, D. Wooldridge, John Wiley and Sons, Inc., New York, 1958.

[6] Schuerger, Th., "Computing-Control Applied to a Sintering Process", Control Engineering, September, 1957.

[7] Ragazzini, J. and G. Franklin, "Sampled Data Control Systems", McGraw-Hill Book Company, Inc., New York, 1958.

[8] Boughton, E. Michael, "Definition and Synthesis of Optimum Smoothing Processes in Filter Terms". IRE Transactions of Instrumentation, Vol. I—7, No. 1, March 1958.

[9] Birmingham, H. P. and F. V. Taylor, "A Design Philosophy for Man-Machine Control Systems", Proc. IRE, Vol. 42, December 1954, page 1748.

Glossary of Computer Terms

The following list is a short explanation of terms used in this book and generally in the computer field. The definitions given arose from the authors' own experience and mainly from the two following sources:

IRE Standards on Electronic Computers, Definitions of Terms, 1956. Proc. Proc. I.R.E. 44, No. 9, 1956.

M. H. Weik, A Second Survey of Domestic Electronic Digital Computing Systems. Ballistic Research Laboratories, Aberdeen Proving Ground, Maryland, Report No. 1010, June 1957.

Absolute Programming: A term used in programming when addresses, functions, or other information is expressed by machine numbers, i. e. in machine language (also: absolute coding).
Access Time: The time required to communicate with a storage unit.
Accumulator: A storage device of the arithmetic unit in which are formed sums and other arithmetical and logical results.
Accuracy: Freedom from error. Not synonymous with precision, e. g. a four place table correctly computed is accurate, a six place table containing an error is more precise, but not accurate.
Adaptive Control System: A control system which automatically adjusts the characteristics of its compensation elements according to the ones of the constraints in order to maintain a desired behavior.
Adder: A device which can form the sum of two quantities.
Address: An expression such as an integer or other set of characters which identifies a storage unit, usually a word.
Algebraic Compiler: A compiler capable of translating mathematical formulas.
Allocate: To assign absolute addresses to programs and subroutines.
Analog: The representation of numerical quantities by means of physical variables.
Analog Computer: A collection of physical components (together with the means of control) used to simulate the physical system under study.
And-Gate; And-Circuit: A logical circuit with two or more inputs, which has the property to give an output signal only if all inputs coincide.
Arithmetic Unit: That part of a computer in which arithmetical and logical operations are performed.
Assemble: To combine an absolute program with the necessary subroutines in the memory such that the complete program is ready for execution.
Asynchronous Computer: A computer whose internal operations are not controlled by equally spaced signals from a clock.
Automatic Coding: The process, performed automatically by the computer, of transforming a problem stated in a formal computer-oriented language into an absolute machine program.
Automatic Programming: The process, performed automatically by the computer, of transforming a problem stated in a formal problem oriented language into an absolute machine program.
Automatic Typewriter: Typewriter which prints out symbols according to electrical signals and provides electrical signals according to the keyboard button which is pressed. Similar to a teletype machine.

Base: A number base, a quantity used to define some positional notation for numbers; radix.
Binary: (a) Pertaining to numbers to the base two.
(b) Having but two alternatives or conditions.
Binary-Coded Decimal System: A system of number representation in which each decimal digit is represented by a group of bits.
Binary Number System: A system of positional number notation, using the base two.

Biquinary Number System: A system of positional number notation using the bases two and five.

Bit: (a) A binary digit, either 0 or 1.
(b) A unit of storage capacity, or of information in general.

Block: A group of words considered as a unit.

Block Access: The referencing of words of a memory in fixed groups of consecutively stored data.

Bootstrap: A method of loading information into a computer with only a few instructions initially in the memory.

Branch: Synonym for conditional jump.

Breakpoint: A point in a program at which the computer may be stopped for visual check or manual operations.

Buffer: (a) A relatively small storage device for temporary storage of data.
(b) An isolating device, generally used to transfer data between two storage units that are not synchronized.

Bus: A path for transmitting information; common to several units.

Calculator: A machine for automatically carrying out arithmetical or logical operations the sequence of which being controlled manually (desk calculator) or from tape or cards (card programmed calculator).

Capacity: (a) The number of digits, or the largest number, which can be held in a computer register.
(b) The amount of information which can be held in a storage device.

Cell: (a) Smallest unit of storage of a memory, identified by an address; can store one word.
(b) Elementary storage unit; can store one bit or one character.

Channel: In a circulating storage a channel is one re-circulating path.

Character: Any single digit, letter, or other printable symbol. Also, the corresponding binary code.

Check: The testing for the occurrence of errors or of machine malfunctions.

Check Sum: The sum of all words of a block of information, used to verify accuracy.

Clear: To set a storage device to the condition corresponding to no information (zero).

Clock: The primary source of signals required for sequencing computer operation.

Closed Shop: A mode of operation of a computer facility where all problems are programmed by members of a specialized group whose only concern is the use of computers.

Code: (a) A system of symbols for representing information.
(b) To prepare a program in machine language for a specific computer.

Coefficient Potentiometer: Potentiometer to perform a fixed coefficient multiplication on a variable of a DC Analog Computer.

Collate: To combine ordered sets of items into one ordered set, which must not necessarily contain all the original items.

Command: Synonym for instruction.

Compensation, Elements or Functions: In an automatic control loop, the elements which have to be inserted to obtain a desired behavior under considerations of the given constraints.

Compiler: A program designed to accept manually prepared programs (usually in symbolic language), translate them into an absolute machine program, and combine it with the necessary subroutines into a program ready for execution.

Computer: (a) A machine for carrying out sequences of calculations automatically.
(b) A machine for carrying out sequences of specified transformations on information automatically.

Computer System: Comprises the basic computer and connected external (peripheral) equipment.

Conditional Jump: An instruction which will cause the proper one of two addresses to be used in obtaining the next instruction, depending on some condition.

Constraints: In the design of a control circuit, characteristics which are given and cannot be changed.

Controller: In a process control loop, the components which perform the compensation function.

Control Unit: That part of a digital computer which governs the sequence of all operations.

Convert: To change numerical information from one notation to another.

Converter: A machine which changes information from one form to another so as to make it acceptable to another machine.
Curve Follower: Device which allows to use graphically represented functions to use for automatic computations.
Cybernetics: Synonym for control system theory.

Data Reduction: The art or process of transforming masses of experimentally obtained data into useful, ordered, or simplified intelligence.
DC Analog Computer: Analog Computer, the components of which are of electrical nature and the variable of which is a DC voltage.
Debug: To find and remove errors in a computer program.
Decision integrator: Special integrator in a Digital Differential Analyzer with an output dependent upon certain conditions.
Delay Line: Any device for producing a time delay of a signal.
Diagnostic Routine: A specific service routine to locate a programming error or a computer malfunction.
Differential Analyzer: An analog computer designed and used primarily for solving differential equations.
Digit: An elementary numerical symbol.
Digital Computer: A computer which operates with information, numerical or other, represented in a digital form.
Digital Differential Analyzer: A computer consisting of a number of digital integrators.
Digitize: To convert an analog measurement of a physical variable to a digital number.
Diode Function Generator: A fully electronic function generator establishing a straight-line approximation of the desired function by using proper combinations of conducting and nonconducting diodes.
Double Precision: Retention of twice as many digits for a number as the computer normally handles, i. e. using two words for a number.
Dump: The output of information of a part or all of the memory for inspection.
Dynamic System: A configuration whose behavior is described mathematically by a differential equation.

Erase: To wipe out, as information stored in the memory.
Error: (a) An error in the usual mathematical sense caused by a numerical method.
(b) A human mistake.
(c) A machine malfunction.
Excess Three Code: A special case of the binary-coded decimal system where a decimal digit is represented by its equivalent in binary plus three.
External Equipment: All parts of a computer system which are not part of the basic computer (e. g. tape units, printers, etc.)
External Memory: That part of the memory accessible only through buffers or input-output circuitry.

File: A sequential set of items.
Filter: An electrical network whose transfer function depends on frequency. Name occasionally used for any dynamic system.
Fixed-Point: The representation of numbers in a computer where the point is implied at some pre-determined or stated position.
Flip-Flop: An electronic circuit capable of assuming two stable states, can be controlled by input signals.
Floating-Point: A number notation where a quantity x is represented by a pair of numbers y and z, such that $x = y \cdot b^z$, b is a known constant, y is called the fraction or mantissa, z is called the exponent.
Flow Chart: A graphical representation of the sequence of operations of a computer program.
Function Generator: Analog computer component which establishes any analytically or empirically defined function of a variable.
Function Plotter: Output device of an analog computer which represents in graphical form a function given by a variable voltage.

Gain: The ratio of output to input signal of any transmission device, particularly an electrical amplifier.
Gate: Synonym for logical element.

Hardware: The physical parts of a computer.
High Gain Amplifier: An amplifier of extremely high gain, operating in the frequency range from 0 to high audio frequencies. Used as main building block to establish operational amplifiers and integrators in analog computation.
Housekeeping: That part of a program which does not directly contribute to the result, but which is necessary to secure the correct sequence, correct initial values, addresses, etc.
Hybrid Computer: A computer which uses both analog and digital representation for data.

Index: A count or tally for keeping track of the number of executions of one or a series of instructions.
Information: An aggregation of data.
Initial Condition Storage: Special storage in a Digital Differential Analyzer which allows an easy resetting of the computer to the conditions prevailing at the start of a computation.
Initialize: To set the addresses and parameters of a program to the values needed at the start.
Input: Information which is transferred from external storage to the internal storage.
Input Function or Signal: Technical name for forcing or exciting function.
Instruction: A completely defined operation for the computer; the principal unit of a computer program. Also, the computer code for such an operation.
Instruction, n-Address: An instruction consisting of an operation and *n* addresses.
Integrator: High gain amplifier with precision resistor in input path and precision capacitor in feedback path.
Interlace: To assign successive addresses to physically separated storage positions for the purpose of reducing access time.
Internal Memory: That part of the memory directly accessible from the control unit.
Interpretive Routine: A program which will examine and properly execute machine-like pseudo instructions.

Jump: An instruction which, conditionally or unconditionally interrupts the normal sequence of operations by specifying the address of the next instruction.

Library: Aggregate storage of frequently used information, e. g. subroutines, programs, tables of data.
Limiter: Device in a Digital Differential Analyzer which performs a limitation on functional values.
Line Printer: A machine capable of printing an entire line of characters across a page simultaneously.
Location: Synonym for address, especially when expressed in symbolic form.
Logical Operation: An operation in which logical (yes-or-no) quantities are the operands.
Loop: A group of instructions in a program which are to be executed repeatedly.

Machine Language: Information is recorded in machine language if it can be picked up and used by the computer without any modification.
Magnetic Core: A ring or wafer made of ferrite, capable of remaining in one of two magnetization states, thus capable of providing storage, or logical functions.
Magnetic Drum: A rotating cylinder on whose magnetic material surface information can be stored in the form of magnetized spots.
Magnetic Tape: A tape or ribbon impregnated or coated with magnetic material on which information may be recorded in the form of magnetized spots.
Malfunction: A failure in the operation of the hardware of a computer.
Marginal Checking: Testing a computer under operating conditions, which are not normal and so chosen as to show computer component weaknesses.
Matrix: An ordered array of quantities or objects.
Memory: A section of the computer used primarily for storing information, synonym: storage.
Merge: To combine ordered sets of items into one ordered set, using the same ordering criterion.
Micro Programming: The logical combination of computer elements necessary for the execution of the machine instructions.
Minimum Access Programming: Selection of the addresses of instructions and operands such that access times are as short as possible.

Mnemonic: Assisting, or intended to assist, memory, especially used for suggestive symbols in programming.
Modifier: A quantity used to alter an address in an instruction.
Monitor: An interpretive service routine which traces certain features in the execution of a program for diagnostic purposes, e. g. the sequence of instructions actually executed, intermediate values of an iteration, etc.
Multiplier: Analog computer component which performs the multiplication of a function by a variable coefficient.

Natural Frequency: The frequency of the oscillations observed in the transient response of a system which is described by a second order differential equation of low damping.

Octal: Pertaining to numbers to the base eight.
Odd-Even Check: A check system where a one or zero is carried along in a code such that the total number of ones is odd (or even).
Operand: Any one of the quantities entering or arising in an operation.
Operation: A defined action.
Operational Amplifier: High gain amplifier with precision resistors in input and feedback paths.
Operational Modes: Specific operational configurations of an analog computer to perform such tasks as insertion of initial conditions, reading out computation results and performing component checks.
Operator: The person who actually manipulates a computer.
Or-Gate; Or-Circuit: A logical circuit with two or more inputs which has the property of giving an output signal if any one of all inputs are present.
Output: Information which is transferred from internal storage to any external equipment.
Output Function or Signal: Technical name for the function describing the reaction of a system or the solution of the equation describing the system.
Overflow: The generation of information exceeding its designated storage space.

Packing Density: The number of units of information recorded within a given dimension of a storage medium, e. g. bits per inch.
Parallel Operation: The processing of the information of a word simultaneously on all digits, using separate facilities for the digits.
Parameter: A quantity used in a general type of calculation, its value specifies the individual calculation.
Parity Check: Synonym for odd-even check.
Patchboard: A board containing the terminals of all connections to the components of a DC analog computer, allowing to connect the components in a proper way to represent the problem under study.
Peripheral Equipment: All equipment which is part of a computer system but not part of the basic computer, e. g. tape units, printer, etc.
Plotter: A device for the automatic recording of computer results in graphical form.
Plugboard: A removable panel containing an ordered array of terminals which may be manually connected by wires in any desired manner.
Post Mortem: A service routine which outputs significant information concerning a program and its data, after execution, to facilitate the search for errors.
Precision: See accuracy.
Process: The configuration over which automatic control is to be exercised. Also called the "plant".
Program: A set of instructions and numbers, arranged in proper sequence, describing all computer operations for the solution of a problem.
Programmer: A person who prepares flow-charts and instruction sequences without necessarily converting them into the detailed codes.
Programming: The process of producing from a given problem a computer program to solve the problem. It consists of problem analysis, selection of the method, and coding.
Pseudo-Code: An arbitrary code, usually for an operation, independent of the hardware of a computer, which must be translated into computer code.
Punch Card: Heavy stiff paper adapted for being punched with an array of holes.

Random Access: Access to storage in which the positions referenced may occur in arbitrary sequence.
Random Numbers: A set of digits devoid of any regularity.
Read: To sense information on a storage medium.
Real-Time Operation: The processing of information obtained from a physical process in synchronism with the process, such that the results are useful to the process.
Recorder: A function plotter which allows only to plot functions of the independent variable "time".
Redundancy: The coding of information with more characters than absolutely necessary.
Redundant Check: A check which uses extra digits, short of complete duplication, to detect malfunctions.
Reference Power Supply: A highly stable power supply providing a DC voltage from which the computer variables in analog computation are derived.
Register: A device capable of retaining information, often that contained in a small subset (e. g. one word) of the aggregate information in a digital computer.
Relative: A term used in programming when addresses are expressed with respect to some reference address in a program.
Relocate: To move an absolute machine program from its original location in storage to another, changing addresses such that the program can be executed in its new location.
Resolver: A device which separates or breaks up a quantity, particularly a vector, into its components, usually by forming the sine and cosine of the given variable.
Restore: To return information in storage to its initial value.
Rock: To move a magnetic tape back and forth over a piece of information in an attempt to read the information without error.
Routine: Synonym for program.
Run: The execution of a program on a computer.

Scalefactor: A coefficient which relates the problem value to the machine value.
Scaling: The process of determining scalefactors.
Sequence Checking Routine: See Monitor.
Serial Operation: The processing of the information of a word taking one digit at a time, using the same facilities for successive digits.
Service Routine: A program, at the disposal of the operator of a computer, to help him perform certain operations.
Servo: Short form for "servo mechanism". In chapter 3 used to mean an electromechanical servo, the command input to which is a voltage and the output of which is a mechanical shaft position.
Servo Function Generator: A servo driven potentiometer, establishing a straight line approximation of the desired function by properly shunting the potentiometer on a multiplicity of taps.
Servo Multiplier: A servo driven potentiometer allowing multiplication of a function by a variable coefficient.
Set Point: A constant input signal to a control circuit. It commands a constant output signal in the presence of internal disturbances in the system.
Shift: To move the characters of a unit of information right or left.
Sign Changer: Operational amplifier with an effective gain of unity.
Software: A collection of standard programs and operational procedures needed for the efficient use of a digital computer.
Spot Check: Checks which are intermittently performed to see whether computer results satisfy original equations.
Square Law Multiplier: A fully electronic multiplier using square law characteristics established by Diode Function Generators.
Stated Point: Synonym for fixed-point.
Statement: A line of coding in a symbolic program.
Storage: Synonym for memory, also the process of storing.
Subroutine: A program for a frequently used calculation, to be called upon by other programs.
Summer: Operational amplifier with a multiplicity of input paths.
Symbolic: A term used in programming when addresses, functions, or other information are expressed by symbols, i.e. arbitrary sets of characters.
Synchro: A transducer representing the position of a mechanical shaft by an AC voltage, either in terms of amplitude or relative phase.

Synchronous Computer: A computer whose internal operations are controlled by equally spaced signals from a clock.
System: A functional entity of technical components and/or operating principles.

Temporary Storage: A portion of the memory set aside by the programmer to hold intermediate results.
Test Routine: A program designed to show whether a computer is functioning properly or not, possibly giving clues to bad components.
Time Division Multiplier: A fully electronic multiplier working on the principle of simultaneous pulse-with and pulse-amplitude modulation.
Trace Routine: Synonym for monitor.
Transfer: To jump to another location.
Transfer Function: The ratio of the output to the input functions of a dynamic system, where both input and output are defined as functions of the independent variable "frequency".
Translate: To change information from one language to another without affecting the meaning.

Variable Increment Computer: A computer somewhat similar to a Digital Differential Analyzer but with variable step size.

Word: An ordered set of characters which is the normal unit in which information may be handled within a computer.
Word Time: In serial computers the time required to process all characters of a word.
Write: To record information in a storage medium.

(Index)